GUIDE TO
NEW YORK CITY
LANDMARKS

Second Edition

GUIDE TO NEW YORK CITY LANDMARKS

New York City Landmarks Preservation Commission

PRESERVATION PRESS

JOHN WILEY & SONS, INC.

New York / Chichester / Weinheim / Brisbane / Singapore / Toronto

Published by John Wiley & Sons, Inc.

A cooperative publication with the New York City Landmarks Preservation Foundation, established in 1965 to designate, monitor, and preserve landmark buildings and historic districts in Manhattan, Brooklyn, Queens, Staten Island, the Bronx, and Governors, Liberty, Ellis, and Roosevelt Islands.

Published simultaneously in Canada.

This publication is designed to provide accurate and authoritative information in regard to the subject matter covered. It is sold with the understanding that the publisher is not engaged in rendering legal, accounting, or other professional services. If legal advice or other expert assistance is required, the services of a competent professional person should be sought.

Maps copyright © 1998 Protonic, New York, New York. All rights reserved. Maps licensed to the New York City Landmarks Preservation Foundation, Inc.

Page layout and typographical design by Jay Anning, Thumb Print.

Library of Congress Cataloging-in-Publication Data:

Dolkart, Andrew
    Guide to New York City landmarks / New York City Landmarks Preservation Commission ; [written by Andrew S. Dolkart]. —2nd ed.
      p.   cm.
    Includes bibliographical references and index.
    ISBN 0-471-18289-3 (alk. paper)
    1. New York (N.Y.)—Guidebooks. 2. Historic Sites—New York (State)—New York—Guidebooks. 3. New York (N.Y.)—Buildings, structures, etc.—Guidebooks. I. New York (N.Y.). Landmarks Preservation Commission. II. Title.
F128.18.D65 1998   97-21378
917.47'1—dc21

Printed in the United States of America

10 9 8 7 6 5 4 3 2

CONTENTS

FOREWORD

New York, one of the world's great cities, has long been famous especially for its cutting-edge creativity and dynamism. But New York is also a historic city, three and one-half centuries old. And a vital part of New York's history is its architecture, the wonderful buildings and neighborhoods that help us understand the city's past and present. The New York City Landmarks Preservation Commission plays an important role in protecting those buildings and neighborhoods, by recognizing them as official city landmarks and historic districts.

The preservation of historic sites is more than just honoring the past, important as that is. The city's great landmarks and historic districts make an enormous contribution to the well-being of our city. They are stable, attractive places where New Yorkers live, work, and play. And by attracting attention, care, and investment, they have become engines of economic development.

New York is a very big city, and few people, native or visitor, have seen it all. If you want to see the best our city has to offer, there is no better guidebook than this *Guide to New York City Landmarks*. From cover to cover, you'll be able to see why New York City is the Capital of the World.

RUDOLPH W. GIULIANI
Mayor
New York City

New York City Hall (Joseph-François Mangin and John McComb, Jr., 1802–11) with the Municipal Building (McKim, Mead & White, 1907–14) in the background. Photo by John Barrington Bayley.

PREFACE

As chairman of the New York City Landmarks Preservation Commission, I am delighted to welcome you to this revised and updated *Guide to New York City Landmarks*. This book is your key to New York City's officially designated landmarks and historic districts. You can use its maps and descriptions to find your way to the city's treasures, from famous monuments known around the world to well-kept secrets known only to New Yorkers.

THE LANDMARKS PRESERVATIONCOMMISSION

Created in 1965 in response to mounting public concern over the destruction of so many of New York's historic buildings, the Landmarks Preservation Commission is responsible for identifying and protecting the city's historic, architectural, and cultural heritage. The results of over three decades of historic preservation have borne out the fondest hopes of those who shaped the Commission. As of this writing, landmark designation protects almost 1,000 individual landmarks and over 20,000 buildings in 68 historic districts.

Our landmarks fall into four categories: individual landmarks, interior landmarks, scenic landmarks, and historic districts. An individual landmark is a building or a site, at least thirty years old in whole or in part, which has, in the words of the landmarks law, a "special character or special historical or aesthetic interest or value as part of the development, heritage or cultural characteristics of the city, state or nation." An interior landmark is a publicly accessible interior space that meets that same standard. Scenic landmarks are city-owned open spaces, usually public parks. Historic districts are areas of the city with special architectural or historical value that gives them a sense of place.

All landmarks, however, fall into one category more important than any other: that of major asset to the city of New York. It is our job at the Commission to see that each one is given the protection that is its due, so that all of them survive and prosper, both for us and for succeeding generations of New Yorkers.

NEW YORK'S LANDMARKS AND HISTORIC DISTRICTS

New York's landmarks are the buildings and sites of all description that help make this the great city that it is. From early colonial houses to Victorian city neighborhoods to modern skyscrapers, they help us understand our city's past—its three and one-half centuries of history—while contributing to its vital present. Here are the first tentative steps of Dutch settlers, fortifications from the Revolutionary War, elegant town houses from the early Republic. There stand the fireproof cast-iron warehouses of the Civil War era, miles of Victorian brownstones and churches, the synagogues of the immigrant Lower East Side. Marvel at the twin-towered Art Deco apartments for skyscraper living along Central Park West, or stroll through the leafy planned suburbs of Jackson Heights in Queens and Prospect Park South in Brooklyn, Riverdale in the Bronx and Saint George in Staten Island. Sidewalk clocks and cemetery gates, subway viaducts and East River bridges, parks and parkways, theaters and restaurants, firehouses and police stations —even a tree growing in Brooklyn—such are the city riches celebrated and protected by landmark status, for New Yorkers and visitors alike.

But landmarks and historic districts are not simply relics of the past, however grand or impressive. Throughout New York, landmarks and historic districts have become prime locations—or better, destinations, places where New Yorkers want to live and work, and tourists want to visit, because of their architectural and historical character. They have become, and remain, stable, desirable places that attract people, renovation, and economic development. The designation of the SoHo–Cast Iron Historic District helped secure the survival of what has become the city's vibrant arts capital. The designation of the Ladies' Mile Historic District, with its huge late 19th-century department store buildings, has helped transform that area into a magnet for large new late 20th-century department stores in a newly prospering commercial district.

The First Precinct Police Station (Hunt & Hunt, 1909–11) is now the home of the Landmarks Preservation Commission. Photo by Carl Forster.

And in dozens of residential historic districts throughout the five boroughs, designation has helped create and support stability, community, and pride. Residents and home owners regularly petition the Commission to join the select company of neighborhoods with landmark status — and real-estate advertisements now routinely include the word *landmark* as an added attraction. The value of landmarks protection today is widely understood, and New York's landmarks are greatly coveted.

Why? What better way to find out than to put this book in your pocket and set out to see the city?

Whether you plan a detailed route or flip to a page at random, whether you walk, bike, or hop the subway, with the *Guide to New York City Landmarks* as your companion you will see the best that New York has to offer. And you will know that each and every site is valued and protected through its designation as a New York City landmark.

JENNIFER J. RAAB
Chairman
New York City Landmarks
Preservation Commission

ACKNOWLEDGMENTS

Foremost acknowledgment must be given to the American Express Corporation and to Furthermore, the publication program of the J. M. Kaplan Fund, which provided the grants that enabled us to map every landmark and historic district. It is the maps that set this book apart from its predecessors. With them, the book is no longer just a resource book but a *guidebook* in the truest sense. It is our hope that the addition of these maps will encourage residents and tourists to set out by foot, subway, bus, bicycle, or car to explore the abundant landmark treasures scattered throughout the five boroughs. And, of course, many thanks are due Ted Ostindien, manager of Protonic, a New York company specializing in custom maps and real estate graphics. Ted's skill at structuring the vast quantity of data and at mapmaking is manifest in the beautiful maps contained herein. He was a welcome member of the team.

This revised guide, produced under the auspices of the New York Landmarks Preservation Foundation, is the result of a truly collaborative effort. Andrew S. Dolkart continued his excellent work from the previous edition. He provided concise and erudite entries for new landmarks, expanded entries on historic districts and contributed new entries for notable buildings within the Greenwich Village and Brooklyn Heights Historic Districts. He also provided helpful suggestions on most aspects of the book. Marjorie Pearson, the director of research at the New York City Landmarks Preservation Commission, brought to this project her encyclopedic knowledge of New York City landmarks, an extraordinary attention to detail, and a deep-felt enthusiasm for the book. Members of the Commission's research department, under Ms. Pearson's direction, conducted the research and wrote the designation reports on which most of the entries are based. Almost all the photographs were taken by Commission staff, including current members Caroline Kane Levy and Carl Forster. Susan Ball, president of the New York Landmarks Preservation Foundation, and Anthony W. Robins, director of special projects at the Commission, were responsible for convincing American Express and Furthermore of the worthiness of improving the guidebook. Jennifer Field helped edit and organize the "Guide to Row-House Architectural Styles" found in Appendix 1. Catherine Barrier and Katy McNabb provided invaluable assistance throughout the project. Matthew A. Postal provided many thoughtful comments and suggestions on the arrangement of entries and photographs. Paul, Weiss, Rifkind, Wharton & Garrison provided pro bono legal assistance. Warm thanks must also be extended to David Sassian and Jan Cigliano, our editors at John Wiley & Sons, whose editorial direction made this book possible.

Finally, this revised guidebook would never have come to fruition without the leadership and energy of Jennifer J. Raab, chairman of the Commission. She championed the project from the very beginning, recognizing the importance of providing New Yorkers and visitors with the only comprehensive guidebook to all New York City landmarks.

MARK A. SILBERMAN
Project Director
New York City Landmarks
Preservation Commission
November 1997

GUIDE TO
NEW YORK CITY
LANDMARKS

INTRODUCTION: HOW TO USE THIS GUIDE

This guide includes information on all individual landmarks, interior landmarks, scenic landmarks, and historic districts designated by the New York City Landmarks Preservation Commission from October 14, 1965 (when the Commission made its first designations) through February 1997. During this time the Commission designated 962 individual landmarks, 98 interior landmarks, 9 scenic landmarks, and 68 historic districts. The entries, written by the architectural historian Andrew S. Dolkart, briefly explain the architectural and historical significance of the landmark properties. The information underlying most of the entries has been collected from the Commission's research department staff under the direction of Marjorie Pearson, the Commission's director of research. Errors in earlier editions of this guide have been corrected (for example, names inaccurately assigned to properties at the time of designation have been emended), and newly discovered information previously unpublished (for example, the accurate historical names of many buildings) has been incorporated. Listings have been divided among New York City's five boroughs: Manhattan, Brooklyn, Queens, the Bronx, and Staten Island. Governors, Liberty, Ellis, and Roosevelt Islands, which are under the jurisdiction of the borough of Manhattan, appear in a chapter of their own for easier reference.

Protonic subdivided Manhattan in its entirety into eighteen maps, while it created more geographically specific maps appropriate for Brooklyn, Queens, the Bronx, and Staten Island. Overview maps at the beginning for each borough depict the subdivisions. Within each map or area, historic districts are listed first, followed by the entries for individual landmarks.

Each individual, interior, and scenic landmark has been assigned a number (for example, Manhattan's landmarks are numbered from 1 through 508; Staten Island's landmarks are numbered from 1 through 67). Each such number is contained

within an oval or circle. It should be noted that individual entries can encompass more than one landmark structure (see, for example, Staten Island No. 20) or more than one type of landmark within a single building (see, for example, Manhattan No. 197, which has both interior and exterior designations), and thus there are only approximately 750 entries, covering a total of over 1,000 landmarks.

Historic-district boundaries have been drawn where appropriate. Historic districts (sometimes abbreviated "H.D.") are numbered separately, and the number is contained within a diamond shape that is incorporated into the boundary line. Each borough's landmarks and historic districts have been numbered separately, beginning with "1." In addition, this guidebook for the first time contains entries on notable buildings that are not individual landmarks but that are found within the Greenwich Village or Brooklyn Heights historic districts. Each such notable building is identified by a capital letter contained within a square.

Having abandoned the alphabetical listing of entries used in the previous edition of the guidebook, we were faced with a significant challenge in numbering and ordering entries within each map and geographic section. For ease of reference, entries are listed in numerical order within each section. With respect to the numbering, it was our goal to group entries in a way that would appear logical to a reader using the book to plan an itinerary. This endeavor, of course, required the vexing task of predicting how readers actually move through the city. For example, do people traveling in Manhattan tend to walk north and south along avenues, or east and west along numerical streets? With no definitive answers to such questions, we, somewhat arbitrarily, adopted the following rules: Numbering generally goes from west to east, and from south to north, in Manhattan and the Bronx, and from north to south in Brooklyn, Queens, and Staten Island. (This corresponds to the general historical development pattern of the boroughs.) In Manhattan, where a map covers a large geographic area or contains many landmarks, we have subdivided the map and grouped entries —using these same general rules—within each subdivision. In Map 8 for example, we have subdivided the area under headings "West of Union Square and Park Avenue South" and "Union Square and East of Park Avenue South." Manhattan Maps 12 and 13 are exceptions to the west-east rule. There, under the assumption that many readers would be orienting themselves from Central Park, the subdivisions and entries run from east to west.

Entries for landmarks begin with the number that corresponds to the location of the landmark on the map. The historic name is listed first, followed, where applicable, by other names associated with the property, and then the address. In a few cases where use of a historic name might lead to confusion or where a later name is much better known, the entry begins with the common name (for example, Fordham University, rather than Saint John's College). Architects associated with the original construction and any relevant additions to the property, along with the dates indicating the widest determinable span of work (from design to completion), are cited next. Interior landmarks are indicated in two ways. Where only the interior is a landmark, the word "interior" is contained in parentheses after the name. Where both the exterior and the interior are landmarks, the interior landmark designation is indicated by the word **interior** in boldface type within the text. (Compare the entries for numbers 211 and 212 in Manhattan.)

After the section on Governors, Liberty, Ellis, and Roosevelt Islands, the reader will find "A Guide to Row House Architectural Styles" in Appendix I. The guide is a very general introduction to the history of the row house—which is far and away the most common type of landmark building in New York City—and its architectural styles, as well as thirteen line drawings that depict the most prevalent and salient features of each style. It is our hope that the guide will help teach the reader to identify the different styles of row-house architecture that are commonly found within the city.

Finally, the reader should be aware that the Commission continues to designate new landmarks and historic districts. A listing of designations made between February 1997 (when this book went into production) and December 1997 is given in Appendix 3. In addition, information on new designations can be obtained by visiting the Commission's web site at http://www.ci.nyc.ny.us/html/lpc/home.html.

Please note that the New York City Landmarks Preservation Commission does not own or operate any landmark properties. In many cases landmark properties are private residences, and the reader is asked to respect the privacy of owners and occupants. Viewing a landmark from a street or other public way is of course quite permissible. However, permission must be obtained from the owner or occupant before venturing onto the property. The entries indicate which properties are museums or otherwise open to the public; visitors to these properties are, in many cases, charged a fee. Interior landmarks are customarily open to the public. Depending on the nature and use of the space, a ticket may be required or a fee charged.

The Commission recognizes that ongoing research on the city's architecture and history will continue to bring new information to light about designated landmarks. The Commission would be pleased to receive such information directed to the attention of its research department. Corrections of errors that might inadvertently have crept into this edition of the guide may also be addressed to:

Research Department
The New York City Landmarks
Preservation Commission
100 Old Slip
New York, NY 10005

HISTORIC DISTRICTS

❶ Fraunces Tavern Block Historic District. The low-rise buildings of this square block provide an unusual illustration of the early building history of Lower Manhattan. Dating primarily from the early 19th century, these buildings stand in marked contrast to the surrounding 20th-century skyscrapers. The block escaped the fire of December 1835 that devastated most of Lower Manhattan. Thus the district retains eleven early buildings, erected between 1827 and 1833, including a rare example of a warehouse in the Federal style (62 Pearl Street, 1827) and several Greek Revival

countinghouses. Also in the district is Fraunces Tavern (see No. 38). Much of the block was saved from demolition in 1974.

❷ Stone Street Historic District. This small historic district, incorporating a part of the colonial street plan of New Amsterdam (see No. 1), is an extraordinary remnant of New York's small-scale commercial architecture, set amid tall 20th-century skyscrapers. The area, initially built up in the 17th and 18th centuries, was destroyed in the fire of December 1835. Immediately after the fire, Greek Revival–style countinghouses, with granite bases of post-and-lintel construction and brick

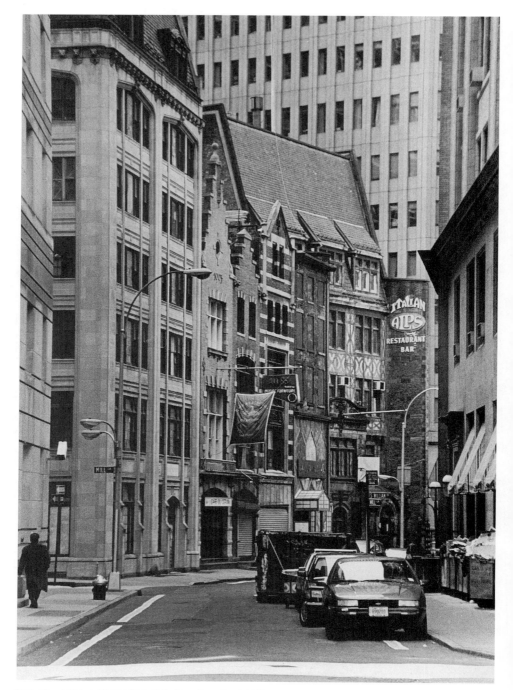

Stone Street Historic District (H.D. 2) looking down South William Street. Nestled among towering skyscrapers, the Stone Street Historic District is a remnant of an earlier period in New York's commercial development. Photo by Caroline Kane Levy.

upper stories, were erected for importers, dry goods dealers, and other merchants. Many of these four-story commercial structures survive on Stone and Pearl Streets; most extend through the block and thus have two street facades. In the mid-19th century, the austere Greek Revival style was superseded by the Italianate style, as exemplified by the major commercial building from this era in the district, the Hanover Bank (now India House; see No. 36) on Hanover Square. In the first years of the 20th century, major changes began occurring in the district, initiated by the Eno family, which had extensive real-estate holdings in New York. In 1903 Amos F. Eno commissioned the prominent architect C. P. H. Gilbert to design new street facades on the building at 13 South William Street/57 Stone Street for his family's real-estate office. Gilbert's picturesque neo–Dutch Renaissance design (expanded in 1908 with another new front at 15 South William Street), with its stepped gables and strapwork detail, is a nostalgic reminder of the area's colonial heritage. During the next several decades, other facades were redesigned or new buildings constructed in a variety of revival styles, notably the neo-Renaissance front of 17 South William Street (Edward L. Tilton, 1906), the neo-Tudor club at 21–23 South William Street (William Neil Smith, 1927–28), the neo-Renaissance facade with exposed metal lintels designed by Arthur C. Jackson (1919) for marine underwriters Chubb & Son at 54 Stone Street, and the neo-Gothic office building for the marine insurance firm William H. McGee & Co. (William Neil Smith, 1929) at 9–11 South William Street. In 1995 Beyer Blinder Belle prepared a master plan for the upgrading and economic revitalization of the area.

3 **South Street Seaport Historic District.** This district contains the largest concentration of early 19th-century commercial buildings in New York. It is an unparalleled physical representation of the extraordinary development of trade and commerce in the early decades of the 19th century as New York City became the economic and financial capital of the nation. The streets are lined with the countinghouses where New York's merchants had their offices and warehoused their goods. Among the very early buildings are those of 1811–12 that make up the Georgian-Federal-style Schermer-

horn Row on Fulton Street (see No. 40). More common are the Greek Revival countinghouses of the 1830s, most with first stories of granite post-and-lintel construction with brick above, such as 247 Water Street (1837; restored, Peter Talbot and James D'Auria, 1992–93) and the trio at 207–211 Water Street (1835–37). A few of the countinghouses have stone fronts, such as the granite Hickson W. Field Store (see No. 39) at 170–176 John Street and the brownstone building erected for A. A. Low & Brothers in 1849 at 167–171 John Street (see Schermerhorn Row Block, No. 40; Low Memorial Library at Columbia University is named for Abiel Abbot Low; see No. 457). By the second half of the 19th century, the South Street area had lost its prominence in New York's commercial life. Many buildings were converted for the wholesale Fulton Fish Market, and a few new structures were built. Among the prominent later buildings designed by noted New York architects are 116–119 South Street (John B. Snook, 1873), which became Meyers Hotel in 1881; 142–144 Beekman Street, a Romanesque Revival building designed by George B. Post in 1885 for fish dealers and ornamented with terra-cotta fish keystones and seashell cornice and iron starfish tie-rods; and Richard Morris Hunt's 1873 red brick building with black brick decorative trim at 21–23 Peck Slip. The area deteriorated in the 20th century, but restoration began in the early 1970s with the creation of the South Street Seaport Museum and Marketplace. Notable new construction in the area has included 15–19 Fulton Street (Beyer Blinder Belle, 1977–83), which is faced with steel panels emulating cast iron, and the Seamen's Church Institute (James Stewart Polshek & Partners, 1989–91) at 241 Water Street.

INDIVIDUAL LANDMARKS

1 **Street Plan of New Amsterdam and Colonial New York,** including all or part of Beaver, Bridge, Broad, Hanover, Marketfield, New, Pearl, South William, Stone, Wall, Whitehall, and William Streets; Exchange Place; Hanover Square; Mill Lane; and Broadway. The financial center of the United States was built on the 17th-century street pattern of colonial New Amsterdam. The Dutch colonial street plan of Lower Manhattan, south of Wall Street, underwent only minor additions and alterations by the British. These narrow streets are the only visible aboveground evidence in Manhattan of the colonial settlement. Streets developed in an organic manner from the original waterfront at Pearl Street. Broadway was the major colonial street, running north along a ridge from the original fort at the Battery. Broad Street ran from the waterfront and contained a canal, which explains its exceptional width.

2 **Pier A,** Battery Park (George Sears Greene, Jr., engineer, 1884–86; addition, 1900). Jutting into New York Bay at the southern end of Manhattan, Pier A was built for the city's Department of Docks and Harbor Police and was designed by the department's chief engineer. It is the last surviving historic pier in Manhattan. Additions include the three-story pier head (1900) and the clock located in the tower at the west end of the pier, which was installed in 1919 as a memorial to servicemen who died in World War I; the clock peals the time on ship's bells. As of 1997, plans called for the wooden siding to be restored in conjunction with the conversion of the building into a restaurant and visitors' center and museum for the New York State Harbor Park.

3 **Castle Clinton,** now Castle Clinton National Monument, Battery Park (Lt. Col. Jonathan Williams and John McComb, Jr., 1808–11). Originally built on an artificial island off the Battery, and referred to as West Battery, Castle Clinton—so named in 1815—was one of a series of forts, including Castle Williams on Governors Island (see Governors Island Historic District), erected to protect New York Harbor. Although the design of the brownstone fort is often attributed to John McComb, Jr., he was probably responsible only for the entrance. After becoming the property of New York City in 1823, the former fort served as a theater (Castle Garden), an immigrant station, and an aquarium before it was restored by the federal government in the early 1970s.

4 **Whitehall Ferry Terminal,** now the Battery Maritime Building, 11 South Street (Walker & Morris, 1906–09). The ferry terminal with its three slips was designed in a Beaux-Arts style and built with exposed steel reminiscent of French ex-

position architecture. The only survivor of the many historic ferry terminals that once lined New York's waterfront, it now serves ferries running to Governors Island and Bay Ridge, Brooklyn.

5 **James Watson House,** now the Rectory of the Shrine of Saint Elizabeth Ann Seton, 7 State Street (attributed to John McComb, Jr., 1793; extension, 1806). In 1793–1806, when this house was erected, Lower Manhattan was still a fashionable residential area. The original Georgian structure has an elegant addition in the Federal style with an Ionic portico conforming to the curve of the street. The building is now a shrine to the first native-born American (and New Yorker) granted sainthood by the Roman Catholic Church.

6 **United States Custom House,** now Alexander Hamilton Custom House (National Museum of the American Indian and Federal Bankruptcy Court), Bowling Green (Cass Gilbert, 1899–1907). In 1899 the Minnesota architect Cass Gilbert won the competition for New York's new customhouse with a masterful essay in Beaux-Arts design. The building has bold three-dimensional massing and an extensive sculptural program on themes related to commerce and trade; the most notable sculptures are Daniel Chester French's *Four Continents,* which flank the grand entrance stairway. The **interiors** on the main floor are as ornate as the exterior. The richly detailed marble entrance hall leads to an oval rotunda embellished with a mural cycle by Reginald Marsh installed in 1936–37 as part of the Treasury Department's Depression-era arts project. Magnificently decorated offices are arranged along the front of the building. After standing empty for many years, most of the landmark spaces have been restored for the National Museum of the American Indian under the direction of Ehrenkrantz & Eckstut Architects.

7 **Interborough Rapid Transit System:** Numerous sites in Manhattan and Brooklyn, including **Control Houses,** Battery Park and West 72nd Street (Heins & La Farge, 1904–05); **Manhattan Valley Viaduct,** Broadway from West 122nd to West 135th Streets (William B. Parsons, engineer, 1900–04); **Underground Stations,** Wall Street, Fulton Street, City Hall, Bleecker Street, Astor Place, and 33rd Street, Manhattan, and Borough Hall,

Brooklyn, on the Lexington Avenue IRT Line; 59th Street–Columbus Circle, 72nd Street, 79th Street, 110th Street, and 116th Street–Columbia University on the Seventh Avenue IRT Line (Heins & La Farge, architect, and William B. Parsons, engineer, Contract 1, 1899–1904; Contract 2, 1902–08). Following a succession of aborted attempts to build a subway system in Manhattan, a contract was signed in 1899 for the construction of the Interborough Rapid Transit Company's first subway. The original IRT line (Contract 1) ran from City Hall to Grand Central Terminal and then turned west to Times Square and north along Broadway to the Bronx. In 1902 Contract 2 extended the system south from City Hall through Lower Manhattan and into Brooklyn. Chief engineer Parsons and his staff were responsible for the construction of the system. One of the most spectacular engineering features planned by Parsons is the Manhattan Valley Viaduct, which carries the Broadway line over a valley at West 125th Street and which consists of approaches faced with rock-fronted granite blocks, steel viaducts, and a central span with three parabolic arches. Although the engineers sited and planned each subway station, the architecture firm of Heins & La Farge designed the ornamentation. The architects were required to use white tile and light-colored brick except where color was "introduced for architectural effect." Color was used for the mosaic sign panels and for the terra-cotta and faience plaques (provided by the Rookwood Pottery of Cincinnati and the Grueby Faience Company of

United States Custom House (No. 6). The Custom House is an essay in Beaux-Arts design and also has an extensive sculptural program on themes relating to commerce and trade. The park in the foreground is Bowling Green (No. 8). Photo by Carl Forster.

Boston) that embellish each station. At many stations the plaques were designed with an attribute unique to that stop. These include the beavers at Astor Place (John Jacob Astor made his initial fortune in beaver pelts), a sailing ship at Columbus Circle, and the seal of Columbia University at 116th Street. In addition to the subterranean stations, Heins & La Farge designed the aboveground entrance structures. Although all the original cast-iron entrance canopies have been removed (a canopy has been reconstructed at Astor Place), two of the Flemish-inspired brick and terra-cotta control houses still stand in Manhattan—at Battery Park just south of Bowling Green and at Broadway and West 72nd Street.

8 **Bowling Green Fence,** Bowling Green Park (1771). This simple iron fence was erected in 1771 to protect a statue of King George III. Although the statue was destroyed in 1776, the fence survives as a unique example of pre–Revolutionary War craftsmanship in New York City.

9 **International Mercantile Marine Company Building,** 1 Broadway (Walter B. Chambers, 1919–21). This austere neoclassical office building, a recladding of an 1880s structure, has facades that are appropriately ornamented with symbols of the sea (seashells, ropes, tridents, dolphins, etc.) and mosaic shields representing many of the world's great port cities. The project was commissioned by the International Mercantile Marine Co., a firm organized in 1902 by J. P. Morgan that combined several independent steamship companies into one powerful entity later known as the United States Lines. The Battery Place entrances, marked "First Class" and "Cabin Class," led into an elegant ticketing hall (now a bank).

10 **Bowling Green Offices Building,** 5–11 Broadway (W. & G. Audsley, 1895–98). This massive office building was designed by British-immigrant architects who described it as a work in the "Hellenic Renaissance" style. The use of Greek, or "Hellenic," forms is evident in the basic tripartite massing (resembling the base-shaft-capital form of a column), in the line of bold pilasters at the base, and in the impressive Grecian entrance enframements. The building initially housed steamship lines and many firms involved with shipping.

11 **Cunard Building,** 25 Broadway (Benjamin Wistar Morris; Carrère & Hastings, consulting architect, 1917–21). Benjamin Wistar Morris worked on the design of this building in 1917–19, experimenting with many massing ideas and a variety of styles before settling on a powerful Renaissance form with subtle nautical detail. The simplicity of the exterior contrasts with the extraordinary richness of the **interior,** which served as the booking hall for the great ocean liners owned by Cunard. The entrance lobby and the Great Hall are two of the finest spaces of their era. The groin-vaulted lobby contains nautical ceiling sculpture carved by Carl Jennewein and painted by Ezra Winter. Gates by master ironworker Samuel Yellin of Philadelphia lead into the spectacular Great Hall (now a post office), with its complex spatial arrangement and superb ceiling frescoes by Winter, wall murals by Barry Faulkner, and rich travertine and marble detail.

12 **Standard Oil Building,** 26 Broadway (Carrère & Hastings; Shreve, Lamb & Blake, associate, 1920–28). Thomas Hastings was largely responsible for the Renaissance-inspired design of this impressive limestone skyscraper, which served as the corporate headquarters and a powerful symbol of Standard Oil, the huge oil company founded by John D. Rockefeller. The complex design takes into consideration the alignment of Broadway and the irregular pentagonal plot, resulting in a curved base and skewed tower capped by a bronze brazier. The tower is a prominent feature of the skyline when viewed from the harbor. The building was constructed in five sections beginning in 1921, so that office tenants, including Standard Oil itself, could be conveniently relocated, and a Childs Restaurant on Beaver Street, which refused to move, could be accommodated until its lease expired in 1928. The facades are ornamented with symbolic lamps, flaming torches, and "SO" ciphers. Standard Oil sold the building in 1956.

13 **American Express Company Building,** now J. J. Kenny Co., 65 Broadway (James L. Aspinwall of Renwick, Aspinwall & Tucker, 1914–17). American Express was established in 1850 to provide reliable transport of packages and valuables. Among the founders were Henry Wells and William Fargo. In the late 19th century, the firm branched into financial services, instituting the money order in

1882 and inventing the traveler's check in 1891. American Express purchased the property on Broadway, stretching through the block to Trinity Place, in 1903 and began planning a towering new home in 1914. Two years later construction began on this 21-story neoclassical-style concrete and steel-framed building faced with white brick and terra cotta over a granite base. American Express retained its headquarters here until 1975.

14 Empire Building, 71 Broadway (Kimball & Thompson, 1895–98). The richly decorative classically inspired detail on the Empire Building's three street elevations exemplify the manner in which skyscraper architects in New York adapted traditional architectural styles to the new skyscraper building type. Francis Kimball, a pioneer in the design of steel-skeleton-frame skyscrapers, created a boldly detailed structure with a triumphal-arch entry. It was the headquarters of the United States Steel Corporation from its establishment by J. P. Morgan in 1901 until 1976. In 1997 work began on the conversion of the building into apartments.

15 Trinity Church (Episcopal) and Graveyard, Broadway at Wall Street (Richard Upjohn, 1839–46; sacristy, Frederick Clarke Withers, 1876–77; All Saints' Chapel, Thomas Nash, 1911–13; Manning Wing, Adams & Woodbridge, 1966). One of the first Gothic Revival buildings in New York and one of Upjohn's earliest works, Trinity Church was for many years the tallest structure in the city, its spire towering over New York's business district. The present church is the third built on this site for New York's oldest Episcopal congregation. The building was constructed of New Jersey brownstone, whose original light and varied hues were revealed when the exterior was cleaned in 1990–91 by Brisk Waterproofing Co. The church has had several important additions, including the sacristy, the chapel, and Manning Wing at the west end, and the bronze entrance doors (1890–96) donated as a memorial to John Jacob Astor III, which were designed by Richard Morris Hunt in collaboration with the sculptors Karl Bitter, J. Massey Rhind, and Charles Niehaus. The surrounding graveyard contains the tombs of such famous Americans as Alexander Hamilton, Albert Gallatin, Francis

Lewis, William Bradford, and Robert Fulton, as well as many fine 18th-century gravestones.

16 Trinity Building and United States Realty Building, 111 and 115 Broadway (Francis H. Kimball, 1904–07). These two skyscrapers were designed with Gothic detail to harmonize with neighboring Trinity Church (see No. 15) and were dubbed by the *New York Times* "twin examples of Gothic splendor." The construction of these enormous slabs was a major undertaking, entailing the relocation of Thames Street and the construction of caissons 80 feet into the marshy subsoil. The limestone-faced buildings are carefully detailed with towers, gables, and fanciful carved ornament.

17 United States Realty Building. See No. 16.

18 Equitable Building, 120 Broadway (Ernest Graham & Associates, Peirce Anderson, architect in charge, 1913–15). At its completion in 1915, the Equitable Building was the largest office building in the world in square footage. This massive structure, with its entrances in the form of triumphal arches and its classical ornamental detail, was a speculative venture, largely planned by Thomas Du Pont, that housed the headquarters of Equitable Life, as well as the offices of many small firms. The bulk of the H-shaped building, rising 38 stories with no setbacks, provoked great controversy and was cited by opponents of unregulated growth as an example of the evils of skyscraper construction. Its presence helped insure the passage of the first zoning law in the United States in 1916. A restoration by Ehrenkrantz, Eckstut & Whitelaw was completed in 1990.

19 Chamber of Commerce of the State of New York, now the International Commercial Bank of China, 65 Liberty Street (James B. Baker, 1900–01). This imposing Beaux-Arts building was erected by the chamber of commerce to symbolize the chamber's importance in New York's commercial life. The marble structure, occupied by the chamber until 1980, was restored in 1990–91 (Haines, Lundberg, Waehler, architect) as part of its conversion into a bank.

20 Liberty Tower, 55 Liberty Street (Henry Ives Cobb, 1909–10). This handsome neo-Gothic skyscraper—clad entirely in white terra cotta and enlivened with fanciful ornament, including birds and alligators—is an important antecedent to the Woolworth Building (see No. 48). The freestanding building, which at the time of its construction was known as "the tallest building in the world on so small an area of ground," was also one of the earliest residential conversion projects in Lower Manhattan. The facade is undergoing major restoration of damaged terra cotta by Merritt Engineering Consultants.

㉑ Federal Reserve Bank of New York, 33 Liberty Street (York & Sawyer, 1919–24). The massive rusticated walls of the Federal Reserve Bank, constructed of stone in two colors, symbolize the strength of the Federal Reserve system and the impregnability of this building, which stores a significant part of the world's gold reserves. The Florentine palazzo form was chosen by York & Sawyer for its association with the Medicis and other leading Renaissance families whose fortunes were made, at least in part, from banking. The iron detail was crafted by the master ironworker Samuel Yellin of Philadelphia.

㉒ John Street Methodist Church, 44 John Street (attributed to Philip Embury, 1841). John Street is the oldest Methodist congregation in North America. Founded in 1766 as the Wesleyan Society in America, the congregation erected its first church in 1768. The well-proportioned Georgian-inspired building with a brownstone facade is the third church on the site.

㉓ 90–94 Maiden Lane Building (attributed to Charles Wright, 1870–71). One of the few mid-19th-century commercial structures still standing in Lower Manhattan, this small French Second Empire building has an iron front, cast at Daniel D. Badger's Architectural Iron Works, that united three early 19th-century warehouses. The facade was commissioned by Roosevelt & Son, the nation's leading importer of plate glass and mirrors, among whose principals was Theodore Roosevelt, the father of the country's twenty-sixth president.

㉔ 56–58 Pine Street Building (Oswald Wirz, 1893–94). This 12-story office building, originally called the Wallace Building after its developer James Wallace, was designed by his company's architect, Oswald Wirz, with Romanesque Revival characteristics. Faced with brick, stone, and terra cotta, the building is distinguished by its round-arched openings, deeply set windows, and truncated columns, and embellished by some of the finest Byzantine carving in New York, including intricate foliate panels and fantastic heads.

㉕ Down Town Association Building, 60 Pine Street (Charles C. Haight, 1886–87; addition, Warren & Wetmore, 1910–11). This elegant Romanesque Revival–style clubhouse was designed by Charles C. Haight for one of New York's earliest private clubs. Faced with Roman brick and highlighted by terra-cotta ornament, the building has a large round-arched entranceway and arched window openings. A two-bay extension to the east of the original building by Warren & Wetmore echoes the Haight building in its materials, fenestration, and details.

㉖ Bankers Trust Building, 14 Wall Street (Trowbridge & Livingston, 1910–12; addition, Shreve, Lamb & Harmon, 1931–33). The stepped pyramid that crowns this great neoclassical limestone tower is one of the most prominent elements of the Lower Manhattan skyline and was such an icon that it became the corporate logo of Bankers Trust. Bankers Trust was organized in 1903 by a group of commercial banks that wanted to enter the lucrative market of trusts and estates; it became a full-service bank in 1917. This office building, containing space for bank offices as well as offices to produce rental income, is located at one of the most important intersections in the financial district. A major addition with subtle Art Deco detail, erected early in the 1930s, was carefully designed to be subordinate to the original structure. Bankers Trust sold the building in 1987.

㉗ New York Stock Exchange, 8–18 Broad Street (George B. Post, 1901–03). This marble-fronted building has been the home of America's principal securities market since 1903. The exchange—which dates back to 1792, when stock dealers met under a buttonwood tree on Wall Street—had been housed at a number of sites before it moved into a building at 12 Broad Street (John Kellum, architect), just south of Wall Street, in 1865. That building was enlarged in 1880–81

(James Renwick, Jr., architect) and eventually replaced by the present structure, whose six monumental Corinthian columns support a pediment containing an allegorical sculptural ensemble entitled *Integrity Protecting the Works of Man,* designed by John Quincy Adams Ward and executed by Paul Wayland Bartlett.

28 **J. P. Morgan & Company,** 23 Wall Street (Trowbridge & Livingston, 1913). At a time when skyscrapers were being erected throughout Lower Manhattan, the Morgan Bank erected this small headquarters building on one of the most valuable pieces of land in New York City, the juncture of Wall and Broad Streets. The low-scaled, austere

New York Stock Exchange (No. 27). The home, since 1903, of America's principal securities market. The statue of George Washington in the foreground stands on the steps of Federal Hall (No. 29). Photo by Caroline Kane Levy.

classical building, clad in white marble, symbolized the wealth and power of this banking institution. The importance of the bank was further underscored by the absence of a name on the exterior; for those wealthy enough to bank at Morgan, no introduction was needed. The building now functions as an entrance pavilion to the larger skyscraper rising behind it.

29 **United States Custom House,** later the U.S. Sub-Treasury, now Federal Hall National Memorial, 28 Wall Street (Town & Davis, Samuel Thompson, William Ross, and John Frazee, 1833–42). This building at the juncture of Wall, Broad, and Nassau Streets in the heart of New York's financial district occupies one of the most historic locations in New York—the site of the original Federal Hall, where George Washington took the oath of office as the nation's first president (commemorated by John Quincy Adams Ward's 1883 sculpture of Washington on the building's steps). Town & Davis designed the imposing marble Custom House, adapting the form of the Parthenon to the needs of a great 19th-century civic monument. The job of supervising construction went to the builder Samuel Thompson. Thompson and his successors, Ross and Frazee, were responsible for design changes that distressed A. J. Davis. **Interior:** The rotunda is among the finest Greek Revival rooms in New York, especially noteworthy for its Corinthian columns, saucer dome, and elegant iron railings cast in the form of classical maidens and twining vines. In 1862, when the U.S. Custom Service moved to the old Merchants' Exchange (see National City Bank, No. 31), this building became a branch of the Sub-Treasury. The building was designated a National Historic Site in 1939 and a National Memorial in 1955.

30 **Manhattan Company Building,** now the Trump Building at 40 Wall Street, 40 Wall Street (H. Craig Severance; Yasuo Matsui, associate architect; Shreve & Lamb, consulting architect, 1929–30). Among the most visible buildings in Lower Manhattan, this 927-foot-tall skyscraper, capped by a pyramidal roof and French Gothic spire, was planned as the world's tallest building (the Chrysler Building won the battle of height). The tower was a speculative venture built by a syndicate of investors that included the Manhattan Company, parent to the Bank of the Manhattan Company, New York's second-oldest bank. The Bank of Manhattan occupied the previous building on the site; it maintained a bank and office space in this skyscraper until 1960. In an extraordinary construction campaign, builders Starrett Brothers & Eken erected the structure in less than one year. In 1996–97 the base of the building was rehabilitated by architect Der Scutt.

31 **National City Bank** (incorporating the Merchants' Exchange), later Citibank, 55 Wall Street (Isaiah Rogers, 1836–41; additions, McKim, Mead & White, 1907–10). The National City Bank building appears to be a single unified structure but is actually the result of two building campaigns begun sixty-eight years apart. The Boston architect Isaiah Rogers designed the original building for the Merchants' Exchange. The three-story Greek Revival structure of Quincy granite with a dome and a colonnade of twelve Ionic columns, each a single block of stone, was one of the most impressive early 19th-century buildings in America. In 1862 the U.S. Custom Service moved from its home at 28 Wall Street (see No. 29) into this building, where it remained until a new custom-house (see No. 6) was erected on Bowling Green. In 1907 James Stillman, president of the National City Bank, recognized that this freestanding Wall Street landmark would be a fitting home for his growing bank, and he arranged for its purchase from the government. Charles F. McKim was commissioned to enlarge the building. The dome was removed, the interior was gutted, four floors were added, and a second granite colonnade was carefully proportioned to align with the original.

32 **City Bank–Farmers Trust Company Building,** 20 Exchange Place (Cross & Cross, 1930–31). This tower, designed with a combination of classical and Art Deco forms, in a style often referred to as "Modern Classic," exemplifies the dramatic exploitation of the requirements of the 1916 zoning law. The base of the freestanding building hugs the lot line and rises up through a series of setbacks to a relatively thin tower that soars 685 feet, 7⅛ inches to create one of the most prominent features of the Lower Manhattan skyline. The building has superb ornament that alludes to the National City

City Bank–Farmers Trust Company Building (No. 32). The setbacks of this building were a response to the 1916 zoning law. Photo by Carl Forster.

Bank, one of the original tenants, including freestanding stylized heroic figures at the first setback, known as the "giants of finance." At the street level are spectacular doors and grilles created in nickel silver (an alloy of nickel, zinc, and copper) by sculptor David Evans.

33 **Beaver Building,** later the New York Cocoa Exchange Building, 82–92 Beaver Street/1 Wall Street Court (Clinton & Russell, 1903–04). Clinton & Russell was the leading architecture firm active in the design of speculative office buildings in New York at the turn of the century. This "flatiron"-shaped 15-story office building incorporates the Classical and Renaissance details and tripartite massing that the firm favored. The brick-clad structure was among the first skyscrapers ornamented with polychromatic glazed terra cotta.

From 1904 to 1921 this was the headquarters of the Munson Steamship Company, and from 1931 to 1972 the building housed the New York Cocoa Exchange and other businesses involved in the cocoa trade.

34 **Delmonico's Building,** 56 Beaver Street (James Brown Lord, 1890–91). The legendary Delmonico's Restaurant was established as a modest café on William Street in 1827 by Swiss immigrants John and Peter Delmonico. After that building burned in 1835, the business moved to this Beaver Street location. In 1890 a luxurious new restaurant with offices above was constructed at this irregularly shaped corner site. The elegant Renaissance-inspired building is faced in beautiful orange brick with a brownstone base and terracotta trim. The columns that flank the corner en-

15

trance, reputedly from Pompeii, were reinstalled from the portico of the 1835 building.

35 **J. & W. Seligman & Co. Building,** later Lehman Brothers, now Banca Commerciale Italiana, 1 William Street (Francis H. Kimball with Julian C. Levi, 1906–07; alterations, Harry R. Allen, 1929; addition, Gino Valle, 1982–86). Francis Kimball's Beaux-Arts skyscraper, with its crowning *tempietto,* exploits an awkwardly shaped site to create an important focal point on William Street south of Wall Street. The building was erected as the headquarters of the investment banking firm established by the Seligmans, who were leaders of New York's German-Jewish community. In 1929, when the building was sold to Lehman Brothers, the main entrance was relocated to the rounded corner, closer to Wall Street. Italian architect Gino Valle's addition skillfully abstracts and complements Kimball's original design.

36 **Hanover Bank,** now India House, 1 Hanover Square (1852–53). The former Hanover Bank is the only survivor of the many Italianate banks erected in Manhattan's financial district in the 1850s. The sandstone-fronted building was modeled on Italian Renaissance palazzo prototypes, appropriate since many of the Renaissance families made their fortunes in banking. The building served as the Cotton Exchange and as the headquarters of W. R. Grace & Co. before being converted into India House, a private club whose founders were involved in foreign trade. The name was chosen because "India" and "the Indies" suggest exotic (and profitable) trading centers.

37 **First Precinct Police Station,** now New York City Landmarks Preservation Commission, 100 Old Slip (Hunt & Hunt, 1909–11). Hunt & Hunt, the firm established by the sons of the famed Richard Morris Hunt, designed this limestone police station in the form of an Italian Renaissance palazzo. The arched openings, rustication, and imposing cornice have been compared to those of the 15th-century Palazzo Riccardi in Florence. After standing vacant for many years, the building was renovated by the New York City Department of General Services. Since 1993 it has housed the offices of the Landmarks Preservation Commission.

38 **Fraunces Tavern,** 54 Pearl Street (1719; reconstruction, William H. Mersereau, 1904–07). The original building on this site was erected in 1719 by Stephen DeLancey. In 1763 the house was converted into a tavern by Samuel Fraunces, and it was here that George Washington gave his famous farewell address to his officers. The building suffered several additions and fires in the 19th century. In 1904 the heavily altered and deteriorated building was purchased by the Sons of the Revolution, which sponsored a somewhat speculative reconstruction that is an important example of Colonial Revival design. Fraunces Tavern is now a museum and restaurant.

39 **Hickson W. Field Stores,** also known as the Baker, Carver & Morrell Building, 170–176 John Street (1840; addition, Buttrick, White & Burtis, 1981–82). Erected for a commission merchant, this building is a rare surviving example of a Greek Revival warehouse with an all-granite front. This building type, characterized by an austere facade and a ground floor articulated by post-and-lintel construction, represents a form first perfected in Boston and introduced to New York in 1826 by Ithiel Town at his Tappan Store (demolished) on Pearl Street. At the time of designation in 1968, the building housed the Baker, Carver & Morrell ship's chandlery. The top story was added in 1981–82 during conversion into a restaurant and apartments.

40 **Schermerhorn Row Block,** 2–18 Fulton Street, 189–195 Front Street, 159–171 John Street, and 91–92 South Street (1811–49). Historically and architecturally, this block is the most important in the South Street Seaport area. All the buildings were erected as warehouses or countinghouses for New York's rapidly expanding mercantile sector. The oldest buildings on the block are 191 and 193 Front Street, both probably erected circa 1793 but redesigned in the 19th century. The principal developer on the block was Peter Schermerhorn, a leading merchant and a member of a prominent New York family. He was responsible for the famous Schermerhorn Row (1811–12), the four-story brick warehouses on Fulton and intersecting streets that were built in the Georgian-Federal style and were originally linked by distinctive sloping roofs with tall chimneys (the mansard on the building at the corner of Fulton and South Streets was added in 1868, when the building was a hotel). Contemporaneous with Schermerhorn Row was a group of six countinghouses on John Street, only one of which (No. 165) survives. In the 1830s Greek Revival buildings began to appear throughout New York's business district. Among the finest of these is A. A. Low & Brothers' stone warehouse at 167–171 John Street (1849), built for one of the most important firms involved in the China trade. Simpler Greek Revival brick warehouses are located at the corner of Front and John Streets (1835–36). In the early 1980s all these buildings were restored (Jan Hird Pokorny, architect) for the South Street Seaport Museum and Marketplace.

Schermerhorn Row Block (No. 40). These buildings were erected as warehouses or countinghouses for New York's rapidly expanding mercantile sector. Photo by Caroline Kane Levy.

HISTORIC DISTRICTS

4 **African Burial Ground and the Commons Historic District.** This district incorporates the land associated with the Commons laid out by the Dutch government in colonial New Amsterdam as well as the site of the 18th-century African Burial Ground. The Commons was set aside by the Dutch for pastureland, located adjacent to the freshwater Collect Pond. Later the Commons became a site for parading troops, public gatherings and celebrations, and executions. Buildings that needed to be located at a distance from the general population, including a powder magazine, an almshouse, and a jail, were erected in the 18th

century. A portion of the Commons finally became a public park in the 1780s and was later incorporated into a park setting for City Hall (see No. 50). The portion of the Commons between Chambers and Duane Streets became a cemetery used for the interment of African slaves and freed men and women in the 18th century and possibly earlier. Its location north of the settled parts of the colony resulted because people of African descent could not be buried in churchyards, which were generally reserved for white residents of the community. During the colonial period, New Amsterdam, and later New York, had one of the largest African populations in North America; in 1746 the 2,444 Africans in New York, both free and enslaved, represented 20.9 percent of the population. The African Burial Ground was undoubtedly a center for African-American spiritual and community life in the 18th century and today is the one surviving tangible reminder of the life of the black residents of colonial New York. The earliest document mentioning this burial ground dates from 1712–13, although the cemetery may have been in use prior to that date. Archaeological investigations have shown that those buried here were generally wrapped in shrouds fastened with brass pins and then laid out in wooden coffins (the majority were hexagonal) with their arms folded or placed at their sides and their heads facing west. By the early 19th century, the burial ground had largely been forgotten as residential development moved into the area north of Chambers Street. As with so many older cemeteries in New York City, real estate development occurred on this site with little respect for those interred there. Miraculously, ex-

tensive amounts of fill were added to the site, and an L-shaped alley running through the block was never developed, so large segments of the cemetery survived successive waves of residential, five-story commercial, and skyscraper construction. The cemetery was uncovered during investigations preliminary to the construction of a federal court house. Sections of the burial ground were completely excavated so that the government building could be erected, but other sections have been preserved in situ as a memorial to New York's earliest African residents.

5 6 7 8 **Tribeca Historic Districts (Tribeca South, Tribeca East, Tribeca West, and Tribeca North).** The four Tribeca historic districts provide an incomparable history of the development of commercial and industrial architecture in New York City from about 1850 through the early years of the 20th century. In the late 18th century,

Tribeca East Historic District streetscape (H.D. 6). The four Tribeca historic districts provide an incomparable history of the development of New York City's commercial and industrial architecture from about 1850 through the early years of the 20th century. Photo by Oliver Allen.

the Lower West Side area now known as Tribeca (from "triangle below Canal") was largely in the hands of two owners—Trinity Church in the western section and the Lispenard family in the eastern section. As development in the city spread north, these owners laid out separate grids of streets (generally separated by Hudson Street) and then leased or sold plots for residential development. Tribeca became New York City's first residential neighborhood. Several early houses survive, notably at 2 White Street (1808–09; see No. 76). With the opening of the A. T. Stewart Store on the corner of Broadway and Reade Street in 1846 (see No. 54), the transformation of Tribeca into a commercial area began. In the 1850s and 1860s, large numbers of store and loft buildings modeled after Italian Renaissance palazzi were constructed along Broadway and on the nearby side streets, many housing retail and wholesale dry goods stores and other establishments, with storage and manufacturing space above. Most of these buildings are faced with Tuckahoe marble from Westchester County, New York, with a smaller number exhibiting facades of cast iron or Dorchester stone, a yellowish sandstone imported from New Brunswick, Canada. All these buildings had cast-iron storefronts with large plate-glass windows. Excellent examples of this type of commercial design can be seen on the north side of Reade Street between Broadway and Church Street and on the south side of Duane Street between Church Street and West Broadway in the Tribeca South Historic District and on Franklin, White, and Walker Streets between Broadway and Church Street in the Tribeca East Historic District. The architects, including Isaac Duckworth, Henry Fernbach, James H. Giles, John B. Snook, and Samuel Warner, were specialists in this building type. Of special note is the concentration of buildings in the sperm-candle mode, with their slender two-story columns resembling candles made of sperm-whale oil. Examples include the cast-iron Kitchen, Montross & Wilcox Store (1860–61; see No. 67) and the Condict Store, 55 White Street (1861; see No. 70), and the marble buildings at 80–82 (James H. Giles, 1860–62), 83 (1860–65), and 87–89 (1860–63) Leonard Street and 388 (King & Kellum, 1858–59), 392 (1859–60), and 394 (1864–65) Broadway between White and Walker Streets, all in the Tribeca East Historic District. In the late 19th

century, development moved west into the area adjoining the Washington Market, the city's major source of fresh produce. Many of the buildings of the 1880s and 1890s, primarily in the Tribeca West Historic District, are Romanesque Revival–style structures with brick facades and stone and cast-iron trim, erected to house produce-related businesses. The development of boldly massed commercial and industrial buildings with Romanesque-inspired round arches began at 173–175 Duane Street, an extraordinary essay in the use of arched openings and subtle brickwork and terracotta detail designed by Babb & Cook in 1879. Other exceptional individual buildings from this period include 36–38 Hudson Street (Babcock & Morgan, 1891–92) and the D. S. Walton & Co. printed wrapping paper factory at 1–9 Varick Street at the corner of Franklin Street (Albert Wagner, 1887–88), both with Romanesque Revival brick facades; the picturesque Dutch Renaissance–inspired 168 Duane Street (Stephen Decatur Hatch, 1886–87); and Hatch's Schepp Building at 45–53 Hudson Street, a Romanesque Revival red brick spice warehouse with black brick trim, designed in 1880. On Jay Street between Staple and Greenwich Streets and Franklin Street between Varick and Hudson Streets are examples of the unified blockfronts of five-story brick commercial buildings popular in the late 19th century. At the end of the 19th century and during the first years of the 20th century, huge, often block-square, rectilinear warehouses were erected, primarily in the Tribeca North Historic District, near the Hudson River Railroad freight terminal on Hudson Square. Prime examples of these buildings are 415–427 Greenwich Street (Charles B. Meyers, 1912–13); 443–453 Greenwich Street (Charles C. Haight, 1883–84), erected for the Trinity Church Corporation, which still owned a great deal of land in Tribeca; and 32–54 Hubert Street (William H. Birkmire, 1903–06). With the removal of the Washington Market to Hunt's Point in the Bronx in the early 1960s and the exodus of industry from the city, Tribeca became a backwater with a significant amount of empty space. Artists began to move into the area in the 1970s. Since the 1980s, large-scale conversion has virtually transformed this former commercial neighborhood into a thriving residential district.

INDIVIDUAL LANDMARKS

41 **Barclay-Vesey Building,** 140 West Street (McKenzie, Voorhees & Gmelin, Ralph Walker, architect in charge, 1923–27). The first major design of Ralph Walker, this brick-faced building, whose name derives from its location between Barclay and Vesey Streets, was commissioned by the New York Telephone Company for its headquarters. It is one of the most significant structures in the annals of skyscraper design, since it was the first building in New York City to exploit the requirements of the 1916 zoning code, leading to the tower's dramatic massing. Walker also pioneered in the use of complex, nontraditional, naturalistic, carved ornament. **Interior:** Exterior ornamental motifs are repeated in the lobby, which contains veined marble walls, travertine floors with bronze medallions, and a vaulted ceiling embellished with murals depicting the stages in the evolution of human communication.

42 **Hopkins Store,** also known as the 75 Murray Street Building (1857). The Venetian Renaissance–inspired cast-iron facade of this five-story commercial structure, built to house the glassware business of Francis and John Hopkins, was probably cast in the foundry of James Bogardus. It is among a handful of surviving buildings with iron elements attributed to Bogardus, the self-proclaimed inventor of cast-iron architecture. The building was rehabilitated in 1994–96 when it was converted to residential use.

43 **Bennett Building,** 139 Fulton Street (Arthur D. Gilman, 1872–73; addition, James M. Farnsworth, 1890–92 and 1894). The Bennett Building, with three fully designed, ten-story cast-iron facades, is thought to be the tallest cast-iron building ever erected. It was built in three campaigns, beginning in 1872 when *New York Herald* publisher James Gordon Bennett, Jr., commissioned a seven-story French Second Empire building that would be rented for stores and offices. In 1892–93 the original mansard roof was removed and four stories were added in a design that replicated the original castings. Architect James Farnsworth returned in 1894, adding a 25-foot-wide section on Ann Street that is also indistinguishable from the original.

44 **Saint Paul's Chapel (Episcopal) and Graveyard,** Broadway at Fulton Street (1764–66; porch, 1767–68; tower, James C. Lawrence, 1794). Manhattan's oldest surviving church is also one of the finest Georgian buildings in the United States. Saint Paul's, the "uptown" chapel for Trinity Church, is a simplified version of James Gibbs's London masterpiece, Saint Martin-in-the-Fields on Trafalgar Square. Built of local stone with brownstone trim, the church has a modest portico on its towered front facade, which faces the 18th-century graveyard. The rear elevation on Broadway features an imposing brownstone Ionic porch—part of the original plan, but not built until 1767–68—sheltering a large Palladian window. The design of the church is often ascribed to Thomas McBean, but no evidence supports this attribution. George Washington worshiped at Saint Paul's during the brief period when New York was the nation's capital.

Saint Paul's Chapel (Episcopal) and Graveyard (No. 44). Built of local stone, Saint Paul's is Manhattan's oldest surviving church. Photo by Carl Forster.

45 **New York County Lawyers' Association,** 14 Vesey Street (Cass Gilbert, 1929–30). This building, designed in the 18th-century English Georgian style, is a late work by Gilbert. Commissioned by an organization that had been founded in 1908 to serve the public interest and the legal profession, the building handsomely complements the 18th-century Saint Paul's Chapel (see No. 44) across the street.

46 **New York Evening Post Building,** 20 Vesey Street (Robert D. Kohn, 1906–07). Built as the offices and printing plant of the *New York Evening Post,* this 13-story limestone-faced structure is a rare example of a New York City building inspired by the early 20th-century Central European artistic reform movement known as the Vienna Secession. Kohn designed several buildings in the style, notably this structure and the meetinghouse of the New York Society for Ethical Culture (see No. 312). The building's refined classicism, rational expression of structure, and stylized ornament are evocative of Viennese precedents. Of special note are the four statues on the tenth floor known as the *Four Periods of Publicity;* two are by Gutzon Borglum, the sculptor of Mount Rushmore, and two are by Estelle Rumbold Kohn, the architect's wife.

47 **Saint Peter's Roman Catholic Church,** 22 Barclay Street (John R. Haggerty and Thomas Thomas, 1836–40). Saint Peter's is the oldest Roman Catholic parish in New York City. This imposing Greek Revival granite church, with its six Ionic columns, replaced an earlier building of 1785. Although a pagan Greek temple might seem an unusual model for a Catholic church, this was a popular form for buildings erected by all denominations.

48 **Woolworth Building,** 233 Broadway (Cass Gilbert, 1910–13). The Woolworth Building was commissioned by F. W. Woolworth, who instructed his architect to design the world's tallest building. Cass Gilbert's neo-Gothic masterpiece, faced almost entirely in terra cotta, rapidly became one of the symbols of New York City. The building's prominence on the skyline was a constant advertisement for Woolworth's stores. When the building was completed, the Woolworth firm occupied only one and one-half stories but profited from the rental of offices on other floors. The F. W. Wool-

worth Company, which still owns and occupies part of the building, undertook a major rehabilitation of the facade (Ehrenkrantz & Associates, architects) in the 1980s that included the replacement of much of the terra cotta with cast stone. **Interior:** The symmetrically planned lobby is among the most spectacular of the early 20th century in New York City. Its rich decorative treatment includes an Early Christian–inspired mosaic barrel vault; a stained-glass skylight; marble walls; bronze furnishings; murals entitled *Labor* and *Commerce* on the mezzanine balconies; and plaster grotesques depicting some of the men involved with the building's construction, among them Woolworth (counting his nickels and dimes) and Gilbert (cradling a model of the building).

49 **Potter Building,** 38 Park Row and 145 Nassau Street (Norris G. Starkweather, 1882–86). Real-estate investor and politician Orlando B. Potter commissioned this picturesque Queen Anne/neo-Grec office building after his previous building on the site burned. He used the most advanced fireproofing then available, employing rolled-iron beams, cast-iron columns, brick walls, and tile arches for structural support, as well as red brick, brownstone-colored terra cotta, and cast iron on the exterior load-bearing walls, which are forty inches thick at the ground level. The extensive terra-cotta detail provided by the Boston Terra Cotta Company so pleased Potter that he established his own firm, the New York Architectural Terra Cotta Company, in Long Island City (see Queens No. 3). The building was converted into apartments in 1979–81.

50 **Home Life Insurance Company Building** (incorporating the **Postal Telegraph Building**), 256–257 and 253 Broadway (Napoleon Le Brun & Sons, Pierre Le Brun, architect in charge, 1892–94; Harding & Gooch, 1892–94). Home Life, founded in Brooklyn in 1860, opened a branch office on this site in 1866. The company held a competition for the design of a new Manhattan office in 1892. The result was Pierre Le Brun's Renaissance-style marble-clad building, an early steel-skeleton-framed skyscraper. The building is a fine example of the tripartite expression of high-rise design, with its ornate arcaded base, simple shaft, and impressive pyramidal crown. Adjacent to the former Home Life building is Harding & Gooch's Postal Telegraph Building, erected for a major competitor of Western Union. In 1947 Home Life purchased the neighboring structure and connected the two buildings internally.

51 **City Hall,** City Hall Park (Joseph-François Mangin and John McComb, Jr., 1802–11). City Hall is one of the most beautiful early 19th-century public buildings in the United States. Mangin and McComb's design was the winning entry in a competition held in 1802. It is generally believed that the French-trained Mangin was responsible for the exterior, since it closely resembles 18th-century French civic structures. The exterior stonework, originally Massachusetts marble with a brownstone rear elevation, deteriorated so extensively that in 1954–56 it was replaced with Alabama limestone above a Missouri granite base. The building's cupola is undergoing restoration by Cabrera Barricklo, architect. The **interior** is especially remarkable. The main entrance hall leads to a central rotunda in which a pair of spectacular cantilevered stairs curve upward to the second floor, where a series of marble Corinthian columns support a coffered dome. The lobby, stairs, and columns are original features; the dome is part of a restoration undertaken by Grosvenor Atterbury in 1912.

52 **New York County Courthouse,** also known as the Tweed Courthouse, 52 Chambers Street (John Kellum and Leopold Eidlitz, 1861–81). This marble building just north of City Hall is intimately associated with New York's corrupt political boss William M. Tweed. The New York County Courthouse was the first permanent government building erected by New York City after the completion of City Hall (see No. 51) in 1811. As conceived by John Kellum, the courthouse was a grand Italianate monument with a Corinthian portico and a long staircase (later removed) facing Chambers Street. Kellum died before the building was completed, and Leopold Eidlitz then designed the south wing in a medieval-inspired style. The building contains some of the finest mid-19th-century **interiors** in New York, including Kellum's cast-iron staircases; an octagonal rotunda (largely the work of Eidlitz) with brick arcades; and Eidlitz's courtroom, which is distinguished by its encaustic tile floors, foliate columns, fireplace, and

Gothic detail. Architect John Waite is guiding a long-term restoration project.

53 **Emigrant Industrial Savings Bank,** 51 Chambers Street (Raymond F. Almirall, 1908–12). The Emigrant Industrial Savings Bank was organized in 1850, under the auspices of Roman Catholic bishop John Hughes and the Irish Emigrant Society, to protect the savings of newly arrived Irish immigrants. In 1908 the bank commissioned designs for a new building that would front both Chambers and Reade Streets. This limestone-faced skyscraper in the Beaux-Arts style was the first to be laid out on an H-plan, providing light and air to almost all office spaces. The building is now owned by New York City and used for municipal offices. **Interior:** The Department of Motor Vehicles occupies the banking hall. This richly decorated space has marble walls and floors, bronze grilles, original tellers' cages, and a series of stained-glass skylights with allegorical figures representing mining, manufacturing, agriculture, and other modes of employment.

54 **A. T. Stewart Store,** later the New York Sun Building, 280 Broadway (Joseph Trench & Co., 1845–46; additions: Trench & Snook, 1850–51 and 1852–53; Frederick Schmidt, 1872; Edward D. Harris, 1884; 1921). The A. T. Stewart Store was one of the most influential buildings ever erected in New York City, as its style, materials, use, and location helped determine the course of architecture and commerce in the city. In 1846 Alexander Turney Stewart opened New York's first department store. Located on the corner of Broadway and Reade Street, the store inaugurated the commercial development of Broadway north of City Hall. As the first Italianate commercial building in New York, it established what would become the style of choice for hundreds of stores and warehouses erected through the succeeding decades. In addition, the store was the first major commercial structure faced with Tuckahoe marble, a material that would later become common on such buildings; it was innovative also in its use of imported French plate glass for the ground-floor windows. The store expanded along Broadway, Reade Street, and Chambers Street, with three-bay modules echoing those of the original design (the final bays were built in 1884). By the early 1850s, cast iron was employed on the ground floor to support the upper walls. The building served as Stewart's retail store until 1862, when it became a warehouse. The sixth and seventh floors are 1884 additions (the seventh-floor corners were added in 1921), built when the store was converted into offices. Offices of the *New York Sun* occupied the building between 1919 and 1952. The A. T. Stewart Store now houses municipal offices.

55 **Broadway-Chambers Building,** 277 Broadway (Cass Gilbert, 1899–1900). Cass Gilbert's first New York City building epitomizes the tripartite columnar base-shaft-capital form popular on early steel-skeleton-frame skyscrapers in New York. The use of materials is especially fine here, with a classically inspired pink granite base, a shaft of red and beige brick, a capital faced in beige terra cotta highlighted with blue, green, yellow, and pink glazed detail, and a crowning green copper cornice.

56 **287 Broadway Building** (John B. Snook, 1871–72). This cast-iron commercial building in the French Second Empire style was erected as a speculative venture. To increase its allure for potential tenants, the building was crowned with an impressive mansard roof featuring lacy iron cresting and was equipped with a very early Otis passenger elevator. The iron elements were cast by Jackson, Burnet & Co., which maintained foundries on Centre Street and on East 13th Street.

57 **Cary Building,** 105–107 Chambers Street (King & Kellum, 1856–57). A masterpiece of cast-iron design, the Cary Building extends through the entire block between Chambers and Reade Streets. Its Italian Renaissance facades, with their arched windows supported by Corinthian columns, were cast in the form of rusticated stone blocks at Daniel D. Badger's Architectural Iron Works on East 14th Street. Erected by the dry goods firm of Cary, Howard & Sanger, the building reflects the mid-19th-century transformation of the area west and north of City Hall into an important commercial district. Badger pioneered in the manufacture of rolling iron shutters, and many of these are still visible on the Cary Building's windows.

58 **Hall of Records,** now Surrogate's Court–Hall of Records, 31 Chambers Street (John R.

Thomas and Horgan & Slattery, 1899–1907). This boldly detailed Beaux-Arts structure was erected by New York City as a representation of the importance of civic government. Designed by Thomas, the building was completed, following his death, by a firm closely allied with New York's Tammany politicians. Built of Maine granite, the building supports a profusion of sculptural details that depict New York's history. The decoration is at its most lavish in the magnificent **interior**, particularly the foyer, with its Siena marble walls and vaulted mosaic ceiling by the artist William de Leftwich Dodge; the double-height marble lobby with a skylight and a divided stair; the encircling corridors; and the two fifth-floor courtrooms, one paneled in Santo Domingo mahogany and the other in quartersawn English oak.

59 **Brooklyn Bridge.** See Brooklyn, No. 15.

60 **Municipal Building,** 1 Centre Street (McKim, Mead & White, William M. Kendall, partner in charge, 1907–14). In 1907 New York City announced a competition for the design of a skyscraper office building to be erected on a site straddling Chambers Street; the building was to house administrative agencies and to incorporate a large subway station. McKim, Mead & White partner William M. Kendall's brilliant functional solution won the competition and was constructed between 1909 and 1914. The base of the limestone building is articulated by a screen of Corinthian columns flanking a central triumphal arch that bridges Chambers Street. The intricate terra-cotta vault above the street is modeled on the entrance treatment of the Palazzo Farnese in Rome. At the south end of the building is the subway entrance, an arcaded plaza covered by dramatic vaults of Guastavino tile construction. The simple office shaft rises 25 stories to a templed cupola crowned by Adolph Weinman's gold statue *Civic Fame;* Weinman also created the allegorical relief panels at the base. A major rehabilitation project was completed in 1992 (Wank Adams Slavin, architect).

61 **United States Courthouse,** 1 Foley Square (Cass Gilbert, 1933–36). Cass Gilbert's last building is a Classical Revival skyscraper that rises from a base of monumental Corinthian columns to a golden pyramidal crown. The building is carefully aligned with the New York County Courthouse (see No. 62) to the north and the Municipal Building (see No. 60) to the south, and its tower balances that of Gilbert's earlier Woolworth Building (see No. 48), located on the opposite side of City Hall Park.

62 **New York County Courthouse,** now the New York State Supreme Court, 60 Centre Street (Guy Lowell, 1913–27). In 1927 the New York County Court moved from the old "Tweed Courthouse" (see No. 52) to this spacious granite-faced building. The Boston architect Guy Lowell won a competition in 1913 with a design for a round building. Construction was delayed and the design altered to

a hexagonal form; work finally began in 1919. The Roman classical style chosen was popular for courthouse architecture in the first decades of the 20th century. The monumental character of the exterior continues on the **interior,** with its central rotunda and radial corridors. In the 1930s, under the sponsorship of the federal government's artists' relief programs, Attilio Pusterla painted a series of murals on the vestibule ceiling and on the rotunda dome; restoration work on these began in 1992.

63 **Fire Engine Company No. 7/Hook & Ladder Company No. 1,** now Hook & Ladder Company No. 1 and Fire Department Bureau of Fire Communication, 100 Duane Street (Trowbridge & Livingston, 1904–05). At the turn of the century,

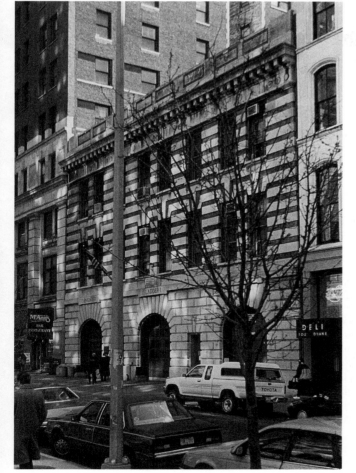

Fire Engine Company No. 7/ Hook & Ladder Company No. 1 (No. 63). At the turn of the century, the New York City Fire Department commissioned new firehouses, like this bold French Renaissance building. Photo by Caroline Kane Levy.

the fire department commissioned new firehouses from various architects, including such prestigious firms as Trowbridge & Livingston. The firm designed a bold French Renaissance building with a rusticated limestone base set below brick with heavy limestone banding. This is among the most impressive small-scale civic structures of the period.

64 David S. Brown Store, also known as the 8 Thomas Street Building (J. Morgan Slade, 1875–76). A manufacturer of laundry and toilet soaps commissioned this rare New York City example of Victorian Gothic masonry design from J. Morgan Slade, who, before his untimely death at age thirty in 1882, distinguished himself as an exceedingly accomplished architect of commercial buildings. The use of banded stone arches and other Venetian Gothic motifs reflects the influence of the English theorist John Ruskin, while the honest use of cast iron on the ground floor indicates Slade's interest in French architectural theory.

65 319 Broadway Building (D. & J. Jardine, 1869–70). The lone survivor of a pair of buildings known as the Thomas Twins that once occupied the two western corners of Broadway at Thomas Street, this Italianate structure has facades of iron that were cast at Daniel D. Badger's Architectural Iron Works.

66 New York Life Insurance Company Building, 346 Broadway (Stephen Decatur Hatch and McKim, Mead & White, 1894–99). The New York Life Insurance Company, one of America's oldest life insurance firms, erected its headquarters building on Broadway between Catherine Lane and Leonard Street in 1868–70. In 1894 Hatch was commissioned to extend the building eastward. Shortly thereafter he died, and the commission was taken over by McKim, Mead & White. Hatch's rear extension was built, but the company then decided to replace its earlier building. The elevations facing the narrow side streets continue Hatch's design, while McKim, Mead & White's Broadway frontage is a flamboyant palazzo-like pavilion crowned by a clock tower. Although now housing municipal offices, the building retains many of New York Life's original **interior** spaces, including a marble lobby, a 13-story stair hall, a banking hall, executive offices, and the clock tower machinery room.

67 Kitchen, Montross & Wilcox Store, also known as the 85 Leonard Street Building (1861). Commissioned by a firm of dry goods merchants, this cast-iron-fronted structure is one of the few surviving buildings in New York known to have been fabricated at the ironworks of the pioneer cast-iron founder James Bogardus. It is also one of a small group of mid-19th-century commercial buildings in the sperm-candle style, identifiable by its two-story columns resembling candles made from sperm-whale oil.

68 359 Broadway Building (1852). This Italianate commercial building with its unusual window enframements reflects the rapid shift from residential to commercial tenancy that occurred on Broadway south of Canal Street following the construction of the A. T. Stewart Store (see No. 54) in 1845. The stone building is of special historic importance because the upper three floors were occupied by the photographer Mathew Brady's portrait studio between 1853 and 1859. Brady, one of the most important photographers in American history, is renowned for his portraits and Civil War images.

69 361 Broadway Building, also known as the James S. White Building (W. Wheeler Smith, 1881–82). While most early examples of cast-iron construction appear to be attempts to simulate stone, cast-iron buildings of the late 1870s and 1880s were designed to exploit the properties of the material itself and are often extremely flamboyant. Commissioned by James S. White, this late example of a building with cast-iron facades contains very large windows set in a framework of elaborately decorated iron columns and piers.

70 Condict Store, also known as the 55 White Street Building (John Kellum & Son, 1861). Commissioned by John and Samuel Condict to house their saddlery business, this structure is one of New York City's most significant commercial buildings of the mid-19th century. It is also the largest surviving example of a cast-iron sperm-candle design, with its thin two-story columns resembling the expensive candles made of sperm-whale oil. The facade, whose iron components were cast at Daniel D. Badger's Architectural Iron Works, was restored in 1988–89 as part of a residential conversion (Liebman Melting Partnership, architect).

71 **Woods Mercantile Buildings,** 46–50 White Street (1865). The Woods Mercantile Buildings are handsome examples of the Italianate commercial palaces faced in Tuckahoe marble that transformed the streets adjacent to Broadway just north of City Hall into a prime business district in the 1850s and 1860s. The two buildings, designed as a single unit, have cast-iron shop fronts and are crowned by an unusual pedimented cornice emblazoned with the name and date of the buildings.

72 **Ahrens Building,** 70–76 Lafayette Street (George H. Griebel, 1894–95). The facades of this narrow seven-story steel-framed corner commercial building in the Romanesque Revival style are unified by three-story round-arched arcades. The building is covered with rough sandstone at the base, contrasting smooth buff brick on the superstructure, and rock-faced brown brick trim; on Lafayette Street it is embellished with three-story metal oriels. The building was erected as a speculative venture at the time when New York City was widening Lafayette Street to create a major traffic artery.

73 **Fire Engine Company No. 31,** now the Downtown Community Television Center, 87 Lafayette Street (Napoleon Le Brun & Sons, 1895). The firm of Napoleon Le Brun & Sons was responsible for the design of many of the city's late 19th-century firehouses. Engine Company No. 31, modeled on early 16th-century Loire Valley châteaux in the style of Francis I, is the firm's most impressive civic design.

74 **254–260 Canal Street Building** (1856–57). Resembling an Italian Renaissance palazzo, this building is an important early example of cast-iron architecture in New York City. There is strong evidence to suggest that this commercial palace, with its seemingly endless array of arched windows, contains iron elements cast by James Bogardus, a pioneer in the construction of cast-iron buildings, little of whose work survives.

75 **Long Distance Building of the American Telephone & Telegraph Company,** now AT&T Headquarters, 32 Sixth Avenue (Voorhees, Gmelin & Walker, Ralph Walker, partner in charge, 1930–32). This massive Art Deco office building

and communications center, conceived as a major enlargement and redesign of an earlier structure, was the world's largest long-distance communications center at the time of its completion. The rough-textured brick facade, with its bold sculptural massing and linear ornament, reflects a technology-inspired aesthetic in keeping with the building's function. **Interior:** The lobby has ceramic tile walls with marble trim, a terrazzo floor, and bronze doors and highlighting. Its artistic detail reinforces the building's purpose: One wall is decorated with a vast tile map of the world; the ceiling features stucco and glass mosaic allegories of long-distance communication to Africa, Asia, Australia, and Europe.

76 **2 White Street House** (1808–09). A brick-fronted frame house with a gambrel roof and dormers, this corner building is one of the few survivors from the period when the Lower West Side area now known as Tribeca was developing as a residential area. The house, built for Gideon Tucker, owner of the nearby Tucker & Ludlum plaster factory, has probably always had a ground-floor store.

77 **175 West Broadway Building** (Scott & Umbach, 1877). A Newark, New Jersey, architecture firm designed this exceptional late 19th-century example of a commercial building with a polychromatic brick facade. The design was inspired by European, particularly German, sources. The corbeled window arches and the corbeled brick cornice are without parallel in New York City architecture.

78 **Western Union Building,** 60 Hudson Street (Voorhees, Gmelin & Walker, Ralph Walker, partner in charge, 1928–30). This massive brick-clad building, which occupies an entire block, shows the influence of Dutch and German Expressionist design on American architecture. The influence is especially evident in Walker's exploitation of brick—both on the exterior, where the color lightens as the building rises in bold setbacks, and in the **interior** vestibules and lobby, with their complexly patterned orange brick walls and matching barrel-vaulted Guastavino tile ceiling. Erected as the headquarters of Western Union, the building contained the corporation's offices, equipment rooms, an auditorium, a cafeteria, shops, and classrooms for company messengers. The building now houses a variety of firms, many of them in the communications industry.

79 **Harrison Street Houses,** 25–41 Harrison Street (1796–1828). Around 1800 the Lower West Side area now known as Tribeca developed into a residential neighborhood of modest brick and frame houses in the Federal style. The houses near the waterfront were gradually engulfed by the expansion of Washington Market, and many of the older buildings in the area were altered for commercial use. As part of an urban renewal project begun in the late 1960s, the nine houses in this L-shaped enclave were incorporated into the Independence Plaza housing complex; three of the houses were moved from Washington Street, including two designed by John McComb, Jr.—at No. 25 (1819), and the architect's own home, now at No. 27 (1796–97). All the houses were extensively rehabilitated by Oppenheimer & Brady.

80 **Fleming Smith Warehouse,** 451–453 Washington Street (Stephen Decatur Hatch, 1891–92). Crowned by eccentric gables and dormers, Hatch's brick warehouse is a skillful combination of Romanesque Revival and Flemish Renaissance design. The central gable contains the date of design and the owner's initials, all wrought in metal. The building was one of the first in Tribeca to be converted for residential use.

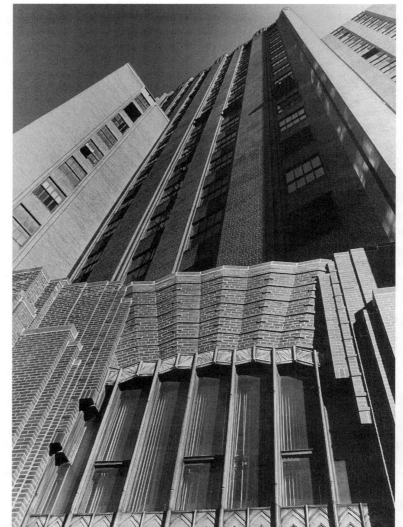

Western Union Building (No. 78). The former headquarters of Western Union, this building shows the influence of Dutch and German Expressionist design. Photo by Caroline Kane Levy.

HISTORIC DISTRICTS

9 **SoHo–Cast Iron Historic District.** SoHo (from "south of Houston") is a commercial district, developed in the mid- to late 19th century to serve the wholesale dry goods trade. The district contains the world's largest collection of buildings with cast-iron fronts. Such buildings were popular between the 1850s and early 1880s because of the speed with which they could be erected and the material's strength and facility for imitating the more expensive stone traditionally used in the construction of commercial palaces. The iron parts were mass-produced at local foundries, such as Daniel D. Badger's Architectural Iron Works, and assembled at the building site. The SoHo district includes a large number of Italianate and French Second Empire cast-iron buildings from the 1850s and 1860s, including the masterful Haughwout Building (see No. 84). Some of the finest mid-19th-century cast-iron streetscapes in America can be seen on Greene Street between Canal and Grand Streets and between Broome and Spring Streets. Besides cast-iron buildings, the district also has a significant number of the masonry structures (largely Tuckahoe marble or Dorchester stone) that the cast-iron buildings sought to emulate. After the Civil War, cast-iron buildings were erected that did not imitate stone but exhibited the technical proficiency of the foundries. Major examples of these late cast-iron designs were the work of such prominent architects as Richard Morris Hunt (Roosevelt Building, 478–483 Broadway, 1873–74), Vaux & Withers (448 Broome Street, 1871–72), Renwick & Sands (34 Howard Street, 1868), and William A. Potter (435 Broome Street, 1873). By the turn of the century, cast iron was no longer favored by architects and builders, and steel-framed brick and terra-cotta loft buildings were erected in SoHo to house garment factories. The most extraordinary of these is the Little Singer Building (Ernest Flagg, 1902–04), at 561 Broadway. In the 1960s artists began moving into the district's underutilized loft spaces, leading to the growth of SoHo as a major arts center. Artists were followed by visitors attracted to the area's new cultural life and then by shoppers who came to visit SoHo's fashionable new stores. Today the area is a mix of residential, cultural, commercial, industrial, and office uses, all housed in an incomparable collection of commercial and industrial buildings, many of which have been beautifully restored.

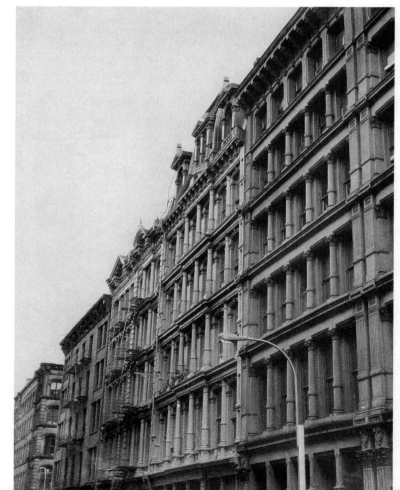

SoHo–Cast Iron Historic District (H.D. 9). One of the world's major arts centers, the district also contains the world's largest collection of buildings with cast-iron fronts. Photo by John Barrington Bayley.

10 Charlton-King-Vandam Historic District. Now located at the edge of an industrial area, this historic district is an extraordinary remnant of early 19th-century residential New York, containing the city's largest concentration of row houses in the Federal style, as well as a significant concentration of Greek Revival houses. The district was once the site of Richmond Hill, a Georgian mansion that served variously as George Washington's headquarters, the official vice presidential residence, and the home of Aaron Burr. Burr had the land surveyed and mapped out the present block and street system in 1797, but he lost the property to John Jacob

Astor, who was responsible for the area's development into a residential neighborhood beginning in the 1820s. Exceptional examples of Federal-style row houses line the north sides of Charlton and Vandam Streets, and King Street has fine examples of Greek Revival houses. Later additions to the district include Public School 8 (David I. Stagg, 1886), a lively Queen Anne–style building at 29 King Street, now converted into apartments.

INDIVIDUAL LANDMARKS

81 149 Mulberry Street House, also known as the Stephen Van Rensselaer House (c. 1816). This brick-faced, wood-frame house exemplifies the small row houses in the Federal style that were once common in Manhattan south of 14th Street. The

Haughwout Building (No. 84). The insistent repetition of round arches and Corinthian columns of this masterpiece of early cast-iron construction was adapted from the facade of the Sansovino Library in Venice. Photo by Caroline Kane Levy.

Flemish bond brickwork, paneled stone lintels, gambrel roof, and dormer windows are characteristic of the style. The house was one of many in the area erected by Stephen Van Rensselaer; it was originally located on the northwest corner of Mulberry and Grand Streets, and was moved in 1841.

82 **Odd Fellows Hall,** 165–171 Grand Street (Trench & Snook, 1847–48; roof addition, John Buckingham, 1881–82). The former Odd Fellows Hall is one of the city's earliest Italianate buildings, designed only a few years after Joseph Trench had introduced the style to New York in the A. T. Stewart Store (see No. 54). The Independent Order of Odd Fellows, which was incorporated in New York in 1844, occupied the building from 1848 until the early 1880s, when the northward movement of the city's affluent residents led to a relocation uptown. The building was subsequently converted for commercial and industrial use.

83 **New York City Police Headquarters,** now the Police Building Apartments, 240 Centre Street (Hoppin & Koen, 1905–09). Following the creation of Greater New York in 1898, the city's police department expanded rapidly, and a large new headquarters building was planned. In 1905 Mayor George McClellan laid the cornerstone of this monumental limestone-faced, steel-framed Edwardian Baroque structure whose tall dome is visible from the City Hall area to the south. The police department relocated in 1973, and after standing empty for over a decade, the building was converted into luxury housing (Ehrenkrantz Group & Eckstut, architect).

84 **Haughwout Building,** 488–492 Broadway (John P. Gaynor, 1856–57). A masterpiece of early cast-iron construction, the Haughwout Building was commissioned by E. V. Haughwout for his fashionable china, silver, and glassware emporium. The iron components were manufactured at Daniel D. Badger's Architectural Iron Works and were originally painted a color referred to in 1859 as "Turkish drab." The attempt to create a beautiful building using a limited number of mass-produced

31

parts is evident in this structure's insistent repetition of round arches and Corinthian columns, motifs adapted from the facade of the Sansovino Library in Venice. After years of neglect, the building's facades were beautifully restored and repainted their original color in 1995 under the direction of Joseph Pell Lombardi, architect.

85 **Roman Catholic Orphan Asylum**, now Saint Patrick's Convent and Girls' School, 32 Prince Street (1825–26). The Roman Catholic Orphan Asylum, founded in 1817, was operated by the Sisters of Charity. This large brick building with an elegant doorway is the most significant institutional building in the Federal style surviving in New York City. Originally housing both boys and girls, the asylum became a girls' institution in 1851. In 1886 the asylum was converted into a school.

86 **Saint Patrick's Old Cathedral**, Mott Street at Prince Street (Joseph-François Mangin, 1809–15; restoration, 1868). New York City's Roman Catholic cathedral was dedicated to the patron saint of Ireland. This original cathedral complex was built on Mott Street, in what was a rapidly developing residential neighborhood in the early 19th century. It is the oldest Roman Catholic church building in New York City. Mangin, the architect of City Hall, designed the original Saint Patrick's Cathedral in a rather fanciful Gothic-inspired style. The church was built of local stone, with facades facing Mott and Mulberry Streets. The building was extensively restored following a disastrous fire in 1866. The cathedral moved uptown to Fifth Avenue between East 50th and 51st Streets in 1879 (see No. 254) and this building became known as Saint Patrick's Old Cathedral.

87 **Saint Patrick's Chancery Office**, later Saint Michael's Chapel, now Saint Michael's Russian Catholic Church, 266 Mulberry Street (James Renwick, Jr., with William Rodrigue, 1858–59). This small Gothic Revival building was designed to harmonize with the nearby cathedral. The architects were James Renwick, Jr., the designer of the new Saint Patrick's Cathedral (see No. 254), which was under construction at the time, and William Rodrigue, a relative of Archbishop John Hughes. Rodrigue, who also assisted Renwick at

Saint Patrick's, had previously designed buildings for Fordham University (see Bronx No. 31).

88 **Fourteenth Ward Industrial School of the Children's Aid Society (Astor Memorial Building)**, 256–258 Mott Street (Vaux & Radford, 1888–89). In the late 1880s and 1890s, the Children's Aid Society erected a series of schools to serve the city's poor, the earliest of which was this superb Victorian Gothic building with beautiful naturalistic terracotta ornament. The school, founded to teach skills to immigrant children, was built with funds provided by John Jacob Astor II as a memorial to his wife, a longtime supporter of the society. The building has been converted into housing.

89 **Puck Building**, 295–309 Lafayette Street (Albert Wagner, 1885–86 and 1892–93; Herman Wagner, 1899). With its seemingly endless round-arched arcades and complex brickwork, the Puck is a masterpiece of late 19th-century New York commercial architecture. The Romanesque Revival building was erected to house the offices and printing plant of *Puck,* a prominent humor magazine, and the J. Ottman Lithographing Co., which printed the magazine's famous chromolithographic cartoons. The two original wings, designed by Albert Wagner, fronted only on Houston and Mulberry Streets. In the late 1890s, Lafayette Street was extended through the block, and two bays of the Puck Building's Houston Street facade and the building's entire west wall were demolished. Herman Wagner, who was related to Albert, designed the new Lafayette Street elevation to conform to the original design. The main entrance was moved from the corner of Houston and Mulberry to Lafayette Street. Both the original and later entrances are marked by statues of Shakespeare's Puck; the statue at the original entrance is by Casper Buberl, and the one on Lafayette Street is the work of Henry Baerer. The building was handsomely rehabilitated in 1983–84 and is now being used for offices and galleries. Extensive additional restoration was undertaken in 1995 by Beyer Blinder Belle, architects.

90 **83 and 85 Sullivan Street Houses** (1819). This pair of modest houses retains original Federal-style doorways with leaded transoms (among the earliest surviving in the city), low stoops with wrought-iron railings, Flemish bond brickwork, and multipaned wooden sash windows. The houses were originally 2½ stories tall, but full third floors were added when the former single-family homes became multiple dwellings. In 1900, No. 85 housed five families.

91 **116 Sullivan Street House** (1832; upper two floors, 1872). This house in the Federal style retains an extremely unusual doorway. In the manner of many local doorways, the six-paneled door is flanked by Ionic colonnettes and crowned by a fanlight. The sidelights, however, are unique survivors: each one is broken into three ovals with wooden frames carved to simulate a cloth curtain drawn through a series of rings.

92 **203 Prince Street House** (1834). This handsomely restored house in the late Federal style was built on land that was once part of Aaron Burr's estate. Originally 2½ stories tall, the house received a full third floor in 1888. The reconstructed, elliptically arched entranceway above a high stoop is a fine example of Federal-style design.

93 **326 Spring Street House,** also known as the James Brown House (c. 1817). A rare survivor from the period when the Lower West Side was a residential area, this gambrel-roofed house in the Federal style was probably erected in 1817 for the tobacconist James Brown. Original features include a facade of brick laid in Flemish bond, splayed window lintels, and a pair of dormers.

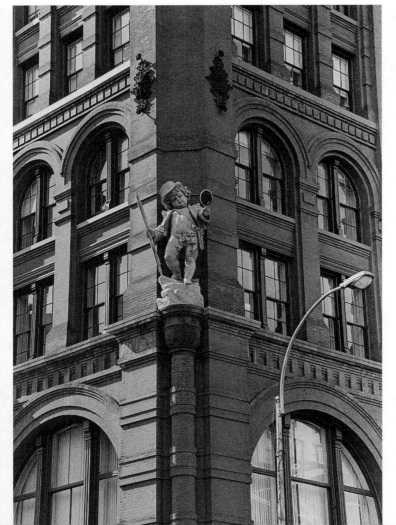

Puck Building (No. 89). This Romanesque Revival building was built to house the offices of *Puck,* a prominent humor magazine. Photo by Carl Forster.

INDIVIDUAL LANDMARKS

94 **Saint James Roman Catholic Church,** 32 James Street (1835–37). Saint James, the second oldest Roman Catholic church building in New York, is constructed of fieldstone and has an impos- ing pedimented Greek Revival brownstone facade that features a pair of Doric columns. The detailing of the facade is modeled on designs published by the architect Minard Lafever, and while the build- ing has frequently been attributed to Lafever, there is no supporting documentary evidence.

95 **Shearith Israel Graveyard,** 55–57 Saint James Place (1683–). This tiny graveyard is all that remains of the earliest surviving burial ground of Congregation Shearith Israel, the oldest Jewish congregation in North America. The graveyard is one of three small Manhattan cemeteries once used by the congregation. The others are on West 11th Street (in the Greenwich Village Historic District, see No. 12) and West 21st Street (in the Ladies' Mile Historic District, see No. 15).

96 **Oliver Street Baptist Church,** now Mariners' Temple (Baptist), 12 Oliver Street (attributed to Isaac Lucas, 1844–45). This building is one of several brownstone-fronted Greek Revival churches erected in Manhattan's newly developing residential neighborhoods in the 1830s and 1840s. The facade of the Mariners' Temple features a pair of slender Ionic columns. The little-known architect Isaac Lucas is mentioned in the 1844 church minutes, but it is not clear whether he was the architect or simply the building superintendent.

97 **Edward Mooney House,** 18 Bowery (c. 1785–89). Built for merchant Edward Mooney at some point between 1785 and 1789, this house in the Georgian style is thought to be the oldest surviving row house in Manhattan. At the time of construction, the Chatham Square area was developing as a fine residential neighborhood, but by the 1840s the house had become a brothel. Today the building boasts many original features above its carefully reconstructed ground story.

98 **Zion English Lutheran Church,** now the Church of the Transfiguration (R.C.), 25 Mott Street (1801; additions, Henry Engelbert, 1868). This former Lutheran church, one of four Georgian-Gothic landmark churches built of locally quarried Manhattan schist on the Lower East Side, became a Roman Catholic church in 1853. In 1868 the tower was added; the heavy Gothic window frames probably also date from this remodeling.

99 **William and Rosamond Clark House,** also known as the 51 Market Street House (1824–25). This row house in the late Federal style, apparently erected for the grocer William Clark and his wife, was built when the Lower East Side was an affluent residential neighborhood. The house re-

Eldridge Street Synagogue (Congregation Khal Adath Jeshurun) (No. 101). This was the first Orthodox synagogue built by the large numbers of Eastern European Jews who settled on the Lower East Side in the late 19th century. Photo by Carl Forster.

tains a beautiful fanlighted entrance, as well as original ironwork and window lintels. The two upper floors were added later in the 19th century.

100 **Northern Reformed Church,** also known as the Market Street Reformed Church, later the Sea and Land Church, now the First Chinese Presbyterian Church, 61 Henry Street (1817–19). This is the most elegant of the four surviving Georgian-Gothic-style churches of the Lower East Side. Built of locally quarried Manhattan schist, the church still has its beautifully proportioned one- and two-story clear-glass windows. The Reformed Church became known as the Sea and Land Church in 1866 when it began ministering to local sailors. The present Chinese congregation reflects the ethnic character of the surrounding neighborhood.

101 **Eldridge Street Synagogue** (Congregation Khal Adath Jeshurun), 12–16 Eldridge Street (Herter Brothers, 1886–87). In the late 19th century, large numbers of Eastern European Jews settled on Manhattan's Lower East Side. The Eldridge Street Synagogue, the first Orthodox synagogue erected by these immigrants, is the most lavish synagogue ever built in the neighborhood. The brick and terra-cotta facade combines Moorish, Gothic, and Romanesque features in a fanciful and imposing manner. Currently undergoing a major restoration (Giorgio Cavaglieri, architect), the building will continue to serve as a synagogue and as a center for education, celebrating American Jewish and immigrant history.

102 **Manhattan Bridge Arch and Colonnade,** Manhattan Bridge Plaza at Canal Street (Carrère & Hastings, 1910–15). Carrère & Hastings's monumental gateway to the Manhattan Bridge was designed in the form of a triumphal arch flanked by curved colonnades. This "City Beautiful" project placed a grand entry at one of the key links between Manhattan and Brooklyn. Preliminary designs for the Manhattan approach were drawn in 1910, the year after the bridge opened. In 1912 Carrère & Hastings prepared final designs that included pylons carved by Carl A. Heber and a frieze by Charles Rumsey entitled *Buffalo Hunt*—a rather odd theme for a New York project. The New York City Department of Transportation is about to begin a restoration of the arch and colonnade.

103 **Bowery Savings Bank,** now GreenPoint Bank, 130 Bowery (McKim, Mead & White, Stanford White, partner in charge, 1893–95). The present bank building is the third erected at this location since the Bowery Savings Bank opened its doors in 1834. For this especially challenging L-shaped site, Stanford White designed two limestone street fronts, each in a Roman classical style with Corinthian columns supporting pediments sculpted by Frederic MacMonnies. White was the first to popularize the Roman classical style for bank design, and his choice established a trend; the Bowery became a prototype for other banks in New York and throughout the United States. The skylighted, L-shaped steel-framed **interior** creates the image of an ancient Roman temple. To the primarily poor immigrants who invested their mea-

Manhattan Bridge Arch and Colonnade (No. 102). A fittingly grand gateway to one of the key links between Manhattan and Brooklyn. Photo by Carl Forster.

ger incomes at this bank, entering this luxurious space must have been an awe-inspiring experience. By employing screens of monumental Corinthian columns, White created a square banking hall within a trapezoidal space. Among the major decorative features of the interior are marble mosaic floors, a yellow Siena marble teller's counter, scagliola (faux marble) columns, marble walls, coffered ceilings, and cast-iron skylights and stairs.

104 Forward Building, 173–175 East Broadway (George A. Boehm, 1912). This prominent 11-story Classical Revival building, erected on the Lower East Side as the home of the *Jewish Daily Forward,* the most significant Yiddish-language newspaper published in America, symbolizes the importance of the publication to the local Eastern European Jewish community. The *Forward* was a socialist paper that fought for the Jewish masses and was closely allied with Jewish labor and social improvement organizations, notably the Amalgamated Clothing Workers Union and the Workmen's Circle (which had offices in the building). The political

leanings of the *Forward* are evident in the building's ornamentation, which includes a series of flaming torches (symbols of the socialist vanguard) as well as low-relief portraits of such socialist leaders as Karl Marx and Friedrich Engels on the frieze (now covered by signage) above the entrance. The Chinese characters currently found on the facade are a reflection of the building's current ownership and the change in the ethnic makeup of the neighborhood.

105 All Saints' Free Church (Episcopal), later Saint Augustine's Chapel, now Saint Augustine's Episcopal Church, 290 Henry Street (1827–29; enlargement, 1849). This "free" church (i.e., rent was not charged for pews) is the most imposing of the four Georgian-Gothic landmark churches constructed of Manhattan schist on the Lower East Side. The design incorporates a double pediment and a projecting tower. In 1945 Trinity Church took over the operation of All Saints'. Four years later Trinity's Saint Augustine's Chapel moved into the building. Saint Augustine's became an independent parish in 1976.

106 Henry Street Settlement, 263 and 265 Henry Street (1827; later alterations) and 267 Henry Street (Buchman & Fox, 1900). In 1893 Lillian Wald, a middle-class woman of German-Jewish descent, founded the Nurses' Settlement, later renamed the Henry Street Settlement, to assist the Lower East Side populace and to help educate and Americanize the Eastern European Jewish immigrant population settling in the area. Two years later the German-Jewish philanthropist Jacob Schiff purchased 265 Henry Street for use by the organization. A single story was added to this well-preserved Federal-style row house, a survivor from a once affluent residential neighborhood; Schiff donated the building to the settlement in 1903. Three years later another German-Jewish philanthropist, Morris Loeb, purchased No. 267 from the Hebrew Technical School for Girls and gave it to the settlement. This Greek Revival house had received a Colonial Revival facade in 1900 when Buchman & Fox donated their services for the redesign of the technical school. The settlement's third building on Henry Street, No. 263, a Federal-style house with an extensively altered facade, was leased for use as classrooms and apartments in 1938 and was acquired by the settlement in 1949. Nos. 263 and 265 were restored in 1989 and 1992.

Hamilton Fish Park Play Center (No. 110). In 1898 it was hoped that this sophisticated municipal building would exert a positive influence on the area's poor immigrant population. Photo by Carl Forster.

107 **Willett Street Methodist Episcopal Church,** now Bialystoker Synagogue, 7–13 Bialystoker Place (1826). The simplest of the four early 19th-century landmark religious buildings of Manhattan schist surviving on the Lower East Side, this building has housed the Bialystoker Synagogue since 1905. The history of the building reflects the changes that occurred in this neighborhood at the turn of the century as tens of thousands of Eastern European Jews arrived in New York. The present congregation was founded in 1878 by Jews from Bialystok, then a part of the Russian Empire and now located in Poland.

108 **Norfolk Street Baptist Church,** now Beth Hamedrash Hagodol Synagogue, 60–64 Norfolk Street (1850). America's oldest congregation of Orthodox Russian Jews, established in 1852, converted this Gothic Revival church into a synagogue in 1885. Among the notable original features are the Gothic woodwork and the iron fence. The building was erected by a Baptist congregation that followed its members north, finally becoming Riverside Church.

109 **Anshe Chesed Synagogue,** later Anshe Slonim Synagogue, 172–176 Norfolk Street (Alexander Saeltzer, 1849–50). Built for the city's third Jewish congregation, this is the oldest surviving building in New York City erected specifically for use as a synagogue and is the earliest synagogue on the Lower East Side. Curiously, the building was designed in a Gothic Revival style and, at the time of construction, was even compared to Cologne Cathedral. The building is now in use as artists' studios.

110 **Hamilton Fish Park Play Center,** 130 Pitt Street (Carrère & Hastings, 1898–1900). The monumental Beaux-Arts Petit Palais in Paris was the model for this small pavilion. The play center and adjacent park were constructed as part of a movement to create parks in New York City's most densely crowded neighborhoods. Rather than a simple utilitarian structure, the building was intended as a sophisticated work that, it was hoped, would exert a positive influence on the area's poor immigrant population. The park has been redesigned several times, and the pavilion was restored in 1989–91.

HISTORIC DISTRICTS

⑪ MacDougal-Sullivan Gardens Historic District. MacDougal-Sullivan Gardens, a small enclave planned around a central garden, became a prototype for related New York developments of the 1920s. In 1920 William Sloane Coffin, president of the Hearth and Home Corporation, purchased twenty-two deteriorated Greek Revival row houses, built between 1844 and 1850, and commissioned a rehabilitation from the architects Francis Y. Joannes and Maxwell Hyde. All the stoops were removed, the two street facades were given a homey Colonial Revival appearance, and, most important, the rear yards were combined to create a private community garden. Each row house was divided into spacious, airy, and well-lit apartments affordable to middle-income people.

⑫ Greenwich Village Historic District. Greenwich Village is one of New York City's oldest and most diverse residential neighborhoods. The architecture within this district reflects the physical growth and continuing change that have occurred in Greenwich Village since the small rural community of Greenwich began to be urbanized in the 1820s. In addition, many of the buildings in the district are a reflection of the rich social and cultural history of this singular neighborhood. Streets in the village of Greenwich were initially laid out

Greenwich Village Historic District (H.D. 12). Federal houses built between 1825 and 1834 on the south side of Grove Street between Bedford and Hudson Streets. Photo by Carl Forster.

in the late 18th century. By the early 19th century, the population was growing, as people moved here to escape crowding and epidemics in the more densely populated metropolis to the south. This was especially true in the 1820s, when a significant number of Federal-style row houses were erected, either of brick or of wood with brick facades. Primarily located on the streets west of Sixth Avenue, they were leased or purchased by a wide variety of middle-class households. A few were grand 3½-story houses with ornate fanlighted entrances, such as 59 Morton Street (1828), but most were more modest 2½-story structures. Excellent examples survive on Grove, Barrow, Commerce, and Hudson Streets. In the 1830s and 1840s, wealthy New Yorkers began moving to Greenwich Village as it became increasingly urbanized and lost its village character. The area between Fifth and Sixth Avenues north of Washington Square was especially popular with these affluent households. The most prestigious houses were the Greek Revival rows with freestanding templed porticoes and elaborate iron railings on Washington Square North (1833–37). More typical Greek Revival row houses with austere entrances framed by heavy stone surrounds can be found throughout the district, most notably at 14–54 West 11th Street (1840–46). Somewhat more modest houses from this period can be found in the less affluent sections of the Village, farther west, especially on Bank and Bethune Streets, west of Seventh Avenue South. By the 1850s, as tastes changed, rows of brownstone-fronted houses were erected in Greenwich Village, although these were never as common as in neighborhoods to the north, since the area was already heavily built up. Perhaps the most significant brownstone row is the Anglo-Italianate terrace at 20–38 West 10th Street (1856–58), with low stoops and unified rusticated bases and iron balconies. Among the finest Italianate houses are those in the brick row with brownstone trim that lines the north side of Saint Luke's Place between Seventh Avenue South and Hudson Street (1851–54). In the post–Civil War period, the population of Greenwich Village changed as many middle-class families moved to newer neighborhoods uptown and poor immigrants crowded into the former single-family row houses, which were converted into multiple dwellings. In the late 19th century, large numbers of five- and six-story tenements were built, especially west of Sixth Avenue, and by the early 20th century, the Village had a significant population of Italian immigrants, as well as considerable Irish and German populations. The blocks north of Washington Square were an exception, retaining a population of middle-class native-born households. The row houses in this area were augmented by a series of early apartment buildings with elevators, spacious apartments, and servants' quarters, such as the Portsmouth and Hampshire (Ralph S. Townsend, 1882–83) at 38–50 West 9th Street, and the Ardea (J. B. Snook & Sons, 1895–1901), at 31–33 West

12th Street. In the early 20th century, the low rents and heterogeneous population of Greenwich Village began to attract artists and political and social radicals. Many buildings were converted in whole or part into artists' studios with large windows facing north, and commercial spaces began to attract coffeehouses and restaurants. The new bohemian community soon drew visitors, and Greenwich Village became an important tourist area. The nontraditional character of the Village also began to attract a large number of gay men and lesbians, establishing Greenwich Village as a center of gay life in New York. The southern extension of Seventh Avenue and the opening of the IRT subway beneath the avenue in 1917 made the neighborhood convenient to downtown and midtown commercial districts (the Sixth Avenue subway, opened in 1930, making the neighborhood even more accessible). Property values rose, and a significant number of new apartment houses were erected, such as the Shenandoah (Emory Roth, 1928–29), at 10 Sheridan Square, and 614 Hudson Street (Emory Roth, 1929–31). Many of these buildings have small apartments planned for single people and childless couples. They attracted large numbers of young educated working women who were for the first time beginning to establish independent households and found the relatively liberal social attitudes of Village residents welcoming. In the 1950s and 1960s, Greenwich Village became one of the first city neighborhoods in America to draw residents interested in living in older urban environments and restoring the residential architecture. Greenwich Village is one of the city's most popular neighborhoods, one that maintains its reputation for welcoming a wide variety of people while it retains an extraordinary array of 19th- and 20th-century buildings.

Within the boundaries of the Greenwich Village Historic District are some of New York City's most important buildings. A selection of these is discussed individually below:

A Saint Luke's Episcopal Church, later Saint Luke's Episcopal Chapel, now Church of Saint Luke-in-the-Fields (Episcopal), 485 Hudson Street (attributed to Clement Clarke Moore, 1821–22). As increasing numbers of people moved north into Greenwich Village, Trinity Church donated land for construction of an Episcopal church. A modest

Federal-style brick structure was erected as the centerpiece of an extraordinary urban complex that included a series of adjoining 2½-story row houses (1825–26). Church records indicate that a "plan" was drawn up by Clement Clarke Moore, a member of the congregation who would later lay out Chelsea and fund construction of Saint Peter's Episcopal Church (see H.D. 14, Map 7). The contract to build the church was given to John Heath. By the late 1880s, the surrounding neighborhood was becoming home to an increasingly poor immigrant community, and the church corporation relocated to Convent Avenue and West 141st Street (see H.D. 34, Map 17); in 1891 Saint Luke's, which retained some of its old congregation, became a chapel of Trinity Parish, becoming an independent congregation again only in 1976. The building burned in 1886 and again in 1981. An extensive reconstruction by Hugh Hardy of the firm Hardy Holzman Pfeiffer Associates was completed in 1985. The congregation remains one of the most active and diverse in the neighborhood.

B **Eighth Presbyterian Church,** later Saint Matthew's Episcopal Church, now Saint John's Evangelical Lutheran Church, 81 Christopher Street (1821–22; altered, Berg & Clark, 1886). This Federal-style church is one of the oldest religious buildings in Greenwich Village. Although altered in 1886, when the Romanesque Revival first story was installed, the building retains elegant Federal-style decorative detail and a domed cupola. Eighth Presbyterian was organized in 1819 and dissolved in 1842; the building was then sold to an Episcopal congregation. In 1858, in response to the growth of the German community in the area, a Lutheran congregation purchased the structure and has maintained it ever since.

C **Stonewall Inn,** 51–53 Christopher Street. At about 1:00 A.M. on June 28, 1969, the gay bar known as the Stonewall Inn was raided by the police, setting off events that resulted in the birth of the modern gay and lesbian rights movement. Although the raid itself was not an unusual event, the fact that bar patrons fought back, forcing the police to retreat, galvanized the community. The anniversary of the riot is celebrated annually around the world with parades and other gay pride events.

D **Northern Dispensary,** 165 Waverly Place (Henry Bayard, carpenter, and John C. Tucker, mason, 1831; third-floor addition, 1855). The Northern Dispensary opened as a private medical clinic for the poor. Established in 1824, it moved into this simple triangular Federal-style building, originally only two stories tall, in 1831. The building has been vacant since the dispensary closed in 1989.

E **Jefferson Market Courthouse (Third Judicial District Courthouse),** now New York Public Library, Jefferson Market Branch, 425 Sixth Avenue (Vaux & Withers, 1874–77). The Jefferson Market Courthouse, the most prominent building in Greenwich Village, is not only a monument of American High Victorian Gothic design, but also of seminal importance in the history of the historic preservation movement. The courthouse is the masterpiece of English-born architect Frederick Clarke Withers, whose knowledge of English public architecture is evident on this building. The courthouse is faced with red brick and has black brick and yellow Ohio sandstone trim. The facades are richly ornamented with sculptural detail, including a pediment with the trial scene from *The Merchant of Venice* and a corner water fountain appropriately decorated with a wading bird, cattails, a snail, a salamander, and other water plants and animals. The building originally contained a police court, a district court, and, in the tall bell tower, a fire watch. In 1885 a survey among architects sponsored by the *American Architect and Building News* voted the courthouse the fifth best building in the United States. The courthouse was vacated in 1958, and its future was in doubt. In 1959 a group of preservationists organized the Committee of Neighbors to Get the Clock on Jefferson Market Courthouse Started as a way of drawing attention to the building and its precarious condition. Soon this group was campaigning to have the building converted into a library, and in 1961 the New York Public Library agreed. Giorgio Cavaglieri was commissioned to design one of the earliest adaptive reuse projects in America, and the rejuvenated building reopened in 1967. Additional work, including the restoration of the slate roof, was undertaken in 1994 by Joseph Pell Lombardi.

F **Saint Joseph's Church** (R.C.), 365 Sixth Avenue (John Doran, 1833–34). The parish of Saint Joseph's was established in 1829 just as Greenwich Village was becoming a populous residential district. Saint Joseph's is the second oldest Roman Catholic church building extant in New York City (after Saint Patrick's Old Cathedral—see No. 86). Built of Manhattan schist with a stuccoed front focusing on a Doric portico, this is one of the most beautifully proportioned Greek Revival church edifices in the city. The arched windows of the facade date from 1885, when architect Arthur Crooks rebuilt the fire-damaged structure.

G **Washington Square Methodist Church,** 135–139 West 4th Street (Gamaliel King, 1859–60). This Early Romanesque Revival–style marble church is a major work by Gamaliel King, an important but little-known mid-19th-century New York architect. The congregation was established on Sullivan Street in 1842, expanding into this building as the size of the congregation increased.

H **Washington Memorial Arch,** Washington Square (McKim, Mead & White, Stanford White, partner in charge, 1889–95; sculptural figures completed 1918). As part of the 1889 celebration of the centennial of George Washington's inauguration as the nation's first president, Stanford White designed a temporary wooden arch for Washington Square. It proved to be so popular that funds were raised to provide a permanent arch at the base of Fifth Avenue. The form is an adaptation of ancient Roman triumphal arches, perhaps symbolizing the triumph of republican democracy in America. The marble structure is embellished with figures of Washington by Herman MacNeil and Alexander Stirling Calder and spandrel panels by Frederick MacMonnies. In January 1917 the arch became a symbol of bohemian Greenwich Village when John Sloan, Marcel Duchamp, and a group of friends climbed to the top and proclaimed that Greenwich Village had seceded from the Union and would thenceforth be the Free and Independent Republic of Washington Square.

I **MacDougal Alley.** Most of the buildings on MacDougal Alley are 19th-century stables erected by the owners of the large row houses on Wash-

Jefferson Market Courthouse (Greenwich Village Historic District Entry E). A monument of American High Victorian Gothic design, the courthouse was also the focus of one of the early, pivotal preservation battles in New York City. Photo by John Barrington Bayley.

ington Square North and West 8th Street. By 1900 the mews had become a slum, but early in the 20th century the stables were discovered by artists who converted them into studios and homes, turning the street into what was known as the "Art Alley de Luxe." Large, north-facing studio windows were added to many of the buildings. The first stable converted into a studio was No. 6, leased by sculptor Frederick Triebel in 1902. Among the artists who soon moved into the former stables were painters Guy Pène du Bois and Ernest Lawson and sculptors Henry Bush-Brown, Jo Davidson, James Fraser, Daniel Chester French, Philip Martiny, and Gertrude Vanderbilt Whitney.

J **Whitney Museum of American Art,** now New York Studio School of Drawing, Painting and

Sculpture, 8–12 West 8th Street (1838; altered, Noel & Miller, 1931). In 1914 sculptor Gertrude Vanderbilt Whitney established the Whitney Studio at 8 West 8th Street, adjoining her MacDougal Alley studio. Here she planned to organize exhibits of the work of the young avant-garde American artists whose work she supported. Whitney assembled a substantial collection of new artworks, and after the Metropolitan Museum rejected her offer of a gift in 1929, she established the Whitney Museum of American Art. In 1931 Auguste L. Noel transformed the three former row houses at 8–12 West 8th Street into a museum and residence for Whitney, covering the facade with a reddish stucco and redesigning the entrance in a modern classical manner. The fledgling museum remained here until 1954. Its history as an art center continues under the auspices of the New York Studio School. A partial restoration of the building was undertaken by Li-Saltzman Architects in 1993.

K **Lockwood de Forest House,** now New York University, Edgar M. Bronfman Center for Jewish Student Life, 7 East 10th Street (Van Campen Taylor, 1887). Lockwood de Forest was a leading decorative designer of the late 19th century and a founder, with Louis Comfort Tiffany, of the Associated Artists (see Seventh Regiment Armory, No. 392). After visiting India, de Forest established a wood workshop in Ahmadabad and incorporated Indian decorative pieces into his designs, including the library at the Andrew and Louise Carnegie House and the extraordinary teak detail on the facade of this row house, which he commissioned in 1887. The house was restored by Helpern Associates in 1994–96 after its acquisition by NYU.

L **Church of the Ascension (Episcopal),** 36–38 Fifth Avenue (Richard Upjohn, 1840–41; parish house, McKim, Mead & White, 1888–89). This symmetrically massed Gothic Revival–style brownstone church, with its central square tower, is an early work of Richard Upjohn that closely relates to his slightly earlier Trinity Church (see No. 15) and slightly later Christ Church, Brooklyn (see H.D. 5, Brooklyn Map 3). In 1885–88 Stanford White was hired to redesign the interior. This early McKim, Mead & White project was one of the great collaborative efforts of the era and includes a mural and a stained-glass window by John

La Farge, marble reredos by Louis Saint-Gaudens, mosaics by D. Maitland Armstrong, and a pulpit by Charles F. McKim. Following the completion of this interior project, McKim, Mead & White redesigned an earlier building to create the elegant Northern Renaissance–inspired yellow brick parish house with bottle-glass windows at 12 West 11th Street.

M **First Presbyterian Church,** 48 Fifth Avenue (Joseph C. Wells, 1844–46; chapel, McKim, Mead & White, 1893–94; church house, Edgar Tafel, 1958–60). First Presbyterian, established in 1716, built its first church on Wall Street in 1719. By 1840 Wall Street was the city's business center, and the congregation chose to move to more residential Greenwich Village. Joseph C. Wells provided the congregation with one of the finest English-inspired Gothic Revival churches in New York. The brownstone building focuses on an impressive pinnacled entrance tower. The chapel on West 11th Street was designed by McKim, Mead & White to complement Wells's original design, while the church house on West 12th Street was inspired by Prairie School design, here infused with Gothic detail.

N **New School for Social Research,** 66 West 12th Street (Joseph Urban, 1929–31). The New School was established in 1919 as a progressive center for adult education, catering especially to women. Initial courses were largely in the social sciences, but the curriculum soon expanded into the arts, psychology, and other liberal arts fields. In 1929 construction began on a new building in Greenwich Village that was as modern in its design as the school was in its educational mission. The New School is among the earliest examples of the influence of European Modernism in New York City. Viennese immigrant architect Joseph Urban was attuned to contemporary developments in Europe and designed a building of black and buff brick with ribbon windows and without applied ornament that stands in marked contrast to the earlier row houses and apartment buildings on West 12th Street. On the **interior,** Urban designed a magnificent egg-shaped auditorium (restored in 1992 by Prentice & Chan Olhausen) that was a model for Radio City Music Hall (see No. 252). The building also contains a series of murals executed by Mexican muralist José Clemente Orozco in 1930–31.

0 **171 West 12th Street Apartments** (Emilio Levy, 1922). In the 1920s large numbers of apartment houses were erected in Greenwich Village, many with small apartments that appealed to single people and couples with no children. As social constraints were liberalized, many single women, including many lesbians, began seeking places to live on their own, and the progressive Greenwich Village community was a welcome place in which to settle. The twenty-four apartments in this building attracted many notable women, including a significant number in the circle of Eleanor Roosevelt. Among those who lived here in the years after the building's completion were Mary

Dewson, one of the most important women active in the Democratic Party during the 1930s and 1940s, and her partner, radical activist Polly Porter; Communist Party leaders Grace Hutchins and Anna Rochester; and Nancy Cook and Marion Dickerman, a couple who founded the private Todhunter School and, along with Roosevelt, established the Val-Kill furniture company.

INDIVIDUAL LANDMARKS

111 **United States Appraisers' Store,** later the U.S. Federal Building, now the Archives Apartments, 641 Washington Street (Willoughby J. Edbrooke and others, 1892–99). The U.S. Department of the Treasury built this Romanesque Re-

The New School for Social Research (Greenwich Village Historic District Entry N) is an early example of the influence of European Modernism in New York City. Photo by Carl Forster.

vival brick building, occupying an entire square block, as a warehouse for imported goods awaiting customs appraisal. The two lowest floors were built to the designs of Supervising Architect of the Treasury Willoughby J. Edbrooke. While Edbrooke designed an additional eight stories, as did one of his successors, William M. Aiken, the upper floors, as constructed, differ from the published designs of both architects. The massive building was used as archival storage for many years and has now been converted into 479 apartments.

112 **131 Charles Street House** (1834). This well-preserved 2½-story brick house in the Federal style provides a contrast to the later lofts and warehouses of its West Village neighborhood.

113 **26, 28, and 30 Jones Street Houses** (1844). These virtually intact Greek Revival row houses typify vernacular residential design of the 1840s. Of special note are the original stoops, wrought-iron railings, modest temple-like entrances (at Nos. 26 and 28), and dentiled cornices.

114 **Judson Memorial Church, Tower, and Hall,** 51–55 Washington Square South (church, 1888–93; tower and hall, 1895–96—all McKim, Mead & White, Stanford White, partner in charge). Built as a memorial to Adoniram Judson, the first American Baptist missionary in Asia, by his son, the Reverend Dr. Edward Judson, and funded in part by John D. Rockefeller, Judson Memorial is one of Stanford White's most elegant works. White combined Italian Early Christian and Renaissance features into a rich composition that remains one of the key elements of the Washington Square skyline. The architect's choice of mottled yellow Roman brick with extensive white terra-cotta trim introduced light coloration into American church architecture. The activist congregation continues to occupy the church, but the hall and tower are now residences for New York University. Adjacent to the hall is an 1877 building designed by John G. Prague as a young men's boardinghouse.

115 **Irad Hawley House,** now the Salmagundi Club and Museum, 47 Fifth Avenue (1853). This Italianate mansion was built for Irad Hawley, president of the Pennsylvania Coal Company, which had its yards along the Greenwich Village waterfront. The house is the last survivor of the mansions that once lined fashionable lower Fifth Avenue. The Salmagundi Club, established in 1871 for "the promotion of social intercourse among artists and the advancement of art," has occupied the house since 1917.

116 **New York County National Bank,** 77–79 Eighth Avenue (DeLemos & Cordes, with Rudolph L. Daus, 1906–07). The New York County National Bank, founded in 1855, erected this small but imposing neoclassical limestone-faced bank with Beaux-Arts motifs on a prominent intersection at the northern edge of Greenwich Village. The French influence is especially evident in the arched windows, with their visible iron framing, and in the exuberant quality of the carving.

117 **New York Savings Bank,** now Central Carpet Co., 81 Eighth Avenue (R. H. Robertson, 1896–97). This corner building, designed to be a visual landmark at the intersection of West 14th Street and Eighth Avenue, is an early example of Classical Revival bank design, begun only a year after the completion of McKim, Mead & White's pioneering Bowery Savings Bank (see No. 103). Faced entirely in Vermont marble, the bank has a temple front supported by a pair of Corinthian columns and is crowned by a commanding copper dome with a clerestory of twenty stained-glass windows. The **interior** of the L-shaped building consists of a grand banking hall with a shallow coffered vault supported by columns and pilasters of Siena marble. A restoration was undertaken by Robert Scarano, Jr., architect, when the building was converted into a rug and carpet emporium in 1994.

118 **Andrew Norwood House,** 241 West 14th Street (1845–47). This beautifully restored house is a survivor from a row of three transitional Greek Revival/Italianate residences erected by the stockbroker Andrew Norwood, who was an active developer in the 14th Street area. Norwood built this house, the central unit of the trio, for himself. As the first masonry buildings on the block, these houses marked the beginning of the transformation of 14th Street into a fashionable residential thoroughfare.

HISTORIC DISTRICTS

13 **Saint Mark's Historic District.** The land within this district was once part of Peter Stuyvesant's "bouwerie," or farm. The transformation of the area into an urban neighborhood began in the late 18th century when Petrus Stuyvesant, the great-grandson of the Dutch governor, began to subdivide the land into building lots. Stuyvesant Street, running due east-west (at an angle to the later grid), dates from this era, as do the Nicholas and Elizabeth Stuyvesant Fish House (1803–04; see No. 135), the Nicholas William Stuyvesant House (1795) at 44 Stuyvesant Street, and Saint Mark's-in-the-Bowery Church (see No. 136). Major development in the district began in 1839 with the construction of 102 East 10th Street and continued through the 1860s with the construction of Greek Revival, Italianate, and Anglo-Italianate row houses. The Fish House had a large garden that was not developed until 1859–61, when "the Triangle" was erected. This magnificent unified complex of Anglo-Italianate brownstone and brick houses faces onto Stuyvesant and East 10th Streets.

INDIVIDUAL LANDMARKS

■ *WEST OF SECOND AVENUE*

119 **Bayard-Condict Building,** 65–69 Bleecker Street (Louis Sullivan; Lyndon P. Smith, associate architect, 1897–99). New York City's only work by Louis Sullivan, the Bayard-Condict is a superb illustration of Sullivan's ideas on skyscraper design. The structure of this 12-story steel-frame loft building, clad entirely in white terra cotta, is clear-

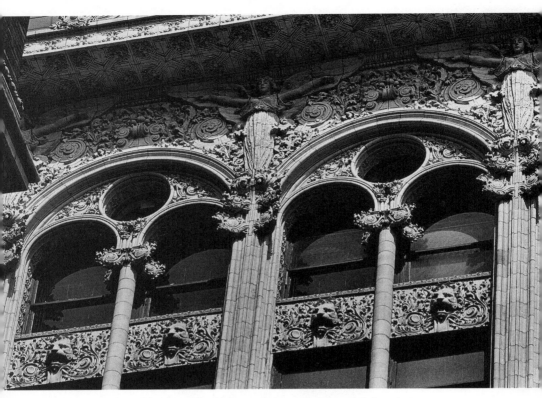

The Bayard-Condict Building (No. 119), with its organic terra-cotta ornament, is the only work by renowned architect Louis Sullivan in New York City; it illustrates Sullivan's theories on skyscraper design. Photo by Caroline Kane Levy.

ly manifested in the six emphatic vertical bays of the facade. The building is divided horizontally into three sections, demonstrating Sullivan's conviction that a skyscraper should have an ornate base to attract people's attention, a shaft of identical stories stacked atop one another, and a decorated crown to cap the building's upward thrust. The design is enhanced by Sullivan's distinctive organic ornament. In 1996 a restoration project was begun under the guidance of Wank Adams Slavin Architects.

120 **Robbins & Appleton Building,** 1–5 Bond Street (Stephen Decatur Hatch, 1879–80). The Robbins & Appleton Building is an impressive French Second Empire cast-iron commercial structure erected as a factory for a firm that manufactured watch cases. Three of the floors were leased to D. Appleton & Co., a prominent pub-

lishing firm of the era. The facade, with its rows of large windows and its massive mansard roof, has been restored and repainted in imitation of stone.

121 **Bond Street Savings Bank,** now the Bouwerie Lane Theater, 330 Bowery (Henry Engelbert, 1873–74). The Atlantic Savings Bank commissioned this Italianate cast-iron building in 1873; by the time the bank was completed, it was known as the Bond Street Savings Bank. This institution soon failed, and in 1879 the property was conveyed to the German Exchange Bank, which catered to the area's large German immigrant population. The former bank has housed a theater since 1963.

122 **New York Marble Cemetery,** interior of the block bounded by East 2nd and 3rd Streets, Second Avenue, and the Bowery (1830–). Entered through an alley off Second Avenue, Manhattan's first non-sectarian cemetery was founded in 1830 as a commercial venture in a then-fashionable section of the city. The cemetery consists of 156 underground vaults of Tuckahoe marble. There are no monuments, only plaques set into the north and south walls bearing the names of the original vault owners.

123 Fire Engine Company No. 33, 44 Great Jones Street (Flagg & Chambers, 1898–99). This Beaux-Arts firehouse is one of the grandest small-scale civic buildings in New York City. The design is dominated by a monumental arch capped by a flamboyant cartouche. The metal infilling of the arch and the metal brackets of the cornice are evidence of the influence that contemporaneous French design had on Ernest Flagg, one of the most sophisticated French-trained architects active in New York.

124 Schermerhorn Building, also known as the 376–380 Lafayette Street Building (Henry J. Hardenbergh, 1888–89). With its varied materials and colors and its use of wide, segmentally arched openings, this corner building is among New York's most monumental commercial structures of the 1880s. Although the solidity of the masonry walls is mitigated by wide window openings, enormous squat stone columns resting on granite bases accentuate the weight of the building's structure. William C. Schermerhorn replaced the old family mansion and rented the new building to a manufacturer of boys' clothing.

125 Old Merchant's House, also known as the Seabury Tredwell House, 29 East 4th Street (1831–32). The Old Merchant's House was built on speculation by Joseph Brewster as part of a row of six identical dwellings. Brewster lived here for a few years, then sold the house to the prosperous hardware merchant Seabury Tredwell in 1836. Gertrude, Tredwell's eighth child, was born in a second-floor bedroom in 1840 and lived in the house until her death in 1933, maintaining the house "as Papa wanted it." At Gertrude's death, a relative saved the house and its contents, converting the building into a museum that illustrates the life of an affluent 19th-century family. The 3½-story row

Old Merchant's House, also known as the Seabury Tredwell House (No. 125). This house museum, with its landmark-designated interior, shows the life of an affluent 19th-century family. Photo by Carl Forster.

De Vinne Press Building (No. 127). Note the sophisticated fenestration pattern on this 19th-century commercial building. Photo by Carl Forster.

house is in a transitional late Federal–Greek Revival style. The exterior is basically Federal in design, distinguished by its Flemish bond brickwork, marble entrance enframement with a Gibbs surround, sloping roof punctuated by dormers, and delicate railings (restored). The **interior**, on the other hand, contains stylish Greek forms, notably the Ionic column screen that separates the front and rear parlors on the main floor. In 1971 a major restoration of the house was undertaken by the architect Joseph Roberto and the designer Carolyn Roberto; continuing restoration has been undertaken by Jan Hird Pokorny Architects.

126 **Samuel Tredwell Skidmore House,** 37 East 4th Street (1845). This 3½-story Greek Revival row house with a freestanding Ionic portico is one of the few surviving houses from the period in the mid-19th century when the East Village was an affluent residential neighborhood. The house was built for the businessman Samuel Tredwell Skidmore, a cousin of Seabury Tredwell, whose house still stands to the west at 29 East 4th Street (see No. 125). The house has been vacant for many years.

127 **De Vinne Press Building,** 393–399 Lafayette Street (Babb, Cook & Willard, 1885–86; addition, 1890–92). Theodore De Vinne, who was in the forefront of the revival of printing as an art form, was responsible for the printing of many major magazines, including *The Century* and *Scribner's Monthly.* De Vinne's Romanesque Revival printing house is a masterpiece of 19th-century commercial architecture with a sophisticated fenestration pattern and subtle terra-cotta detail. The focus of the front elevation is a trio of three-story arches with deeply recessed window frames that accent the massive quality of the walls.

128 **Astor Library,** now the Joseph Papp Public Theater, 425 Lafayette Street (south wing, Alexander Saeltzer, 1849–53; center section, Griffith Thomas, 1856–69; north wing, Thomas Stent, 1879–81). New York's first public library was built with a bequest from John Jacob Astor. The building, which appears to be a single unified structure, was actually erected in three campaigns, each with a different architect of record. The German-born Alexander Saeltzer established the building's form with his use of the German round-arched, or *Rundbogenstil,* style, with its roots in Northern Italian Romanesque design. The building served for many years as the headquarters of the Hebrew Immigrant Aid Society (HIAS) but was vacant and endangered in 1965 when the theatrical producer Joseph Papp persuaded the city to acquire it. In 1966 architect Giorgio Cavaglieri converted the building for use by one of America's most innovative theatrical institutions. In recent years all the windows have been beautifully restored by Buck Cane Architects.

129 **La Grange Terrace,** also known as Colonnade Row, 428, 430, 432, and 434 Lafayette Street (attributed to Seth Geer, 1832–33). These four houses survive from a row of nine Greek Revival marble-fronted residences that, at the time of their completion, were among the grandest dwellings in New York and were occupied by members of New York's leading families. Erected, and possibly designed, by the developer Seth Geer and named for the Marquis de Lafayette's estate in France, the row is unified by the use of a Corinthian colonnade that was once crowned by a continuous band of anthemia (now visible only at No. 434). The buildings began to deteriorate in the post–Civil War era as the wealthy moved out of this neighborhood, and the houses were subdivided into apartments and commercial spaces. The row now contains apartments, restaurants, and theaters.

130 **Cooper Union,** Cooper Square (Frederick A. Peterson, 1853–59; later rooftop additions). Dedicated to "the advancement of science and art," Cooper Union was established as a school offering free education to working-class men and women. The Italianate building, faced in brownstone, was

La Grange Terrace, also known as Colonnade Row (No. 129). For a brief period one of the city's toniest addresses, only four of these grand dwellings survive. Photo by Carl Forster.

among the first structures to employ rolled iron beams (fabricated at Peter Cooper's Trenton, New Jersey, foundry) and was also among the earliest buildings designed to accommodate an elevator. The original structure rose only five stories, with income-producing stores on the first floor. Several rooftop additions have led to significant structural alterations, including the replacement in 1886 of the original rectangular second-floor windows with segmental arched openings (Leopold Eidlitz, architect). In 1975–76 the cast-iron storefronts were restored (new pieces were cast in aluminum by the school's art students) and the street level was converted into a library; these changes were part of an extensive renovation designed by John Hejduk, the dean of Cooper Union's architecture school.

131 **Metropolitan Savings Bank,** now the First Ukrainian Evangelical Pentecostal Church, 9 East 7th Street (Carl Pfeiffer, 1867). Built to serve the largely German inhabitants of this East Village neighborhood, the Metropolitan Savings Bank is a significant example of French Second Empire design. Pfeiffer handled the Second Empire idiom in a sophisticated manner, creating a dynamically massed structure on a relatively small site. In 1937 the marble building was purchased by the First Ukrainian Assembly of God, and it has since served as a church.

132 **20 Saint Mark's Place House,** also known as the Daniel Leroy House (1832). In the 1830s the south side of Saint Mark's Place between Second and Third Avenues was developed with an elegant row of 3½-story brick houses erected on speculation by Thomas E. Davis. The sole intact survivor is No. 20, whose exceptional marble entrance surround is ornamented with vermiculated blocks. The original residents appear to have been the South Street merchant Daniel Leroy and his wife, Elizabeth Fish.

133 **New York Free Circulating Library, Ottendorfer Branch,** now the New York Public Library, Ottendorfer Branch, 135 Second Avenue (William Schickel, 1883–84). The German-American philanthropists Oswald Ottendorfer, publisher of the *Staats-Zeitung,* and his wife, Anna, built this library and the adjacent German Dispensary (see No. 134) as part of their efforts to improve the

minds and bodies of their fellow German immigrants. The library is an ornate red brick Queen Anne– and Renaissance-inspired building with extensive terra-cotta detail that incorporates such symbols of wisdom and knowledge as globes, owls, books, and torches. Even before it was completed, the Ottendorfers donated their library to the New York Free Circulating Library, a privately funded library system (see No. 356). The Ottendorfer is now the oldest operating branch of the New York Public Library system. Its **interior** retains its original character, with reading rooms on the first and second floors and cast-iron book stacks at the rear of the first floor and on the glass-floored mezzanine.

134 **Deutsches (German) Dispensary,** now Stuyvesant Polyclinic, 137 Second Avenue (William Schickel, 1883–84). The German Dispensary and the neighboring Ottendorfer Library (see No. 133) were commissioned by Anna and Oswald Ottendorfer, philanthropists concerned with the welfare of New York's German immigrant community. This exuberant Italian Renaissance–inspired structure, designed by the German-born architect William Schickel, is among the first buildings in New York to display extensive ornamental terra cotta, including busts of important figures in the history of medicine.

135 **Nicholas and Elizabeth Stuyvesant Fish House,** also known as the Stuyvesant-Fish House, 21 Stuyvesant Street (1803–04). The Fish House was built by Petrus Stuyvesant, great-grandson of the last director general of New Amsterdam, on land owned by the Stuyvesant family since the 17th century. The brick dwelling in the Federal style was a wedding gift to Stuyvesant's daughter Elizabeth and her husband, Nicholas Fish, a veteran of Valley Forge.

136 **Saint Mark's-in-the-Bowery Church (Episcopal),** East 10th Street at Second Avenue (1799; tower, Town & Thompson, 1826–28; portico, 1854). The second oldest church building in Manhattan, Saint Mark's is a survivor from the period when the East Village was sparsely populated. The land on which the church is built, the former site of Dutch governor Peter Stuyvesant's private chapel (Stuyvesant is buried in the churchyard),

New York Free Circulating Library (No. 133) and Stuyvesant Polyclinic (No. 134). These two buildings were built by philanthropists Oswald and Anna Ottendorfer to help their fellow German immigrants. Photo by Carl Forster.

was sold to the Episcopal Church for one dollar by Stuyvesant's great-grandson. The original field-stone church was a simple pedimented structure with beautifully proportioned window openings. In 1828, by which time the area around the church was developing into the city's most affluent residential neighborhood, a stylish Greek Revival tower was constructed, turning the church into one of the most prominent buildings in the vicinity. An Italianate cast-iron portico was added in 1854. As the community changed over the years, the church building deteriorated significantly; at the same time the Saint Mark's congregation developed into one of the most politically and socially committed in the city. A restoration project was begun in 1975 that included training local residents in construction; this project, which continued even after a fire severely damaged the church in 1978, was completed in 1983.

137 **Louis N. Jaffe Art Theater (Yiddish Art Theater/Yiddish Folks Theater)**, now Village East City Cinemas, 189 Second Avenue (Harrison G. Wiseman, 1925–26). In the 1920s Second Avenue below 14th Street was known as the Yiddish Rialto. Erected as a home for the Yiddish Art Theater by Jewish civic leader Louis Jaffe, this is the most prominent of the theaters that once housed Yiddish productions. The design, with its large central arch, gold-hued cast-stone facing, and symbolic Judaic ornament, resembles the form of contemporary synagogues designed in what was known as the "Semitic" style, an original combination of Moorish, Byzantine, and Middle Eastern motifs. Although the Yiddish Art Theater, a company inspired by the European "art theater" movement, only performed in this building for four seasons, the theater remained a Yiddish stage, generally known as the Yiddish Folks Theater. With the Yiddish theater in decline, the building was converted into a movie house in 1946. It again became a legitimate stage in 1953, hosting the famous Phoenix Theater repertory company, which produced classic and modern plays with such great actors as Hume Cronyn, Jessica Tandy, Eli Wallach, Farley Granger, Lillian Gish, and Eva LeGallienne. Later the theater premiered *Oh! Calcutta!* and *Grease.* In 1990–91 the **interior** was converted into a multiplex cinema, preserving much of the exotic polychromatic ornament of the lobby, proscenium, and auditorium walls and ceiling.

138 **Grace Church (Episcopal) Complex,** 800 and 804 Broadway and 92, 94–96, and 98 Fourth Avenue (church, James Renwick, Jr., 1843–46; with additions, James Renwick, Jr., Edward T. Potter, Heins & La Farge, and William W. Renwick; rectory, James Renwick, Jr., 1846–47; Grace House, James Renwick, Jr., 1880–81; Grace Church Houses, now Grace Church School: Memorial House, James Renwick, Jr., 1881–83; Clergy House, Heins & La Farge, 1902–03; Neighborhood House, Renwick, Aspinwall & Tucker, 1906–07). Grace Church is one of the most significant early examples of Gothic Revival architecture in America. Designed in a French Gothic mode, the marble church and its picturesque rectory were among the first works of James Renwick, Jr. The church is strategically sited at a point where Broadway curves, so that the vista up Broadway from the Battery terminates with the church tower. This location underscores the Episcopal parish's standing as one of the most prestigious religious organizations in New York City. Over the years the church has had many additions and alterations, all of them in keeping with Renwick's original scheme. Among these are Renwick's Grace House (1880–81), which connects the church and rectory; his 1883 replacement of the original wood spire with the present marble spire; Edward T. Potter's Chantry (1879; alterations by William W. Renwick, 1910); and a chancel extension (Heins & La Farge, 1903). As the nature and needs of the congregation changed in response to population changes in the surrounding area, new buildings were added to the complex, including a series of structures on Fourth Avenue that display great stylistic coherence. In 1881 James Renwick designed Grace Memorial House in a Gothic style that echoes his earlier church design. This building is thought to

have housed New York's first day-care center. Twenty-one years later the building was expanded to the south with the addition of the Clergy House, an exact copy of the original building. The complex was further expanded in 1907 with the more austere Neighborhood House. An addition to the Grace Church School was built behind the facades of the Memorial House, the Clergy House, and part of the Neighborhood House in 1974–75.

■*EAST OF SECOND AVENUE*

139 **New York City Marble Cemetery,** 52–74 East 2nd Street (1831–). Opened one year after the nearby New York Marble Cemetery (see No. 122), this cemetery was the second nonsectarian burial ground in the city. Among the distinguished citizens buried beneath the stone markers and monuments are members of the Fish, Kip, Lenox, and Roosevelt families.

140 **First Houses,** 29–41 Avenue A and 112–138 East 3rd Street (Frederick L. Ackerman, 1935–36). First Houses was the nation's earliest public-sponsored low-income housing project and the first effort of the city's newly established Housing Authority. The L-shaped complex was planned as a renovation of older tenements; every third building was to be removed, creating a series of courtyards. As work proceeded, however, the remaining buildings had to be substantially reconstructed. The open space to the rear of the buildings was landscaped with trees, benches, fanciful sculpture, and playgrounds.

141 **Grace Chapel (Episcopal) and Hospital,** now Immaculate Conception Church (R.C.) and Clergy House, 406–412 East 14th Street (Barney & Chapman, 1894–96). Barney & Chapman designed two distinguished and distinctive Episcopal church complexes in the French Gothic style—Grace Chapel and the Church of the Holy Trinity (see No. 441). This chapel of brick and terra cotta was built by Grace Church (see No. 138) as a free church that would minister to all, regardless of income—that is, no pew rents were charged. Adjoining the church is an austere complementary structure erected as a hospital. In 1943 the Episcopal chapel was converted into a Roman Catholic church, and the hospital became a clergy house.

HISTORIC DISTRICT

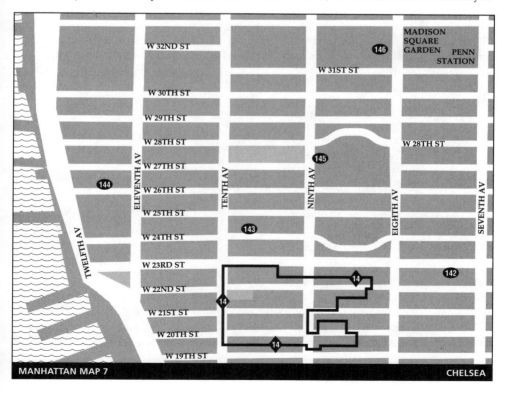

14 **Chelsea Historic District.** In 1750 Captain Thomas Clarke purchased a large plot of land along the Hudson River and laid out a country estate that he called Chelsea. A portion of the property was deeded to Clarke's grandson Clement Clarke Moore in 1813. Moore, a wealthy, well-educated scholar, poet, and country gentleman, is remembered today as the author of "A Visit from Saint Nicholas." As the city moved northward, Moore realized that his land would soon be ripe for development. With the advice and assistance of James N. Wells, Moore had the area divided into building lots with restrictions placed on the design and quality of new housing. Between 1825 and 1860, almost the entire area was built up. The district is especially rich in Greek Revival row houses, notably Cushman Row (1839–40), at 408–418 West 20th Street between Ninth and Tenth Avenues, and also contains New York City's largest concentration of Anglo-Italianate row houses, identifiable by their low stoops and sunken base-

ments. Moore donated land on West 20th Street for Saint Peter's Episcopal Church (1836–38), an early example of the Gothic Revival in America, and also gave the land on which the General Theological Seminary was constructed. The oldest surviving building on the Episcopal seminary's block is a small Gothic Revival stone structure of 1836; most of the campus was the work of Charles C. Haight, who prepared a master plan in 1883 and designed a series of Collegiate Gothic buildings.

INDIVIDUAL LANDMARKS

142 **Chelsea Apartments,** now the Chelsea Hotel, 222 West 23rd Street (Hubert, Pirsson & Co., 1883–85). The famous Chelsea Hotel was built as one of the city's earliest cooperative apartment houses. The facade of the picturesque Queen Anne building, executed in a variety of materials, is enhanced by tiers of remarkable iron balconies ornamented with flowers. Since its conversion into a hotel in 1905, the Chelsea has attracted many famous writers, artists, and musicians, including Brendan Behan, Thomas Wolfe, Dylan Thomas, Mark Twain, Tennessee Williams, Virgil Thomson, and Sid Vicious; it was also the location for Andy Warhol's movie *Chelsea Girls.*

143 **437–459 West 24th Street Houses** (1849–50). This long row of twelve paired houses was erected by the builder Philo V. Beebe to provide housing for the merchants and professionals who moved into the Chelsea neighborhood in the 1840s. Most of these transitional Greek Revival/Italianate dwellings have deep landscaped

yards and retain their original stoops, iron railings, and other details.

144 **Starrett-Lehigh Building,** 601–625 West 26th Street (Cory & Cory; Yasuo Matsui, associate; consulting engineers, Purdy & Henderson, 1930–31). The striking Starrett-Lehigh Building is an enormous freight terminal and warehouse, occupying an entire block. It was built as a joint venture of the Starrett Investing Corporation and the Lehigh Valley Railroad (trains could pull right into the ground story of the building). The building—with its setback massing, polygonal corners, and

The Chelsea Hotel (No. 142) attracts many famous artists and musicians. Its picturesque Queen Anne facade is enhanced by tiers of iron balconies. Photo by Peter Choy.

Starrett-Lehigh Building (No. 144). This huge freight terminal and warehouse was one of the few American designs included in the Museum of Modern Art's International Style exhibition of 1932. Photo by Carl Forster.

horizontal bands of steel ribbon windows alternating with brick spandrels and concrete floorplates—was in the forefront of modern design when it was erected in 1930–31. This was one of only a handful of American designs included in the Museum of Modern Art's pioneering International Style exhibition of 1932.

145 **Church of the Holy Apostles (Episcopal),** 300 Ninth Avenue (Minard Lafever, 1845–48; additions, Minard Lafever, 1853–54; transepts, Richard Upjohn & Son, 1858). Lafever's only surviving building in Manhattan is a rare New York example of an Italianate church. The brick building, which has a prominent spire, has been enlarged several times. In 1853–54 it was extended 25 feet with the construction of a new chancel, and in 1858 transepts were constructed to the designs of Charles Babcock of the firm Richard Upjohn & Son. The

building contains several stained-glass windows designed by William Jay Bolton that survived a devastating fire in 1990. Following the fire, the socially active congregation raised money for its continuing efforts to feed the hungry while at the same time restoring this exceptional church building.

146 **United States General Post Office,** now the James A. Farley Building, Eighth Avenue at West 31st Street (McKim, Mead & White, William M. Kendall, partner in charge, 1908–13). The McKim, Mead & White firm designed this enormous granite structure as a companion to Pennsylvania Station, which once stood across the street. The building features a colonnade of 20 Corinthian columns, each 53 feet high, and stretches along two full city blocks. Studies are under way to determine the feasibility of converting the building into a railroad station.

■ *WEST OF UNION SQUARE AND*
 PARK AVENUE SOUTH

HISTORIC DISTRICT

⑮ Ladies' Mile Historic District. The Ladies' Mile Historic District developed largely in the decades following the Civil War, when commerce intruded on the residential neighborhoods between Union and Madison Squares. In the late 1860s, businesses such as Arnold Constable (881–887 Broadway; Griffith Thomas, 1868–76) and Lord & Taylor (see No. 157) erected imposing Italianate and French Second Empire marble or cast-iron department stores along Broadway. They were soon joined by Gorham Silver Manufacturing Company (see No. 156), W. & J. Sloane (880–886 Broadway; W. Wheeler Smith, 1881–82), and other prestigious emporiums. Sixth Avenue also became a center for department stores, with B. Altman & Co. opening on the southwest corner of West 19th

Ladies' Mile Historic District (H.D. 15). The large store windows on the second floor of many of these buildings allowed riders of the elevated railway to peer into the stores on Sixth Avenue. Photo by Caroline Kane Levy.

Street in 1877 (D. & J. Jardine, architect; additions, 1880–1909). Altman's was followed by a succession of other stores, culminating in the 1895–97 construction of the monumental Siegel-Cooper Department Store (DeLemos & Cordes, architect) between West 18th and West 19th Streets. Fifth Avenue attracted smaller shops, publishing houses (see Scribner's, No. 160), the offices of charitable institutions such as the Methodist Book Concern (Edward Hale Kendall, 1888–90) at No. 148–152 and the Presbyterian Building (Rowe & Baker, 1894–95) at No. 154–158, and skyscrapers (see Flatiron Building, No. 161). With the exception of 23rd Street, with its large depart-

ment stores (notably Stern Brothers, 32–46 West 23rd Street; Henry Fernbach, 1878, with later additions), the side streets in the district were redeveloped at the turn of the century with loft buildings in which many of the goods sold in the nearby stores were manufactured. The finest of these is the Viennese Secession–influenced Spero Building (Robert D. Kohn, 1907–08) at 19–27 West 21st Street. A wave of restoration and rehabilitation began in the 1980s as the area was rediscovered by architects, photographers, publishing houses, advertising firms, and other businesses. These businesses have in turn attracted restaurants, boutiques, and other fashionable shops to Broadway, Fifth Avenue, and the adjacent side streets, while many of the former department stores on Sixth Avenue have been restored for national merchandising chains.

INDIVIDUAL LANDMARKS

147 **126, 128, 130–132, 136, and 140 West 18th Street Stables** (1864–65). These five landmark buildings are rare survivors of a row of thirteen private carriage houses designed in a utilitarian round-arched style. Erected on a street devoted exclusively to stables, they served the large residences built north of 14th Street in the mid-19th century.

148 **New York House and School of Industry,** now the Young Adults Institute, 120 West 16th Street (Sidney V. Stratton, 1878). Founded in 1850, the New York House and School of Industry was organized by members of several of New York's wealthiest families to assist destitute women by providing them with employment in the form of needlework, ranging from mundane sewing to the production of fancy embroidery. The charity's

1878 headquarters is thought to be the earliest building in the Queen Anne style in the city. The stone, terra-cotta, and slate trim, the paneled oriel with multipaned windows, and the free use of classical motifs are characteristic of highly sophisticated Queen Anne design. The building has been restored by Anderson Associates, architects.

149 **574 Sixth Avenue Building** (Simeon B. Eisendrath, 1903–04). Erected as a retail store for the Knickerbocker Jewelry Company, this building has a simple, rationally massed facade crowned by an exuberant cornice that was designed to attract the attention of riders on the Sixth Avenue Elevated, which ran in front of the building.

150 **5, 7, 9, 17, 19, 21, and 23 West 16th Street Houses** (c. 1845–46). In the 1840s the streets adjacent to Fifth Avenue just north of 14th Street were developed with row houses. Most of these structures were demolished as commerce invaded the area in the late 19th century, but West 16th Street retains a significant number of Greek Revival houses. The most impressive are the four survivors

126, 128, 130–32, 136, and 140 West 18th Street Stables (No. 147). A reminder of New York's equestrian past. Photo by Caroline Kane Levy.

of a row of nine wide houses—Nos. 5, 7, 9 and 17—each of which has a full-height curving bay on its front facade, an extremely rare feature in New York. In 1930 the family-planning pioneer Margaret Sanger moved her Birth Control Clinical Research Bureau into No. 17. Nos. 19 and 21 are simpler houses displaying fine ironwork, while No. 23 has a magnificent cast-iron balcony and stoop railing. All the houses have wide stone entrance enframements with battered sides and eared corners; this is a classic Greek form copied from the window surrounds on Greek temples.

151 **Lincoln Building,** 1–3 Union Square West (R. H. Robertson, 1889–90). The Lincoln Building is representative of the early skyscraper form as it evolved in New York, where architects chose to adapt already-popular styles to this new building type. Robertson designed the Lincoln Building in the same Romanesque Revival style that he used for churches, houses, and other structures. The building, faced in limestone, granite, red brick (now painted), and terra cotta, marks an important transitional phase in skyscraper engineering; it was constructed with a metal framing in combination with traditional masonry bearing walls.

152 **Bank of the Metropolis,** 31 Union Square West (Bruce Price, 1902–03). Price was an important early skyscraper designer with a particular interest in adapting the tripartite form of the column to tall buildings. This neo-Renaissance limestone-faced example is clearly massed in Price's preferred base-shaft-capital manner. The Bank of the Metropolis, founded in 1871 to serve the needs of businesses in the Union Square area, maintained its offices on the square until 1918, when it was absorbed by the Bank of Manhattan (now Chase Bank).

153 **Decker Building,** now the Union Building, 33 Union Square West (John Edelmann in the employ of Alfred Zucker, 1892–93). A rare example of a Moorish-inspired skyscraper, the headquarters of the Decker Piano Company was designed by John Edelmann, mentor and friend of Louis Sullivan. Many features of the Decker Building, most notably the naturalistic ornament, reflect Sullivan's influence. The base of the building was handsomely restored in 1995.

154 **Century Building,** now Barnes & Noble Bookstore, 33 East 17th Street (William Schickel, 1880–81). The red brick Century Building is a rare New York example of a Queen Anne commercial structure. Erected to house the prestigious Century Publishing Company, publisher of *The Century* and *St. Nicholas* magazines, the building is characteristic of the finest Queen Anne design in its free use of classical motifs in stone and terra cotta and its employment of the style's trademark sunflowers. After standing vacant for many years, the building was converted into a bookstore, and the facade received an award-winning restoration by Li-Saltzman Architects in 1994–95.

155 **Everett Building,** 200 Park Avenue South (Goldwin Starrett & Van Vleck, 1908). Located on the north side of Union Square, the Everett Building exemplifies an important development in the design of commercial high-rise buildings—the construction of functional, fireproof structures with large windows, open floor space, and simple classical detail. This emphasis on functionalism reflects the influence of Chicago skyscraper designs; in fact, the architect, Goldwin Starrett, had worked for four years in the Chicago office of Daniel Burnham.

156 **Gorham Manufacturing Company Building,** 889–891 Broadway (Edward Hale Kendall, 1883–84; alteration, John H. Duncan, 1912). This commercial building in the Queen Anne style was erected for the Gorham Manufacturing Company, a leading American silver firm, for its retail outlet in the exclusive Ladies' Mile shopping district. The Gorham is an early example of a mixed-use building: only the lower two floors were occupied by the store; the upper floors were rented as bachelor apartments. By 1893, however, the building was entirely in commercial use. The architect John H. Duncan is responsible for a remodeling of the building in 1912 that entailed the removal of a corner tower and the addition of roof dormers. The building now contains shops at street level and apartments above.

157 **Lord & Taylor Store,** 901 Broadway (James H. Giles, 1869–70). Two English immigrants, Samuel Lord and George Taylor, founded the dry goods firm Lord & Taylor around 1830. The business joined the northward migration of Manhattan's commercial establishments when it opened this impressive French Second Empire store in the fashionable Ladies' Mile shopping district. James H. Giles's original cast-iron building was considerably larger than the present structure; much of the Broadway frontage was rebuilt after Lord & Taylor moved in 1914 to its present home on Fifth Avenue at 39th Street. The building is noteworthy for its bold three-dimensional massing, its large windows, and the chamfered corner topped with a mansard roof that was designed to attract the attention of shoppers traveling south on Broadway from uptown residential neighborhoods. The facade has been restored and given a new ground story by Kutnicki Bernstein Architect.

158 **Theodore Roosevelt Birthplace,** now the Theodore Roosevelt Birthplace National Historic Site, 28 East 20th Street (Theodate Pope Riddle, 1923). At his death in 1919, Theodore Roosevelt was revered as a great American hero. Three years earlier his boyhood home, a modest Gothic Revival row house on East 20th Street (much altered after the Roosevelt family moved uptown in 1872), had been demolished. The Woman's Roosevelt Memorial Association, founded with the intention of honoring Roosevelt's memory, purchased the birthplace site, along with the adjacent home (also significantly altered) of Theodore's uncle, Robert Roosevelt. The association proceeded to demolish the uncle's house and to commission Theodate Pope Riddle, one of the first female architects in America, to reconstruct Theodore Roosevelt's childhood home as it had existed in 1865, when a mansard roof had been added and the interiors redesigned. A modest museum wing was built on the adjoining site. In 1963 the house was donated to the National Park Service.

159 **Church of the Holy Communion (Episcopal) Complex,** Sixth Avenue at West 20th Street (church, 1844–46; rectory and parish house, c. 1850; Sisters' House, 1854—all Richard Upjohn). Although a small building, the former Church of the Holy Communion had one of the most influential designs of the 19th century. Holy Communion was the first asymmetrical Gothic Revival church edifice in the United States and was the prototype for hundreds of similar buildings erected all across the country. Upjohn designed the building to resemble a small me-

dieval English parish church; the rectory and other additions complement the church in style and massing. The church's founder, the Reverend William Muhlenberg, a leader of the evangelical Catholic movement within the Episcopal Church, was closely involved with the design; it was apparently he who suggested the use of transepts and other features that were more common in Roman Catholic churches of the era. As part of his work at Holy Communion, Muhlenberg organized Saint Luke's Hospital, established a library that became the Muhlenberg Branch of the New York Public Library, and founded the first boys' choir and the first Episcopal sisterhood in America. The small three-story building on Sixth Avenue was the Sisters' House. The Holy Communion parish consolidated with Calvary and Saint George's (see H.D. 16 and H.D. 17, Map 8), and its complex of buildings has been converted for secular purposes.

160 **Scribner Building,** now the United Synagogue of America, 153–157 Fifth Avenue (Ernest Flagg, 1893–94). The publishing firm Charles Scribner's Sons commissioned this building for use as a bookstore and corporate headquarters. The limestone-fronted building, Flagg's first commercial work, indicates the architect's sophisticated understanding of contemporary French design, especially evident in the use of heavy load-bearing corner piers that flank a more open central area with large windows, attenuated iron colonnettes, and a wide shop front. The Scribner company was founded in 1846 by Charles Scribner and flourished, under various names, until Scribner's death in 1871. By the late 1870s, Scribner's sons had taken over the firm, which grew into one of America's most prestigious publishing houses, introducing works by Henry James, Edith Wharton, F. Scott Fitzgerald, and Ernest Hemingway, among others. The Fifth Avenue building, designed by Charles Scribner II's brother-in-law, was the first built specifically for the company. In 1913 the company moved into a new store farther north on Fifth Avenue (see No. 249).

161 **Flatiron Building,** Broadway and Fifth Avenue at 23rd Street (D. H. Burnham & Co., 1901–03). The Chicago architect Daniel Burnham designed this triangular steel-framed skyscraper on what was, at the turn of the century, among the most promi-

Flatiron Building (No. 161) Daniel Burnham's memorable design for this prominent site.
Landmarks Preservation Commission collection.

nent sites in New York City—Madison Square at the junction of Fifth Avenue and Broadway—anchoring the north end of the prestigious Ladies' Mile shopping district. Built as offices for the Fuller Construction Company (see No. 272), the skyscraper was dubbed the Flatiron because its shape resembles that of a clothing iron. Many early 20th-century painters and photographers were inspired by the building's singular form, and it became a world-famous symbol of the romantic New York skyline. The slender 22-story building is clad in traditional Italian Renaissance ornament, most of it white terra cotta; the light coloration was again revealed in 1991 when the building was cleaned and restored (Hurley & Farinella, architect). The small metal and glass extension (known as the cowcatcher) at the apex of the building was designed by the Burnham firm in 1902.

162 **Sidewalk Clock,** 200 Fifth Avenue at West 23rd Street (Hecla Iron Works, 1909). Clocks were once an important part of the street fabric of American cities. Large cast-iron sidewalk clocks, many of which served as advertisements for jewelers and other businesses, proliferated in the early 20th century. In Manhattan four such clocks are landmarks (see Nos. 247, 365, and 440). There are, in addition, two landmark clocks in Queens (see Nos. 6 and 35) and one in Brooklyn (see No. 8). This clock, as the words on its faces announce, was installed by the Fifth Avenue Building (now the Toy Center), which opened in 1909. It is the most ornate sidewalk clock in New York City. A fluted Ionic column supports the clock, which is framed by wreaths of oak leaves and crowned by a cartouche.

163 **Metropolitan Life Insurance Company Tower,** 1 Madison Avenue (Napoleon Le Brun & Sons, Pierre Le Brun, architect in charge, 1907–09). The 54-story tower that rises along the east side of Madison Square was planned by the Metropolitan Life Insurance Company as the world's tallest building and was intended as a corporate symbol. Designed by Pierre Le Brun, the tower evokes the form of the famous campanile in the Piazza San Marco in Venice. Despite the fact that much of the tower's ornament was removed in a renovation of 1960–64, the tower's form is intact, as are the most prominent features of the design,

the ornate four-faced clock and the crowning cupola and lantern.

164 **Appellate Division Courthouse,** Appellate Division, New York State Supreme Court, 27 Madison Avenue (James Brown Lord, 1896–99). This small Beaux-Arts limestone courthouse is especially notable for the manner in which art is incorporated into the design to create a structure that is unified architecturally and symbolically. The three-dimensional exterior, with its projecting Corinthian porticoes, supports an extensive display of sculpture by sixteen artists on themes relating to the law. Of special note are Daniel Chester French's *Justice,* at the peak of the pediment; Frederick Ruckstuhl's *Wisdom* and *Force,* flanking the entrance stair; and statues representing important figures in the history of justice standing along the roofline. **Interior:** The magnificent main hall, courtroom, and anteroom are richly decorated with furniture designed specifically for the courthouse by Herter Brothers and with an elaborate series of allegorical murals painted by ten American artists, including Edwin Blashfield, Kenyon Cox, and H. Siddons Mowbray.

165 **Trinity Chapel (Episcopal) Complex,** now the Serbian Orthodox Cathedral of Saint Sava and Parish House, 15 West 25th Street (chapel, Richard Upjohn, 1850–55; clergy house, R. & R. M. Upjohn, 1866; parish school, Jacob Wrey Mould, 1860). This symmetrically massed, Early English Gothic–inspired building was erected to serve the congregants of Trinity Church (see No. 15) who in the mid-19th century were moving to the newly developing neighborhoods around Madison Square. To the east of the church and the adjoining clergy house is the parish school (now the parish house), a small polychromatic building that is an early and notable example of the Victorian Gothic style in the United States as well as Mould's only surviving building in New York City. In 1943 the complex was sold to the Serbian Orthodox Church.

166 **Gilsey House,** 1200 Broadway (Stephen Decatur Hatch, 1869–71). The exuberant French Second Empire cast-iron building that dominates the intersection of Broadway and West 29th Street was a premier 19th-century New York hostelry. With its projecting frontispieces and extraordinary

Gilsey House (No. 166). An exuberant French Second Empire cast-iron building.
Photo by Carl Forster.

mansard roof, the baroque structure was erected when this section of Broadway was being transformed into New York's entertainment district. In 1979 the building was converted into housing. In 1992 the facades were restored and repainted in a cream color by Building Conservation Associates.

167 **Church of the Transfiguration (Episcopal),** also known as the Little Church Around the Corner, 1 East 29th Street (church and rectory, 1849–50; church addition, 1852; lych-gate, Frederick Clarke Withers, 1896; lady chapel, 1906; mortuary chapel, 1908). The Church of the Transfigura-

tion consists of a series of Gothic Revival structures built around a quiet garden. The original one-story church and adjoining rectory were designed by an unidentified architect in 1849, and the guildhall, transepts, and tower were added a few years later. Frederick Clarke Withers's English-inspired lychgate was described by a contemporary critic as "the one touch necessary to make the surroundings of the church . . . the most picturesque and charming of any in New York." The church acquired its sobriquet in 1870, when the minister of a fashionable church nearby, declining to conduct a funeral service for an actor, referred the mourners to "the little church around the corner." The church has welcomed actors ever since.

168 **Marble Collegiate Church,** 272 Fifth Avenue (Samuel A. Warner, 1851–54). Like West End Collegiate (see No. 334) on the Upper West Side, Marble Collegiate traces its history back to the city's first church, a Reformed congregation established by Dutch colonists in 1628. This Early Romanesque Revival building, with its Gothic trim and Wren-like steeple, is clad entirely in the Tuckahoe marble from which the church derives its name. The church has had a number of famous preachers, most prominent among them the Reverend Norman Vincent Peale.

169 **Colony Club,** now the American Academy of Dramatic Arts, 120 Madison Avenue (McKim, Mead & White, Stanford White, partner in charge, 1904–08). Founded in 1903, the Colony Club was the first private women's club in New York City to erect its own clubhouse. Stanford White's building was modeled on 18th-century houses in Annapolis, Maryland (he even escorted building committee members on a trip to view the original houses), with header-bond brickwork laid in a diaper pattern. By 1914 the club had outgrown this building, and a new clubhouse was erected on Park Avenue (now in H.D. 29, Map 14). Since 1963 the building has housed the American Academy of Dramatic Arts, the oldest professional acting school in the English-speaking world.

170 **Grand Hotel,** 1232–1238 Broadway (Henry Engelbert, 1868). The Grand Hotel is a handsome marble-fronted building erected at a time when Broadway between Madison and Herald Squares was being transformed into a glittering entertainment district. French Second Empire in style, the hotel is distinguished by its pavilion massing, its chamfered corner, and its imposing mansard roof with large pedimented dormers and ocular windows.

171 **Grolier Club,** now the Graler Club, 29 East 32nd Street (Charles W. Romeyn, 1889). Founded in 1884 for "the literary study and promotion of the arts pertaining to the production of books," the Grolier Club occupied this building from 1890 until 1917, when it moved to larger quarters on

East 60th Street. The highly original late Romanesque Revival design was executed in Roman brick and stone. The building is now in use as a club and restaurant.

172 **Della Robbia Bar (The Crypt),** now Fiori Restaurant (interior), 4 Park Avenue (Warren & Wetmore with R. Guastavino Company and Rookwood Pottery Company, 1910–13). The Della Robbia Bar, also known as the Crypt, of the former Vanderbilt Hotel, is an outstanding example of a ceramic interior and one of the few such early 20th-century spaces that survive. The vaulted space is constructed from structural, textured, ivory-colored Guastavino tiles (similar to those used at the Oyster Bar at Grand Central Terminal—see No. 239) combined with colorful ceramic ornament, embellished with flowers, faces, and other motifs, produced by the Rookwood Pottery Company of Cincinnati, one of the country's leading art pottery manufacturers.

173 **Empire State Building,** 350 Fifth Avenue (Shreve, Lamb & Harmon, 1929–31). Among the best-known symbols of New York City, the Empire State Building was designed to be the world's tallest building and is a product of the frenzy of skyscraper construction that produced the great Art Deco towers of the late 1920s and early 1930s. The building was conceived by General Motors vice president John Raskob and was promoted by former New York governor Al Smith, who served as president of the Empire State Corporation. Unfortunately, the Depression left much of the office space vacant; the building was saved from bankruptcy by the popularity of its observation deck. The brick-clad edifice with a stone base was massed in accordance with zoning laws while accommodating the constraints of elevator placement, a restricted budget, and an effort to have no office space more than 28 feet from a window. **Interior:** The lobby is laid out in a functional manner with all corridors leading to the elevators. The walls are covered with two varieties of German marble highlighted by aluminum detailing. Major ornamental features include aluminum bridges, bronze medallions depicting the crafts and industries involved with the building's construction, and a marble panel with an aluminum relief of the building superimposed on a map of New York, the Empire State.

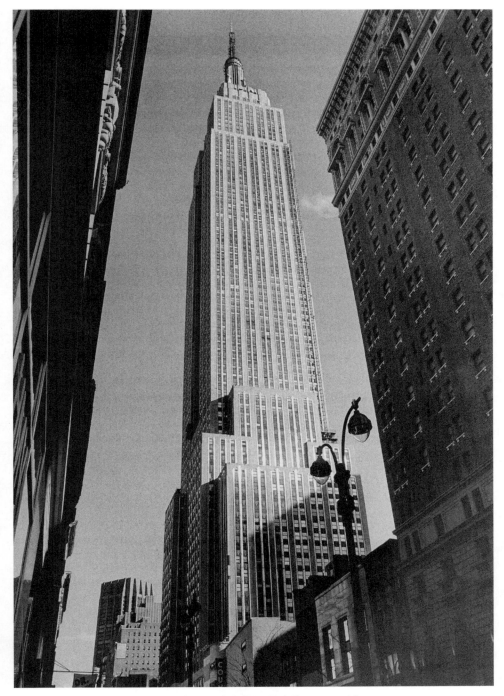

Empire State Building (No. 173). This prominent symbol of New York City was saved from bankruptcy during the Depression by the popularity of its observation deck. Photo by Carl Forster.

■ *UNION SQUARE AND EAST OF PARK AVENUE SOUTH*

HISTORIC DISTRICTS

16 **Gramercy Park Historic District.** The special character of Gramercy Park is largely the result of a plan established by the developer Samuel B. Ruggles, who purchased a large tract of land in 1831 with the intention of creating a prime residential neighborhood around a small private park open only to the owners of adjacent lots. To attract builders, Ruggles not only planned the park and enclosed it with a tall iron fence (still extant), but also laid out Irving Place and Lexington Avenue. It was not, however, until the 1840s that fine row houses, many still standing on the west and south sides of the park, were erected and sold to prominent citizens. Somewhat smaller row houses were built on the blocks to the south of the park; several fine examples from the 1850s can be found on East 18th Street. In conjunction with this residential development, impressive buildings such as Calvary (Episcopal) Church (Park Avenue South at East 21st Street; James Renwick, Jr., 1846) and the Friends Meeting House (see No. 180) were constructed, helping to establish Gramercy Park as a neighborhood of great prestige. Later in the century, as the area's preeminence waned, several early apartment houses were built; the Queen Anne–style Gramercy (34 Gramercy Park East; George DaCunha, 1883) and the neo-Gothic 36 Gramercy Park East (James Reily Gordon, 1908–10) are prime examples. Clubs were also attracted to the neighborhood—both the Players (see No. 182) and the National Arts Club (see No. 181) are housed in converted residences. By the early 20th century, the Gramercy Park area was home to an affluent, artistic group of people living in older buildings, in new duplex cooperatives (e.g., 24 Gramercy Park South; Herbert Lucas, 1908), and in renovated row houses. On several blocks the old-fashioned row houses were rediscovered and redesigned with stucco facades embellished with simple artistic details. This is especially evident on East 19th Street between Irving Place and Third Avenue, known as the Block Beautiful, where, beginning in 1909, the architect Frederick H. Sterner renovated many houses.

17 **Stuyvesant Square Historic District.** Stuyvesant Square was laid out in 1846 on land donated to the city by Peter Gerard Stuyvesant. The square is divided by Second Avenue, and each of its two parts is surrounded by an original cast-iron fence. Stuyvesant Square provides a fine setting for two of New York's most distinguished landmarks, the Friends Meeting House and Seminary (see No. 177) and Saint George's Church (Episcopal) (see No. 178). The earliest Greek Revival houses in the district were erected in 1842–43 at 214–216 East 18th Street, when residential development reached north of 14th Street. Most of the district's houses, however, were built in the 1850s, when late Greek Revival, Italianate, and Anglo-Italianate rows were constructed. One of the latest single-family dwellings in the district is the Sidney Webster House (1883) at 245 East 17th Street, the only surviving residence in New York City designed by the architect Richard Morris Hunt.

INDIVIDUAL LANDMARKS

174 **Union Square Savings Bank,** 20 Union Square East (Henry Bacon, 1905–07). The bold academic classicism of this white granite bank building with its Corinthian temple front reveals the design aesthetic of Henry Bacon, an architect best known for the monumental Lincoln Memorial in Washington, D.C. The Institution for the Savings of Merchants' Clerks, established in 1848, was renamed the Union Square Savings Bank in 1904. The bank remained an independent institution until 1968, when it merged with another bank. The building has been vacant since 1992.

175 **Century Association Building,** now Century Center for the Performing Arts, 109–111 East 15th Street (Gambrill & Richardson, 1869). Not only is this the oldest surviving clubhouse building in Manhattan, but it appears to be an early work of Henry Hobson Richardson, who would later become one of America's most influential architects. Charles Gambrill began planning the clubhouse in 1866, before Richardson was a member of the club or Gambrill's partner, but by the time the building was erected, the firm Gambrill & Richardson had been formed and Richardson had become a Centurion. Although it is not clear what the relative contribution of each partner was to the design, the massing and the employment of a mansard roof and stylized neo-Grec detail resemble features on other early buildings by Richardson and may reflect his French training. In 1996–97 the building was rehabilitated and converted into a theater by Beyer Blinder Belle, architect.

176 Germania Life Insurance Company Building, now the Guardian Life Building, 201 Park Avenue South (50 Union Square East) (D'Oench & Yost, 1910–11). Prominently located on a corner site overlooking Union Square, the headquarters of the Germania Life Insurance Company (renamed Guardian Life in 1918 in response to anti-German sentiment during World War I) is a 20-story tower with a tripartite massing. The building is crowned by an enormous mansard roof atop which stands an early example of electric signage.

177 Friends Meeting House and Seminary, 15 Rutherford Place and 226 East 16th Street (attributed to Charles T. Bunting, 1861). This austere brick meetinghouse and the adjoining seminary, with its finely proportioned massing and original multipaned windows, were erected by a group of Quakers known as the Hicksites, who were more traditional in their mode of worship than the Orthodox Quakers (see No. 180). Having been divided since the mid-19th century, the two groups reconciled in 1958, retaining this building as their meetinghouse.

178 Saint George's Church (Episcopal), Rutherford Place at East 16th Street (Blesch & Eidlitz, 1846–56). This massive round-arched stone building dominating Stuyvesant Square is one of the first and most significant examples of Early Romanesque Revival church architecture in America. The exterior, probably the work of the Bavarian-born architect Otto Blesch, reflects the influence that the German round-arched style known as *Rundbogenstil* had on American design in the 1840s. The interiors were the work of Leopold Eidlitz, who also restored the church after it was damaged by fire in 1865. The design was ideally suited to the requirements of its rector, Stephen Higginson Tyng, an ardent leader of the evangelical wing of the Episcopal Church and one of the greatest preachers of his time. The original stone spires

were removed in 1889; the church's facade was restored in the 1980s. The church is only one part of a larger complex (included in the Stuyvesant Square Historic District) composed of Saint George's Chapel (M. L. & H. G. Emery, 1911–12), a neo-Romanesque building located to the north of the church; the rectory, set to the rear of the church, designed in the early 1850s by Eidlitz; and the romantic, asymmetrically massed Saint George Memorial House (now apartments), a gift from J. P. Morgan that was designed by Leopold Eidlitz's son, Cyrus L. W. Eidlitz, in 1886.

179 326, 328, and 330 East 18th Street Houses (1853). These three Italianate brick row houses form a pleasant enclave in the middle of the blockfront of East 18th Street between First and Second Avenues. The houses have deep front yards, a rarity in Manhattan, and superb cast-iron verandas.

180 Friends Meeting House, now Brotherhood Synagogue, 144 East 20th Street (King & Kellum, 1857–59). A doctrinal split in the Quaker community led to the construction of two Manhattan meetinghouses in the mid-19th century (see No. 177). New York's Orthodox Quaker community, the more worldly of the city's two Quaker congregations, commissioned the prominent firm King & Kellum to design a meetinghouse for this site on Gramercy Park. The chaste but beautifully detailed Italianate building was constructed of extremely fine yellow sandstone from Ohio. The meetinghouse was carefully restored (James Stewart Polshek, architect) in the 1970s as part of its conversion into a synagogue.

181 Samuel Tilden House, now the National Arts Club, 15 Gramercy Park South (Vaux & Radford, 1881–84). Calvert Vaux's masterful Victorian Gothic facade resulted from a remodeling of two earlier row houses. This work was undertaken for Samuel J. Tilden, a lawyer who resigned as governor of New York to run for the presidency in 1876, losing in the electoral college to Rutherford B. Hayes. Reflecting the influence of John Ruskin's architectural theories, the house's polychromatic facade is enlivened with sculptural ornament depicting various plants, animals, and birds native to the New York area as well as with busts of notable writers and thinkers, chosen to reflect Tilden's literary interests. At his death, Tilden's private library, and a considerable fortune, helped to establish the New York Public Library (see No. 237). In 1906 the National Arts Club, an organization dedicated to supporting the arts, purchased the building.

182 **The Players,** 16 Gramercy Park South (1845; redesign, McKim, Mead & White, Stanford White, partner in charge, 1888–89). This single-family Gothic Revival–style brownstone house has been occupied as a club by the Players since 1888. Original Gothic drip lintels on the upper floors survive from the original rowhouse facade. Edwin Booth, who established the Players as a club for men in the theatrical profession, commissioned his friend Stanford White to redesign the building. White removed the stoop and added the elegant Italian Renaissance–inspired two-tiered porch with its magnificent ironwork, as well as the stained-glass windows and the cornice that incorporates theatrical masks.

183 **Church Missions House,** now the Protestant Welfare Agencies Building, 281 Park Avenue South (Robert W. Gibson and Edward J. N. Stent, 1892–94). Beginning in the late 19th century, the area immediately south of East 23rd Street became a center for the offices of charitable organizations.

The Players (No. 182) was established as a club for men in the theatrical profession. Photo by Peter Choy.

Public Baths (No. 185). Designed according to Roman prototypes, this building was constructed to address appalling sanitary conditions in New York City's slums. Photo by John Barrington Bayley.

The Church Missions House, a steel-frame structure whose facade was modeled on a medieval Flemish guildhall, was the headquarters for the missionary activities of the Episcopal Church. The building was restored in the early 1990s by Kapell & Kastow; it continues to house social service organizations.

184 **Sixty-ninth Regiment Armory,** 68 Lexington Avenue (Hunt & Hunt, 1904–06). The 69th Regiment Armory was the first New York City armory built after the Seventh Regiment Armory (see No. 392) that was not designed in the form of a medieval fortress. Hunt & Hunt rejected the medieval form in favor of a French Beaux-Arts mode with a severe military aspect. The armory is famous as the home of "the Fighting 69th," New York's only official Irish regiment, and as the site of the legendary 1913 Armory Show, which introduced modern art to the American public.

185 **Public Baths,** Asser Levy Place at East 23rd Street (Brunner & Aiken, 1904–06). In the late 19th century, progressive social reformers lobbied for the creation of public baths that would help alleviate sanitary problems in New York City's slum neighborhoods, where few residents had access to a

bath or a shower. Appropriately, the design precedent for the Asser Levy Place baths was the public baths of ancient Rome, as evidenced by the paired columns and semicircular thermal windows. Now a swimming pool and recreation center, the building was restored by the Parks Department in 1989–90.

186 **New York School of Applied Design for Women,** later Pratt–New York Phoenix School of Design, now Touro College, Lexington Avenue Campus, 160 Lexington Avenue (Harvey Wiley Corbett, 1908–09). In the late 19th century, women began to enter the art world in increasing numbers and became especially active in the decorative arts. The New York School of Applied Design for Women was established in 1892 to offer "women instruction which may enable them to earn a livelihood . . . in the application of ornamental design to manufacture and the arts." The school, which specialized in such fields as book illustration, textile and wallpaper design, and interior decoration, was unusual in that its programs were geared specifically to the education of poor women. The architect of the school's facility, Harvey Wiley Corbett, was also an instructor there. He designed an idiosyncratic version of a classical temple, complete with casts from the Parthenon frieze.

INDIVIDUAL LANDMARKS

■ *WEST OF SEVENTH AVENUE*

187 **New Amsterdam Theater,** 214 West 42nd Street (Herts & Tallant, 1902–03). As home to the Ziegfeld Follies, as well as Eva Le Gallienne's Civic Repertory Theater and George White's "Scandals," this legendary theater has presented scores of great actors in memorable productions. The theater has a narrow Beaux-Arts-inspired entrance facade on West 42nd Street with a vertical sign dating from 1937,

when the theater was used as a movie house. The **interior** is adorned with splendid Art Nouveau decoration. The lobby, foyers, reception room, staircases, smoking room, and auditorium contain ornate terracotta panels evoking theatrical themes; murals by George Peixotto, Robert Blum, and others; faience stairway balustrades; art tiles designed by Henry Mercer; and ornate plaster, stone, and wood carving. The theater closed in 1985. In 1995–97 the Walt Disney Company undertook a major restoration under the direction of Hardy Holzman Pfeiffer, architect, that rejuvenated the extraordinary interior.

188 **McGraw-Hill Building,** 330 West 42nd Street (Raymond Hood, Godley & Fouilhoux, 1930–31). The 35-story McGraw-Hill Building is a major work of the great skyscraper architect Raymond Hood. The massing, with horizontal setbacks that allow the building to be read as a modern slab, and the simple detailing illustrate the transition between the decorative Art Deco style and the more austere slab forms of International Style design. With the McGraw-Hill Building, Hood also introduced to New York the idea of horizontal ribbon windows, a feature that would become common on modern skyscrapers. Color was an important element of the design. Almost the entire building is faced in blue-green terra cotta; the metal windows were originally apple green with a band of vermilion across the top; the entranceway is clad in alternating bands of blue and green metal; and the building is crowned by a sign with the corporate name spelled out in 11-foot-tall letters originally painted white with an orange stripe. The building was erected west of Eighth Avenue in an area zoned for industrial use because it housed not only McGraw-Hill's corporate offices but also its printing plant. McGraw-Hill moved to another building on Sixth Avenue in the late 1960s, but this building remains in use as offices.

189 **Paramount Building,** 1501 Broadway (Rapp & Rapp, 1926–27). The theater architects Rapp & Rapp designed this dramatically massed skyscraper (at its completion, the tallest in the Times Square area) as offices for Paramount Pictures, as a home for the Paramount Theater (demolished), and as an advertisement for the Paramount Corporation. The motion picture company's trademark, a mountain encircled by five-pointed stars, is echoed in the mountainlike massing of the building and its surmounting four-faced clock, on which the hours are marked by five-pointed stars. The clock is crowned by a glass globe that, when illuminated, is visible for miles and is a focal point of the Times Square area. The clocks and globe were restored in 1997.

New Amsterdam Theater (No. 187). This legendary theater has splendid Art Nouveau decoration throughout the interior. It has recently been completely restored. Photo courtesy of Whitney Cox.

Theaters along West 44th Street, between Broadway and Eighth Avenue. Photo by Carl Forster.

190 **Little Theater,** now the Helen Hayes Theater, 238 West 44th Street (Ingalls & Hoffman, 1912; interior remodeling, Herbert J. Krapp, 1917–20). The construction of the Little Theater marked a new direction in Broadway theater design. The theater was commissioned by the producer Winthrop Ames to house the type of drama known as intimate theater. The small size (the theater seated only 299 people) and the use of the primarily domestic Colonial Revival style on both the exterior and **interior** contribute to the feeling of intimacy. The balcony was added in 1917 in an effort to make the theater more profitable.

191 **Erlanger Theater,** now the Saint James Theater, 246–256 West 44th Street (Warren & Wetmore, 1926–27). The restrained Beaux-Arts facade of this theater is the work of an important New York architecture firm. Commissioned by the producer Abraham Erlanger, the theater was renamed the Saint James by new owners following Erlanger's death in 1930. The **interior,** which contains a large auditorium, is unusual in its reliance on spatial organization rather than on ornament for effect. The

Saint James has housed such great American musicals as *Oklahoma!, The King and I,* and *Hello, Dolly!*

192 **Shubert Theater,** 221–233 West 44th Street (Henry B. Herts, 1912–13). This is the flagship playhouse of the Shubert Organization, a major force in the construction of theaters and the production of plays in New York and elsewhere in the United States since the early 20th century. Built as a memorial to Sam Shubert, the oldest of the three Shubert brothers, the building also served as the headquarters of the Shubert theatrical empire. The theater was designed in a lavish manner with Venetian Renaissance sgraffito decoration on the exterior and, on the **interior,** elaborate plasterwork and murals by J. Mortimer Lichtenauer. The Shubert has been home to many hit productions, among them the record-breaking *A Chorus Line.* In 1996 architect Francesa Russo of Campagna & Russo restored the original color scheme and murals and re-created the central ceiling mural.

193 **Broadhurst Theater,** 235–243 West 44th Street (Herbert J. Krapp, 1917–18). One of many

Broadway theaters built by the Shuberts, the Broadhurst opened under the personal management of the playwright George Broadhurst. Built as a companion to the Plymouth Theater (see No. 200), the building has a handsome neoclassical facade of patterned brick and terra cotta. The plan of the Adamesque **interior** is characteristic of the many theaters designed by Krapp: the space is wider than it is deep and has a single curving balcony. Among the celebrated actors to have appeared in plays at the Broadhurst are Eva Le Gallienne, Lionel and Ethel Barrymore, Leslie Howard, Barbara Stanwyck, Humphrey Bogart, Karl Malden, Rosalind Russell, Joel Grey, Katharine Hepburn, George C. Scott, and Dustin Hoffman.

194 **Majestic Theater,** 245–257 West 44th Street (Herbert J. Krapp, 1926–27). The Majestic, a large musical house (seating 1,800), was built by Irwin Chanin as one of a trio of theaters; the others were the Royale (see No. 199) and the Theater Masque (see No. 198). The eclectic exterior is in a style that Chanin and his architect referred to as "modern Spanish." The **interior** is decorated in a neoclassical manner and is laid out in the so-called stadium plan that Chanin and Krapp first introduced at their Forty-sixth Street Theater (see No. 204). Among the hit musicals that have played the Majestic are *Carousel, South Pacific, The Music Man, Camelot, The Wiz,* and *The Phantom of the Opera.*

195 **Actors Studio,** originally the Seventh Associate Presbyterian Church, 432 West 44th Street (c. 1858). The Actors Studio, founded in 1947, is best known for its association with Lee Strasberg, who became director of the studio in 1949. Strasberg was the leading American advocate of the Method acting technique pioneered by Konstantin Stanislavsky at the Moscow Art Theater. In 1955 the Actors Studio purchased this late Greek Revival church structure and converted it for use as a drama school. In 1995 the building was restored by Davis, Brody & Associates, architect.

196 **Film Center Building** (interior), 630 Ninth Avenue (Ely Jacques Kahn, 1928–29). The ground-floor vestibule, lobby, and hallway of the Film Center, composing one of the most beautiful Art Deco interiors in New York, were designed by Kahn in his idiosyncratic manner. Much of the in-

The Martin Beck Theater (No. 197) is a Moorish-inspired building with lavish interior details. Photo by Justin Van Soest.

terior reflects a pre-Columbian influence. Of special interest are the geometrically patterned terrazzo floors, the ziggurat shape of the plaster ceilings, the superb metalwork, and—the lobby's most striking feature—the polychromatic mosaic on the wall between the elevator banks.

197 **Martin Beck Theater,** 302–314 West 45th Street (C. Albert Lansburgh, 1923–24). Among the most spectacular theaters in the Broadway theater district, this Moorish-inspired structure was built by the producer Martin Beck, who operated the theater until his death in 1940. The **interiors** reflect Beck's desire to build the most lavish legitimate theater in the Broadway area. The fantastical Moorish-Byzantine-style spaces were designed by Lansburgh in collaboration with the painter Albert Herter. Since the 1960s the Martin Beck Theater has been a popular venue for musicals and has housed such hits as *Bye Bye Birdie, Man of La Mancha,* and *Into the Woods.* A major restoration of the interior was completed in 1996 by Francesa Russo Architects.

198 **Theater Masque,** now the Golden Theater, 252–256 West 45th Street (Herbert J. Krapp, 1926–27). Built by Irwin Chanin in conjunction with the Majestic (see No. 194) and the Royale (see No. 199), the Theater Masque, which was renamed for the producer John Golden in 1937, is a small house planned for intimate dramas. Both the exterior and the **interior** of the theater were designed in the "modern Spanish" style used by Krapp for several of his Chanin commissions. *Tobacco Road* premiered at the Masque in 1933 and was followed by many other successful productions, including, in recent years, *The Gin Game, Crimes of the Heart, 'Night Mother,* and *Glengarry Glen Ross.*

199 **Royale Theater,** 242–250 West 45th Street (Herbert J. Krapp, 1926–27). The Royale and its neighbors the Theater Masque (see No. 198) and the Majestic (see No. 194) were built as a trio by Irwin Chanin; all were designed in the "modern Spanish" style that he favored. The **interior** continues the Spanish-inspired detail and is particularly notable for the groin-vaulted ceiling of the auditorium, which features a large mural by Willy Pogany entitled *Lovers of Spain.* One of the most popular theaters on Broadway, the Royale has been home to *Diamond Lil* (starring Mae West), *The Magnificent Yankee,* Moss Hart's *Light Up the Sky,* Julie Andrews's American debut in *The Boy Friend,* Thornton Wilder's *The Matchmaker,* Laurence Olivier in *The Entertainer,* Tennessee Williams's *Night of the Iguana,* and *The Subject Was Roses.*

200 **Plymouth Theater,** 234–240 West 45th Street (Herbert J. Krapp, 1917–18). The Plymouth, planned by the Shuberts as a companion to the Broadhurst (see No. 193), has always been one of Broadway's most successful theaters. It has housed *Abe Lincoln in Illinois, Private Lives, Dial 'M' for Murder, The Caine Mutiny Court Martial, The Odd Couple, Plaza Suite,* and *Equus.* The Plymouth and the Broadhurst were the first designs of the prolific theater architect Herbert J. Krapp, and they reflect his interest in the use of patterned

brickwork on the exterior and Adamesque design for the **interior.**

201 **Booth Theater,** 222–232 West 45th Street (Henry B. Herts, 1912–13). The Italian Renaissance–inspired Booth and the neighboring Shubert Theater (see No. 192) were designed as a pair by the prominent theater architect Henry B. Herts. The **interior** of the Booth was planned as an intimate setting for drama. The theater has been enormously successful, housing such important American plays as *You Can't Take It with You; The Time of Your Life; Come Back, Little Sheba; That Championship Season; For Colored Girls . . . ; Sunday in the Park with George;* and *Having Our Say.*

202 **Music Box Theater,** 239–247 West 45th Street (C. Howard Crane & E. George Kiehler, 1920). Producer Sam Harris built this theater to house Irving Berlin's *Music Box Revues.* The revues ran for five years, after which time the theater housed many successful plays and musicals, including George S. Kaufman and George and Ira Gershwin's *Of Thee I Sing,* Kaufman and Edna Ferber's *Dinner at Eight* and *Stage Door,* Moss Hart and Irving Berlin's *As Thousands Cheer,* and several hits by Kaufman and Hart, including *The Man Who Came to Dinner.* The elegant English-inspired neoclassical exterior is articulated by a porch supported by four attenuated columns; the Adamesque **interior** features delicate plasterwork and murals.

203 **Imperial Theater (interior),** 249 West 45th Street (Herbert J. Krapp, 1923). Built by the Shuberts, the Imperial has long been one of the most successful Broadway theaters. Planned as a showcase for musicals and revues, the theater has premiered such hits as *Rose-Marie; Oh, Kay!; Annie Get Your Gun; Gypsy; Oliver!; Fiddler on the Roof; Cabaret; Dreamgirls;* and *Les Miserables.* The Imperial has an elegant Adamesque interior with fine plasterwork.

204 **Forty-sixth Street Theater,** now the Richard Rodgers Theater, 226–236 West 46th Street (Herbert J. Krapp, 1924). The first Broadway theater built by the Chanin Organization, the Forty-sixth Street is an elaborate Renaissance-inspired work that features several innovations in theater design, notably a single entrance and, on the interior, stadium-type seating with a steeply raked orchestra and a single balcony (Irwin Chanin thought such seating would democratize theatergoing). Many hit musicals have played the Forty-sixth Street, including *Good News, Finian's Rainbow, Guys and Dolls, Damn Yankees,* and *1776.*

205 Globe Theater, now the Lunt-Fontanne Theater, 203–217 West 46th Street (Carrère & Hastings, 1909–10). Built as the headquarters of the influential Broadway producer Charles Dillingham, the Beaux-Arts Globe is the only surviving theater designed by Carrère & Hastings. After serving as a movie house for many years, the Globe was returned to legitimate theater use in 1958; at the same time, however, its interior was gutted and its name was changed. Dillingham had been able to attract many major stars to play the Globe, including Sarah Bernhardt, Lynn Fontanne, Fred and Adele Astaire, and Fanny Brice. In more recent years the theater has been favored for musicals, chief among them *The Sound of Music* and *Sophisticated Ladies.*

206 Mansfield Theater, now the Brooks Atkinson Theater, 256–262 West 47th Street (Herbert J. Krapp, 1925–26). Named originally for the 19th-century American actor Richard Mansfield, and renamed in 1960 for the theater critic Brooks Atkinson, this theater is one of six erected in the 1920s by the Chanin Organization. The theater was designed in the "modern Spanish" style favored by Irwin Chanin. The exceptional **interior** reflects the expertise of Chanin, Krapp, and Roman Meltzer, the former architect to Czar Nicholas II who supervised the ornamental scheme, which includes fine plasterwork and murals. The theater has housed a number of successful dramas and comedies, including *Green Pastures, Come Blow Your Horn, Talley's Folly,* and *Noises Off.*

207 Biltmore Theater (interior), 261–265 West 47th Street (Herbert J. Krapp, 1925–26). One of six Broadway theaters built by Irwin Chanin, the Biltmore has a handsome Adamesque interior laid out in an unusual horseshoe-shaped plan. The relatively small house, which has been home to such long-running hits as Neil Simon's *Barefoot in the Park* and the classic rock musical *Hair,* has been vacant for many years.

208 Barrymore Theater, 243–251 West 47th Street (Herbert J. Krapp, 1928). Built by the Shuberts to honor their star performer, Ethel Barrymore, this theater is among Krapp's most interesting designs—its facade takes the form of a giant classical Roman window with a terra-cotta grid. The **interior** is unusual for its mock-Elizabethan decoration. Ethel Barrymore appeared in the first production at the theater as well as in three other plays performed there between 1929 and 1931. Among the theater's many successful productions were *Gay Divorce* (with Fred Astaire), *The Women, Key Largo, A Streetcar Named Desire,* and *Raisin in the Sun.*

209 Longacre Theater, 220–228 West 48th Street (Henry B. Herts, 1912–13). The Longacre was designed in the French neoclassical style for the Broadway producer and baseball magnate Harry Frazee (who owned the Boston Red Sox). The **interior,** with its simple French-inspired decor (now somewhat altered), incorporated many innovations in design, planning, and ventilation. Although the theater has had a checkered history, it has housed a number of long-running hits, notably *Ain't Misbehavin'* and *Children of a Lesser God.*

210 Forrest Theater (interior), later the Coronet Theater, now the Eugene O'Neill Theater, 230–238 West 49th Street (Herbert J. Krapp, 1925–26). Built by the Shuberts, the Forrest was named for the celebrated American actor Edwin Forrest (see Fonthill, Bronx No. 46) and renamed in honor of the great American playwright Eugene O'Neill in 1953. The auditorium is an elegant example of the Adamesque design favored by Krapp. The most famous production staged in this theater was *Tobacco Road,* which moved to the Forrest in 1934, several months after opening at the Theater Masque (see No. 198), and which ran for 3,182 performances, then a Broadway record. In 1994 a restoration of the interior was undertaken by Francesa Russo of Campagna & Russo, architect.

211 Ambassador Theater (interior), 215–223 West 49th Street (Herbert J. Krapp, 1919–21). Krapp made lavish use of paint and plaster in the Adamesque style to create the illusion of opulence on the interior of this theater. The Ambassador is one of numerous Broadway houses commissioned by the Shuberts in the 1920s; it has since housed more than 120 different productions, including in recent years *Bring In 'Da Noise, Bring In 'Da Funk.*

■ *EAST OF SEVENTH AVENUE*

212 **Greenwich Savings Bank,** 1352–1362 Broadway (York & Sawyer, 1922–24). This "temple of thrift" is a sophisticated rendition of academic classicism by the noted bank architects York & Sawyer. The firm manipulated such features as a high rusticated base and Corinthian colonnades on each of the three street fronts to create a monumental architectural statement. The irregular shape of the site is masterfully handled on the **interior** where a majestic elliptical banking hall is set within a trapezoid. Limestone, sandstone, and varicolored marbles create an impressive classical space that retains many of its original bronze furnishings. The building is currently vacant.

213 **Knickerbocker Hotel,** 1462–1470 Broadway (Marvin & Davis, with Bruce Price, 1901–06; annex at 143 West 41st Street, Trowbridge & Livingston, 1906). At the turn of the century, several grand hotels were erected in the Times Square area; the only survivor is the Knickerbocker. Financed by John Jacob Astor IV, this Beaux-Arts red brick building with terra-cotta detail and a prominent mansard roof was among the city's most lavish hostelries and was a popular dining and dancing spot in New York's new theater district. The hotel closed during the Depression, and the building was converted for office use.

214 **Bush Tower,** 130–132 West 42nd Street and 133–137 West 41st Street (Helmle & Corbett, 1916–18, 1921). The setback massing of Bush Tower, built by the Bush Terminal Company as an international merchandise market, became a prototype for the skyscrapers erected in New York City in the following decade. According to Corbett, the setbacks were a purely aesthetic solution, planned prior to the passage of the 1916 zoning law. The narrow neo-Gothic midblock building is unusual for its decorated brick side elevations.

215 **Henry Miller's Theater,** 124–130 West 43rd Street (Allen, Ingalls & Hoffman, 1917–18). This theater was designed to the specifications of the actor/producer/director Henry W. Miller and was the venue of Miller's own productions until his death in 1926. Before its conversion into a movie house in 1969, and later into a succession of dance clubs, the theater housed such notable plays as *Born Yesterday, The Cocktail Party, Under Milk Wood,* and *Enter Laughing.*

216 **Town Hall,** 113–123 West 43rd Street (McKim, Mead & White, Teunis J. van der Bent, partner in charge, 1919–21). Town Hall was built by the League for Political Education as a meeting hall for the city. It was planned to accommodate lectures, concerts, and movies and to serve as a clubhouse for members of the league. As soon as it opened, Town Hall became a popular venue for speaking engagements; guest speakers included many of the most eminent figures of the 20th century, among them Theodore Roosevelt, Henry James, Booker T. Washington, Margaret Sanger, Winston Churchill, and Woodrow Wilson. The **interior** includes a simple lobby and a Colonial Revival–style auditorium that is celebrated for its acoustics.

217 **Lambs Club,** now the Manhattan Church of the Nazarene, 128 West 44th Street (McKim, Mead & White, Stanford White, partner in charge, 1903–05; addition, George A. Freeman, 1915). Founded in 1874, the Lambs was a club for actors and theater enthusiasts. In 1903 the commission for the Lambs' new clubhouse went to the firm McKim, Mead & White—all three principals were members. Stanford White was responsible for the Colonial Revival design ornamented with lambs' and rams' heads. The size of the building was doubled in 1915 when an addition to the west, a virtual copy of White's original, was constructed.

218 **Belasco's Stuyvesant Theater,** now the Belasco Theater, 111–121 West 44th Street (George Keister, 1906–07). The actor, director, and manager David Belasco, one of the most important figures in the history of the American stage, conceived this theater as a "living room" in which actors and audience would come in close contact. The use of the homey Colonial Revival style for the exterior heightens the domestic theme. The **interior** is especially noteworthy for its Tiffany glass lamps, column capitals, and ceiling panels and for the eighteen murals by the Ashcan school artist Everett Shinn.

The Lyceum Theater (No. 221) has the most imposing facade in the Broadway theater district. Photo by Carl Forster.

219 **Hotel Gerard,** now the Gerard Apartments, 123 West 44th Street (George Keister, 1893–94). The Gerard exhibits an unusual combination of Romanesque, Gothic, and Northern European Renaissance forms. This apartment hotel was in the vanguard of the movement that was to transform the low-rise residential area north of Times Square into a district of theaters, hotels, and related facilities.

220 **Hudson Theater,** now Hudson Theater of the Millennium Hotel, 139–141 West 44th Street (J. B. McElfatrick & Son and Israels & Harder, 1902–04). The Hudson, one of the oldest Broadway theaters, was built by the producer Henry B. Harris as a showcase for his stars. The theater has a restrained Beaux-Arts facade and an exuberant **interior** with elegant plasterwork and stained glass. It was restored in 1990 by Stonehill & Taylor, archi-

tect, as part of the construction of the adjacent Millennium Hotel.

221 **Lyceum Theater,** 149–157 West 45th Street (Herts & Tallant, 1902–03). The Beaux-Arts facade of the Lyceum is the most imposing in the Broadway theater district. Built for the early 20th-century theater impresario Daniel Frohman, the playhouse was designed by New York's most talented theater architects. Although it is a two-balcony house, the **interior** is relatively small and was planned for intimate plays. Lush plaster detail embellishes walls and ceilings and is adorned with the initial *L*. The theater is further enhanced by marble paneling and lobby murals by James Wall Finn. The Lyceum has housed many of Broadway's most famous comedies and dramas, including a run of classic plays produced in the late 1960s by the APA-

Phoenix Theater. The list of great stars who have performed at the Lyceum is unparalleled and includes William Gillette, Ethel Barrymore, Billie Burke, Walter Huston, Bette Davis, Miriam Hopkins, Cornel Wilde, Joseph Cotton, Maurice Evans, John Garfield, Montgomery Clift, Ruth Gordon, Melvyn Douglas, Alan Bates, Lauren Bacall, Angela Lansbury, Billy Dee Williams, Helen Hayes, Rosemary Harris, Brian Bedford, and Nancy Marchand.

222 **Public School 67**, later the High School of the Performing Arts, now the Jacqueline Kennedy Onassis High School for International Careers, 120 West 46th Street (C. B. J. Snyder, 1893–94). P.S. 67 is the first school known to have been designed by C. B. J. Snyder, who as superintendent of school buildings for New York City's Board of Education for thirty years was responsible for the design of many of the city's finest school buildings. This Romanesque Revival structure enjoyed fame as the home of the High School of the Performing Arts from the founding of the school in 1948 until 1985, when it moved to a new facility. The school's curriculum emphasizes studies in music, drama, and dance, and its graduates include Eliot Feld, Arthur Mitchell, Rita Moreno, Liza Minnelli, Al Pacino, Ben Vereen, and Edward Villella. After a fire, the building was restored in 1991–93 by Jack L. Gordon, architect.

223 **Church of Saint Mary-the-Virgin (Episcopal) Complex**, 133–145 West 46th Street (Napoleon Le Brun & Sons, Pierre Le Brun, architect in charge, 1894–95). This Midtown church complex consists of a French Gothic–inspired limestone-clad church, its flanking brick-faced clergy house and mission house, and a brick-clad rectory and lady chapel that face onto West 47th Street. The church was built for a congregation in the forefront of the American Anglo-Catholic movement, and the buildings were planned to further Anglo-Catholic worship. J. Massey Rhind's extensive sculptural decoration complements Pierre Le Brun's design. Saint Mary's is thought to be the first church built with a steel frame.

224 **Embassy Theater (interior)**, now the Embassy I Theater, 1556–1560 Broadway (Thomas W. Lamb, with Rambusch Studio, 1925). The Embassy Theater, planned as an experiment to deter-

mine whether an elegant, intimate movie house would attract an exclusive high-society audience, has an ornate French-inspired interior designed by architect Thomas W. Lamb and the decorating firm of Rambusch Studio that features elaborate plasterwork and murals by Arthur Crisp. As part of the effort to create a salonlike atmosphere, a woman (the heiress Gloria Gould) was appointed manager of the theater. The exclusivity lasted only a few years; in 1929 the Embassy became the first newsreel theater in the country.

225 **Palace Theater (interior)**, 1564–1566 Broadway (Kirchhoff & Rose, 1912–13). The legendary Palace Theater, built as a vaudeville house, has hosted a greater number of stars and a greater variety of entertainment than any other Broadway theater. Although built by Martin Beck, it was operated primarily by Beck's rival E. F. Albee of the Keith-Albee Circuit, which produced vaudeville nationwide. The first production at the Palace was a flop, but the appearance of Sarah Bernhardt in May 1913 marked the beginning of an era of unprecedented success. The Palace featured such great vaudeville stars as Bob Hope, Ed Wynn, Sophie Tucker, George Jessel, Will Rogers, Jimmy Durante, the Marx Brothers, W. C. Fields, Harry Houdini, and Eddie Cantor. Succumbing to changes in the entertainment industry, the Palace became a movie house in 1932, but since the opening of *Sweet Charity* in 1966 it has become a theater for musicals. The theater was refurbished in 1990–91 (Fox & Fowle, architect) and reopened, appropriately, with *The Will Rogers Follies*.

226 **Cort Theater**, 138–146 West 48th Street (Thomas W. Lamb, 1912–13). Among the oldest and most beautiful Broadway theaters, the Cort is an adaptation of the Petit Trianon (1762) at Versailles. The theater was designed for the producer John Cort by one of America's most prominent theater architects. The elegant **interior** is decorated with French neoclassical detail and a mural depicting a dance in the gardens of Versailles. The theater has housed a large number of dramas, including many revivals. Among the long-running shows that have played the Cort are *The Diary of Anne Frank, Sunrise at Campobello, The Magic Show, Sarafina,* and *The Heiress.* It is regularly used for productions of the Lincoln Center Theater.

MAP 14

MAP 11

MAP 9

MAP 8

CENTRAL PARK S

E 59TH ST

W 58TH ST
E 58TH ST

W 57TH ST
E 57TH ST

W 56TH ST
E 56TH ST

W 55TH ST
E 55TH ST

W 54TH ST
E 54TH ST

W 53RD ST
E 53RD ST

W 52ND ST
E 52ND ST

W 51ST ST
E 51ST ST

E 50TH ST

E 49TH ST

W 48TH ST
E 48TH ST

W 47TH ST
E 47TH ST

W 46TH ST
E 46TH ST

W 45TH ST
E 45TH ST

W 44TH ST
E 44TH ST

W 43RD ST
E 43RD ST

W 42ND ST
E 42ND ST

E 41ST ST

W 40TH ST
E 40TH ST

W 39TH ST
E 39TH ST

W 38TH ST
E 38TH ST

W 37TH ST
E 37TH ST

W 36TH ST
E 36TH ST

W 35TH ST
E 35TH ST

W 34TH ST
E 34TH ST

W 33RD ST
E 33RD ST

W 32ND ST
E 32ND ST

SIXTH AV

AV OF THE AMERICAS

FIFTH AV

MADISON AV

PARK AV

VANDERBILT AV

LEXINGTON AV

THIRD AV

SECOND AV

FIRST AV

UNITED NATIONS PLZ

TUDOR CITY PL

ROCKEFELLER CENTER

ROCKEFELLER PLAZA

BROADWAY

■ *WEST OF PARK AVENUE*

INDIVIDUAL LANDMARKS

227 **B. Altman & Co. Department Store**, now B. Altman Advanced Learning Super Block (New York Public Library, Science, Industry and Business Library; Oxford University Press; and City University of New York, Graduate School and University Center), 355–371 Fifth Avenue and 188–198 Madison Avenue (Trowbridge & Livingston, 1905–13). The imposing B. Altman & Co. store was among the first of the great department stores on Fifth Avenue. Designed to complement the nearby mansions, the store was a major catalyst for the transformation of Fifth Avenue into a boulevard lined with magnificent stores. Although the building appears to be a single unified Italian Renaissance–inspired structure, it was erected in several stages, with the first Fifth Avenue wing opening in 1906. B. Altman went out of business in 1989. The exterior of the vacant building was restored by Hardy Holzman Pfeiffer, architects, and the interior has been reconfigured for three separate organizations, largely by Gwathmey Siegal & Associates, architect.

228 **Thomas and Fanny Clarke House**, now the Collectors Club, 22 East 35th Street (McKim, Mead & White, Stanford White, partner in charge, 1901–02). For his friend the art collector and dealer Thomas Benedict Clarke, Stanford White designed one of his most delightful town houses. The street facade combines what is basically a Colonial Revival brick front with an unusual medieval-inspired multipaned bowed window reminiscent of those favored by the British architect Richard Norman Shaw in the 1870s. In 1937 the house was purchased by the Collectors Club, a leading organization devoted to philately.

229 **Church of the Incarnation (Episcopal) and Rectory**, 205 and 209 Madison Avenue (church, Emlen T. Littell, 1864; restoration and additions, D. & J. Jardine, 1882; rectory, Edward P. Casey, 1905–06). The Church of the Incarnation was erected at the time Murray Hill was being developed as a prestigious residential neighborhood. Built of brownstone with light-colored sandstone trim, the Gothic Revival structure's most prominent feature is its tall broached spire. D. & J. Jardine restored and enlarged the building following a fire in 1882. The church contains some of the finest ecclesiastical artwork in America, including stained-glass windows designed by William Morris, Edward Burne-Jones, Louis Comfort Tiffany, and John La Farge; sculpture by the American masters Daniel Chester French and Augustus Saint-Gaudens; and a monument designed by Henry Hobson Richardson. A rectory built adjacent to the church in 1868–69 was largely rebuilt and given a new facade in a neo-Jacobean style in 1905–06 and is currently used as a parish house. A major restoration of the church was undertaken in 1991 (Jan Hird Pokorny, architect).

230 **Pierpont Morgan Library and Annex**, 29–33 East 36th Street (McKim, Mead & White, Charles F. McKim, partner in charge, 1902–07; annex, Benjamin Wistar Morris, 1927–28). When J. P. Morgan commissioned a library to house his collection of books and manuscripts, Charles F. McKim responded with an architectural masterpiece. McKim based his design on the attic story of the Nymphaeum of 1555, built in Rome for Pope Julius III. The facade of Tennessee marble laid up without mortar centers on an entrance in the form of a Palladian arch. To either side are lions carved by Edward Clark Potter and roundels and panels by Andrew O'Connor and Adolph Weinman. The refined simplicity of the exterior belies the richness of the **interior**. The original library has three public rooms, each magnificently decorated. The colorful marble entrance hall is crowned by a domed ceiling adorned with murals and plasterwork by H. Siddons Mowbray, a leading muralist of the period, who derived his inspiration from the work of Raphael. The East Library is dominated by triple tiers of bookcases and is ornamented with lunettes by Mowbray. The West Library, which was Morgan's study, has been called "one of the great achievements of American interior decoration." In 1927–28 a harmonious addition in the Classical Revival style was erected to the west of the original library; a glass pavilion designed by Voorsanger Mills was added to the rear in 1990–91.

231 **Tiffany & Co. Building**, 397–409 Fifth Avenue (McKim, Mead & White, Stanford White, partner in charge, 1903–06). Upon the completion of this Italian Renaissance–inspired white marble palace, Tiffany & Co. became one of the first large stores to move north of 34th Street on Fifth Avenue. Stanford White's sophisticated design, closely modeled on the 16th-century Palazzo Grimani in Venice, adapted Michele Sanmicheli's residential design to the needs of a prestigious jewelry emporium.

232 **Joseph Raphael De Lamar House**, now the Consulate General of the Republic of Poland, 233 Madison Avenue (C. P. H. Gilbert, 1902–05). This Beaux-Arts mansion, the largest in Murray Hill and one of the grandest in all of New York, was designed for a Dutch-born entrepreneur who made his fortune in the California Gold Rush. The subtly asymmetrical house, with an entrance that is flanked by marble columns and crowned by a pair of putti, is surmounted by an exceptionally imposing mansard.

233 **Knox Building**, now part of the Republic National Bank Building, 452 Fifth Avenue (John H. Duncan, 1901–02). With its limestone and white brick facades, the Knox Building is a fine example of Beaux-Arts commercial architecture. Erected for a prominent hat company at a time when business development was sweeping north along Fifth Avenue, the building is conspicuously sited on the corner immediately south of the New York Public Library's plaza.

234 **American Radiator Building**, 40 West 40th Street (Raymond Hood, 1923–24). Raymond Hood's first New York City skyscraper is highlighted by conservative Gothic-inspired detail but was, at the time of its construction, quite daring in its dramatic exploitation of the setback massing required by the 1916 zoning law. The building's most unusual feature is its black brick, chosen by Hood in an attempt to devise a unified facade (the facades of most earlier skyscrapers were light-colored masonry punctuated by dark window openings). The gold crown of the building was originally brightly lit at night to simulate the glow of a hot radiator.

235 **Bryant Park Studios**, 80 West 40th Street (Charles A. Rich, 1900–01). The Bryant Park Studios, like a handful of other buildings erected in New York City around 1900, was designed as com-

The Bryant Park Studios (No. 235) was designed as combined living and studio spaces for artists. Photo by Carl Forster.

bined living and studio spaces for artists. The large windows with unobstructed north light (Bryant Park is across the street) illuminate the double-height studios. The building was commissioned by successful portrait painter Abraham Anderson, who kept a studio here. Among the building's other residents were the artists Edward Steichen and Fernand Leger. The studios continue to be used by design firms, although residential occupancy has ended.

236 **Bryant Park Scenic Landmark**, Sixth Avenue at West 42nd Street (east end, Carrère & Hastings, 1898–1911; main park, Lusby Simpson, 1933–34; redesign, Hanna/Olin, landscape architect, and Lynden B. Miller, garden designer, 1988–91). Bryant Park was built on the site of two of New York's most famous 19th-century structures, the Crystal Palace and the Croton Reservoir. Established in 1884, the park was not actually laid out until the 20th century. The terraces and kiosks at the east end were designed by Carrère & Hastings as part of the New York Public Library (see No. 237) commission and include the sculptor Herbert Adams's Bryant Memorial. The main park, planned in the tradition of formal French gardens, was laid out as a Depression-era public works project. The park was restored and sections of it were redesigned in 1988–91, creating one of the most successful oases in New York City. Of special interest, at the west end of the park, is the Josephine Shaw Lowell Fountain (Charles Platt, 1912), the first major monument in New York dedicated to a woman; Lowell was a pioneering social reformer.

237 **New York Public Library, Astor, Lenox and Tilden Foundations,** 476 Fifth Avenue (Carrère & Hastings, 1898–1911). The main building for the New York Public Library, the design for which was won in competition by Carrère & Hastings, is perhaps the greatest masterpiece of Beaux-Arts architecture in the United States. The library, a private foundation housed in a city-owned building, was established in 1895 when the Astor Library (see No. 128), the Lenox Library, and the Tilden Trust (see No. 181) consolidated their holdings. The majestic building, constructed of Dorset marble from Vermont, is enormous in scale, yet its broad front stairs and projecting central pavilion are not overpowering. They draw the public into one of the world's leading research institutions. The exterior is embellished with sculpture by Edward Clark Potter (the lions), Frederick MacMonnies (the fountains), Paul Wayland Bartlett (figures above the entrances), and George Gray Barnard (the end pedi-

New York Public Library, Astor, Lenox, and Tilden Foundations (No. 237). Arguably the greatest masterpiece of Beaux-Arts design in the United States. Photo by John Barrington Bayley.

ments). The **interiors**, notably the main lobby (Astor Hall), the staircases, and the central hall, are distinguished by the outstanding quality of their design, materials, and construction. A major restoration of both the exterior and the interior was undertaken in the 1980s (Davis, Brody & Associates, architect), and further renovations continue.

238 **Park Avenue Viaduct**, also known as the Pershing Square Viaduct, Park Avenue from East 40th Street to Grand Central Terminal (Warren & Wetmore, design, 1912; construction, 1917–19). Grand Central Terminal (see No. 239) was designed with complex systems for the efficient circulation of trains, surface traffic, and pedestrians. The Park Avenue Viaduct was conceived in 1903 by the architecture firm Reed & Stem as an expeditious way of moving traffic along Park Avenue and around the massive terminal. As designed by Warren & Wetmore in 1912, the viaduct consists of three low, broad arches—all originally open—composed of steel girders cantilevered from granite piers; ornate iron railings run along the roadway above the arches.

239 **Grand Central Terminal**, East 42nd Street at Park Avenue (Reed & Stem and Warren & Wetmore; William Wilgus, engineer, 1903–13). One of the world's great railway terminals, often referred to as the gateway to the nation, Grand Central is an outstanding Beaux-Arts design. The engineer William Wilgus and the architects Reed & Stem were responsible for the terminal's innovative plan, with its extensive tunnels, ramp system, and upper and lower concourses. The monumental facades and the sumptuous interior spaces were the work of Whitney Warren. Grand Central was designed on an axis with Park Avenue; Jules-Felix Coutan's clock and *Transportation* statue at the apex of the building terminate the avenue's northward vista. The **interiors** are laid out in a formal, axial Beaux-Arts manner with a grand waiting room and an even grander concourse, famous for its windowed east and west elevations—through which shafts of light penetrate the space—and its high vaulted ceiling appropriately decorated with constellations highlighted by electric stars. Ramps lead down to the more modest lower concourse, planned for suburban trains, and to the famous Oyster Bar,

Grand Central Terminal (No. 239). Once considered the "gateway to the nation," the Beaux-Arts Grand Central Terminal also played a seminal role in the history of the American historic preservation movement. Photo by John Barrington Bayley.

whose vaulted ceiling is covered in Guastavino tiles. The landmark designation of Grand Central Terminal sustained a series of legal challenges that culminated in a 1978 United States Supreme Court decision affirming the validity of New York City's landmarks law. Under the auspices of the Metropolitan Transportation Authority, the terminal is being restored by Beyer Blinder Belle, architect.

240 Century Association Clubhouse, 7 West 43rd Street (McKim, Mead & White, 1889–91). McKim, Mead & White's design for the Century Association, a club organized in 1847 "to promote the advancement of art and literature," established the Italian Renaissance palazzo mode as the favored style for the many private clubhouses built in American cities in the late 19th and early 20th centuries. In New York City this influence is evident in such later buildings as the Metropolitan Club (see No. 367) and the University Club (see No. 261). The facade of the Century, combining light-colored stone, Roman brick, and terra cotta, is highlighted by magnificent ironwork. The club moved here from its previous home on East 15th Street (see No. 175). The building was restored in 1992 by Jan Hird Pokorny, architect.

241 Fire Engine Company No. 65, 33 West 43rd Street (Hoppin & Koen, 1897–98). Erected at a time when West 43rd Street between Fifth and Sixth Avenues was being developed as the location of some of the city's most prestigious clubs and hotels, this four-story Italian Renaissance–inspired firehouse was designed to resemble the nearby Century Association Clubhouse (see No. 240).

242 Algonquin Hotel, 59–61 West 44th Street (Goldwin Starrett, 1902). The Algonquin Hotel is famous for playing host to literary and theatrical visitors, most prominently the legendary Round Table, a group of critics, writers, and humorists including Robert Benchley, Heywood Broun, George S. Kaufman, Ring Lardner, Dorothy Parker, and Alexander Woollcott, who convened on the premises almost daily in the 1920s.

243 New York Yacht Club, 37 West 44th Street (Warren & Wetmore, 1899–1900). This clubhouse in the Beaux-Arts style was the first building by the

architects Warren & Wetmore, best known for their later work at Grand Central Terminal (see No. 239). It is one of the most lighthearted buildings of the era. As befits the home of the nation's most prestigious yacht club, the building presents a limestone facade designed on a nautical theme. The most prominent feature is the trio of windows carved to resemble the sterns of baroque galleons. Elsewhere on the ornate street front, restored in the early 1990s by the architecture firms Beyer Blinder Belle and Paino/Soffes, are seashells, dolphins, dripping seaweed, and other marine ornament.

244 Harvard Club of New York City, 27 West 44th Street (McKim, Mead & White, Charles F. McKim, partner in charge, 1893–94; rear addition on West 45th Street, 1900–05; west wing, 1913–16). Appropriately, the Harvard Club was designed in a colonial-inspired style reminiscent of the early buildings on the university's Cambridge, Massachusetts, campus. Charles F. McKim, who had unsuccessfully studied engineering at Harvard and later designed several buildings and memorial gates on the Harvard campus, was responsible for the original building of dark red "Harvard brick" with limestone trim. The same style and materials were used by McKim, Mead & White for the two additions.

245 Association of the Bar of the City of New York, 42 West 44th Street (Cyrus L. W. Eidlitz, 1895–96). This imposing limestone building, with street facades on both 43rd and 44th Streets, illustrates Eidlitz's individualistic approach to the handling of classical architectural forms. Eidlitz designed the building for the Association of the Bar, New York's leading legal organization, which was founded in 1870 "for the purpose of maintaining the honor and dignity of the profession of the law, of cultivating social relations among its members, and increasing its usefulness in promoting the due administration of justice."

246 Mechanics' and Tradesmen's Institute, 20 West 44th Street (Lamb & Rich, 1890; additions, Ralph S. Townsend, 1903–05). The Mechanics' and Tradesmen's Institute was built in two separate campaigns that created a single unified design. The original building was erected by the Berkeley School, a private boys' school that emphasized military drill exercise. In 1899 the property was acquired by the General Society of Mechanics and Tradesmen, an organization founded in 1785 to foster education in the mechanical trades. In 1903 Andrew Carnegie, who was a member of the society, provided a gift of $250,000 to renovate the building. The original top story was replaced with three stories, and the building's magnificent wrought-iron fire escapes were installed.

247 **Sidewalk Clock** (see No. 162), 522 Fifth Avenue at West 44th Street (Seth Thomas Company, 1907). Installed on Fifth Avenue at 43rd Street by the American Trust Company, this clock was moved to its present location, a block farther north, in the 1930s. The clock has an unusually ornate base and is crowned by a cast-iron pineapple.

248 **Fred F. French Building,** 551 Fifth Avenue (H. Douglas Ives and Sloan & Robertson, 1926–27). The prominent Fred F. French real-estate firm erected this skyscraper with massed setbacks for its corporate headquarters and for rental income. The use of detail inspired by ancient Mesopotamian art is an indication of the exotic historicism that was prevalent during the 1920s. The exotic influence is especially evident at the base, where the bronze entrances and storefronts are embellished with mythological figures and Near Eastern ornament, and at the crown, with its vivid polychromatic terra-cotta decoration. **Interior:** The ornamental motifs in the magnificent lobby pick up exterior design elements. The lobby has a vaulted ceiling, bronze doors, and other elaborate Near Eastern features. Wiss, Janney, Elstner Associates and Li-Saltzman Architects completed a restoration of the building in 1992.

249 **Scribner Building,** now Benetton, 597 Fifth Avenue (Ernest Flagg, 1912–13). Almost two decades after moving into its building at 153–157 Fifth Avenue, between 21st and 22nd Streets (see No. 160), Charles Scribner's Sons followed Manhattan's fashionable retailers to Midtown. Ernest Flagg, Charles Scribner II's brother-in-law, was again commissioned to design a store and office building for the firm. Flagg elaborated on his earlier design, which had become an identifiable image of the Scribner firm, and created a 10-story French-inspired limestone-fronted building with a

facade that reflects the nature of the steel skeleton frame. As befitted a prestigious bookstore, the vaulted **interior** was designed to resemble a small library. Appropriately the plaster ceiling contains cartouches embellished with the initials *CS,* as well as open books and lamps of learning. The 1996 conversion into a clothing store entailed regilding the elegant iron shop front and extensively restoring the interior (Phillips Janson Group, architect).

250 **Goelet Building,** now Swiss Center Building, 608 Fifth Avenue (Victor L. S. Hafner and Edward Hall Faile, 1930–32). The Goelet family, one of New York's major landowners and developers, erected a large mansion on the corner of Fifth Avenue and West 49th Street in 1880. Robert Goelet replaced the house with this Art Deco building, which consists of a two-story commercial base articulated by large glass display windows and eight office floors clad in green and white marble. The central decorative element on the second story of the Fifth Avenue front is the Goelet crest—a swan set above intertwined *G*s. Swans are also evident on the ceiling of the **interior** vestibule. The vestibule and lobby are among the finest Art Deco spaces in New York, with their complex floor plan, varicolored marbles, aluminum and aluminum-leaf highlights, nickel silver doors, and stylized ornamentation. The lower floors were restored in 1997 in the spirit of the original design by the firm Garrison & Siegel, architect.

251 **Saks Fifth Avenue,** 611 Fifth Avenue (Starrett & Van Vleck, 1922–24). The department store specialists Starrett & Van Vleck designed this luxurious emporium in 1922 in a Renaissance-inspired style appropriate to the exclusive commercial character of Fifth Avenue. Saks's relocation from Herald Square to Fifth Avenue at East 50th Street marks the final chapter in the northward migration of Manhattan's large retail stores, a development that began early in the 20th century.

252 **Rockefeller Center** (Associated Architects; other architects as noted): **RCA Building and Lobby,** now the General Electric Building, 30 Rockefeller Plaza (1932–33); **RCA Building West,** now the General Electric Building, 1250 Sixth Avenue (1932–33); **RKO Building,** now the Amax Building, 1270 Sixth Avenue (1931–32); **Radio**

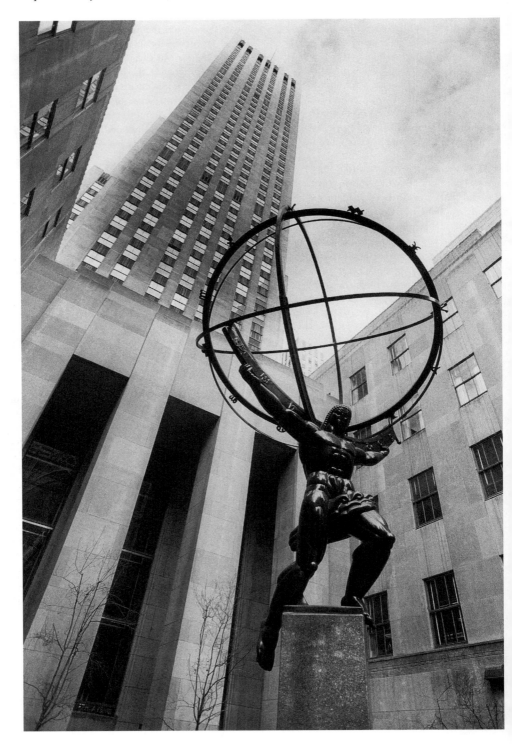

City Music Hall, 1260 Sixth Avenue (1931–32); British Empire Building, now the British Building, 620 Fifth Avenue (1932–33); La Maison Français, 610 Fifth Avenue (1933); Palazzo d'Italia, 626 Fifth Avenue (1933–34); International Building and Lobby, 630 Fifth Avenue (1933–34); International Building North, 636 Fifth Avenue (1933–34); the former Time-Life Building, now 1 Rockefeller Plaza (1936–37); Associated Press Building, 50 Rockefeller Plaza (1938); the former Eastern Airlines Building, now 10 Rockefeller Plaza (1939); U.S. Rubber Company Building, now the Simon & Schuster Building, 1230 Sixth Avenue (1939; extension, Harrison & Abramovitz, 1954–55); Esso Building, now the Warner Communications Building, 75 Rockefeller Plaza (Carson & Lundin, 1946–47); Manufacturers Hanover Trust Building, now 600 Fifth Avenue (Carson & Lundin, 1950–52); Promenade, also known as Channel Gardens; Sunken Plaza; Rockefeller Plaza; and Rooftop Gardens. Rockefeller Center, one of America's most significant architectural and urban design projects, has been copied many times, but it has never been equaled. The center, which incorporates office buildings, stores, theaters, and open space, unites a sophisticated business sense with good design in the largest privately sponsored real-estate venture ever undertaken in New York City. The genesis of Rockefeller Center was the desire of John D. Rockefeller, Jr., to help the Metropolitan Opera build a new home. Rockefeller agreed to lease a large plot of land—bounded by 48th and 51st Streets, Fifth and Sixth Avenues—on which the new opera house would be built and where he would erect a series of profitable office buildings. Unfortunately, the stock market crash of 1929 forced the Met to abandon the project. Despite the Depression and the withdrawal of the opera company, Rockefeller and his advisers continued to plan a large commercial complex. The layout and the design of the original buildings were handled by the Associated Architects, a group directed by Raymond Hood that in-

cluded the architects Reinhard & Hofmeister, advisers to Rockefeller since the inception of the project, and Corbett, Harrison & MacMurray, specialists in skyscraper design. The plan consisted of a monumental central building—the RCA Building—surrounded by smaller office towers, low-rise buildings on Fifth Avenue that were to be leased to foreign tenants, and strategically placed open spaces such as the promenade (popularly known as the Channel Gardens because it runs between the British and French buildings) and the sunken plaza that would draw people into the underground shops. The limestone-faced buildings combine simple modern massing with a traditional artistic scheme. All the artworks in Rockefeller Center have humanistic themes—for example, progress through science, and technology and peace through international understanding. Among the most famous pieces are Paul Manship's *Prometheus* and Lee Lawrie's *Atlas*. Several of the buildings have significant interiors. The ground floor of the RCA Building is most famous for its lobby murals by José Maria Sert (in part replacing murals by Diego Rivera) and Frank Brangwyn. The International Building's lobby is a dramatic four-story space embellished with rich materials and metallic sculptures by Michio Ihara installed in 1978. The success of the initial project led Rockefeller to plan additional buildings on sites adjacent to the original complex.

The major entertainment facility at Rockefeller Center is Radio City Music Hall. Opened in 1932, this 6,200-seat theater—the world's largest at the time of its construction—was planned by the impresario Samuel Rothafel (better known as Roxy) for live entertainment, but it soon became a movie theater in which the feature films were preceded by stage shows starring the precision dancers known as the Roxyettes (later the Rockettes). On the interior, the huge auditorium was planned to be as intimate as possible. It consists of a great arched proscenium in the form of a rising sun and a large orchestra with three shallow balconies. The decoration of the theater was undertaken by Donald Deskey, who created a modern, well-integrated scheme for the carpets, wall coverings, and furnishings. Like other Rockefeller Center buildings, the theater contains several major artworks, including Ezra Winter's monumental foyer mural, *Fountain of Youth,* and a series of murals in the men's and women's lounges.

Rockefeller Center (No. 252), the largest privately sponsored real-estate venture ever undertaken in New York City, was in the forefront of urban design. Lee Lawrie's statue of Atlas rises in front of the International Building. Photo by Stephen Senigo.

253 **Villard Houses,** later the Helmsley Palace Hotel, now the New York Palace Hotel and the Urban Center, 451–457 Madison Avenue and 24 East 51st Street (McKim, Mead & White, Joseph M. Wells, designer, 1882–85). Commissioned by the railroad entrepreneur Henry Villard, this masterpiece of late 19th-century urban design involved the skillful combination of six brownstone houses into a single monumental U-shaped unit set around an open court. The complex is not only one of the most beautiful in New York but was also among the first major projects in the United States to adapt specific European architectural precedents. In this case, the architect Joseph M. Wells of the McKim, Mead & White office took as a model the Palazzo della Cancelleria in Rome. The massing, arcades, window enframements, and rosette details of the Roman palace were used in the New York project, but in a novel manner, to accord with the New York site and with the demands of a late 19th-century residential commission. In the early 1970s, demolition of the complex was threatened, but in 1975–76 the houses were incorporated into the Palace Hotel and the north wing was reserved as office and gallery space for organizations involved in architectural and design issues.

254 **Saint Patrick's Cathedral (R.C.) Complex,** Fifth Avenue between East 50th and 51st Streets (cathedral, rectory, and cardinal's residence, James Renwick, Jr., 1853–88; lady chapel, Charles T. Mathews, 1901–06). In 1852, when New York's Roman Catholic archdiocese purchased the site for a new cathedral, the area near Fifth Avenue and 50th Street was relatively uninhabited, but by the time Saint Patrick's was inaugurated in 1879 (the spires were not completed until 1888), the area had become one of the city's finest residential districts. James Renwick, Jr.'s design was influenced by continental Gothic buildings, in particular Cologne Cathedral. Although the marble building was not constructed exactly to Renwick's specifications (several major structural changes were made), his Fifth Avenue facade, with its three entrances and twin spires, is among the most impressive 19th-century ecclesiastical works in America. Early in the 20th century, Renwick's east front was removed and reconstructed at Our Lady of Lourdes Church (see No. 465) and the present lady chapel was built.

255 **647 Fifth Avenue House,** also known as the George W. Vanderbilt House, now Versace (Hunt & Hunt, 1902–05; addition, Charles L. Fraser, 1917). This town house in the Louis XV style and its neighbor the Morton and Nellie Plant House (see No. 256) are reminders of the residential character of Fifth Avenue early in the 20th century. The house, one of a pair known as the Marble Twins, was commissioned by George W. Vanderbilt and sold to his brother William K. Vanderbilt before it was completed. It is the last survivor of a group of Vanderbilt residences built on this section of Fifth Avenue. The house was designed by the sons of Richard Morris Hunt, the architect of George Vanderbilt's famous Biltmore estate in North Carolina. Robert Goelet and his wife, Elsie, were the only residents prior to the 1917 sale of the house to the art dealers Gimpel & Wildenstein. Versace sponsored an extensive restoration of the facade in 1995–96 (Laboratorio Associati, architect).

256 **Morton and Nellie Plant House** and **Edward and Frances Holbrook House,** now Cartier, Inc., 651–653 Fifth Avenue and 2–4 East 52nd Street (Robert W. Gibson, 1903–05 and C. P. H. Gilbert, 1904–05). The banker, yachtsman, and baseball club owner Morton Plant built an elegant Italian Renaissance–inspired house, which is the finest surviving mansion on Fifth Avenue south of 59th Street. The Plant house and the adjacent Holbrook house at 4 East 52nd Street were successfully converted into a shop for the Cartier jewelry company by William Welles Bosworth around 1917.

257 **Racquet and Tennis Club,** 370 Park Avenue (McKim, Mead & White, William S. Richardson, partner in charge, 1916–19). The Racquet and Tennis Club is one of the few survivors from the period when Park Avenue north of Grand Central Terminal was lined with luxurious masonry apartment houses and institutional buildings. In keeping with the prestige of the site chosen for its new home, the club engaged the services of McKim, Mead & White, even though by 1916 the firm's two leading designers, McKim and White, were no longer alive. A younger partner, William S. Richardson, was responsible for this project, designed in the form of an Italian Renaissance palazzo, the style that the firm had established for clubhouses almost thirty years earlier with its Century Association (see No. 240). The most interesting features of the subdued front elevation are the recessed loggia and the frieze in the form of a tennis net with crossed rackets.

258 **Lever House,** 390 Park Avenue (Skidmore, Owings & Merrill, Gordon Bunshaft, partner in charge, 1950–52). The construction of the 24-story glass and stainless steel Lever House heralded the beginning of a new wave in American skyscraper design and a turning point in the history of modern architecture. Lever House established the suitability of the International Style for office building design and signaled the transformation of the style from one associated with an idealistic European social movement into one symbolizing corporate America. Lever House also signaled the beginning of the transformation of Park Avenue south of 59th Street from a street of masonry apartments and institutions into an avenue of glass towers. Lever House was the first skyscraper in the form of a vertical slab erected in New York City after the passage of the 1916 zoning resolution; the setbacks required by the 1916 law were not necessary if a building occupied only 25 percent of its lot. Bunshaft's design is especially dramatic because the slab is set perpendicular to Park Avenue and appears to float above the street and above the one-story base and open plaza. In 1997 Skidmore, Owings & Merrill was rehired, in conjunction with the construction firm Lehrer McGovern Bovis, to plan a major restoration of the deteriorated facades.

259 **Saint Thomas Church (Episcopal) and Parish House,** Fifth Avenue at West 53rd Street (Cram, Goodhue & Ferguson, 1906–13). Saint Thomas, a major design by Cram, Goodhue & Ferguson, is a limestone-faced building that makes dramatic use of its corner site. Replacing a church that burned in 1905, the neo-Gothic design, with an asymmetrically placed tower, combines features from English and French medieval architecture. The initial plan for the church was devised by Ralph Adams Cram, but it appears to have been Bertram Goodhue who developed the idea into the magnificent building that was erected in 1911–13. Beyer Blinder Belle were the architects for a facade restoration completed in 1997.

260 **William H. and Ada S. Moore House,** now Banco di Napoli, 4 East 54th Street (McKim, Mead & White, 1898–1900). This marble-fronted house was commissioned by W. E. D. Stokes, builder of the Ansonia Hotel (see No. 329), but four months before its completion, Stokes sold the house to Ada S. Moore. Moore and her husband, the Chicago lawyer and corporate titan William H. Moore, a founder of U.S. Steel and other large corporations, moved into one of McKim, Mead & White's most beautiful Italian Renaissance–inspired town houses. After Ada Moore's death in 1955, the house had a succession of philanthropic and commercial tenants. In 1993 Banco di Napoli acquired the house, and SCI Design undertook renovation and restoration work.

261 **University Club,** 1 West 54th Street (McKim, Mead & White, Charles F. McKim, partner in charge, 1896–1900). Charles F. McKim designed the University Club in the spirit of Italian High Renaissance palazzi. The nine-story structure is divided into three horizontal sections, each defined by the tall arched windows that light the clubhouse's major rooms (lounge, library, and dining room); subsidiary floors are subtly placed between them. The building is faced with pink Milford granite and ornamented with the seals of various universities, executed in marble by Daniel Chester French, and a large club seal by Kenyon Cox.

262 **Moses Allen and Alice Dunning Starr House,** now Petrola House, also known as the 5 West 54th Street House (R. H. Robertson, 1897–99). The neurologist Moses Allen Starr commissioned this meticulously detailed town house at a time when many wealthy New Yorkers were building houses in the area; it is one of five adjacent town houses erected in the late 1890s that are designated landmarks. The subtle Renaissance-inspired building has a limestone base; its upper floors are clad in Roman brick trimmed with limestone.

263 **Philip and Carrie Lehman House,** also known as the 7 West 54th Street House (John H. Duncan, 1899–1900). Philip Lehman, son of a founder of the banking firm Lehman Brothers and himself a partner in the firm, commissioned this limestone-fronted Beaux-Arts town house, one of five adjacent landmark residences on the north side of West 54th Street. After Philip's death in 1947, the house was occupied by his son Robert, who amassed an extraordinary art collection; this collection was later given to the Metropolitan Museum of Art, where it is now installed along with interiors removed from the house.

264 **James J. and Josephine Goodwin Residence,** now U.S. Trust Company, also known as the 9–11 West 54th Street House (McKim, Mead & White, Charles F. McKim and William Mead, partners in charge, 1896–98). The wealthy businessman James Junius Goodwin, a cousin and business partner of J. P. Morgan's, was responsible for commissioning one of McKim, Mead & White's finest Colonial Revival residences. Modeled on Charles Bulfinch's Third Harrison Gray Otis House (1806) in Boston, this elegant brick structure was planned as a double house; the Goodwins resided in the larger unit at No. 11. The building underwent an award-winning restoration and conversion into a bank between 1980 and 1981 (Haines, Lundberg, Waehler, architect).

265 **13 and 15 West 54th Street Houses** (Henry J. Hardenbergh, 1896–97). This pair of houses was built as a speculative venture. Hardenbergh's love of Northern European architecture, evident at his famous Dakota Apartments (see No. 317), is also seen in these residences with their banded window enframements and tapered pilasters. In 1906 No. 13 was purchased by John D. Rockefeller; it was the home of his son, John D. Rockefeller, Jr., until about 1918. Later, Governor Nelson Rockefeller of New York used the house as an office; he died here in 1979. Nelson Rockefeller purchased No. 15 in 1955, and for many years it housed the Museum of Primitive Art (now the Michael Rockefeller Collection at the Metropolitan Museum of Art).

266 **Rockefeller Apartments,** 17 West 54th Street and 24 West 55th Street (Harrison & Fouilhoux, 1935–37). In their simplicity, their use of industrial materials, their smooth wall surfaces, and especially their fenestration, these two brick apartment houses exemplify early International Style design in the United States. The windows consist of bands of metal sash, often grouped in curving bays, that provide 15 percent more light

than required by city building codes. Commissioned by Nelson Rockefeller, these buildings represent the first of many collaborations between Rockefeller and Wallace K. Harrison. In 1997 the cooperative organization undertook a major restoration, most notably of the extraordinary windows, under the supervision of William Leggio Architects.

267 **Gotham Hotel,** now the Peninsula Hotel, 696–700 Fifth Avenue (Hiss & Weekes, 1902–05). The Italian Renaissance–inspired Gotham Hotel is among the handsomest surviving early 20th-century luxury hotels in New York City. The 20-story limestone building was designed to harmonize with the adjoining University Club (see No. 261) and to complement the St. Regis Hotel (see No. 268), begun one year earlier on a site across Fifth Avenue.

268 **St. Regis Hotel,** 699–703 Fifth Avenue and 2 East 55th Street (Trowbridge & Livingston, 1901–04; extension, Sloan & Robertson, 1927). Planned by Colonel John Jacob Astor as New York's finest luxury hotel, the St. Regis is among the most elegant Beaux-Arts buildings in the city. As befits its location on New York's most prestigious avenue, the hotel "established a new standard of excellence . . . superior to that of any hotel in this country, and probably over any hotel in the world," commented one critic on the occasion of the hotel's opening. The 1927 addition complements the original design. The hotel reopened, following an extensive refurbishing, in 1991.

269 **712 Fifth Avenue Building,** later the Rizzoli Building, now part of the Henri Bendel Store, 712 Fifth Avenue (Albert S. Gottlieb, 1907–08). When the Fifth Avenue Presbyterian Church commissioned this commercial building for a site adjacent to the church, Fifth Avenue was primarily residential. Thus the building was designed in accordance with 18th-century French prototypes as a five-story limestone-fronted structure that would blend with the nearby houses and maintain the elegant character of the street. The first tenant was the fashionable decorating establishment of L. Alavoine & Co. From 1964 to 1985, the Rizzoli bookstore and publishing company occupied the premises.

270 **Coty Building,** now part of the Henri Bendel Store, 714 Fifth Avenue (Woodruff Leeming, 1907–08; glass front, René Lalique, 1910). The former Coty Building, originally a row house erected in 1871, received a new commercial front in 1907–08. The building was leased in 1910 by the French perfumer François Coty, who commissioned what is now the only extant architectural glasswork in New York City designed by the great French glassmaker René Lalique. Lalique's composition of intertwining vines initially rose from the second through the fifth floors (the narrow second-floor level has been lost) and was designed to fit within the preexisting commercial frame. The facade, including the glass, was restored in 1989–90 by Beyer Blinder Belle, architect.

271 **Harry B. and Evelina Hollins Residence,** later the Calumet Club, now the Consulate General of Argentina, 12–14 West 56th Street (McKim, Mead & White, 1899–1901; alteration, J. E. R. Carpenter, 1924). The banker and broker Harry B. Hollins commissioned this handsome Colonial Revival brick house in 1899, at a time when many town houses were being built in north Midtown. Commerce soon overwhelmed the neighborhood, and in 1914 the house was converted into the Calumet Club. Ten years later the club removed the original central entrance and constructed the porch and wing to the east. Since 1947 the house has been occupied by the Argentine consulate.

272 **Fuller Building,** 41 East 57th Street (Walker & Gillette, 1928–29). Erected as the headquarters of the Fuller Construction Company, this prominently sited corner building was planned to house retail stores and art galleries on the first six floors and offices above. The design, with its modernist interpretation of classical architectural forms, reflects the conservative aspects of the Art Deco style. The building has a black Swedish granite base; the upper floors are clad in a light-colored limestone. A pair of figures by the noted sculptor Elie Nadelman crowns the imposing three-story entrance. The stylized modern classicism of the exterior continues on the **interior,** where the vestibules and lobby are richly decorated with marble walls, mosaic floors, and bronze detail. Of special note are the round mosaic floor panels rep-

resenting the company's three successive headquarters buildings—the Tacoma Building in Chicago, the Flatiron Building (see No. 161), and the Fuller Building—and the bronze elevator doors depicting scenes of building construction.

■ *EAST OF PARK AVENUE*

HISTORIC DISTRICTS

18 **Sniffen Court Historic District.** New York City's smallest historic district consists of ten round-arched stables erected in 1863–64 on a small court set perpendicular to East 36th Street between Lexington and Third Avenues. Although the source of the court's name is obscure, it is believed that it recalls John Sniffen, a local builder. In the 1920s the modest two-story brick buildings were converted into stylish residences. One stable became the home and studio of the sculptor Malvina Hoffman, several of whose works adorn the wall at the far end of the alley.

19 **Tudor City Historic District.** Fred F. French, one of New York's most active developers following World War I, began buying dilapidated row houses and tenements on the far east end of 42nd Street in 1925. In December of that year he announced that construction would begin on "the largest housing project ever undertaken in mid-Manhattan." French and his architectural staff, headed by H. Douglas Ives, designed a complex of apartment houses and apartment hotels with Tudor detail. The choice of a Tudor style and "olde English" names such as The Cloister, Essex House, and Windsor Tower, the location of the development on a bluff set apart from its surroundings, the absence of through streets, and the presence of two small private parks lent a suburban character to the complex. This ambience was appropriate since Tudor City sought to attract middle-class tenants who might have moved to the suburbs had they not been sufficiently impressed by the community's amenities and its convenient proximity to the nearby Midtown commercial district.

20 **Turtle Bay Gardens Historic District.** As part of a movement to reclaim the deteriorated brownstone row houses of the east Midtown area, Charlotte Martin purchased twenty run-down houses on East 48th and 49th Streets in 1919–20. She commissioned Edward C. Dean and William Lawrence Bottomley to renovate the houses into single-family units and apartments, to redesign the facades, and to combine the rear yards into an Italian Renaissance–inspired garden, although as an amateur architect Martin is thought to have had significant input into the designs. Iron turtles were placed on the fence posts, and Martin dubbed the development Turtle Bay Gardens. Ever since, the beautiful enclave has attracted people in the arts, including the architect Edward Dean, Katharine Hepburn, Mary Martin, Tyrone Power, Stephen Sondheim, Leopold Stokowski, and E. B. White.

INDIVIDUAL LANDMARKS

273 **Civic Club,** now Estonian House, 243 East 34th Street (Thomas A. Gray, 1898–99). The Civic Club was founded by Frederick Goddard, a wealthy New Yorker involved in turn-of-the-century social reform efforts who sought specifically to improve the lives of people residing between 23rd and 42nd Streets east of Fourth (now Park) Avenue. Goddard not only founded the Civic Club but also erected its Beaux-Arts clubhouse. The building remained in the Goddard family until 1946, when it was sold to the Estonian Educational Society, an organization that sponsors activities for Estonian-Americans.

274 **James F. D. and Harriet Lanier House,** 123 East 35th Street (Hoppin & Koen, 1901–03). At the turn of the century, many of the old residences in Murray Hill were replaced by imposing new town houses. The banker James Franklin Doughty Lanier and his wife demolished two modest houses of 1854 and erected this richly detailed Beaux-Arts dwelling designed by architects who had studied at the École des Beaux-Arts and worked in the offices of McKim, Mead & White.

275 **Adelaide L. T. Douglas House,** now the Guatemalan Permanent Mission to the United Nations and Guatemalan Consul General, 57 Park Avenue (Horace Trumbauer, 1909–11). New York socialite Adelaide L. Townsend Douglas commis-

sioned this house from the fashionable Philadelphia architect Horace Trumbauer a year after her divorce from William Douglas, the initial developer of Douglaston, Queens. Trumbauer designed the house in the Louis XVI style that he favored for urban residences. The facade contains especially interesting sculpted friezes.

276 **152 East 38th Street House** (1858; redesign, Robertson Ward, 1934–35). This house is an example of the extensive redesign that many of New York's older houses underwent in the 1920s and 1930s. Set far back from the lot line, the house appears originally to have been an outbuilding on an estate belonging to a member of President Martin Van Buren's family. In 1934 the developer Russell A. Pettengill commissioned Robertson Ward to convert the building and its neighbor into a residence and office for his own use. The old facade was stuccoed, and a low wall with thin colonnettes and other Regency-inspired detail was constructed near the front of the lot. In 1944 the house was sold to the publisher Cass Canfield.

277 **Bowery Savings Bank Building,** 110 East 42nd Street (York & Sawyer, William Louis Ayres, partner in charge, 1921–23 and 1931–33). In 1920 the Bowery Savings Bank decided to move its headquarters from its historic bank on the Bowery (see No. 103) to a site on East 42nd Street in the rapidly developing Midtown office district. The prominent architecture firm York & Sawyer was responsible for the Italian Romanesque–inspired building with its enormous arched entrance and monumentally scaled **interior.** The vast basilica-like banking hall (65 feet high, 80 feet wide, and 197 feet 6 inches long), with its plaster ceiling designed in imitation of wood beams, is richly decorated with a variety of marbles, sandstones, and limestone, bronze screens and tellers' cages, and an intricate marble Cosmati floor. Most recently it has housed a branch of the GreenPoint Bank. The elevator lobby is especially notable for its blue mosaic ceiling with gold stars. In 1931–33 a six-story addition, dubbed the chapel, with fine interior detail, was erected to the east of the original building.

278 **Chanin Building,** 122 East 42nd Street (Irwin S. Chanin, with Sloan & Robertson, 1927–

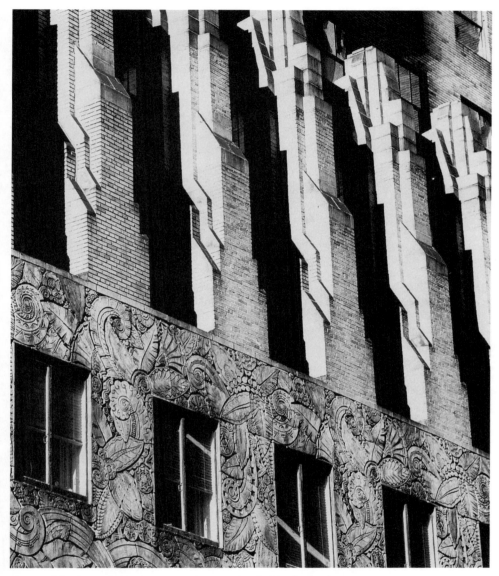

Chanin Building (No. 278). A major Art Deco skyscraper. Detail of the decorated terra-cotta frieze by Rene Chambellan. Photo by Stephen Senigo.

29). This Art Deco structure, designed in part by its builder, Irwin S. Chanin, is one of the most significant New York skyscrapers of the 1920s, as it is one of the earliest with a solid base, setback massing, and a buttressed crown inspired by the form of Eliel Saarinen's influential entry in the 1922 Chica-

go Tribune Building competition. The base is ornamented with decoration by Rene Chambellan, including a terra-cotta frieze with stylized curvilinear and angular naturalistic forms set in a complex pattern that is the quintessence of Art Deco design. Below this frieze is a bronze band illustrating the

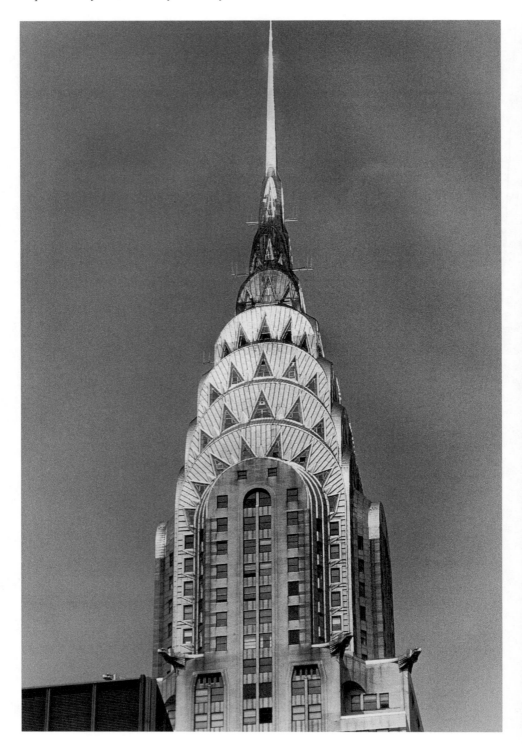

theory of evolution—beginning with primitive marine life and extending as far as birds.

279 **Chrysler Building,** 405 Lexington Avenue (William Van Alen, 1928–30). The Chrysler's stunning Art Deco design is the embodiment of the romantic New York skyscraper. The 77-story edifice, distinguished by its abundant automotive imagery (for example, silver hood ornaments embellish the setbacks and stylized racing cars appear at the thirty-first floor) and a striking crown, was a personal symbol of Walter P. Chrysler and an advertisement for his corporation, as well as a speculative investment in office space. The black Belgian granite entrance arches lead into the spectacular **interior.** The lobby contains red Moroccan marble walls and yellow Siena marble floors; a ceiling mural by Edward Trumbull, which, according to a contemporary source, depicts "the vision, human energy, and engineering ability which made possible the structure"; steel, aluminum, and onyx ornament; and elevator cabs richly detailed in exotic woods that are among the most glorious ever created.

280 **Daily News Building,** 220 East 42nd Street (Raymond M. Hood, 1929–30). Joseph Patterson, founder of the *Daily News,* commissioned this building as the home and symbol of America's first tabloid and the country's largest newspaper. As designed by Hood, the building combines Art Deco and modernist forms in a striking manner. The flat roof and freestanding slablike massing are significant modern innovations, but Hood's use of striped brickwork and an entrance adorned with a large relief panel of light rays shining on a diverse urban populace are characteristic decorative forms of Art Deco design. The *Daily News* remained a major tenant until 1995.

281 **Beaux-Arts Institute of Design,** now American Federation of Musicians and Employers Pension Welfare Fund, 304 East 44th Street (Frederic C. Hirons, of the firm Dennison & Hirons, 1928). The Society of Beaux-Arts Architects, dedicated to furthering the architectural ideas promulgated at the École des Beaux-Arts in Paris, held a competi-

tion for the design of a new school in 1927. The winning entry combines traditional Beaux-Arts ideas of symmetry, solidity, monumentality, and the use of symbolic artwork (by Rene Chambellan) with ornament reflecting the contemporary Art Deco design aesthetic. The building was rehabilitated in 1989–92 (Milo Kleinberg Design Associates, architect) as offices for its current occupant.

282 **Beaux-Arts Apartments,** 307 and 310 East 44th Street (Kenneth M. Murchison and Raymond M. Hood, of the firm Raymond Hood, Godley & Fouilhoux, 1929–30). This pair of apartment houses was among the first in New York City to reflect the trend toward modernism, as evidenced in the horizontal massing, the use of steel casement windows, and the lack of applied ornament. The buildings contain studio and one-bedroom apartments planned for artists and others who wished to live in the artistic community that grew up around the nearby Beaux-Arts Institute of Design (see No. 281).

283 **New York Central Building,** now the Helmsley Building, 230 Park Avenue (Warren & Wetmore, 1927–29). The New York Central Building, set astride Park Avenue just north of Grand Central Terminal (see No. 239), was the linchpin of the Terminal City complex of hotels and office buildings sponsored by the New York Central Railroad. Designed by the same architects responsible for the exterior of the railroad terminal, this tower once dominated Park Avenue and the surrounding Midtown business district with its distinctive design and monumental pyramidal roof capped by an ornate cupola (undergoing restoration). **Interior:** The impressive lobby, planned as a corridor connecting East 45th and 46th Streets, echoes the magnificence of the exterior. The building's design and ornamentation celebrate the prowess of the New York Central Railroad, which had its headquarters on the premises. A sense of imperial grandeur is created by the marble walls and bronze detail, which includes extensive use of the railroad's initials. The Chinese red elevator doors open into cabs with red walls, wood moldings, gilt domes, and painted cloudscapes.

Chrysler Building (No. 279). A romantic Art Deco symbol of New York City. Photo by Carl Forster.

284 **William Lescaze House and Office,** 211 East 48th Street (William Lescaze, 1933–34). The pioneer modern architect William Lescaze designed this house for his family and incorporated an office into the basement level. The building, actually a re-design of an old row house, is generally considered to be the first truly "modern" house in New York. It has a complex, rationally designed street front with precisely balanced solids and voids. The stuccoed facade is pierced by casement ribbon windows and expanses of glass block; this is the first use of glass block in New York City.

285 **Amster Yard,** 211–215 East 49th Street (1869–70; renovation, Harold Sterner, 1945). In 1945 James Amster commissioned Sterner to convert a group of run-down buildings of the late

1860s into shops, offices, and apartments grouped around a landscaped courtyard.

286 **Waldorf-Astoria Hotel,** 301 Park Avenue (Schultze & Weaver, Lloyd Morgan, partner in charge, 1929–31). The famous Waldorf-Astoria Hotel on Park Avenue is the modern reincarnation of the legendary pair of hotels erected by the Astor family (John Jacob Astor immigrated from Waldorff, Germany) in the 1890s on the present-day site of the Empire State Building. The Park Avenue building combines a transient hotel with a pair of vertically massed residential skyscraper towers each surmounted by a crowning beacon. The hotel has a gray limestone base with matching gray brick

William Lescaze House and Office (No. 284). The first truly modern house in New York City. Photo by David Bishop.

above and is ornamented at street level with Art Deco–style storefronts, lamps, entries, and screens, a soaring winged statue, and other features in nickel silver, a silver-colored alloy of nickel, zinc, and copper that was extremely popular in the late 1920s and early 1930s.

287 **Saint Bartholomew's Church (Episcopal) and Community House,** Park Avenue at East 50th Street (Bertram Goodhue, 1914–19; community house, Mayers, Murray & Phillip, 1926–28). Superbly sited in a terraced garden amid the corporate towers of Park Avenue, the Byzantine-inspired Saint Bartholomew's is an outstanding example of the work of Goodhue. The church is constructed of fine materials—salmon-colored brick highlighted with bands of limestone—and is ornamented with carvings, many of them representative of the life of Saint Bartholomew. The famous triple-arched entrance portal (1900–03), designed by Stanford White of the firm McKim, Mead & White for the congregation's previous home on Madison Avenue, was a memorial to Cornelius Vanderbilt II; Goodhue was required to incorporate this element into his design. The entrance, with its bronze doors and carved panels, the work of Daniel Chester French and Andrew O'Connor (central bay), Herbert Adams (north), and Philip Martiny (south), was modeled on the portal to the Provençal Romanesque church Saint Gilles-du-Gard near Arles, France. The community house, designed by Goodhue's successor firm after his death, is completely in harmony with the church.

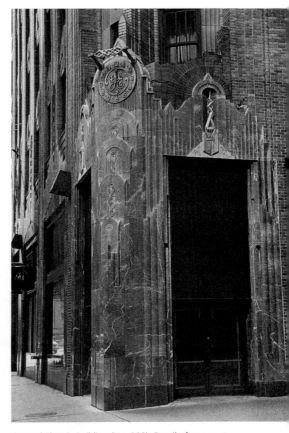

General Electric Building (No. 288). Detail of corner at East 51st Street, with signature clock. Photo by Carl Forster.

288 **General Electric Building,** 570 Lexington Avenue (Cross & Cross, 1929–31). The Radio Victor Corporation of America (RCA) was a subsidiary of General Electric when it commissioned this Art Deco building as its headquarters. But when, in 1931, as part of an effort to gain corporate independence, the firm moved to Rockefeller Center, it deeded this building to General Electric. The octagonal brick tower, rising from a base with rounded corner, is one of the most expressive skyscrapers of its era. Especially noteworthy features are the complex brickwork and terra cotta in colors chosen to blend with the neighboring Saint Bartholomew's Church (see No. 287) and the use of details symbolic of the building's tenant: the corner clock whose projecting arms grasp electric bolts; the spec-

tral figures with boltlike bodies above the shop fronts; and the stylized figures at the building's crown, each with a halo of electric rays. In 1995, after the building was donated to Columbia University, an extensive restoration was completed by Ernest de Castro of the WCA Design Group.

289 **Seagram Building,** 375 Park Avenue (Ludwig Mies van der Rohe, with Philip Johnson and Kahn & Jacobs, 1955–58). The only building in New York designed by the modern master Mies van der Rohe, the Seagram Building is considered to be the greatest of the International Style skyscrapers erected in the postwar era, when this style became a symbol of corporate America. Seagram's president, Samuel Bronfman, and his daughter, the architect

Phyllis Lambert, selected Mies and gave him a virtually unlimited budget for the project. The juxtaposition of the extruded bronze frame with the rectangular bronze spandrel panels and transparent glass surfaces of the curtain wall creates the tight geometry and the contrast between solid and void that typify the finest International Style design. The tower rises behind a plaza with a pair of fountains. **Interior:** The fine materials and careful detailing of the exterior are evident in the lobby, designed by Philip Johnson, with its travertine walls and floor, bronze mullions, and elevator cabs with stainless steel and bronze mesh panels. The stairs at the rear lead to the Four Seasons Restaurant (see No. 290).

290 **Four Seasons Restaurant (interior),** 99 East 52nd Street (Philip Johnson, 1958–59). An integral part of Mies van der Rohe's Seagram Building (see No. 289), the Four Seasons Restaurant has one

of the most notable International Style interiors in the United States. Planned as a first-class restaurant, the beautifully proportioned interior spaces display travertine, bronze, aluminum, wood, rawhide, and other materials, all of which have been installed with expert craftsmanship that accentuates their natural beauty. For this design Johnson collaborated with an interior designer, a lighting consultant, horticulturists, artists, and furniture and industrial designers to create a unified series of environments, including the long narrow lobby, the Grill Room, and the Pool Room.

291 **312 East 53rd Street House** (1865–66). One of a pair, this small frame mansard-roofed house in the French Second Empire style is an intact example of a type of modest dwelling that was once common in New York City but is now exceptionally rare.

Seagram Building (No. 289). The only building in New York designed by the master architect Mies van der Rohe, the Seagram Building is considered the greatest International Style skyscraper. Photo by Carl Forster.

292 **Central Synagogue** (Congregation Ahavath Chesed), 652 Lexington Avenue (Henry Fernbach, 1871–72). Central Synagogue is the oldest building in New York State in continuous use by a single Jewish congregation. The congregation was founded in 1846 on the Lower East Side by Jews from Bohemia. Following the city's population northward, the congregation purchased a corner site on Lexington Avenue at East 55th Street and commissioned the design of a new sanctuary from the Prussian-born Jewish architect Henry Fernbach. The masterful Moorish-inspired form re- flects the heritage of Jews in Moorish Spain and was a response to the 19th-century debate on the appropriate style for synagogues. The earliest Moorish-inspired synagogues were in Germany, but beginning with the 1866 design for America's oldest Reformed congregation, Congregation B'nai Jeshurun in Cincinnati, Moorish temples were erected throughout the United States. The brownstone-faced Central Synagogue, with its banded arches and onion domes, is a masterpiece of the style. In 1995 the Philadelphia firm Kopple & Associates undertook a facade restoration.

Central Synagogue (Congregation Ahavath Chesed; No. 292). The Moorish-inspired form reflects the heritage of Jews in Spain. Photo by Carl Forster.

INDIVIDUAL LANDMARKS

293 **Winter Garden Theater (interior)**, 1634–1646 Broadway (W. Albert Swasey, 1910–11; remodeling, Herbert J. Krapp, 1922–23). Built around 1885 as the American Horse Exchange, a stable and auction mart, this building was converted into a theater in 1910–11 for the Shuberts. The present seating arrangement and decor date largely from the remodeling of 1922–23. The enormous theater contains some of Krapp's finest Adamesque ornament. In its early years the Winter Garden attracted lavish revues; it premiered with *La Belle Paree*, which introduced Al Jolson. The revamped theater has attracted both revues, such as the *Ziegfeld Follies* of 1934, which starred Fanny Brice, and a series of musicals, including *Wonderful Town, West Side Story, Funny Girl, Mame, Pacific Overtures,* and *Cats,* the longest-running play in Broadway history.

294 **Hollywood Theater,** later the Mark Hellinger Theater, now Times Square Church, 217–239 West 51st Street (Thomas W. Lamb, 1929). The Hollywood, originally entered from Broadway (entry demolished), is the sole survivor of the great Broadway

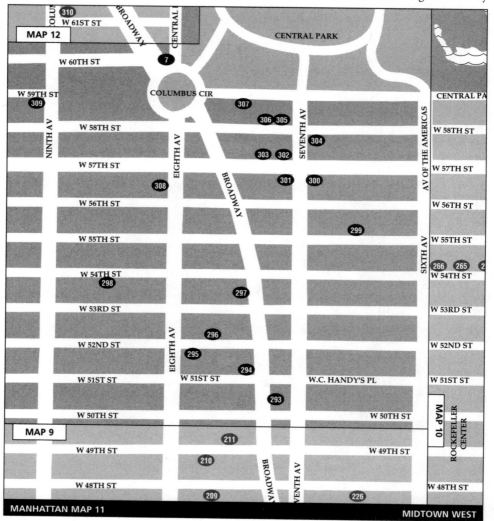

movie palaces. The exterior, with its combination of modernist elements (a massing derived from Frank Lloyd Wright's Unity Temple and a series of figures inspired by those on Eliel Saarinen's Helsinki Railroad Station), hides a lavish Baroque-inspired **interior** with rich gilded plaster surfaces, large mirrors, murals of nymphs and clouds, and ornate chandeliers. Run as a movie theater for only five years, the theater was converted into a legitimate house and renamed for a noted columnist and producer. The building was sold to the Times Square Church in 1991.

295 **Alvin Theater,** now the Neil Simon Theater, 244–254 West 52nd Street (Herbert J. Krapp, 1926–27). Built to house the musical comedies of the producers Alex Aarons and Vinton Freedley (whose names were merged in the theater's original name), the Alvin is one of the prolific theater architect Herbert J. Krapp's most impressive Adamesque designs. **Interior:** The lobbies and auditorium continue the use of the Adamesque detail seen on the exterior. The theater has housed an extraordinary number of hit productions since its debut with George and Ira Gershwin's *Funny Face,* including the Gershwins' *Girl Crazy* and *Porgy and Bess,* Ethel Merman in *Anything Goes,* Henry Fonda in *Mister Roberts,* Judy Holliday in *Bells Are Ringing,* and James Earl Jones in *The Great White Hope.*

296 **Guild Theater,** later the ANTA Theater, now the Virginia Theater, 243–259 West 52nd Street (Crane & Franzheim, 1924–25). The Theater Guild, an organization founded by members of the theater community for the express purpose of presenting high-quality plays, commissioned this building as a theater and a theatrical resource center. The facade design was inspired by 15th-century Tuscan villas. The guild produced a series of classical and modern plays (premiering Eugene O'Neill's *Mourning Becomes Electra* and *Ah, Wilderness!*) with all-star casts before it was forced to give up the theater in 1943. From 1950 to 1981, the American National Theater and Academy (ANTA) owned the theater; among its productions was the American premiere of *A Man for All Seasons.*

297 **Hammerstein's Theater (interior),** now the Ed Sullivan Theater, 1697–1699 Broadway (Herbert J. Krapp, 1927). The neo-Gothic style chosen for the vestibule, lobbies, and auditorium of the former Hammerstein's Theater is unique on Broadway. The theater was built by Arthur Hammerstein (see Arthur and Dorothy Dalton Hammerstein House, Queens No. 25) as a memorial to his father, Oscar Hammerstein I, and no expense was spared in making the interiors as imposing as possible. Unfortunately, the theater was never successful as a legitimate playhouse. It served for many years as a dance hall and then became a radio theater. In 1945 it was converted for use by television and housed *The Ed Sullivan Show,* the longest-running program in television history. Since 1993 it has been the location for *The Late Show with David Letterman,* following an extensive renovation and partial restoration of the theater.

298 **Eleventh District Municipal Court/Seventh District Magistrates' Court,** now the Midtown Community Court, 314 West 54th Street (John H. Duncan, 1894–96). This courthouse is an example of the imposing small-scale civic buildings erected throughout New York City in the late 19th century. For the limestone and brick structure, Duncan employed Renaissance forms ornamented with terra-cotta detail incorporating symbols of justice. After serving several other uses, the building was converted back into a courthouse in 1995.

299 **Mecca Temple,** now the City Center 55th Street Theater, 131 West 55th Street (H. P. Knowles, 1922–24). Famed since 1943 as the home of several of New York's major performing arts organizations, the City Center Theater was originally a temple for the Ancient Order of Nobles of the Mystic Shrine, better known as the Shriners. A Moorish-inspired design, the building is faced in sandstone blocks and is crowned by a huge tiled dome. The facade is enlivened by entrances featuring brightly colored terra cotta and glazed tile in an Islamic design. The temple consists of a huge auditorium above a basement banquet room (now the Manhattan Theater Club) and a 12-story wing to the rear that originally housed lodge and club rooms (now offices). Mecca Temple was never a financial success, and in 1942 New York City foreclosed on the property. Mayor Fiorello La Guardia conceived of the idea of converting the hall into a cultural center that offered tickets at affordable prices. The City Center of Music and Drama was officially organized in 1943. City Center's constituents have included the New York City Ballet, the New York City Opera, the Joffrey Ballet, and the Alvin Ailey Dance Theater.

300 Carnegie Hall, West 57th Street at Seventh Avenue (William B. Tuthill, 1889–91; office wing, William B. Tuthill, 1892–95; studio wing, Henry J. Hardenbergh, 1896–97). Carnegie Hall, one of America's greatest concert halls, was built by steel magnate Andrew Carnegie as part of his efforts toward "the improvement of mankind." Known originally as the Music Hall, the Carnegie Hall auditorium opened in 1891 with the American conducting debut of Tchaikovsky and since then has hosted many of the world's leading musicians. The building, faced in Roman brick and terra cotta and designed in an Italian Renaissance–inspired style, was originally crowned by a mansard roof; this roof was replaced by a full top floor early in

the 1890s. The hall has two major additions: Tuthill's office tower on West 56th Street and Hardenbergh's studio tower on West 57th Street. Carnegie Hall was saved from demolition in 1960 when it was purchased by the city; it was handsomely refurbished in 1981–90 by James Stewart Polshek & Partners. An office tower, designed by Cesar Pelli & Associates and containing improved backstage facilities, was erected immediately to the east of the studio tower in 1986–90.

301 Rodin Studios, 200 West 57th Street (Cass Gilbert, 1916–17). Named for one of the most innovative artists living at the time, the Rodin was the latest of the series of buildings erected in Manhattan in the first years of the 20th century to provide combined studio and residential space for artists. The building contained double-height studios, most of them facing north onto West 57th Street, and duplex living units at the rear. The

Carnegie Hall (No. 300). One of America's greatest concert halls, Carnegie Hall was built by steel magnate Andrew Carnegie as part of his efforts toward "the improvement of mankind." Photo by Carl Forster.

building has a reinforced concrete frame that is faced in polychromatic rough brick with extensive iron and terra-cotta trim in a French Gothic style that complements the American Fine Arts Society (see No. 303) across the street. Cass Gilbert had previously used this style on his Woolworth Building (see No. 48). The Rodin Studios now houses offices, and the duplex units have been subdivided.

302 **Osborne Apartments,** 205 West 57th Street (James E. Ware, 1883–85, enlargement of top story, 1889; addition to west, Alfred S. G. Taylor, 1906). The Osborne, an early luxury apartment building, is located in the area that by the mid-1880s was rapidly becoming the city's first center of apartment-house construction. Ware's robust Italian Renaissance–inspired building with medieval detail is clad in heavy, rock-faced blocks of red sandstone and features elegant carved ornamental panels. The building's plan—the Osborne contains duplex apartment units—is reflected in its elevations. There are twelve floors in the front and fourteen at the rear.

303 **American Fine Arts Society,** now the Art Students League, 215 West 57th Street (Henry J. Hardenbergh, 1891–92). With its design adapted from a hunting lodge erected by Francis I in the forest of Fontainebleau in the early 16th century, this building is one of several New York City landmarks that reflect Hardenbergh's interest in Northern European architecture. The American Fine Arts Society was incorporated in 1889 by the New York Architectural League, the Society of American

The American Fine Arts Society (No. 303) reflects architect Henry Hardenbergh's interest in Northern European architecture. Photo by John Barrington Bayley.

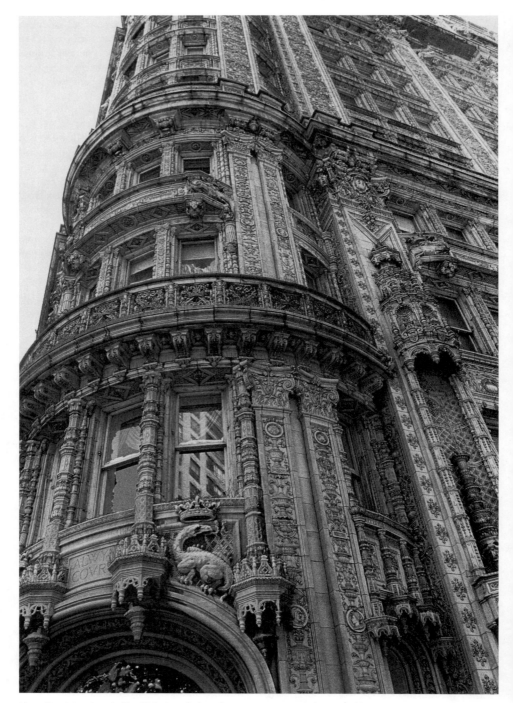

Alwyn Court Apartments (No. 304). A profusion of terra-cotta ornament decorates this early apartment house. Detail of corner bay. Photo by Carl Forster.

Artists, and the Art Students League to raise funds for a building that would contain offices, galleries, and studios for the three organizations. Each originally had space in the building; it is now used solely by the Art Students League.

304 **Alwyn Court Apartments,** 182 West 58th Street (Harde & Short, 1907–09). Almost every inch of this apartment house is covered with terracotta ornament in the Francis I style. Located just south of Central Park, in an area that attracted a significant number of Manhattan's early apartment houses, Alwyn Court originally boasted expansive 14-room apartments (subdivided during the Depression), each with five baths. The facade was cleaned and restored in 1980–81 (Beyer Blinder Belle, architect).

305 **Helen Miller Gould Carriage House,** now the Unity Center of Practical Christianity, 213 West 58th Street (York & Sawyer, 1902–03). Although planned for a utilitarian function, this structure is a sophisticated example of early French Renaissance-

inspired design, resembling a town house on the Place Vendôme in Paris. Built for the eldest daughter of the "robber baron" Jay Gould, the carriage house is an early work of York & Sawyer, an architecture firm best known for its banks.

306 **Fire Engine Company No. 23,** 215 West 58th Street (Alexander H. Stevens, 1905–06). Fire Engine Company No. 23 is a straightforward Beaux-Arts limestone and brick building that served as a model for other early 20th-century firehouses. The building is one of the first to have been designed by the fire department's superintendent of buildings rather than by an outside architect.

307 **Gainsborough Studios,** 222 Central Park South (Charles W. Buckham, 1907–08). The Gainsborough was planned as combined living and studio space for artists. The double-height windows facing Central Park provide north light to the studios; duplex apartments are located at the rear. The facade (restored in 1988) acknowledges the building's artist residents with its bust of Thomas

Gainsborough Studios (No. 307). The building's original artist residents are acknowledged in the bust of Thomas Gainsborough rising above the frieze *A Festival Procession of the Arts*. Photo by Carl Forster.

Gainsborough, a frieze by Isidore Konti entitled *A Festival Procession of the Arts,* and an art tile mural produced at Henry Mercer's Moravian Tile Works.

308 **Hearst Magazine Building,** 951–969 Eighth Avenue (Joseph Urban and George B. Post & Sons, 1927–28). Built as the headquarters of William Randolph Hearst's publishing empire, this building was designed by the Viennese-born and -educated architect Joseph Urban, a leading theater designer of the 20th century. The six-story building, faced in cast limestone, was planned as a base for a skyscraper that was never built. It combines Art Deco ornament, Viennese Secessionist forms, and baroque theatricality that exemplify Urban's architectural vision. Of special note are the paired sculptural figures representing comedy and tragedy, art and music, sport and industry, and printing and science.

309 **Roosevelt Hospital, William J. Syms Operating Theater,** 400 West 59th Street (W. Wheeler Smith, 1890–92). W. Wheeler Smith worked in conjunction with the prominent surgeon Charles McBurney to create the most advanced operating theater in the world for Roosevelt Hospital. McBurney examined modern operating facilities throughout Europe and America before he accepted a final design. Although the building's interior has been altered, its distinctive exterior form (a rectangle with a semiconical roof) and utilitarian appearance continue to express its original function.

Hearst Magazine Building (No. 308). The tower that was designed to go atop this base was never built. Photo by Carl Forster.

■ *EAST OF COLUMBUS AVENUE*

HISTORIC DISTRICTS

21 **Upper West Side/Central Park West Historic District.** Extending westward from the western edge of Central Park, this large district evokes the distinctive qualities of the Upper West Side, from its powerful iconography of twin towers along Central Park West, to its active commerce along Columbus Avenue, to its residential side streets. The district is defined by a large concentration of

Upper West Side/Central Park West Historic District streetscape (H.D. 21). The north side of West 78th Street between Amsterdam and Columbus Avenues. Photo by Caroline Kane Levy.

ment houses, such as the Dakota (see No. 317), were built in this early period, but most apartment-house construction in the district dates to the early years of the 20th century, when the neighborhood's great Beaux-Arts apartment buildings were erected, including the Prasada (Charles Romeyn, 1904–07), the Langham (Clinton & Russell, 1904–07), the Kenilworth (Townsend, Steinle & Haskell, 1906–08), and the Saint Urban (Robert T. Lyons, 1904–05). Beginning in 1902, West 67th Street was transformed into a unique enclave of apartment houses, most designed in a neo-Gothic mode with double-height studio spaces for artists. In the 1920s many large apartment houses and apartment hotels were built along Central Park West and other streets in the district, but most construction ceased with the advent of the Great Depression in 1929. During the entire span of development, important institutional buildings were also erected, including museums, churches, and synagogues, several of which are individual landmarks (see below).

㉒ Central Park West–West 73rd–74th Streets Historic District. Now entirely subsumed within the Upper West Side/Central Park West Historic District (H.D. 21), this square block contains some of the finest residential design on the Upper West Side. The earliest buildings in the district are eighteen row houses on West 73rd Street, which survive from a row of twenty-eight designed by Henry J. Hardenbergh in 1882–85 for Edward S. Clark, president of the Singer [Sewing Machine] Manufacturing Co., in a style compatible with the nearby Dakota Apartments (see No. 317). Clark's grandson Frederick Ambrose Clark developed much of West 74th Street in 1902–04 with a long neo-Georgian row designed by Percy Griffin. The Clarks sold the Central Park West frontage in 1902, and Clinton & Russell's elegant Langham Apartments in the Beaux-Arts style was erected in 1904–07.

㉓ Central Park West–76th Street Historic District. This small historic district is now located entirely within the Upper West Side/Central Park West Historic District (H.D. 21). Row houses began to appear on West 76th Street in 1887; by 1900, forty-four of them had been built within the district. Central Park West retains examples of the

architecturally distinctive buildings erected on the Upper West Side during the fifty years in which substantial development occurred in the neighborhood. The inauguration of the Ninth Avenue elevated railway in 1879 along what is now Columbus Avenue opened the vast unoccupied regions of the Upper West Side to speculative development, and hundreds of neo-Grec, Romanesque Revival, Queen Anne, and neo-Renaissance row houses were built on the side streets between Central Park West and Amsterdam Avenue, while tenements for the working class and French flats for middle-class households were constructed on or near Amsterdam and Columbus Avenues. A few grand apart-three types of buildings erected on that avenue at the turn of the century: the Kenilworth (Townsend, Steinle & Haskell, 1906–08), a Beaux-Arts-style apartment house designed for upper-middle-class families; the neo-Gothic Church of the Divine Paternity (now Fourth Universalist Society; William A. Potter, 1897–98); and the New-York Historical Society (see No. 319), one of two major museums located along the park. The district also includes Harde & Short's Studio Building (1907–09) at 44 West 77th Street, an apartment house that contains two-story artists' studios with attached duplex residential units.

INDIVIDUAL LANDMARKS

310 **Kent Automatic Parking Garage,** later the Sofia Brothers Warehouse, now the Sofia Apartments, 33–43 West 61st Street (Jardine, Hill & Murdock, 1929–30). This flamboyant brick and polychrome terra-cotta Art Deco building was erected as a parking garage that employed a patented automatic parking system: an electrical "parking machine" engaged each car by its rear axle and towed it from an elevator to a parking spot. Unfortunately, the novel system failed. The building served as a more conventional garage until 1941, when it became the Sofia Brothers Warehouse. In 1983–84 the warehouse was converted into luxury apartments.

311 **Century Apartments,** 25 Central Park West (Irwin S. Chanin, 1931). The twin-towered Century, a sophisticated example of residential Art Deco design in New York, is a major element of Central Park West's distinctive skyline. Much of the Century's aesthetic interest lies in the successful manipulation of such features as brickwork, windows, bays, and balconies and the spare use of ornament to highlight entrances, setbacks, towers, and other elements.

312 **New York Society for Ethical Culture,** 2 West 64th Street (Robert D. Kohn, 1909–10). The Ethical Culture meetinghouse is among a small group of exceptional buildings designed by Robert D. Kohn in the Secessionist mode, a reform style that developed in Vienna at the turn of the century. The austere geometry and abstract classicism of

Viennese design are evident in this structure and in Kohn's New York Evening Post Building (see No. 46). For both buildings Kohn's wife, Estelle Rumbold Kohn, provided sculptural decoration.

313 **First Battery Armory,** later the 102nd Medical Battalion Armory, now Capital Cities/ABC, Inc., Studios, 56 West 66th Street (Horgan & Slattery, 1900–03). The First Battery, founded in 1867, was a largely German-American volunteer unit of the National Guard. The unit was one of several in New York City that built medieval-inspired armories at the turn of the century. This relatively small building has a lively facade, with turrets, crenellations, and other castlelike features, some functional and others merely decorative.

314 **Shearith Israel Synagogue** (the Spanish and Portuguese Synagogue), 99 Central Park West (Brunner & Tryon, 1896–97). As the Jewish population in the United States expanded, especially in the second half of the 19th century, debate arose over the appropriate style for synagogues. In the post–Civil War years, Moorish-inspired designs were popular. Late in the century, after archaeologists discovered the ruins of the Second Temple in Jerusalem, built during the Roman occupation of Palestine, this classical monument became the model for new synagogues. Congregation Shearith Israel is believed to have been the first to adopt this style when it erected its new home on Central Park West, and it influenced the design of hundreds of other synagogues nationwide. Shearith Israel, founded in 1654 by Sephardic Jews who arrived in New York from a Dutch colony in Brazil, is the oldest Jewish congregation in North America. This synagogue is the fourth erected by the congregation since it built its initial home in 1730.

315 **Central Park Scenic Landmark,** Fifth Avenue to Central Park West, 59th Street to 110th Street (Frederick Law Olmsted and Calvert Vaux, designed 1858). One of the great man-made monuments of the 19th century, Central Park was the first large-scale public park in the United States, and its success influenced park design all across the country. The design embodies 19th-century attitudes toward nature and the ideals of a democratic society. The park was planned as a naturalistic landscape in which urban dwellers of all back-

Central Park Scenic Landmark (No. 315). The first large-scale public park in the United States, Central Park influenced park design across the country. Also shown are the San Remo Apartments (No. 318). Photo by Carl Forster.

grounds could mingle and find respite from the pressures of life. Olmsted and Vaux transformed what was in part a rugged, swampy area with scattered settlements (including Seneca Village, a small community of African-Americans and Irish immigrants) into a bucolic setting of meadows, lakes, and forests punctuated with modest buildings designed by Vaux. Four separate road and path sys-

Wrey Mould's intricate carved representations of plants and birds native to New York in each season and a fountain by Vaux crowned by Emma Stebbins's sculpture *Angel of the Waters of Bethesda;* the heavily forested 30-acre Ramble; the formal Conservatory Garden; and such beautiful bodies of water as the Lake and Harlem Meer. Major restoration projects undertaken by the Parks Department and the Central Park Conservancy since the 1970s have returned much of Central Park to its original glory.

316 Majestic Apartments, 115 Central Park West (Irwin S. Chanin, 1930–31). The Majestic is one of the four great twin-towered apartment buildings that define the Central Park West skyline. This Art Deco building is the earlier of Irwin Chanin's two Central Park West apartment houses and is somewhat simpler than the nearby Century (see No. 311). The towers are a response to a 1929 building regulation that limited the height of an apartment building's street wall but permitted tall towers on large plots.

317 Dakota Apartments, 1 West 72nd Street (Henry J. Hardenbergh, 1880–84). One of New York's best-known buildings, the Dakota was erected at a time when the Upper West Side was sparsely populated. The building was commissioned by Edward S. Clark, president of the Singer [Sewing Machine] Manufacturing Company and an active West Side developer. Hardenbergh's interest in Northern European architecture is evident in the building's somewhat Germanic design, with its picturesque gables rising above Central Park. In plan, the Dakota has a central courtyard with an entrance in each corner. A cleaning and restoration of the facades has revealed the cream-colored shade of the brick and the beautifully carved stone detailing.

318 San Remo Apartments, 145–146 Central Park West (Emery Roth, 1929–30). Soaring over Central Park, the San Remo is one of the most significant components of the Central Park West skyline. The building was designed by Emery Roth at the pinnacle of his career as a designer of apartment houses. The San Remo and the nearby Beresford (see No. 321) are examples of Roth's sophisticated adaptation of Italian Renaissance forms to high-rise residential design.

tems wend through the park: pedestrian walkways, carriage drives, bridle paths, and transverse roads that carry crosstown traffic. These systems pass over and under one another by way of stone and cast-iron bridges of exceptional beauty. Among the major features of the park are the 33-acre Sheep Meadow; the 1,200-foot-long Mall, with its rows of American elms; Bethesda Terrace, with Jacob

319 **New-York Historical Society,** 170 Central Park West (York & Sawyer, 1903–08; wings, Walker & Gillette, 1937–38). This museum and research facility, designed in a severe Classical Revival style, was built to house a rich repository of artwork and historical material relating primarily to the history of New York City and New York State and collected since the organization of the society in 1804. The granite-faced central pavilion with its Ionic colonnade is complemented by end wings added several decades after the main building was erected.

320 **American Museum of Natural History,** Central Park West at West 77th Street (Vaux & Mould, 1874–77; south and part of west elevation, Cady, Berg & See, 1888–1908; east wing, Trowbridge & Livingston, 1912–34; Theodore Roosevelt Memorial Hall, John Russell Pope, 1931–34; library, Kevin Roche John Dinkeloo Associates, 1990–92). Five years after the museum's incorporation in 1869, construction began on a spacious site known as Manhattan Square with Vaux & Mould's High Victorian Gothic building, now barely visible in a court at the west side of the site. In 1888 Cady, Berg & See prepared a master plan for the institution that envisioned a monumental Romanesque Revival complex to be constructed of pink granite; only the south front and a portion of the west front (undertaken by the architect Charles Volz) were completed. In 1912 Trowbridge & Livingston began planning a series of Classical Revival pavilions; only the east wing was erected. John Russell Pope's Theodore Roosevelt Memorial Hall, now the museum's main entrance, is in the form of a massive triumphal arch. The **interior** of Memorial Hall is among New York's great monumental spaces, with a barrel-vaulted ceiling, giant Corinthian columns, and rich marble walls and floors, all reminiscent of the grandeur of ancient Rome. The room, reopened in 1991 following a restoration by the Roche firm, contains a series of murals by William A. Mackay that depict events in Roosevelt's life. In 1997, construction of Polshek & Partners' new Hayden Planetarium began, replacing an earlier building by Trowbridge & Livingston.

321 **Beresford Apartments,** 211 Central Park West (Emery Roth, 1928–29). The Italian Renaissance–inspired Beresford, with its three prominent octagonal towers, is one of the masterpieces of the famed apartment-house designer Emery Roth. The building is among the most prominent elements of Central Park West's distinctive skyline.

■ *WEST OF COLUMBUS AVENUE*

HISTORIC DISTRICTS

24 **West 71st Street Historic District.** This small, nearly block-long district on a quiet cul-de-sac ends in a wall that separated the street from the railroad tracks to the west. The district consists of thirty-three row houses, erected in six groups over only a three-year period (1893 to 1896), a single town house of 1903–04, and an apartment building erected in 1924. The block's cohesive quality results from the consistent use of Renaissance-inspired detail on all the masonry row houses.

25 **West End–Collegiate Historic District.** Named for the nearby West End Collegiate Church (see No. 334), this historic district consists primarily of row houses that developers built on speculation in the last fifteen years of the 19th century. Many of the city's most talented architects specializing in row-house design—including C. P. H. Gilbert, Lamb & Rich, and Clarence True—were active in the district, creating blockfronts with an eclectic blend of Italian, French, and Flemish Renaissance stylistic forms, among others. Lamb & Rich's 1891 blockfront in the Francis I style on the west side of West End Avenue between West 76th and West 77th Streets is among the most beautiful on the Upper West Side. In the first decades of the 20th century, several apartment houses were built in the district, reflecting the decline in row-house construction as land values rose and as the apartment house became an increasingly acceptable residential alternative for affluent New Yorkers.

26 **Riverside Drive–West 80th–81st Street Historic District.** This small historic district illustrates, in microcosm, the early residential development of the West End section of New York's Upper West Side. Development began on West 81st Street in 1892, with the construction of a row of five transitional Romanesque Revival/neo-Renaissance row houses designed by Charles Israels (Nos. 308–314).

Two years later Israels designed an additional row on West 80th Street (Nos. 307–317). Another wave of row-house construction occurred in 1897–99, when the architect/developer Clarence True built the houses on and adjacent to Riverside Drive. These large brick and stone row houses are characteristic of True's Northern European–inspired designs. Contemporaneous with the row houses are three modest French flats erected on West 80th Street for middle-class families. In 1926 one of True's houses was demolished and replaced by a 16-story neoclassical apartment building designed by Maurice Deutsch.

INDIVIDUAL LANDMARKS

322 **Dorilton Apartments,** 171 West 71st Street (Janes & Leo, 1900–02). Perhaps the most flamboyant apartment house in New York, the Dorilton is an enormous Beaux-Arts pile with striking French-inspired sculptural decoration and an iron gate reminiscent of those that guard French palaces. The Dorilton was erected to cater to the prosperous upper-middle-class families who were moving into apartment houses on the Upper West Side in increasing numbers in the early years of the 20th century. An ongoing restoration of the facade and the mansard roof has rejuvenated the building.

323 **309 West 72nd Street House,** also known as the William E. Diller House (Gilbert A. Schellenger, 1899–1901). William E. Diller, a physician and an active builder of single-family houses, erected this impressive Renaissance Revival town house as a speculative venture (he never lived here). Built on a site with restrictive covenants that required high-quality construction, the house complements the neighboring residences commissioned by the Kleeberg, Prentiss, and Sutphen families (see Nos. 324, 325, and 326).

324 **John and Mary Sutphen House,** 311 West 72nd Street (C. P. H. Gilbert, 1901–02). The Sutphen House and the neighboring Kleeberg and Prentiss Houses (see Nos. 325 and 326) are all French-inspired limestone-fronted dwellings built on oddly shaped lots in accordance with restrictive covenants that required the construction of high-quality residences. These restrictions were inaugu-

rated by John Sutphen's father, who once owned the entire Riverside Drive frontage between West 72nd and West 73rd Streets.

325 **Frederick and Lydia Prentiss House,** 1 Riverside Drive (C. P. H. Gilbert, 1899–1901). One of a group of extraordinary town houses at the southernmost end of Riverside Drive designed by the prolific architect C. P. H. Gilbert, this limestone-fronted Beaux-Arts structure is set on a curved lot and has two visible facades, one of which fronts a triangular court shared with the neighboring Sutphen House (see No. 324).

326 **Philip and Maria Kleeberg House,** 3 Riverside Drive (C. P. H. Gilbert, 1896–98). The Kleebergs' elegant town house, designed in the French Renaissance style, is one of four landmark residences located at the gateway to Riverside Drive. Gilbert's design for this limestone-fronted house takes full advantage of its wide curving lot, incorporating a recessed bay above the entrance, a large projecting bay, and a fourth-story loggia.

327 **Chatsworth Apartments and Annex,** 340 and 344 West 72nd Street (John E. Scharsmith, 1902–04 and 1905–06). Prominently sited at the southern end of Riverside Park and Drive, the Beaux-Arts Chatsworth and its annex were built to house the affluent families moving into Upper West Side apartment houses at the turn of the century. The Chatsworth originally offered such amenities as a conservatory, a sun parlor, a café, a billiards room, a barber shop, a beauty salon, and electric bus service along West 72nd Street to and from Central Park.

328 **Riverside Park and Riverside Drive Scenic Landmark,** West 72nd Street to St. Clair Place (Frederick Law Olmsted, design, 1873–75; initial construction, 1875–80; additions, Clifton Lloyd, 1934–37). Riverside Park was initially established in 1865 as a way of increasing real-estate values on the Upper West Side. Riverside Drive was laid out as a separate entity in 1870. Three years later the city's Parks Department asked Olmsted, one of the landscape architects of Central Park (see No. 315) and Prospect Park (see Brooklyn No. 69), to draw up a formal plan for the park and drive. It was Olmsted's idea to treat the two as a single design that would

Ansonia Hotel (No. 329). The soundproof construction of this grand apartment hotel has made it popular with musicians, singers, and conductors. Photo by Caroline Kane Levy.

take advantage of the natural beauty of the site. The curving drive was landscaped with trees, walkways, and viewing sites, and the hillside leading down toward the New York Central's railroad tracks and the Hudson River was planted. The wide, straight walkway within the park (located on top of the railroad tracks) and the paths and playgrounds alongside the river were not part of Olmsted's design but were laid out by Clifton Lloyd at the time of the construction of the Henry Hudson Parkway, during Robert Moses's tenure as Parks Commissioner. Since the late 19th century, Riverside Drive has acquired some of New York's finest monuments. The most prominent of these are Grant's Tomb (see No. 461) and the Soldiers' and Sailors' Monument (see No. 353). On a

more modest scale are such important works of public sculpture as Anna Hyatt Huntington's *Joan of Arc* (base by John V. Van Pelt) at West 93rd Street, Karl Bitter's *Franz Sigel* (base by William Welles Bosworth) at West 106th Street, and the Firemen's Memorial by Attilio Piccirilli (sculptor) and H. Van Buren Magonigle (architect) at West 100th Street.

329 **Ansonia Hotel,** 2101–2119 Broadway (Paul E. M. DuBoy, 1899–1904). The largest and most exuberant of the multiple dwellings in the Beaux-Arts style erected on the Upper West Side at the turn of the century, the Ansonia was built as an apartment hotel by W. E. D. Stokes, a major developer in the area. Stokes advocated all-masonry fireproof construction, including soundproof partitions between floors and apartments, a feature that has attracted many distinguished musicians, singers, and conductors.

330 **Verdi Square Scenic Landmark,** Broadway and Amsterdam Avenue at West 72nd Street. This small triangular park is dominated by a statue of Giuseppe Verdi, commissioned by New York's Italian community from the Sicilian sculptor Pasquale Civiletti and unveiled in 1906. The granite pedestal is encircled by figures representing characters from four of Verdi's operas. The statue was restored in 1996–97, and relandscaping is planned.

331 **Central Savings Bank,** now the Apple Bank for Savings, 2100–2108 Broadway (York & Sawyer, 1926–28). York & Sawyer, the leading architect of banks in New York City in the 1920s, was responsible for several banks in the Italian Renaissance palazzo style. The freestanding Central Savings Bank is the grandest of these, with its massive rusticated limestone facades and magnificent exterior ironwork crafted by Samuel Yellin of Philadelphia. Like York & Sawyer's earlier Brooklyn Trust Company Building (see Brooklyn No. 18), this building is modeled after the work of the 16th-century Veronese architect Michele Sanmicheli. The **interior** banking hall is among the grandest and most ornate in New York City, with its huge gilded and coffered barrel-vaulted ceiling, marble floor laid in a geometric pattern, rusticated sandstone walls, and marble teller's counter capped by intricate iron screens created by master ironworker Yellin.

332 Beacon Theater (interior), 2124 Broadway (Walter W. Ahlschlager, 1927–28). The lavishly appointed lobbies, stairways, and auditorium of the Beacon, with their eclectic Greek, Roman, Renaissance, and rococo detail, are characteristic of the great movie palaces built in the 1920s. The Beacon, one of the last surviving movie palaces in New York City, is now used primarily for concerts.

333 Belleclaire Hotel, 2171–2179 Broadway (Emery Roth of the firm Stein, Cohen & Roth, 1901–03). The earliest known design by Roth, the Belleclaire is one of the fine apartment hotels erected on the Upper West Side at the turn of the century. The design is unusual in its use of ornamental motifs inspired by contemporary Secessionist architecture in Central Europe in combination with more traditional French Beaux-Arts motifs. The facades contain fine carved detail and complex window sash.

334 West End Collegiate Church and Collegiate School, West End Avenue at West 77th Street (Robert W. Gibson, 1892–93). The West End Collegiate Church traces its roots back to the organization of the first church in New Amsterdam in 1628. Appropriately, when the church was built on the Upper West Side, a style evocative of Dutch Renaissance architecture was chosen. The massing and the use of stepped gables, strapwork ornament, and finials are reminiscent of the design of the early 17th-century Butcher's Market in Haarlem, the Netherlands. The school building, erected to house the oldest private secondary school in America,

founded in 1638, was built as a part of the church complex; the Collegiate School is now an independent institution.

335 Apthorp Apartments, 2201–2219 Broadway (Clinton & Russell, 1906–08). The Astor estate commissioned this monumental apartment house, which covers an entire square block of the Upper West Side. Clinton & Russell's adaptation of an Italian Renaissance palazzo includes a large, landscaped central courtyard separated from the street by handsome iron gates.

336 103, 104, 105, and 107–109 Riverside Drive and 332 West 83rd Street Houses (Clarence True, 1898–99). The architect/developer Clarence True erected these five houses as part of a row of six (No. 102 has been demolished), using his signature Elizabethan Revival mode of design, which combined English and French Renaissance forms; the idiosyncratic style is unique to True's residential work on the Upper West Side. The facades of Nos. 103 and 104 were redesigned by Clinton & Russell and rebuilt in 1910–11 in a manner that recalled the original, after a lawsuit brought by a neighboring property owner forced the removal of the original stoops and bow fronts, which encroached on the public way. The facades of Nos. 105 and 107–109 were redesigned by Bosworth & Holden and Tracy, Swartwout & Litchfield, respectively, and rebuilt in the same years. Because No. 332 was around the corner on West 83rd Street, its facade did not have to be rebuilt.

West End Collegiate Church and Collegiate School (No. 334). The design of the school building is evocative of Dutch Renaissance architecture. Photo by Carl Forster.

■ *EAST OF AMSTERDAM AVENUE*

HISTORIC DISTRICT

㉑ **Upper West Side/Central Park West Historic District.** See Map 12.

INDIVIDUAL LANDMARKS

337 **Claremont Stables,** now the Claremont Riding Academy, 175 West 89th Street (Frank A. Rooke, 1892). Designed in the Romanesque Revival style, the Claremont is the oldest functioning commercial stable in Manhattan. The building was erected as a livery stable for the rental of horses and carriages.

338 **Eldorado Apartments,** 300 Central Park West (Margon & Holder, with Emery Roth, 1929–31). The Art Deco Eldorado is the northernmost of the four great twin-towered apartment buildings that line Central Park West. It is believed that Margon & Holder designed the Art Deco detailing but that Emery Roth, one of the leading apartment-house designers of the period, was responsible for the plan and the massing, which closely resemble Roth's contemporaneous work on the San Remo Apartments (see No. 318).

339 **Trinity School** (including the former Saint Agnes Parish House), 121–147 West 91st Street (school, Charles C. Haight, 1893–94; parish house, William A. Potter, 1888–92). Trinity School, established in 1709, followed New York's population north and settled on the Upper West Side in 1894. Haight designed an English Collegiate Gothic structure not unlike his contemporaneous work at Yale University. The building incorporates large windows that maximize natural light and air circulation. Adjacent to the school is the Romanesque Revival granite-and-red-sandstone parish house originally built for use by Trinity Church's Saint Agnes Chapel. When the church was demolished in 1944, the parish house was converted into classrooms. Restoration work has been undertaken by Buttrick, White & Burtis, architect.

340 **Charles A. Vissani House,** 143 West 95th Street (James W. Cole, 1889). Appropriately, this Gothic Revival town house was commissioned by the Very Reverend Charles A. Vissani, the first Commissary General of the Holy Land for the United States. It housed not only Vissani but also a group of Franciscan priests who worked with him in his mission to develop interest in the preservation of the holy places in Jerusalem and Palestine. The building is now divided into apartments.

Trinity School (No. 339). The large windows were designed to maximize natural light and air circulation. Photo by Carl Forster.

119

Association Residence for Respectable Aged Indigent Females (No. 343). One of Richard Morris Hunt's few surviving buildings in New York City has been converted into a hostel. Photo by Carl Forster.

341 **354 and 355 Central Park West Houses** (Gilbert A. Schellenger, 1892–93). These two survivors from a row of five neo-Renaissance dwellings are rare examples of row houses built on Central Park West.

342 **First Church of Christ, Scientist,** 1 West 96th Street (Carrère & Hastings, 1899–1903). New York City's oldest Christian Science congregation erected this magnificent church, which is built entirely of Concord granite. The building was designed by Carrère & Hastings shortly after the firm won the competition for the New York Public Library (see No. 237). The church displays a rare combination of English Baroque massing (not unlike the churches of Nicholas Hawksmoor) and French Beaux-Arts detail.

343 **Association Residence for Respectable Aged Indigent Females,** now the New York City American Youth Hostel, 891 Amsterdam Avenue (Richard Morris Hunt, 1881–83; addition, Charles

A. Rich, 1907–08). The Association for the Relief of Respectable Aged Indigent Females, one of New York City's first charitable institutions, was chartered in 1814 to aid those who were left poor widows by the Revolutionary War and the War of 1812. As the number of needy clients increased, a large new home was needed; in 1881 the Amsterdam Avenue blockfront between West 103rd and 104th Streets was purchased. This building is among the few extant structures in New York City designed by Richard Morris Hunt; it is also a rare example of 19th-century institutional architecture that has been successfully adapted to a new use. The design of the Gothic-inspired brick-and-stone building clearly reflects Hunt's knowledge of contemporary French architecture. The conversion to New York's first youth hostel was completed in 1990 (Larsen Associates, architect).

344 **New York Cancer Hospital,** later the Towers Nursing Home, 455 Central Park West and 32 West 106th Street (Charles C. Haight, 1884–86, and additions, 1889–90). Founded in 1884, the New York Cancer Hospital was the first institution in the United States (and the second in the world, after the London Cancer Hospital) dedicated to the study and treatment of cancer. Haight's design was inspired by Le Lude, one of the great Renaissance châteaus of the Loire Valley. The five massive round towers were planned to provide a maximum amount of light and air to the wards and to facilitate nursing supervision from the center of each ward; it was also thought that the shape prevented air stagnation and the accumulation of dirt and germs in corners. The building has been vacant for many years.

■ WEST OF AMSTERDAM AVENUE

HISTORIC DISTRICTS

27 **Riverside Drive–West End Historic District.** The West End section, the portion of the Upper West Side located west of Broadway, developed somewhat later than the area near Central Park, which was served by the elevated trains running along Columbus Avenue. Although the earliest buildings in the district are the row houses at 267–271 West 88th Street (Nelson M. Whipple, 1884), development did not begin in earnest until three years later. Between 1887 and 1897, row houses were built on speculation along the length of West End Avenue and adjacent side streets. Notable examples include the neo-Renaissance rows with gold or beige brick and terra-cotta detail designed by Thom & Wilson, C. P. H. Gilbert, and Ralph Townsend in 1893–95 on West 88th and West 89th Streets, and several groups designed between 1890 and 1901 by Clarence True on West End Avenue at West 90th and West 92nd Streets and on West 88th through West 92nd Streets between West End Avenue and Riverside Drive, mostly in his favorite Elizabethan Revival style. The two blockfronts of row houses on West End Avenue between 90th and 91st Streets illustrate the low scale and architectural quality of this avenue prior to its reconstruction as a street of apartment buildings. Most of the multiple dwellings that replaced the West End Avenue row houses in the early decades of the 20th century were the work of specialists in apartment-house design and planning. Among the finest apartment houses are Schwartz & Gross's

Chautauqua (1911–12) at No. 574, with its Sullivanesque ornament; George & Edward Blum's Evanston (1910) at No. 610, with its unusual terra-cotta and iron detail; Neville & Bagge's neo-Renaissance building at No. 590 (1915), with its beautiful ocher-colored terra-cotta ornament; and Emery Roth's No. 580 (1926–27), ornamented with the bold High Renaissance features that this architect favored on his large buildings of the 1920s. In the early 20th century, Riverside Drive also became a prime location for elegant apartment houses, such as the Clarendon (Charles Birge, 1906–07) at No. 137–139. Many of the apartment houses erected on Riverside Drive during its peak period of development in the 1920s follow the curve of the drive: No. 160 (Gaetan Ajello, 1922) has a convex front, while the facade of the block-long building at No. 171–177, between West 89th and West 90th Streets (J. E. R. Carpenter, 1925–26), is concave. The extraordinary Normandy is located on Riverside Drive between West 86th and West 87th Streets (see No. 351). There are two important religious structures in the district. The Gothic Revival Fourth Presbyterian Church (now Annunciation Greek Orthodox Church) on West End Avenue and West 91st Street (Heins & La Farge, 1893–94) served the area's first residents, who were predominantly Protestant. Congregation B'nai Jeshuran (Schneider & Herts, 1917–18) on West 88th Street was built for the increasing number of Jewish residents in the neighborhood; its impressive facade with austere granite walls and a great arched entrance was a prototype for the "Semitic" synagogue designs that became popular in the 1920s.

28 **Riverside Drive–West 105th Street Historic District.** This small district built on the gentle slope leading to Riverside Drive consists of residences erected in 1899–1902. The cohesive quality of the district's row houses and town houses is the result of five factors: the brief construction span; the use of English basements with entries at or near the sidewalk level; the use of similar materials, mainly limestone, to create a unified streetscape; the exuberant Beaux-Arts detail chosen by all four architecture firms active in the district (Janes & Leo, Mowbray & Uffinger, Hoppin & Koen, and Robert D. Kohn); and the covenants that required buildings of "suitable character and such as are a benefit to the neighborhood."

INDIVIDUAL LANDMARKS

345 Red House, 350 West 85th Street (Harde & Short, 1903–04). With its combination of French Gothic and Renaissance elements, the Red House recalls early 16th-century residences in the style of Francis I. This red brick and white terra-cotta building is the first of the four major French Gothic–inspired apartment houses designed by Harde & Short (see Nos. 304, 371, and H.D. 23, Map 12) and is a reflection of the changing character of the Upper West Side in the early years of the 20th century, when apartment houses began to supplant row houses as the dominant type of residence.

346 316, 318, 320, 322, 324, and 326 West 85th Street Houses (Clarence True, 1892). This row of six brick houses trimmed with Maynard red sandstone is among the most unusual designed by Clarence True. The houses were commissioned by Charles Judson, with whom True shared a business address. The well-preserved row is of note for the Spanish tile used on the rectangular oriels and projecting false roofs and for its brickwork laid in a rusticated manner to echo the rusticated stonework on the entrance level.

347 329, 331, 333, 335, and 337 West 85th Street Houses (Ralph S. Townsend, 1890–91). Townsend's row of five Queen Anne/Romanesque Revival brick-and-brownstone houses was erected in the decade when much of the Upper West Side west of Broadway was emerging as a desirable residential neighborhood.

348 John B. and Isabella Leech House, 520 West End Avenue (Clarence True, 1892). The Leech residence is an unusual work by the prolific West Side architect/developer Clarence True. The corner house combines Romanesque, Gothic, and Elizabethan forms and is enlivened by superb carved detail. Built for a wealthy cotton broker, the house is a rare example of an individually designed single-family town house on West End Avenue.

349 Belnord Apartments, 201–225 West 86th Street (Hiss & Weekes, 1908–09). Built at a time when apartment houses were becoming the most popular type of residence on the Upper West Side, the Belnord, designed in the Italian Renaissance style, is an enormous building, encompassing an entire city block. The three main entrance arches on West 86th Street, with their sgraffito decoration, lead to a large landscaped courtyard.

350 Saint Paul's Methodist Episcopal Church and Parish House, now the Church of Saint Paul and Saint Andrew (United Methodist), 540 West End Avenue (R. H. Robertson, 1895–97). The design of Saint Paul's Methodist Episcopal Church and the parish house adjoining the church on West 86th Street reflects a major shift from the picturesque Romanesque Revival to a style dominated by Classical and Renaissance-inspired forms. With its bold octagonal campanile, tiled buttresses, and singular terra-cotta detail, Saint Paul's exemplifies the eclecticism of the 1890s in its successful combination of elements from many sources, including Early Christian, early Italian Renaissance, Spanish Renaissance, and German Romanesque architecture.

351 Normandy Apartments, 140 Riverside Drive (Emery Roth & Sons, 1938–39). The Normandy is a masterpiece of the apartment-house specialist Emery Roth. Overlooking the Hudson River, this twin-towered building is the last of Roth's major prewar apartment houses. The building combines the Italian Renaissance forms that Roth had perfected at the Beresford (see No. 321) and the San Remo (see No. 318) on Central Park West with new Moderne features such as streamlined corners and concave entrances featuring mosaic detail.

352 Isaac L. and Julia B. Rice House, now the Yeshiva Ketana of Manhattan, 346 West 89th Street at Riverside Drive (Herts & Tallant, 1901–03). The Rice mansion is one of only two freestanding houses that survive on Riverside Drive. The noted theater architects Herts & Tallant designed this mansion for the lawyer, writer, and chess expert Isaac Rice and his wife, Julia, a physician who, although she never practiced, was involved in medical issues and was responsible for the creation of quiet zones around New York City hospitals. Villa Julia, as the Rices called their home, combines Georgian and Beaux-Arts forms in a highly individualistic manner. In 1908 C. P. H. Gilbert undertook alterations (most barely visible) for the second owner, Solomon Schinasi, a partner in the tobacco firm Schinasi Brothers (see Morris and Laurette Schinasi House, No. 361).

353 **Soldiers' and Sailors' Monument,** Riverside Drive at West 89th Street (Stoughton & Stoughton, with Paul E. M. DuBoy, 1897–1902). The Soldiers' and Sailors' Memorial Arch in Brooklyn (see Brooklyn No. 68) and this monument on Riverside Drive are physical manifestations of the nostalgia for the Civil War era that swept across the United States in the late 19th century as the horrors of the war faded into history. Although a Civil War monument was proposed as early as 1869, it was not until 1897 that enough interest was generated to hold a design competition. The monument was originally intended for Grand Army Plaza, near the entrance to Central Park; the design that won the competition

needed to be reworked when the site was changed to Riverside Drive. Construction of the marble monument and its related terraces began in 1900. The cylindrical building is an enlarged version of the Hellenistic Monument of Lysicrates in Athens.

354 **Pomander Walk,** 3–22 Pomander Walk, 261–267 West 94th Street, and 260–274 West 95th Street (King & Campbell, 1921). One of the most surprising residential enclaves in New York City, Pomander Walk consists of sixteen two-story neo-Tudor houses facing onto a private walk and eleven additional houses on West 94th and West 95th Streets. This picturesque complex was built by the restaurateur and developer Thomas Healy in an attempt to re-create the village atmosphere evoked in Lewis Parker's popular play *Pomander Walk.*

Pomander Walk (No. 354). An attempt by developer Thomas Healy to re-create a village atmosphere in a dense urban setting. Photo by Carl Forster.

355 **Midtown Theater,** now the Metro Theater, 2624–2626 Broadway (Boak & Paris, 1932–33). In the 1920s and 1930s, Broadway on the Upper West Side was lined with neighborhood movie theaters. The Art Deco Midtown is not only one of the few still functioning, but it also has one of the finest theater facades in New York. The street front is clad entirely in colored terra cotta, primarily beige and black. The focus of the design is a medallion with a bas-relief of figures and masks representing comedy and tragedy. The marquee, with its horizontal chrome banding, is largely original.

356 **New York Free Circulating Library, Bloomingdale Branch,** now the Ukrainian Academy of Arts and Sciences, 206 West 100th Street (James Brown Lord, 1898). The Bloomingdale Branch library was commissioned by the New York Free Circulating Library, an organization established in 1878 by wealthy New Yorkers to provide for the "moral and intellectual elevation of the masses." To serve the increasingly populous Upper West Side, the library erected this fireproof steel-frame building designed in the French classical style. The library became a branch of the New York Public Library in 1901; in 1961 the building was sold to a private organization for use as a research facility devoted to the study of Ukrainian culture.

357 **854, 856, and 858 West End Avenue and 254 West 102nd Street Houses** (Schneider & Herter, 1892–93). These four Queen Anne/Romanesque Revival brownstone houses are the sole surviving examples of a type of site planning commonly employed on West End Avenue corners in the 1890s, when this street was being developed with speculative row houses for upper-middle-class buyers. Each of these groups featured residences along the avenue, a prominent corner house, and an additional house facing the side street.

358 **William and Clara Baumgarten House,** 294 Riverside Drive (Schickel & Ditmars, 1900–01). This Beaux-Arts town house near West 102nd Street is one of the few luxury residences of its type to survive on Riverside Drive. The limestone structure was commissioned by William Baumgarten, who served as head of the famous interior design firm Herter Brothers and later established his own decorating company.

359 **Marseilles Hotel,** 2689–2693 Broadway (Harry Allan Jacobs, 1902–05). The Marseilles is among the most prominent of the grand apartment hotels erected at the turn of the century on the Upper West Side. The Beaux-Arts building—with its limestone base, brick facing, terra-cotta trim, and mansard roof—was built in anticipation of the opening of an IRT subway station at West 103rd Street.

360 **Master Building,** 310–312 Riverside Drive (Harvey Wiley Corbett of the firm Helmle, Corbett & Harrison, with Sugarman & Berger, associated architects, 1928–29). This innovative mixed-use structure is a significant work by Corbett, an influential designer of skyscrapers. The building was planned as a 29-story apartment hotel that would incorporate the Nicholas Roerich Museum—including galleries, a library, and an auditorium—on its ground floor. The building is among the finest Art Deco high-rise structures in New York City. Among its notable features are the patterned brickwork that varies from dark to light as the building rises, the dramatic setbacks and irregular massing of the upper floors, the ornamental crown, and the innovative use of corner windows.

361 **Morris and Laurette Schinasi House,** 351 Riverside Drive (William B. Tuthill, 1907–09). This flamboyant marble residence, one of only two freestanding mansions surviving on Riverside Drive, was built by a wealthy cigarette manufacturer and partner in the tobacco firm Schinasi Brothers. The early 16th-century French Renaissance style popular for the châteaux along the Loire was adapted here to an urban setting overlooking the Hudson.

362 **Manhasset Apartments,** 301 West 108th Street and 300 West 109th Street (Joseph Wolf, 1899–1901; enlarged, Janes & Leo, 1901–05). The Beaux-Arts-style Manhasset is one of the most imposing apartment houses erected on the Upper West Side at the time when this neighborhood was the center of apartment-house construction in New York. The lower eight stories were erected in 1899–1901, but when the developer defaulted, the new owner commissioned Janes & Leo to add three stories, including the monumental mansard roof. Janes & Leo also designed the grand entrance pavilions. Construction was finally completed in 1905, and apartments in the two wings were rented to affluent families.

The Master Building (No. 360) by architect Harvey Wiley Corbett is one of New York City's
finest Art Deco high-rise buildings. Photo by Carl Forster.

E 76TH ST

396

387
E 75TH ST

E 74TH ST

395
E 73RD ST

395

384 385
E 72ND ST

386

E 71ST ST

383 382 381 380
378
E 70TH ST

379

29

377
376
E 69TH ST
375
373
E 68TH ST
374

29
E 67TH ST
372
393 394
371
391
E 66TH ST
392
390
370
389
E 65TH ST

369
29

E 64TH ST

315
388
E 63RD ST

30
E 62ND ST
368
30

E 61ST ST

FIFTH AV
367
E 60TH ST

365
29
GRAND
ARMY
PLZ
364
E 59TH ST
363
366

E 58TH ST
397

E 58TH ST

FIFTH AV

MADISON AV

PARK AV

LEXINGTON AV

THIRD AV

SECOND AV

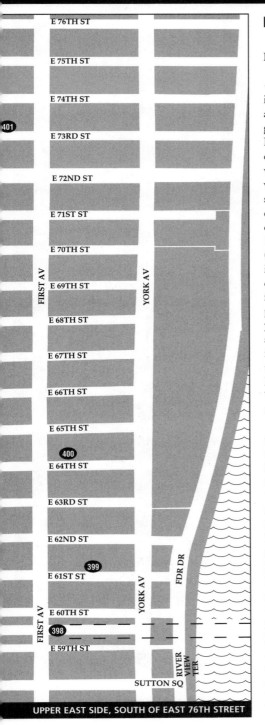

■ *WEST OF PARK AVENUE*

HISTORIC DISTRICT

㉙ Upper East Side Historic District. This district is composed largely of the mansions, town houses, apartment houses, private carriage houses and garages, and institutional buildings erected by or for New York City's wealthiest citizens in the first decades of the 20th century. The earliest wave of development in the district occurred in the 1870s when brownstone and brick row houses were constructed by speculative builders for sale to middle-class households; this movement was spurred by the opening of the Third Avenue elevated railway in 1878. A number of these houses are still extant (largely on Madison Avenue), but most were demolished or redesigned in the late 19th and early 20th centuries when a more affluent population transformed the streets north of 59th Street into the city's premier residential neighborhood. It was in these years that many members of America's financial and social elite commissioned substantial town houses from some of the nation's finest architects. The district contains major residential works by McKim, Mead & White; Carrère & Hastings; Warren & Wetmore; Ernest Flagg; Mott B. Schmidt; Delano & Aldrich; and other leading architects.

There are so many superb houses in the district that not all can be noted. The district contains major town houses in the Beaux-Arts style, such as the Ernesto and Edith Fabbri House (now Johnson O'-Connor Research Foundation, Haydel & Shepard, 1898–1900) at 11 East 62nd Street, the Marshall Orme and Caroline Astor Wilson House (now New India House, Warren & Wetmore, 1900–03) at 3 East 64th Street, and the William and Maria Schieffelin House (now the Lotos Club, Richard Howland Hunt, 1898–1900) at 5 East 66th Street. Important buildings in other styles include the Venetian Renaissance–inspired Joseph and Kate Pulitzer House (McKim, Mead & White, Stanford White, partner in charge, 1900–03) at 11 East 73rd Street; the Roman Renaissance–inspired William and Gladys Ziegler, Jr., House (now New York Academy of Sciences, Sterner & Wolfe, 1919–20) at 2 East 63rd Street; the Jacobean Thomas and Florence Lamont House (now Visiting Nurse Service of New York, Walker & Gillette, 1920–21) at 107 East 70th

Upper East Side Historic District streetscape (H.D. 29), 11 East 62nd Street. One of the many Beaux-Arts townhouses that characterize this district. Photo: Landmarks Preservation Commission collection.

Street; the Colonial Revival–style Park Avenue Houses (see below); and two early Modern works by architect William Lescaze—the Raymond and Mildred Kramer House (1934–35) at 32 East 74th Street and the Edward A. and Dorothy Norman House (1940–41) at 124 East 70th Street. In addition, the neighborhood's residents constructed fine new institutions: churches, such as the neo-Gothic Park Avenue Baptist (now Central Presbyterian, Henry C. Pelton and Allen & Collens, 1920–22) on Park Avenue and East 64th Street and Saint James Episcopal (Ralph Adams Cram, 1923–24) on Madison Avenue and East 71st Street; synagogues, such as the impressive Temple Emanu-El (Robert D. Kohn, Charles Butler, and Clarence S. Stein, associated architects with Mayers, Murray & Phillip, consultants, 1927–29) on Fifth Avenue and East 65th Street; and private clubs, such as the Metropolitan (see No. 367), the Knickerbocker (see No. 368), the Colonial Revival–style Colony (Delano & Aldrich, 1914–16) on Park Avenue and East 62nd Street, and the English Georgian–style Links (Cross & Cross, 1916–17) at 36 East 62nd Street. Some of the wealthiest families also built or purchased private carriage houses (or, after the invention of the automobile, private garages), most of them located on the blocks east of Park Avenue, with the largest and finest concentration on East 69th Street between Third and Lexington Avenues.

By the second decade of the 20th century, as the maintenance of private homes became increasingly expensive and inconvenient, luxurious apartment houses were erected in increasing numbers on Fifth and Park Avenues and other streets in the district. Some of these brick and limestone buildings were designed by the architects who were also responsible for town houses, such as Walter B. Chambers (563 Park Avenue, 1909–10) and York & Sawyer (660 Park Avenue, 1926–27), but most were the work of architects such as J. E. R. Carpenter, George & Edward Blum, and Rosario Candela, who specialized in luxury apartment house design and planning. At the same time the apartment houses were being constructed, Madison Avenue, which had originally been a residential street, was transformed into a fashionable commercial thoroughfare. The lower floors of old row houses were converted into elegant shops, and the upper stories became apartments or offices. Although most of the buildings in the district predate World War II, a few important Modern build-

ings were erected in the 1950s and 1960s for institutional use, notably Philip Johnson's Asia Society (now Russell Sage Foundation and Robert Sterling Clarke Foundation, 1958–60), an early International Style glass structure at 112 East 64th Street, and Marcel Breuer & Associate's expressionistic design for the Whitney Museum of American Art (1964–66) on Madison Avenue and East 75th Street.

INDIVIDUAL LANDMARKS

363 **Plaza Hotel,** 768 Fifth Avenue and 2 Central Park South (Henry J. Hardenbergh, 1905–07; addition, Warren & Wetmore, 1921). The Plaza's status as one of the world's great luxury hotels has been maintained since it opened in 1907. Located on a prominent site—overlooking Central Park (see No. 315), Grand Army Plaza (see No. 364), and Fifth Avenue—this elegant building was designed in a free adaptation of French Renaissance architecture, taking full advantage of the vistas provided by the surrounding open space. Warren & Wetmore's 58th Street addition is a simplified version of Hardenbergh's original design.

364 **Grand Army Plaza Scenic Landmark,** Fifth Avenue at 59th Street (Carrère & Hastings, 1913–16). A modest plaza was laid out on this site as part of the design of Central Park (see No. 315). Although Richard Morris Hunt had proposed a formal plaza for the site as early as 1863, it was the sculptor Karl Bitter's 1898 proposal for a Parisian-inspired plaza that was eventually acted upon. In 1912 Joseph Pulitzer bequeathed $50,000 for the erection of a fountain, and a competition was held for the design. In 1913 the project was awarded to Thomas Hastings, who closely followed Bitter's plan. Hastings laid out one of the most urbane public spaces in the city: a formal, axial, elliptical space divided in half by 59th Street. The plaza is the setting for Hastings's Pulitzer Fountain, which is crowned by Bitter's bronze statue of Pomona, goddess of abundance. North of 59th Street is Augustus Saint-Gaudens's masterful General Sherman Monument, set on a base by Charles McKim. This statue, which had been unveiled in 1903, was moved to align with the new fountain. The fountain was restored and the Sherman statue regilded in 1988–90.

365 Sidewalk Clock, 783 Fifth Avenue at East 59th Street (E. Howard Clock Company, 1927). Located in front of the Sherry-Netherland Hotel, this clock was probably installed around the time the hotel opened in 1927 (see No. 162).

366 Pepsi-Cola Building, now ABN-Amro Bank, 500 Park Avenue (Skidmore, Owings & Merrill, Gordon Bunshaft, partner in charge; Natalie de Blois, senior designer, 1958–60). The Pepsi-Cola Company expanded rapidly in the 1950s under the direction of Alfred N. Steele (who was married to Joan Crawford). The construction of an International Style headquarters on fashionable Park Avenue was part of Steele's efforts to promote the company. Design was directed by noted SOM partner Gordon Bunshaft, who had previously designed Lever House (see No. 258) only a few

blocks to the south. The senior designer, responsible for major work on this project, was Natalie de Blois, among the first women actively involved with corporate architecture. The small building, one of the most elegant of its era, is clad in what appears to be a weightless screen of gray-green glass and aluminum.

367 Metropolitan Club, 1–11 East 60th Street (McKim, Mead & White, Stanford White, partner in charge, 1891–94; addition, Ogden Codman, 1912). The 19th-century architecture critic Montgomery Schuyler described the Metropolitan Club as "the largest, most imposing, and most luxurious of the clubhouses of New York." This building, designed in the Italian Renaissance style, is a masterpiece of late 19th-century American architecture and a major example of the design skills of Stanford

Pepsi-Cola Building (No. 366). An elegant example of corporate identity through architecture. Photo by Carl Forster.

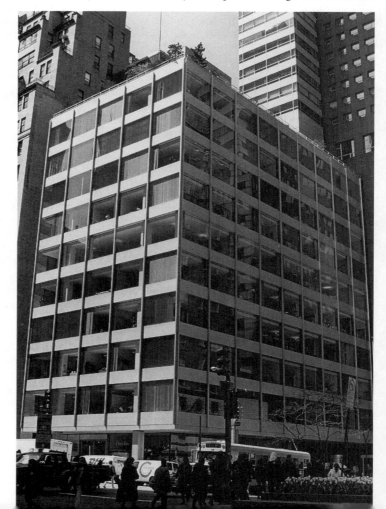

White. The Metropolitan Club was founded in 1891 by a group of prominent New Yorkers disgruntled by the rejection of several of their friends from membership in the Union Club. The marble exterior of the new club was specifically planned to be as unostentatious as possible, with rich detail limited to the interior. Since the club wished to have a lounge overlooking Central Park, the entrance is on the side, through elaborate iron gates and a court demarcated by a two-story wing with a shallow niche. The east side of the court is flanked by an earlier row house (11 East 60th Street) redesigned for the club in 1912. The facades were sensitively cleaned and waterproofed by Nicholson & Galloway in 1991.

368 **Knickerbocker Club,** 2 East 62nd Street (Delano & Aldrich, 1913–15). The exclusive Knickerbocker Club, founded in 1871 in reaction to the relaxation of admissions standards at other private men's clubs, commissioned this clubhouse in 1913. The architects Delano & Aldrich specialized in the design of refined adaptations of 18th- and early 19th-century American and English architecture, as can be seen in this elegant brick building and in several nearby landmark houses. A restoration of the club was completed in 1991.

369 **The Arsenal,** now the Administration Building of the New York City Department of Parks and Recreation, Central Park at East 64th Street (Martin E. Thompson, 1847–51). Built "to house and protect the arms of the state," the Arsenal was designed as a mock-medieval castle, complete with octagonal towers. After only a few years of use as an arsenal, the structure was converted into a police station; it later served as the first home of the American Museum of Natural History. In 1934 the building became the headquarters of New York City's Parks Department.

370 **Sara Delano Roosevelt and Franklin and Eleanor Roosevelt Houses,** now the Sara Delano Roosevelt Memorial House, 47–49 East 65th Street (Charles A. Platt, 1907–08). This double town house of unified English Georgian–inspired design has a single central entrance. Access to the individual units was gained through doors in the vestibule; Sara Roosevelt lived to the left, and her son and daughter-in-law lived to the right. It was in his fourth-floor bedroom in this house that

Franklin Roosevelt convalesced from polio in 1921–22. After Sara's death in 1941, the building was purchased for use by nearby Hunter College.

371 **45 East 66th Street Apartments** (Harde & Short, 1906–08). The firm Harde & Short was responsible for several of New York's most flamboyant apartment buildings in the early years of this century, including the Red House (see No. 345), Alwyn Court (see No. 304), and this impressive structure on

45 East 66th Street Apartments (No. 371). One of several flamboyant apartment buildings built by the architecture firm Harde & Short. Photo by Caroline Kane Levy.

the corner of East 66th Street and Madison Avenue. The building is faced in red brick with black mortar and has a profusion of French Gothic–inspired terra-cotta detail. As is characteristic of the architects' work, the street facades have large multipaned windows. The facades were magnificently restored by engineer Vincent Stramandinoli in 1987–88.

372 **R. Livingston and Eleanor T. Beeckman House,** now the Permanent Mission of Yugoslavia to the United Nations, 854 Fifth Avenue (Warren & Wetmore, 1903–05). This elegant limestone dwelling, one the few mansions still standing on Fifth Avenue, is in the style of the urban town houses erected in France during the reign of Louis XV. It was built for Robert Livingston Beeckman, a member of a prominent New York family, and was purchased by the Yugoslav government in 1946.

373 **J. William and Margaretta C. Clark House,** later Automation House, now Richard Feigen & Co., 49 East 68th Street (Trowbridge & Livingston, 1913–14). The socially well-connected architecture firm Trowbridge & Livingston designed this Colonial Revival house for the family of J. William Clark, heir to the Clark sewing thread fortune. Restored in 1991 by Buttrick, White & Burtis, the town house has elegant Federal-inspired detail, including a pair of arched openings on the ground floor and a variety of window lintels on the upper floors.

374 **Percy and Maud H. Pyne House,** now Center for Inter-American Relations, 680 Park Avenue (McKim, Mead & White, Charles F. McKim, partner in charge, 1906–12). Charles F. McKim designed this house for the financier and philanthropist Percy Pyne and his wife in 1906, but con-

680, 684, 686, and 690 Park Avenue (Nos. 374–377) are among the early mansions constructed on Park Avenue after the railroad tracks were covered. Photo by John Barrington Bayley.

struction did not begin until 1910, when the railroad tracks along Park Avenue were finally covered. One of the earliest town houses on Park Avenue, it set an 18th-century design precedent that was followed by the three succeeding houses on this block, erected between 1916 and 1926. In 1965 demolition began on this house and its two neighbors, the Filley and Sloane houses (see Nos. 375 and 376). In response to a public outcry, the Marquesa de Cuevas, a granddaughter of John D. Rockefeller, purchased the houses at the last minute and donated them to various organizations.

375 **Oliver D. and Mary Pyne Filley House,** now the Spanish Institute, 684 Park Avenue (McKim, Mead & White, 1925–26). The last of the four landmark town houses to be built on this block, this house was erected for the daughter and son-in-law of Percy and Maud Pyne—for whom McKim, Mead & White had designed the adjacent house (see No. 374) sixteen years earlier—on the site of the Pynes' garden.

376 **William and Frances Crocker Sloane House,** now the Italian Cultural Institute, 686 Park Avenue (Delano & Aldrich, 1916–19). Delano & Aldrich excelled at the design of Colonial Revival buildings, and this house, designed for the president of the prominent W. & J. Sloane furniture store, is a characteristic example. It is one of four stylistically related landmark houses on this block and one of three saved from demolition in 1965 (see No. 374).

377 **Henry P. and Kate T. Davison House,** now the Consulate General of Italy, 690 Park Avenue (Walker & Gillette, 1916–17). Henry P. Davison, one of the founders of Bankers Trust, commissioned this English Georgian–style brick house, the second of four related landmark buildings that create the unique blockfront of Park Avenue between East 68th and 69th Streets. The construction of these houses reflects the development of Park Avenue as a prestigious residential neighborhood following the covering of the avenue's railroad tracks around 1910. The building served as a residence until 1952, when it was converted into the Italian consulate.

378 **Gustav and Virginia Pagenstecher House,** also known as the 21 East 70th Street House, now Hirschl & Adler Galleries (William J. Rogers,

1918–19). The last of the five landmark town houses to be erected on the north side of East 70th Street, the Pagenstecher House is a limestone structure designed in an austere French neoclassical style. At the second floor a pair of tall round-arched windows is set in deep reveals.

379 **Dave Hennen and Alice Morris House,** also known as the 19 East 70th Street House, now the Knoedler Gallery (Thornton Chard, 1909–10). This especially austere early Italian Renaissance–inspired limestone town house, built on land previously owned by the wealthy landholder and philanthropist James Lenox, was erected for a client who would later become the U.S. ambassador to Belgium. The building now houses the illustrious Knoedler Gallery, which celebrated its 150th anniversary in 1996.

380 **Alvin W. and Angeline Krech House,** also known as the 17 East 70th Street House (Arthur C. Jackson, 1909–11). The Krech family's French neoclassical limestone town house lends a dignified character to the north side of East 70th Street. Alvin Krech was, according to his obituary, "one of the prominent figures in American finance and industry," serving as chairman of the Equitable Trust Company and as a railroad administrator.

381 **John Chandler and Corinne deBébian Moore House,** also known as the 15 East 70th Street House (Charles I. Berg, 1909–10). This house in the French neoclassical style is one of five adjacent landmarks erected on land that had been owned by James Lenox and the Lenox estate until 1907, when plots were sold to individuals who erected new town houses.

382 **11 East 70th Street House** (John H. Duncan, 1909–10). Of the five landmark town houses on this block, No. 11 was the only one built on speculation. The builder Cornelius Luyster, Jr., commissioned the dwelling from the well-known architect John H. Duncan, who designed a subdued residence in the French neoclassical style.

383 **Henry Clay and Adelaide Childs Frick House,** now the Frick Collection and Frick Art Reference Library, 1 East 70th Street and 10 East 71st Street (Carrère & Hastings, 1913–14; entrance pavilion and library, John Russell Pope, 1931–35; garden addition, Harry Van Dyke, John Barrington Bayley, and G. Frederick Poehler, 1977; garden, Russell Page). The palatial residence of the steel magnate Henry Clay Frick, built on the entire Fifth Avenue blockfront formerly occupied by the Lenox Library, was planned by Thomas Hastings as both a residence and a gallery for the display of Frick's great art collection. Modeled on 18th-century French sources, the house is placed on a terrace set back from Fifth Avenue and surrounded by a retaining wall, thus heightening the structure's formal monumentality. Following the death of Adelaide Frick in 1931, the house was enlarged and converted into a museum, which opened to the public in 1935. This conversion and the construction of the adjoining reference library on East 71st Street were undertaken by John Russell Pope several years before he designed the National Gallery in Washington.

384 **Oliver Gould and Mary Brewster Jennings House,** now Lycée Français de New-York, 7 East 72nd Street (Flagg & Chambers, 1898–99). The Jennings House and the neighboring Sloane House (see No. 385) are two of the finest Beaux-Arts residences in New York City; they lend a note of Parisian elegance to Manhattan's Upper East Side. Appropriately, both houses were designed by French-trained architects, and both are now owned by a French school. Built for a wealthy businessman and his family, the limestone-fronted Jennings House displays a rich surface texture, with vermiculated blocks on the ground floor and rusticated stonework above. The house is crowned by a particularly bold convex mansard with exuberant copper detail.

385 **Henry T. and Jessie Sloane House,** now Lycée Français de New-York, 9 East 72nd Street (Carrère & Hastings, 1894–96). Henry T. Sloane, son of the founder of the W. & J. Sloane furniture store, commissioned this luxuriant Beaux-Arts house from the French-trained architects Carrère & Hastings. Sloane and his wife lived here for only a short time before their scandalous divorce in 1898. After being briefly occupied by Joseph Pulitzer, the house was purchased by James Stillman, president of National City Bank. The house and its complementary neighbor, the Oliver Gould Jennings House (No. 384), are now occupied by the Lycée Français.

386 **Gertrude Rhinelander Waldo House,** now the Polo/Ralph Lauren Store, 867 Madison Avenue (Kimball & Thompson, 1895–98). Designed in the style of the early French Renaissance châteaux of the Loire Valley, this enormous limestone mansion was built by an eccentric society matron who never lived in the house. Rather, she resided across the street, and the house remained empty until 1920, when it was converted for commercial use. Ralph Lauren instituted a major rehabilitation of the property in 1984.

387 **Edward S. and Mary Stillman Harkness House,** now the Commonwealth Fund, 1 East 75th Street (Hale & Rogers, 1907–08). Built by the son of one of the six original partners in the Standard Oil Company, the Harkness House is an Italian Renaissance–inspired mansion faced entirely with marble. Following the death of Mary Harkness in 1950, the house became the headquarters of the Commonwealth Fund, a philanthropic foundation that Edward Harkness's mother had founded in 1918. The building is surrounded by a spectacular cast- and wrought-iron fence that has been restored.

■ *PARK AVENUE TO THIRD AVENUE*

388 **Cyril and Barbara Rutherford Hatch House,** 153 East 63rd Street (Frederick J. Sterner, 1917–19). Shortly after their marriage, the New York socialites Barbara Rutherford (daughter of Mrs. William K. Vanderbilt) and Cyril Hatch commissioned this handsome Mediterranean-inspired town house. Following the Hatches' divorce in 1920, the spacious house, which has an interior courtyard, was occupied by Charles Dillingham, owner of the Globe Theater (see No. 205) and one of the country's most prominent theatrical producers, and then by Charles L. Lawrance, a pioneer in aeronautical engineering. In 1940 the property was purchased by Louise Hovick, better known as the burlesque queen Gypsy Rose Lee. In 1985 it became the home of artist Jasper Johns.

389 **Church of Saint Vincent Ferrer (R.C.) Complex,** 869 Lexington Avenue and 141–151 East 65th Street (church, Bertram Goodhue, 1914–18; priory, William Schickel, 1880–81; Holy Name Society Building, Wilfred E. Anthony,

Gertrude Rhinelander Waldo House (No. 386). This enormous mansion was built in the style of early French Renaissance châteaux found in the Loire Valley. Photo: Landmarks Preservation Commission collection.

1930; school, Elliot L. Chisling-Ferrenz & Taylor, 1948). Shortly after completing Saint Thomas Church (see No. 259), Bertram Goodhue received the commission for this Roman Catholic church erected by the Dominican order. Goodhue's design uses academic Gothic forms in a free manner. The austere exterior is faced in Plymouth granite with white limestone carvings by Lee Lawrie that appear to grow organically from the massive stonework. Immediately south of the church is the older priory, a Victorian Gothic design that is one of the few surviving examples of the ecclesiastical

work of the architect William Schickel. In the 20th century, the church complex expanded along East 65th Street with the construction of the neo-Gothic Holy Name Society Building and Saint Vincent Ferrer School.

390 **131–135 East 66th Street Apartments** (Charles A. Platt and Simonson, Pollard & Steinam, 1905–06). This distinguished limestone-fronted building reflects the popular adaptation of the Italian Renaissance palazzo form to the New York apartment house. The cooperative was the first apartment house designed by the prestigious architect Charles A. Platt, who worked here in association with a firm that specialized in the design of buildings with double-height artists' studios and duplex living quarters. Platt himself moved into the building upon its completion.

391 **130–134 East 67th Street Apartments** (Rossiter & Wright, 1907). This building, on the corner of Lexington Avenue and East 67th Street, was designed as a pendant to the adjacent apartment house at 131–135 East 66th Street (see No. 390). Like its neighbor, the East 67th Street structure is a cooperative building, faced in limestone and designed in the Italian Renaissance style, and it also has double-height studios.

392 **Seventh Regiment Armory,** 643 Park Avenue (Charles W. Clinton, 1877–79). The socially prominent Seventh Regiment was formed in 1806 and in 1824 became the first regiment to adopt the term *National Guard.* In 1874 the city leased this Park Avenue site to the regiment, which raised the money to build a monumental new armory. Clinton, a Seventh Regiment veteran, designed the armory with a 187-by-290-foot drill shed and an administration building in the form of a medieval fortress. The building became a prototype for the later medieval-inspired armories that appeared in large numbers in New York (see Brooklyn No. 48 and Bronx No. 26) and throughout the country. The wealth and importance of the Seventh Regiment are evident in the decoration of the armory's **interiors,** notably the individual regiment rooms used by officers and for formal public occasions on the first floor and the second-floor company rooms. The finest rooms are the exotic Veterans' Room and the Library, extraordinary surviving Aesthetic Movement interiors executed by the Associated Artists (Louis Comfort Tiffany, Stanford White, and others). Other rooms were decorated by such leading American designers as Herter Brothers, Alexander Roux & Co., Pottier & Sty-

Seventh Regiment Armory (No. 392). The medieval style was copied by many other armories in New York and around the country. Photo by Carl Forster.

mus, Sydney V. Stratton, and Kimball & Cabus. The drill room, measuring 200 by 300 feet and 100 feet high, where the regiment practiced, is one of the largest unobstructed spaces in New York and the oldest balloon shed, or barrel-vaulted roof supported on visible arch trusses, in America.

393 **Mount Sinai Dispensary,** also known as the 149–151 East 67th Street Building, now the Kennedy Child Study Center (Buchman & Deisler and Brunner & Tryon, 1889–90). Mount Sinai Hospital, the oldest Jewish hospital in New York City, first opened a dispensary for the treatment of outpatients in 1875. As the demand for services grew, this Italian Renaissance–inspired structure, faced in brick, stone, and terra cotta, was erected to house both an enlarged dispensary and the hospital's nursing school. The design is the combined work of two prominent Jewish architecture firms.

394 **Park East Synagogue** (Congregation Zichron Ephraim), 163 East 67th Street (Schneider & Herter, 1889–90). Park East is a late manifestation of the use of Moorish forms in synagogue design (see Central Synagogue, No. 292). The congregation was organized in 1888 by Rabbi Bernard Drachman, who believed in the importance of adapting Orthodox practices and traditions to American customs. This conviction was a direct response to the increasing popularity of Reform Judaism, especially among the German Jews settling in substantial numbers on the Upper East Side in the late 19th century. This synagogue's architectural style was seen as a link between 19th-century Judaism and the flowering of Jewish culture in Moorish Spain. Restoration of the facade was undertaken in 1996 by Dan Peter Kopple & Associates, architects.

395 161–179 and 166–182 East 73rd Street Buildings (Nos. 161 and 163, Thomas Rae, 1896–97; Nos. 165 and 167, George L. Amoroux, 1903–04; No. 171, 1860; No. 173, Hobart H. Walker, 1893; No. 175, 1860; No. 177–179, Charles F. Hoppe, 1906; No. 166, Richard M. Hunt, 1883–84; No. 168, Charles W. Romeyn, 1899; No. 170, Frank Wennemer, 1890–91; No. 172–174, Frank Wennemer, 1889; No. 178, John H. Friend, 1902; No. 180, William Schickel & Co., 1890–91; No. 182, Andrew Spense Mayer, 1890). Beginning in the final decades of the 19th century, as the blocks

of the Upper East Side between Fifth and Park Avenues were being transformed into streets of mansions and town houses erected for New York's wealthiest citizens, many of the streets to the east were redeveloped with carriage houses. These carriage houses were erected in locations that were convenient to the large houses but sufficiently far away that the smells and noise of the stables did not mar the quality of life on the residential streets. In the years immediately preceding these developments, East 73rd Street between Lexington and Third Avenues was lined with modest row houses erected around 1860; two of these buildings, Nos. 171 and 175, have survived. In 1883 Richard Morris Hunt designed the first private carriage house on the street, a Romanesque Revival building at No. 166, built for Henry G. Marquand, for whom Hunt also designed a lavish mansion on Madison Avenue. The ten carriage houses that followed were erected either by individuals for their own use or by speculative builders who sold the structures to nearby residents. The most distinguished of these is No. 168, a neo-Flemish building complete with stepped gable and strapwork ornament designed for banker William Baylis. Since only the very wealthy could afford to maintain a private carriage house, most people who owned horses boarded them in commercial stables such as the five-story Romanesque Revival building at No. 182. In the early years of the 20th century, the majority of the carriage houses and stables were converted for automotive use. In this same period, commercial garages, such as the handsome building in the Beaux-Arts style at No. 177–179, began to appear in the neighborhood. By the 1920s, as the maintenance of a private garage became prohibitively expensive, most of the carriage houses were converted into private residences. At the same time, the two surviving row houses were rehabilitated, each by a prominent New York architect for his own residence—Erastus D. Litchfield at No. 171 and Francis L. Pell at No. 175.

396 **Saint Jean Baptiste Roman Catholic Church,** 1067–1071 Lexington Avenue (Nicholas Sirracino, 1910–13). Saint Jean Baptiste, built to serve a largely French-Canadian Roman Catholic congregation, is an impressive example of Italian Mannerist–inspired design. Of special note on this limestone-faced church are the Corinthian portico, paired towers, and dome. Construction was funded by the streetcar magnate Thomas Fortune Ryan, who, it is said, sought to replace a smaller building in which he had once been forced to stand during mass. The building was restored in 1995–96 by Hardy Holzman Pfeiffer, architects.

■ EAST OF THIRD AVENUE

HISTORIC DISTRICT

30 **Treadwell Farm Historic District.** Once part of the farm of Adam Treadwell, the older brother of Seabury Tredwell [sic], whose house (see Old Merchant's House, No. 125) is now a museum, this district was transformed by speculative builders into a neighborhood of modest row houses in 1868–76. Later in the 19th century, the neighborhood deteriorated, but it was rediscovered after World War I by affluent New Yorkers searching for housing convenient to the new Midtown commercial area. Between 1919 and 1922, almost every house in the district was altered; many of the facades were simplified by the removal of stoops and other projecting features. In 1930 Martin Hedmark designed the Swedish Baptist Church (now Trinity Baptist) at 250 East 61st Street in an unusual Scandinavian Modern style; the church features exceptional brickwork and ironwork.

INDIVIDUAL LANDMARKS

397 **311 and 313 East 58th Street Houses** (1856–57). These two vernacular houses with Italianate details are reminders of the simple dwellings that once dotted Midtown. Both houses are below sidewalk level as a result of the construction of a new approach to the Queensboro Bridge in 1930.

398 **Queensboro Bridge.** See Queens No. 4.

399 **Abigail Adams Smith Museum,** 421 East 61st Street (1799). In 1795 Colonel William S. Smith and his wife, Abigail, the daughter of John and Abigail Adams, established the estate of Mount Vernon along the East River. In 1798, before all the estate buildings were complete, the Smiths were forced to sell their property to William T. Robinson; it was Robinson who con-

structed the combined coach house and stable that is now the Abigail Adams Smith Museum. The building's conversion into a hotel in 1826 entailed substantial alterations to the interior and the construction of a veranda. The Colonial Dames of America purchased the property in 1924 and converted the hotel into a museum that has been open to the public since 1939.

400 **City and Suburban Homes Company, First Avenue Estate** (in part), 1168–1200 First Avenue, 401–423 East 64th Street, and 402–416 East 65th Street (James E. Ware, James E. Ware & Sons, and Philip H. Ohm, 1898–1915). The First Avenue Estate is the oldest extant project built by the City and Suburban Homes Company, a limited-dividend corporation dedicated to the construction of decent affordable housing for the working poor. The company was founded and supported by some of New York's most prominent citizens, who when investing in City and Suburban shares agreed to limit their return to 5 percent. City and Suburban's development projects were experimental housing; thus the various buildings have different plans and room arrangements. This complex was begun before the Avenue A Estate (see No. 438), but it was completed later. The light-colored brick buildings were designed by James E. Ware, an architect active in the design of housing for the working poor, and by City and Suburban's own architect, Philip H. Ohm. Since their completion, the model tenements have housed large numbers of working people in quality apartments of a sort not easily found in New York City by those with limited income.

401 **Bohemian National Hall (Národní Budova),** 321 East 73rd Street (William C. Frohne, 1895, 1897). In the late 19th century, Yorkville became a center for Czech and Slovak immigrants, and this social hall was erected to serve the community's needs. The ornate Renaissance-inspired building was planned as a general meeting hall for all Czech and Slovak organizations and included a restaurant, a bar, club rooms, bowling alleys, a shooting gallery, a ballroom/theater, and classrooms where children of immigrants were taught Czech language, history, and culture. Czech-born architect Jan Hird Pokorny has undertaken a restoration of the building.

139

E 92ND ST
E 91ST ST
E 90TH ST
E 89TH ST
E 88TH ST
E 87TH ST
E 86TH ST
E 85TH ST
E 84TH ST
E 83RD ST
E 82ND ST
E 81ST ST
E 80TH ST
E 79TH ST
E 78TH ST
E 77TH ST
E 76TH ST

FIRST AV
YORK AV
FDR DR
EAST END AV
YORK AV
FIRST AV

443
442
33
438
437

CHEROKEE PL
GRACIE SQ
GRACIE TER
EAST END AV
FDR DR

EAST RIVER

ROOSEVELT ISLAND

UPPER EAST SIDE, EAST 76TH STREET TO EAST 94TH STREET

■ WEST OF MADISON AVENUE

HISTORIC DISTRICTS

31 **Metropolitan Museum Historic District.** Located across Fifth Avenue from Central Park and the Metropolitan Museum of Art, this district traces the three main stages of residential development on the Upper East Side. Many modest row houses were built on speculation on the district's side streets in the 1870s and 1880s, especially after the Third Avenue Elevated began operation in 1878. Examples of these early houses are still evident in the district, notably at 22 and 26 East 78th Street, two Italianate houses (Silas M. Styles, 1871), and 4 East 78th Street, a Queen Anne–style house (Edward Kilpatrick, 1887–89). The area was then transformed into one of New York's most exclusive residential neighborhoods beginning in the 1890s, when the city's financial and social elite constructed mansions and town houses. Especially fine examples of these houses can be seen on the block bounded by East 78th and 79th Streets and Fifth and Madison Avenues, where the town houses designed by Warren & Wetmore; C. P. H. Gilbert; Ogden Codman; McKim, Mead & White; Horace Trumbauer; and other leading architects remain remarkably intact. In the second decade of the 20th century, such luxury apartment houses as 998 Fifth Avenue (see No. 404) began to replace the mansions. This development continued into the 1920s, when most of the restrained limestone and brick buildings on Fifth Avenue were erected and when the more progressive Art Deco apartment house, designed by Howells & Hood for *Daily News* publisher Joseph M. Patterson, was built in 1927–28 at 3 East 84th Street. The apartment building at 1001 Fifth Avenue, with an early postmodern facade, was designed by Philip Johnson and constructed in 1978–80.

32 **Carnegie Hill Historic District.** The history of building construction in Carnegie Hill (generally the area between East 86th and East 96th Streets and Fifth and Lexington Avenues) is quite complex, with overlapping phases of residential development. By the mid–19th century, this area had scattered houses, including a number of wooden dwellings, such as 120 and 122 East 92nd Street (see No. 430). With the opening of the elevated rail lines on

Third Avenue (1878) and Second Avenue (1880), speculative development of row houses for middle-class residents in the neo-Grec, Romanesque Revival, and Queen Anne styles began on the side streets and along Madison Avenue. There is a hierarchy to these houses, with the largest on the blocks between Fifth and Madison Avenues, close to Central Park, such as Cleverdon & Putzel's row of four-story houses at 5–25 East 94th Street (1892–94) and Thomas Graham's similar row at 6–14 East 92nd Street (1890–92); narrower, three-story houses between Madison and Park Avenues, including James E. Ware's row at 1285–1293 Madison Avenue (1889–90); and the smallest houses to the east of Park Avenue. The most notable ensemble is on East 95th Street between Park and Lexington Avenues, where four obscure architects—Frank Wennemer, Louis Entzer, Jr., Flemer & Koehler, and C. Abbott French & Co.—created one of the city's loveliest streets between 1887 and 1892. A second phase of development was inaugurated by Andrew Carnegie when he purchased the Fifth Avenue blockfront between East 90th and East 91st Streets in 1898 for the construction of a large mansion (see No. 412). In the first decades of the 20th century, other wealthy families moved to the area, building large houses or redesigning the older row houses. Many of the mansions are individual landmarks (see below), but others are not, including the English neoclassical William and Elsie Woodward House at 9 East 86th Street (now the Town Club, Delano & Aldrich, 1916–18); Henry and Annie Phipps' Italian Renaissance town house (now the Liederkranz Society, Grosvenor Atterbury, 1902–04) at 6 East 87th Street; Ogden Codman's French neoclassical house for Archer and Helen Huntington (now the National Academy of Design, 1913–15) at 1083 Fifth Avenue; and the four austere Colonial Revival town houses designed by Delano & Aldrich (1919–22) for R. Fulton Cutting's four children at 15 East 88th Street and 12–16 East 89th Street (now Saint David's School). At the same time that the mansions were being built, apartment houses planned for other wealthy families were beginning to rise in the area. Among the earliest were George & Edward Blum's white brick and terracotta Capitol at 12 East 87th Street (1910–11) and 1067 Fifth Avenue (1914–17), only the second luxury apartment house on Fifth Avenue, designed by C. P. H. Gilbert in an adaptation of the Francis I style that he favored for town-house designs. Major apartment-house construction occurred on Fifth and Park Avenues in the 1920s, including seven Fifth Avenue buildings by the noted designer of luxury apartments J. E. R. Carpenter. As wealthy families moved to Carnegie Hill, several society churches and schools also relocated to the area, notably the Church of the Heavenly Rest (Episcopal), which erected Mayers, Murray & Phillip's neo-Gothic church with facade sculpture by Lee Lawrie in 1927–29 on the corner of Fifth Avenue and East 90th Street; Brick Presbyterian, which commissioned a Colonial Revival church for a site on Park Avenue between East 91st and East 92nd Streets from York & Sawyer in 1937; the Spence School, which moved into a restrained Colonial Revival building (John Russell Pope, 1929) at 20 East 91st Street; and the Colonial Revival Nightingale-Bamford School (Delano & Aldrich, 1929), at 20–24 East 92nd Street. In the second decade of the 20th century, Madison Avenue lost some of its residential character, as the lower stories of row houses were converted into fashionable stores. After World War II some of the mansions were demolished and replaced by undistinguished apartment buildings, and many of the row houses and mansions were converted for school, museum, and other institutional uses. At this time the neighborhood also became home to Frank Lloyd Wright's Guggenheim Museum (see No. 407), one of the great buildings of the mid-20th century. Carnegie Hill now contains a lively mix of residential, commercial, and institutional buildings.

INDIVIDUAL LANDMARKS

402 **James B. and Nanaline Duke House,** now the New York University Institute of Fine Arts, 1 East 78th Street (Horace Trumbauer, 1909–12). This enormous freestanding house, modeled on the 18th-century Château Labottière in Bordeaux, is one of the most magnificent mansions in New York. Duke was born a poor boy in North Carolina and eventually rose to become a figure of unrivaled power in the American tobacco industry. Nanaline Duke and her daughter Doris gave the mansion to New York University in 1957, and it has been successfully adapted for use as the university's graduate school of art history.

403 **Payne and Helen Hay Whitney House,** now the Office of Cultural Services, Embassy of France, 972 Fifth Avenue (McKim, Mead & White, Stanford White, partner in charge, 1902–09). Financier Oliver H. Payne commissioned this house as a wedding gift for his nephew Payne Whitney and Whitney's bride, Helen Hay. The bowfront marble mansion is one of Stanford White's most successful Italian High Renaissance–inspired designs. The Republic of France acquired the building in 1952.

404 **998 Fifth Avenue Apartments** (McKim, Mead & White, William S. Richardson, partner in charge, 1910–12). This magnificent Italian Renais-

998 Fifth Avenue Apartments (No. 404). This early apartment house designed by McKim, Mead & White became the model for hundreds of other buildings later erected on the East Side. Photo by Carl Forster.

sance–inspired building, with street elevations clad entirely in limestone with yellow marble trim and a spectacular copper cornice, was the first luxury apartment house erected on Fifth Avenue north of 59th Street. The expansive simplex and duplex units appealed to an elite clientele, and the building was rapidly rented. In its form and detail, the building became the model for New York City apartment houses, with hundreds later erected on Fifth, Park, and other avenues.

405 **1009 Fifth Avenue House,** also known as the Benjamin N. and Sarah Duke House (Welch, Smith & Provot, 1899–1901). Soon after its completion, this Beaux-Arts town house, erected on speculation, was sold to Benjamin N. Duke, a director of the American Tobacco Company. In 1907 Benjamin's brother James purchased the house, where he lived until the completion of his own nearby mansion (see No. 402) in 1912. Until recently the house was occupied by other members of the Duke family. A superb restoration was completed in 1985.

406 **Metropolitan Museum of Art,** Fifth Avenue at East 82nd Street (major wings by Calvert Vaux and Jacob Wrey Mould, 1870–80; Thomas Weston with Arthur L. Tuckerman, associate, 1883–88; Arthur L. Tuckerman, 1890–94; Richard Morris Hunt, 1894–95; Richard Howland Hunt and George B. Post, 1895–1902; McKim, Mead & White, 1904–26; Kevin Roche John Dinkeloo Associates, 1967–90). In their original design for Central Park (see No. 315), Frederick Law Olmsted and Calvert Vaux sited the Metropolitan Museum of Art on a plot west of Fifth Avenue at 82nd Street. The original museum building, a High Victorian Gothic structure designed by Vaux and Jacob Wrey Mould (and now partially visible as the inner wall of the Lehman Wing), was built set back from Fifth Avenue, although Vaux planned for a larger museum facing the avenue. As the Metropolitan expanded its collections, a series of wings was added. The early wings, such as Weston and Tuckerman's south wing (now visible in the Petrie Sculpture Court), were built in the park; the focus changed, however, with the design of Richard Morris Hunt's Beaux-Arts central pavilion (completed by Richard Howland Hunt following his father's death in 1895) on Fifth Avenue. On the **interior** the vestibule, Great Hall, and stair-

way, designed by Richard Morris Hunt and constructed under the supervision of his son, with George B. Post as consulting architect, provide a fitting introduction to the expanded museum. Beginning in 1904 the Metropolitan undertook additions on Fifth Avenue designed by Charles F. McKim of the firm McKim, Mead & White that represent a simplified version of Hunt's design. Kevin Roche John Dinkeloo Associates was commissioned to prepare a master plan for the museum in 1967; the last of the firm's modern stone-and-glass wings was completed in 1990. Its American Wing, built at the northwest corner of the complex, incorporates the facade of the former Bank of New York (Martin E. Thompson, 1823–25), which was saved from destruction and moved to the museum in 1924.

407 **Solomon R. Guggenheim Museum,** 1071 Fifth Avenue (Frank Lloyd Wright, 1956–59). Established by Solomon R. Guggenheim as a repository of nonobjective (i.e., abstract) art, the Guggenheim Museum is housed in one of the most acclaimed buildings of the 20th century. The museum is the major New York City work of the American master Frank Lloyd Wright and is often considered to be the crowning achievement of his later career. The building's organic form, a reversed spiral, was intended as a reflection of the natural shapes to be found across the street in Central Park. The **interior,** with its vast open space and spiraling cantilevered ramp punctuated by exhibition alcoves, is among Wright's most spectacular. In the basement is a circular auditorium also designed by Wright. In 1989–92 an addition designed by Charles Gwathmey of Gwathmey Siegel & Associates was constructed, and Wright's building was restored.

408 **Grafton W. and Anne Minot House,** also known as the 11 East 90th Street House (A. Wallace McCrea, 1929). The present austere facade of this house was inspired by 18th-century French designs. It replaces the original Beaux-Arts front designed by Barney & Chapman and built in 1902–03 for William and Louise McAlpin. A. Wallace

Solomon R. Guggenheim Museum (No. 407). Many consider the Guggenheim Museum to be the crowning achievement of architect Frank Lloyd Wright's later career. Photo by Caroline Kane Levy.

McCrea specialized in this type of town-house modernization. The building is now part of the Cooper-Hewitt Museum complex (see No. 412).

409 **Emily Trevor House,** also known as the 15 East 90th Street House (Mott B. Schmidt, 1927–28). This red brick house, with its carefully detailed limestone portico and trim, is an essay in English 18th-century design. It was built for the sister of John B. Trevor, whose house is located on East 91st Street (see No. 416).

410 **17 East 90th Street House** (F. Burrall Hoffman, Jr., 1917–19). This handsome Colonial Revival brick house with an unusual street-level arcade was commissioned by Robert and Charlotte Fowler, who apparently never lived here, since the property was sold in 1919.

411 **1261 Madison Avenue Apartments** (Buchman & Fox, 1900–01). This elegant Beaux-Arts apartment house has a characteristic limestone facade with a mansard roof, iron balconies, and three-dimensional carved detail. Its construction in 1900 reflected a change in the character of the area now known as Carnegie Hill, as imposing new apartment houses intended for affluent residents joined the neighborhood's earlier tenements and row houses.

412 **Andrew and Louise Carnegie House,** now the Cooper-Hewitt National Design Museum, Smithsonian Institution, 2 East 91st Street (Babb, Cook & Willard, 1899–1903). After Andrew Carnegie purchased this large plot on a relatively undeveloped section of Fifth Avenue, he evicted a few squatters and demolished a riding academy and several tenements so that he could build what he envisioned as "the most modest, plainest and most roomy house in New York." The 64-room house synthesized "modest and plain" Georgian-inspired brickwork with Beaux-Arts ornament and incorporated the most advanced mechanical and structural systems of the day. Carnegie chose the site because it permitted him to lay out a large garden; the original landscape plan, probably by Schermerhorn & Foulks, is largely extant. In 1972 the mansion became the property of the Smithsonian Institution, which commissioned architect Hugh Hardy to convert the building into a museum of design. The

Carnegie site also includes the Colonial Revival **George L. McAlpin House** at 9 East 90th Street (George Keister, 1902–03), which became the home of Carnegie's daughter in 1920. The two houses were connected in 1996–97 and other changes made (including the skillful addition of a ramp for handicapped access to the front entrance) by James Stewart Polshek & Partners, architects.

413 **Otto and Addie Kahn House,** now the Convent of the Sacred Heart, 1 East 91st Street (J. Armstrong Stenhouse, with C. P. H. Gilbert, 1913–18). British architect J. Armstrong Stenhouse worked with C. P. H. Gilbert to create this magnificent limestone mansion, modeled on the 15th-century Palazzo della Cancelleria in Rome. The client, the banker Otto Kahn, was one of New York's most generous patrons of the arts; he twice aided in saving the Metropolitan Opera, backed many American theatrical organizations, and sponsored the American tours of such European institutions as Stanislavsky's Moscow Art Theater and Diaghilev's Ballet Russe. Since 1934 the house has served as the Convent of the Sacred Heart's prestigious school for girls. The facade was cleaned and restored in 1994 under the direction of Buttrick, White & Burtis, architects.

414 **James A. and Florence Sloane Burden House,** now the Convent of the Sacred Heart, 7 East 91st Street (Warren & Wetmore, 1902–05). William Sloane and his wife, Emily Vanderbilt Sloane, built this house and the neighboring Hammond House (see No. 415) for their daughters on land purchased from Andrew Carnegie, whose own house was across the street (see No. 412) and who acquired a significant amount of property in the neighborhood in order to regulate its development. Warren & Wetmore provided Florence Sloane and her husband, James A. Burden, Jr. (son of the founder of the Burden Ironworks), with a grand, limestone-clad Beaux-Arts mansion with facades fronting both the street and the drive set between the two houses.

415 **John Henry and Emily Vanderbilt Sloane Hammond House,** now Consulate General of the Russian Federation in New York, 9 East 91st Street (Carrère & Hastings, 1902–03). This grand house, designed in the 16th-century Roman manner, and

The Otto and Addie Kahn House (No. 413) was modeled on the 15th-century Palazzo della Cancelleria in Rome. Photo by Carl Forster.

its neighbor, the Burden House (see No. 414), were erected for the daughters and sons-in-law of William and Emily Vanderbilt Sloane on land that the Sloanes had purchased from Andrew Carnegie. The beautifully proportioned limestone-faced mansion is among the most impressive residential designs of Carrère & Hastings. The Hammonds' son John was a famous jazz promoter, and their daughter Alice married jazz great Benny Goodman. The house has been beautifully restored by the current owners.

416 **John B. and Caroline Trevor House,** now Consulate General of the Russian Federation in New York, 11 East 91st Street (Trowbridge & Livingston, 1909–11). The Trevor House is the smallest of the four landmark town houses on the north side of East 91st Street. The simple French neo-

classical residence is faced with limestone articulated by a trio of arched openings on the main floor and is crowned by a mansard roof.

417 **Felix and Frieda S. Warburg House,** now the Jewish Museum, 1109 Fifth Avenue (C. P. H. Gilbert, 1907–08). Gilbert, who specialized in mansions in the style of Francis I, designed similar limestone-faced, Loire Valley château–inspired houses for Isaac D. Fletcher (on Fifth Avenue at East 79th Street, now in the Metropolitan Museum Historic District), F. W. Woolworth (demolished), and the wealthy German-Jewish banker Felix Warburg. In 1944 Frieda Schiff Warburg donated the house as a permanent home for the Jewish Museum. An addition in 1990–93 by Kevin Roche that copied the design of the original house more than doubled the size of the museum.

■ *EAST OF MADISON AVENUE TO LEXINGTON AVENUE*

418 **John S. and Catharine C. Rogers House,** now the New York Society Library, 53 East 79th Street (Trowbridge & Livingston, 1916–17). The most impressive of the four landmark town houses on the north side of East 79th Street, the Rogers House was built for a wealthy lawyer and his wife. The limestone structure, whose design is based on Italian Renaissance prototypes, has housed the New York Society Library since 1937. Established in 1754, the library is the oldest in New York City and the fourth oldest in the country.

419 **John H. and Caroline Iselin House,** also known as the 59 East 79th Street House (Foster, Gade & Graham, 1908–09). The socially prominent lawyer John Iselin and his wife commissioned this house, which is stylistically unusual in its combination of Northern Renaissance and French classic forms, and lived here until 1919. It is one of four adjacent landmark town houses constructed early in the 20th century, when East 79th Street became an especially prestigious residential address.

420 **Thatcher and Frances Adams House,** also known as the 63 East 79th Street House (Adams & Warren, 1902–03). Lawyer Thatcher Adams commissioned this English neoclassical town house. The brick and limestone building is reminiscent of the urban dwellings of 18th-century London. The original mansard roof was replaced by the present fourth and fifth stories in 1945 (Elias K. Herzog, architect).

421 **George and Sarah Rives House,** also known as the 67–69 East 79th Street House, now the Greek Consulate General (Carrère & Hastings, 1907–08). Modeled on the late 17th-century town houses built on la place Vendôme in Paris, this house was commissioned by the lawyer, statesman (he was assistant secretary of state), and historian George Rives and his second wife, Sarah. Rives was an especially active supporter of New York's prominent institutions, serving on the boards of Columbia University (working closely with Seth Low in planning the Morningside Heights campus), the New York Public Library, and New York Hospital, as well as on the New York City Rapid Transit

Commission, which guided construction of the New York City subway. In 1962 the Greek architect Pierre Zannettos altered the top two floors of the house and added a sixth story.

422 **Lewis Spencer and Emily Coster Morris House,** also known as the 116 East 80th Street House (Cross & Cross, 1922–23). The design of this house, the earliest of four adjoining landmark town houses, was based closely on 18th-century London residences. Especially notable features are the house's projecting central pedimented pavilion and the brick arches of the ground-floor windows. Lewis Spencer Morris traced his ancestry back to one of New York's most prominent colonial families. He was a lawyer, trustee of the Cathedral of Saint John the Divine, and a trustee of the New York Society Library.

423 **George and Martha Whitney House,** also known as the 120 East 80th Street House (Cross & Cross, 1929–30). The town house commissioned by George Whitney is the most elaborate of the four adjacent landmark houses on East 80th Street, all modeled on 18th-century London residences. Whitney was an internationally famous financier who served for many years as the head of J. P. Morgan & Co.

424 **Clarence and Anne Douglass Dillon House,** also known as the 124 East 80th Street House (Mott B. Schmidt, 1930). This four-story brick house, the last of the four large landmark town houses in the English neoclassical style erected on the south side of East 80th Street between 1922 and 1930, was commissioned by the financier Clarence Dillon and his wife, Anne. Their son, C. Douglas Dillon, would later serve as secretary of the Treasury. The Dillon House and its neighbor, the Vincent Astor House (see No. 425), are fine examples of the sophisticated work of Mott B. Schmidt, a popular society architect who specialized in the design of residences in 18th-century revival styles.

425 **Vincent and Helen Astor House,** now the Junior League of the City of New York, 130 East 80th Street (Mott B. Schmidt, 1927–28). This grand limestone town house is closely modeled on Robert Adam's Society of Arts Building at the Adelphi in

London. The house was erected by the millionaire real-estate owner and social reformer Vincent Astor, head of the American branch of the Astor family. Astor's fortune was used to establish the Vincent Astor Fund, which has benefited major social welfare projects in New York City and assisted such institutions as the New York Public Library.

426 **Church of Saint Ignatius Loyola (R.C.),** 980 Park Avenue (Schickel & Ditmars, 1895–1900). As is characteristic of Jesuit churches, the design of Saint Ignatius Loyola is modeled on the Jesuits' Renaissance churches in Rome. The symmetrically massed, limestone-faced structure rests on the rough stone base (visible on East 84th Street) of an earlier church, dedicated to Saint Lawrence O'-Toole, that was begun in 1884 but never finished.

427 **Regis High School,** 55 East 84th Street (Maginnis & Walsh, 1913–17). Designed to harmonize in scale with the Church of Saint Ignatius Loyola (see No. 426), across the street, Regis is an imposing five-story Classical Revival limestone building with street fronts on both East 84th and East 85th Streets. The school was founded by the Jesuits in 1912 to provide a liberal arts education to gifted Catholic men. The building was designed by a Boston firm that specialized in work for Roman Catholic institutions.

428 **Lewis Gouverneur and Nathalie Bailey Morris House,** 100 East 85th Street (Ernest Flagg, 1913–14). Flagg designed this idiosyncratic house for a descendant of a prominent colonial New York family. The town house is massed in three sections, all oriented toward East 85th Street: the main residential block, a rear wing with a garage at street level, and a stairway wing recessed behind a narrow court. The design combines American colonial detail with the massing and the free use of 18th-century forms favored by the English architect Richard Norman Shaw.

429 **Reginald and Anna DeKoven House,** 1025 Park Avenue (John Russell Pope, 1911–12). The light-opera composer Reginald DeKoven and his wife, the writer Anna DeKoven, commissioned this brick and limestone mansion from John Russell Pope, an architect best known for his austere classical buildings. The house was built after work was completed on the roofing of the Park Avenue railroad tracks. It was designed in the Jacobean Revival style, providing evidence of Pope's wide-ranging architectural talents.

430 **120 and 122 East 92nd Street Houses** (No. 120, 1871; No. 122, attributed to Albro Howell, carpenter-builder, 1859). These two vernacular frame houses recall the period before intense urbanization altered the semirural character of the Upper East Side. Each of the houses has a deep front porch, heavy window surrounds, and a bracketed cornice—all typical features of Italianate design. No. 122 was built by Adam C. Flanagan, a custom-house officer. In 1871 Flanagan sold adjacent land to John C. and Catherine E. Rennert. John Rennert, a wine merchant, commissioned No. 120.

431 **George F. Baker, Jr., House Complex,** now (in part) the Russian Orthodox Church Outside of Russia, 67, 69, and 75 East 93rd Street (No. 75, main house, 1917–18; No. 71–73, ballroom wing, 1928; No. 69, 1928–29; No. 67, 1931—all by Delano & Aldrich). The main section of this complex, at the corner of Park Avenue and East 93rd Street, was commissioned by the financier Francis F. Palmer. Ten years after it was begun, the elegant town house was sold to George F. Baker, Jr., chairman of the First National Bank (now Citibank). Baker enlarged the house, first by the addition of a ballroom wing at No. 71–73 and garage (No. 69 East 93rd Street) and the creation of an open court to the west of the house, and later by the addition of 67 East 93rd Street, intended as a home for Baker's father, who died before the house was completed. The entire complex is a superb example of Delano & Aldrich's sophisticated handling of English and American 18th-century architectural forms. In 1958 the main house and its ballroom wing were converted for use as a Russian Orthodox church; a courtyard stairway was built to facilitate this new use.

432 **Virginia Graham Fair Vanderbilt House,** now Lycée Français de New-York, 60 East 93rd Street (John Russell Pope, 1930–31). Vanderbilt was a society leader, a racehorse breeder, the ex-wife of William K. Vanderbilt, and the daughter of Senator James Fair of Nevada, who made his fortune tapping the Comstock lode and the Big Bonanza mine. The limestone house resembles the great private *hôtels* built in Paris during the reign of Louis XV. Appropriately, it is one of several French-inspired residences in the neighborhood that now house a French school.

433 **William Goadby and Florence Baker Loew House,** now the Smithers Alcoholism Center of Roosevelt Hospital, 56 East 93rd Street (Walker & Gillette, 1930–31). The scale and austere geometry of this monumental limestone mansion are reminiscent of late 18th-century English design. William Loew was a wealthy stockbroker and socialite with the financial resources to build this mansion during the Depression. The site was acquired soon after Loew's brother-in-law George Baker purchased a house across the street (see No. 431). The facade of the Loew House, with its concave front and refined fluted arches, is among the most unusual in New York. Following Loew's death in 1955, the house was acquired by the theatrical producer Billy Rose, who lived here until his death in 1966.

434 **1321 Madison Avenue House** (James E. Ware, 1890–91). This Queen Anne house with a towering pyramidal roof was originally the end building of a row of five brownstone-fronted dwellings. The brick facade on East 93rd Street has a prominent entrance set above a massive stone stoop.

■ *EAST OF LEXINGTON AVENUE*

HISTORIC DISTRICT

33 **Henderson Place Historic District.** The twenty-four picturesque Queen Anne houses of this district survive from an enclave of thirty-two houses built in 1881 by the developer John C. Henderson for "persons of moderate means." The architecture firm Lamb & Rich composed each blockfront as a unit, emphasizing the ends with small towers and creating lively street fronts. Henderson erected these modest houses as an investment, and most remained in his family until the 20th century. As is characteristic of the Queen

William Goadby and Florence Baker Loew House (No. 433). The facade, with its concave front and refined fluted arches, is among the most unusual in New York City. Photo by Carl Forster.

Anne style, the massing is dynamic and the facades are richly textured. The houses are built of brick and rough stone and are enlivened by projecting bays and oriels, small-paned windows, and a roof line with an eccentric silhouette of gables, dormers, mansards, and stout towers with slate shingles.

INDIVIDUAL LANDMARKS

435 **157, 159, 161, 163, and 165 East 78th Street Houses** (1861). These five brick houses with Italianate elements survive from a row of eleven erected by the builder Henry Armstrong at the time when the Upper East Side was just beginning to attract middle-class home owners. Nos. 163 and 165 have been combined into a single residence.

436 **208, 210, 212, 214, 216, and 218 East 78th Street Houses** (1861–65). These six narrow Italianate row houses, surviving from a speculative venture that included the construction of fifteen identical red brick houses, were built just after the streets of Yorkville were opened in 1860. The unusual elliptically arched doors and windows on the facades lend a rhythmic pattern to the streetscape.

Henderson Place Historic District (H.D. 33). Some of the twenty-four picturesque Queen Anne houses in the district. Photo by Peter Choy.

437 **East River Houses,** later the Shively Sanitary Tenements, now the Cherokee Apartments, 507–523 East 77th Street and 508–522 East 78th Street (Henry Atterbury Smith, 1909–11). The East River Houses were erected in response to two of New York City's most pressing social problems—a serious tuberculosis epidemic and the need for affordable housing. These "model tenements," sponsored by Mrs. William K. Vanderbilt, were intended to house working people, especially families in which a member suffered from tuberculosis. The idea for this complex was conceived by Henry Shively, a physician and an expert on consumption. The tenements were designed by architect and housing reformer Henry Atterbury Smith, with large central courts approached by passageways with Guastavino tile vaults, triple-sash windows, balconies with Guastavino tiles on the undersides, and open stair towers—all features maximizing the amount of sunlight and fresh air that reached each apartment. The buildings underwent an extensive exterior restoration in 1989–90.

438 **City and Suburban Homes Company, Avenue A (York Avenue) Estate,** 1470–1492 York Avenue, 501–555 East 78th Street, and 502–540 East 79th Street (Harde & Short, Percy Griffin, and Philip H. Ohm, 1900–13). The Avenue A Estate was, at the time of its completion, the largest "model tenement" complex ever built. It was a project of the City and Suburban Homes Company (see No. 400). The various buildings have different plans and room arrangements. All are clad in brick and feature modest amounts of ornament. Of special interest are the Potter Memorial buildings at 516 and 520 East 79th Street, designed in an appropriate neo-Gothic style as a memorial to the Episcopal bishop Henry C. Potter. The complex also included the Junior League Hotel for Women at 541–555 East 78th Street, erected to provide inexpensive accommodation for single working women, which has been converted into apartments.

439 **New York Public Library, Yorkville Branch,** 222 East 79th Street (James Brown Lord, 1902).

East River Houses (No. 437). Erected at the turn of the century, these model tenements contained design features that maximized the amount of sunlight and fresh air that reached each apartment. Photo by Carl Forster.

Gracie Mansion (No. 442). The official home of the mayor of New York City, Gracie Mansion was built between 1799 and 1804. Photo by John Barrington Bayley.

The Palladian-inspired Yorkville Library was the first of numerous branch libraries throughout the city built as a result of Andrew Carnegie's 1901 gift to the New York Public Library (see No. 466). This facility had been planned many years earlier by the New York Free Circulating Library, which explains the choice of James Brown Lord as architect; Lord had previously designed the Free Circulating Library's Bloomingdale Branch (see No. 356).

440 **Sidewalk Clock** (see No. 162), 1501 Third Avenue at East 84th Street (E. Howard Clock Company, late 19th century). This unusual sidewalk clock, designed in the form of a giant pocket watch, was erected by the jeweler Adolph Stern in front of his shop at 1508 Third Avenue. When the business relocated across the street in the 1920s, the clock was also moved. At some point after 1900, arms were placed above the watch fob; these once supported the three golden balls that are a traditional symbol of a pawnbroker.

441 **Church of the Holy Trinity (Episcopal) Complex,** 316–332 East 88th Street (Barney &

Chapman; Saint Christopher House, 1896–97; addition, 1897–99). Serena Rhinelander donated this church as a memorial to her father and grandfather, building it on land that had been in her family since 1798. Holy Trinity was planned as a settlement church, run by the affluent Saint James Parish on Madison Avenue, to minister to the poorer residents of Yorkville. The complex—consisting of the church, the parsonage, and Saint Christopher House, all of French Gothic inspiration—is faced with rich tawny brick with extensive terra-cotta trim and is set around a landscaped court anchored by one of New York's most beautiful towers. The church was built three years after Barney & Chapman designed the similarly styled but simpler Grace Chapel (see No. 141). In 1995 the congregation began a long-term restoration project on the complex.

442 **Gracie Mansion,** East End Avenue at East 88th Street (attributed to Ezra Weeks, 1799–1804; Susan B. Wagner wing, Mott B. Schmidt, 1965–66). In 1793 the Scottish-born Archibald Gracie settled in New York, where he established a successful mercantile business. In 1798 Gracie began purchasing land on Horn's Hook, a small peninsula jutting into the East River at Hell Gate; here he erected a country house overlooking the river. The house was expanded in 1802–04. Gracie sold the property in 1823, and it had several owners before it was acquired by the city's Department of Parks in 1896. In 1924 the house was converted for use by the Museum of the City of New York. A major renovation was undertaken by the architect Aymar Embury II in 1934–36, following the museum's move to Fifth Avenue. Gracie Mansion became the official home of the mayor of New York City in 1942. Mott B. Schmidt added a wing to the house in 1965–66, and a major restoration by Charles A. Platt Partners was completed in 1985.

443 **Municipal Asphalt Plant,** now the Asphalt Green Recreational Center, Franklin Delano Roosevelt Drive at East 90th Street (Kahn & Jacobs, 1941–44). The asphalt plant, built adjacent to the FDR Drive, was the first successful American use of the parabolic arch form in reinforced concrete. The radical design was based on principles that

Robert Allan Jacobs had studied while working for Le Corbusier in France. The plant ceased operations in 1968 and, after standing vacant for several years, was converted into a recreation center by Hellmuth, Obata & Kassabaum and Pasanella + Klein.

444 **146, 148, 150, 152, 154, and 156 East 89th Street Houses** (Hubert, Pirsson & Co., 1886–87). Six houses survive from an original group of ten striking Queen Anne dwellings erected by William Rhinelander, whose family had acquired this land in 1812. The narrow houses were designed as a unit with richly textured facades, oriels, and a continuous mansard roof pierced by gables, dormers, and tall brick chimneys.

445 **160 East 92nd Street House** (attributed to Albro Howell, carpenter-builder, 1852–53). One of the few residences to survive from the period when Yorkville was a country village, this vernacular frame house is surprisingly well preserved. The original Corinthian columns of the front porch were replaced around 1930.

Municipal Asphalt Plant (No. 443). This building was the first successful American use of the parabolic arch form in reinforced concrete. Photo by Carl Forster.

HISTORIC DISTRICT

32 **Carnegie Hill Historic District.** See Map 15.

INDIVIDUAL LANDMARKS

446 **Squadron A Armory,** Madison Avenue between East 94th and 95th Streets (John R. Thomas, 1893–95). The picturesque battlemented Madison Avenue facade is all that remains of the monumental Squadron A Armory, which once occupied the entire block between Madison and Park Avenues. The facade was saved when the remainder of the building was demolished in 1966, and it now serves as the entrance to the playground of the Hunter College High School.

447 **Willard and Dorothy Whitney Straight House,** later the National Audubon Society, now

Saint Nicholas Russian Orthodox Cathedral (No. 452). The design of this church derives from 17th-century Baroque churches in Moscow. Photo : Landmarks Preservation Commission collection.

the International Center of Photography, 1130 Fifth Avenue (Delano & Aldrich, 1913–15). This imposing English Georgian Revival house was commissioned by Willard Straight, a diplomat and financier who specialized in Far Eastern affairs. While working as a Far East expert for J. P. Morgan & Co., Straight established India House (see No. 36), a club whose members were involved with foreign ventures. With the financial assistance of his wife, Straight later founded *The New Republic* and *Asia* magazines. The Straights' house is one of Delano & Aldrich's boldest designs. Of special note are the ocular windows on the upper story, which are modeled after similar windows on the wing of Hampton Court Palace in England designed by Christopher Wren.

448 **Mrs. Amory S. Carhart House,** now Lycée Français de New-York, 3 East 95th Street (Horace Trumbauer, 1913–16). Designed to resemble a Parisian town house from the era of Louis XVI, this elegant neoclassical limestone building is the work of the firm of the Philadelphia architect Horace Trumbauer. Mrs. Carhart commissioned the house a year after her husband's death but lived here only briefly before her own death in 1918.

449 **Ernesto and Edith Fabbri House,** now the House of the Redeemer, 7 East 95th Street (Egisto Fabbri and Grosvenor Atterbury, 1914–16). Edith Fabbri, great-granddaughter of Cornelius Vanderbilt, and her husband, the Italian count Ernesto Fabbri, built this L-shaped Italian Renaissance–inspired house; Count Fabbri's family's crest, an arm holding a hammer, is visible in the iron gate of the courtyard. Although Atterbury is the architect of record, it was apparently Count Fabbri's brother, the Italian architect and interior designer Egisto Fabbri, who was responsible for the actual design. In 1949 Mrs. Fabbri transferred the property to the House of the Redeemer, an Episcopal retreat center.

450 **Ogden Codman House,** now Manhattan Country School, 7 East 96th Street (Ogden Codman, 1912–13). Ogden Codman, one of the most important residential architects and interior designers of the early 20th century, designed this house for himself. Codman's advocacy of French design is reflected in the facade, which is modeled after that of an 18th-century Parisian town house.

451 **Lucy Dahlgren House,** later the Pierre Cartier House, 15 East 96th Street (Ogden Codman, 1915–16). The Dahlgren House is a companion to Codman's own house nearby (see No. 450). This French neoclassical town house was built for the socially prominent and enormously wealthy heiress Lucy Drexel Dahlgren, who apparently spent little time here. For many years the house was occupied by Pierre Cartier, founder of the jewelry firm that bears his name.

452 **Saint Nicholas Russian Orthodox Cathedral,** 15 East 97th Street (John Bergesen, 1901–02). Saint Nicholas, the diocesan seat of the Russian Orthodox Church in North America, was built with funds collected throughout the Russian empire. The design of the building, with its five onion domes, polychromatic detail, and *kokoshniki* (ogival pediments), derives from 17th-century Baroque churches in Moscow. The "Moscow Baroque" style was revived in Russia in the late 19th century and was adapted for this New York site by an architect of Russian descent.

453 **Museum of the City of New York,** 1220–1227 Fifth Avenue (Joseph J. Freedlander, 1928–30). Designed in a Georgian colonial style—an appropriate choice for this museum, which specializes in local history—this brick building with a white marble base and trim is massed around a courtyard that opens onto Fifth Avenue and Central Park. The museum was incorporated in 1923 and was originally housed in Gracie Mansion (see No. 442). The city donated the site between East 103rd and East 104th Streets, but funds for construction were privately subscribed.

454 **Public School 72,** later P.S. 107, now Julio de Burgos Cultural Center, 1674 Lexington Avenue (David I. Stagg, 1879–82; annex, C. B. J. Snyder, 1911–13). Erected to serve a rapidly growing im-

migrant community, this neo-Grec-style brick building with stone trim is one of the oldest intact school structures in Manhattan. The building, extending along the entire Lexington Avenue blockfront between East 105th and East 106th Streets, is massed with a series of interlocking cubic forms capped by towers. Architects Lee Barrero and Raymond Plumey restored the former school in 1994–95, converting it for use as a cultural center.

455 **Saint Cecilia's Church (R.C.) and Regina Angelorum,** 112–120 East 106th Street (church, Napoleon Le Brun & Sons, 1883–87; Regina Angelorum, Neville & Bagge, 1907). Founded in 1873, Saint Cecilia's was one of the first Roman Catholic churches in East Harlem. The facade of this Romanesque Revival structure reflects the architects' masterful use of brick and terra cotta, especially evident in the arched panel depicting Saint Cecilia, the patron saint of music, playing an organ. The Regina Angelorum was designed to complement the church; its facade unified two earlier buildings, which were then used as a convent and a home for working girls (now a convent and day nursery).

Public School 72 (No. 454), dating from 1879–82, is one of the oldest intact school structures in Manhattan. Photo by Carl Forster.

■ WEST OF FREDERICK DOUGLASS BOULEVARD

HISTORIC DISTRICTS

34 **Hamilton Heights Historic District.** Located immediately north of City College (see No. 463), the Hamilton Heights Historic District consists almost entirely of row houses and churches erected between 1886 and 1906. The land was once part of Alexander Hamilton's estate, and Hamilton's own house (see No. 464) is preserved at 287 Convent Avenue. The area remained undeveloped until the 1880s, when the new elevated rail line on Eighth Avenue brought it within commuting distance of downtown commercial districts. Speculative developers erected houses in a wide range of styles: Queen Anne–style residences lined Convent Avenue south of West 144th Street; spectacular rows of Northern Renaissance–inspired houses, among the finest in New York, were built at 452–466 and 453–467 West 144th Street (William E. Mowbray,

1886–90); flamboyant Beaux-Arts limestone houses with cartouches and other sculptural detail rose at 280–298 Convent Avenue (Henri Fouchaux, 1899–1902); and a brick, stone, and terra-cotta row was built at 413–423 West 144th Street (Thomas H. Dunn, 1898–1900) combining French and Venetian Renaissance forms in a particularly appealing composition. The one-block-long Hamilton Terrace, initially laid out as a private street, contains an intact array of handsome brick and stone houses erected between 1895 and 1902. Three important churches anchor the edges of the district; architecturally, the most notable is R. H. Robertson's Saint Luke's Episcopal Church (1892–95), on the corner of Convent Avenue and West 141st Street. The latest building erected in the district, the modern brick and concrete Ivey Delph Apartments at 19 Hamilton Terrace, was designed in 1948 by Vertner W. Tandy, the first African-American architect registered in New York State. The first residents of the district were middle-class white New Yorkers, both native and im-

Hamilton Heights Historic District (H.D. 34). Photo: Landmarks Preservation Commission collection.

migrant. In the 1920s and 1930s, prosperous African-American families began purchasing the houses in what came to be known as Sugar Hill.

35 **Audubon Terrace Historic District.** Established on the former estate of artist and naturalist John James Audubon, Audubon Terrace is one of America's first planned cultural centers. The complex was conceived by Archer M. Huntington, philanthropist, Spanish scholar, and heir to the Southern Pacific Railroad fortune. In 1904 Huntington founded the Hispanic Society of America and commissioned his cousin Charles P. Huntington to design a gallery and library for a site on West 155th Street, just west of Broadway. The Hispanic Society (1904–08) was soon joined by the American Numismatic Society (1907), the American Geographical Society (1911; now housing Boricua College), the Museum of the American Indian (1915–22), and the Spanish-language Church of Our Lady of Esperanza (1912), all designed by Huntington. Later the American Academy of Arts and Letters and the National Institute of Arts and Letters (now the American Academy and Institute of Arts and Letters) moved into a building designed by McKim, Mead & White (1921–23) at the west end of the complex; Cass Gilbert designed an auditorium and art gallery addition for these organizations in 1928. The buildings share a unified Italian Renaissance style and are set around a plaza embellished with sculpture by Archer Huntington's wife, Anna Hyatt Huntington.

INDIVIDUAL LANDMARKS

456 **Eglise de Notre Dame (R.C.) and Rectory,** Morningside Drive at West 114th Street (Daus & Otto, 1909–10, and Cross & Cross, 1914; rectory, Cross & Cross, 1913–14). Daus & Otto's imposing limestone sanctuary, dedicated to Our Lady of Lourdes, was completed in 1910. The austere nave, front elevation, and rectory, designed by Cross & Cross, were completed four years later. The formal French neoclassical design, with its pedimented Corinthian portico, was originally intended to be crowned by a dome (never executed) modeled on that of the Pantheon in Paris.

Columbia University, Broadway at West 116th Street. In 1891 Columbia College announced that it would abandon its campus on East 49th Street and Park Avenue and move to the site of New York Hospital's Bloomingdale Insane Asylum. In December 1893 Charles F. McKim was chosen as architect of the new campus; designs were completed in 1894. McKim's axial plan, inspired by Beaux-Arts concepts, called for a central library symmetrically flanked by twelve classroom buildings (nine were constructed), a chapel, and an assembly hall, with a student center and memorial hall to the rear of the library (not built), all to be constructed on a raised platform. Much of this plan was completed, and several of the structures are now designated landmarks. As Columbia grew, land to the south and east was purchased, and McKim, Mead & White enlarged the campus plan.

457 **Low Memorial Library** (McKim, Mead & White, Charles F. McKim, partner in charge, 1894–97). Charles F. McKim's monumental domed library is at the heart of the Columbia campus. The building is raised above its surroundings on a series of plazas linked by stairways and commands the main entrance to the academic precinct. Modeled on the Roman Pantheon, the library is the only building on the original Columbia campus that is faced entirely in stone. The library was a gift from Columbia president Seth Low as a memorial to his father, the China trader Abiel Abbot Low (see Schermerhorn Row Block, No. 40). The grandeur of the exterior is continued on the **interior,** which features a vestibule marked by a pair of Connemara marble columns and an enormous domed octagonal rotunda supported by four great piers and sixteen columns of green Vermont marble. The library's collections were moved to a new building in 1934, and Low became an administrative center.

458 **Saint Paul's Chapel** (Howells & Stokes, 1904–07). Saint Paul's Chapel was a gift of Olivia and Caroline Phelps Stokes, in memory of their parents, and was designed by their nephew, I. N. Phelps Stokes. The building, a magnificent example of Northern Italian Renaissance design, is faced with burned brick, limestone, and marble trim and is surmounted by a tile roof. The Guastavino tilework used for the dome, vaults, and other elements is visible on the ceiling of the exterior portico.

Low Memorial Library (No. 457). Modeled after the Roman Pantheon, this building is the centerpiece of the Columbia University campus. Photo by Peter Choy.

459 **Casa Italiana,** 1151–1161 Amsterdam Avenue (McKim, Mead & White, William M. Kendall, partner in charge, 1926–27). Casa Italiana is located on Columbia's east campus. William M. Kendall appropriately styled this building to copy a 15th-century Roman palazzo. Constructed to house the university's center for Italian studies, Casa Italiana was primarily funded by wealthy New Yorkers of Italian descent, notably members of the Paterno family, leading real-estate developers. The building was rehabilitated and the east facade finished in 1995–96 by Buttrick, White & Burtis, architects.

460 **Union Theological Seminary,** encompassing Brown Memorial Tower, James Tower, and James Memorial Chapel, Broadway at Reinhold Niebuhr Place (Allen & Collens, design, 1906–07; Brown Memorial Tower, base, 1908–10, tower, 1927–28; James Tower and James Memorial Chapel, 1908–10). This Protestant seminary, founded in 1836, followed Columbia University (see Nos. 457–459) to Morningside Heights, purchasing two entire square blocks along Broadway between West 120th (now Reinhold Niebuhr Place) and West 122nd Streets in 1905, primarily with money donated by D. Willis James, a businessman associated with the

161

Phelps-Dodge Company. A 1906 design competition was won by the Boston firm Allen & Collens with its English Perpendicular Gothic–style entry. The landmark elements—the two tall towers and the chapel that faces onto Claremont Avenue—are the three most significant features of the campus. The complex is constructed of Manhattan schist quarried on the site and is trimmed in limestone.

461 General Ulysses S. Grant Tomb, now the General Grant National Memorial, Riverside Drive at West 122nd Street (John H. Duncan, 1891–97). Dramatically sited near the north end of Riverside Park, the Grant Tomb is among the most impressive Classical Revival monuments of its period. Begun six years after Grant's death in 1885, the tomb was erected at a time of increasing nostalgia for the Civil War era with money contributed by some ninety thousand people, including many African-Americans. Duncan's granite monument was modeled on reconstructions of one of the great classical tombs, the Mausoleum of Halicarnassus. The **interior,** incorporating a domed rotunda and dominated by a central crypt with twin sarcophagi (for Grant and his wife), was inspired by the Invalides, the final resting place of Napoleon, in Paris. A major restoration was completed in 1997.

462 Croton Aqueduct, 135th Street Gatehouse, West 135th Street at Convent Avenue (Frederick S. Cook, 1884–90). The granite and brownstone gatehouse is the most impressive local architectural feature of the New Croton Aqueduct (See Nos. 501 and 502). The building was erected to regulate the flow of water from both the new and the old Croton Aqueduct systems. Although relatively small, the building looms like an impregnable medieval fortress, symbolically protecting New York's vital water supply.

463 City College, now City College North Campus, City University of New York, Convent Avenue between West 138th and West 140th Streets (George B. Post and George B. Post & Sons, 1897–1930). What is now City College was founded as the Free Academy in 1847 and was located on Lexington Avenue near East 23rd Street. Renamed in 1866, the college purchased the site of its uptown campus along Convent Avenue in

1897. After Post won the design competition for the new campus, this Collegiate Gothic complex was erected. All the early campus buildings and the three original gates—at West 138th, 139th, and 140th Streets—were constructed of dark Manhattan schist, excavated on the site, and trimmed with contrasting white terra cotta. The buildings are Main Building (now Shepard Hall), 1902–07; Townsend Harris Hall, 1903–06; Chemistry Building (now Baskerville Hall), 1903–08; Mechanic Arts Building (now Compton Hall), 1903–08; Gymnasium (now Wingate Hall), 1903–08; and Technology Building (now Goethals Hall), 1928–30;.

464 Alexander Hamilton House, the Grange, now the Hamilton Grange National Monument, 287 Convent Avenue (John McComb, Jr., 1801–02). Alexander Hamilton's country house, designed in the Federal style, once stood on a 35-acre tract. In 1889, when development threatened its survival, it was given to Saint Luke's Church and moved from Convent Avenue and West 143rd Street to its present site and altered. The house was briefly used as a church and later as a rectory. It was purchased by a preservation organization in 1924, opened to the public nine years later, and donated to the U.S. Department of the Interior in 1962. It is closed to visitors at present.

465 Our Lady of Lourdes Church (R.C.), 467 West 142nd Street (O'Reilly Brothers, 1902–04). This Roman Catholic church, one of the oddest buildings in New York, is composed of pieces salvaged from three of the city's most prominent mid-19th-century landmarks and combined by Cornelius O'Reilly. Much of the High Victorian Gothic facade is a reconstruction of Peter B. Wight's famous National Academy of Design (1863–65), which stood at Fourth Avenue and East 23rd Street. The rear of the church consists of the original east end of James Renwick, Jr.'s Saint Patrick's Cathedral (see No. 254), which was replaced in 1901–06 by a new lady chapel. The stone pedestals that flank the front steps come from the A. T. Stewart mansion (John Kellum, 1864–69), which stood at Fifth Avenue and 34th Street.

466 New York Public Library, Hamilton Grange Branch, 503 West 145th Street (McKim, Mead &

White, Charles F. McKim, partner in charge, 1905–06). In the late 19th century, most of the city's public libraries were run by private organizations such as the New York Free Circulating Library (see Nos. 133 and 356). The New York Public Library, founded in 1895, had an endowment devoted to its research facility and lacked the financial resources to organize and run a circulating system. Andrew Carnegie solved the problem in 1901 when he offered the New York Public Library a gift of more than $5 million for the construction of sixty-seven branch libraries. Because land in Manhattan was expensive, almost all the libraries were conceived as relatively narrow mid-block structures, and a general plan was devised that could easily be adapted to most of these sites. Each library was to be three stories tall, with a Renaissance-inspired limestone facade. This basic arrangement had been successfully employed by the Free Circulating Library (these libraries were merged into the public library system). This branch library, built as a result of the Carnegie donation, has a beautifully proportioned rusticated facade with alternating triangular and segmental window pediments and elegant iron railing, features adapted from the Palazzo Farnese in Rome.

467 **Joseph Loth & Company Silk Ribbon Mill,** 1828 Amsterdam Avenue (Hugo Kafka, 1885–86). One of New York's most exceptional industrial buildings is located on Amsterdam Avenue between West 150th and West 151st Streets. Established in New York in 1875, the Loth company manufactured Fair and Square brand silk ribbons. The factory, a rare example of an architect-designed mill structure, was planned in the shape of a K, which permitted the construction of interior spaces uninterrupted by columns and walls and maximized the light entering the building. The massing of the facades, with their brick facing and large windows separated by narrow pilasters, typifies mill design. The factory, which has undergone some additions and alterations, now houses a variety of industrial and commercial tenants.

468 **32nd Police Precinct Station House,** later the 30th Police Precinct Station House, 1854 Amsterdam Avenue (Nathaniel D. Bush, 1871). After Bush became the police department's first architect in 1862, he designed a series of Italianate and French Second Empire brick precinct houses. When the 32nd Police Precinct Station House was built, the area around it was still largely rural, and the structure, with its large mansard roof and handsome iron cresting, was among the most conspicuous in the vicinity. The building is currently used by Saint Luke's AME Church as the home of the African Methodist Episcopal Church Self Help Program.

469 **James A. and Ruth M. Bailey House,** now the M. Marshall Blake Funeral Home, 10 Saint Nicholas Place (Samuel B. Reed, 1886–88). The circus impresario James A. Bailey (of the famed Barnum & Bailey Circus) commissioned this flamboyant Romanesque Revival limestone house with Flemish gables. At the time of its construction, the house was located in a relatively undeveloped neighborhood and enjoyed fine views to the east, toward Long Island Sound.

470 **409 Edgecombe Avenue Apartments** (Schwartz & Gross, 1916–17). Originally called the Colonial Parkway Apartments, this 12-story building set on a ridge overlooking central Harlem was the most prestigious address for African-American New Yorkers from the 1930s through the 1950s. Among the prominent tenants were singer and actor Julius C. Bledsoe (creator of the role of Joe in *Show Boat* and the first to sing "Ole Man River"); poet and critic William Stanley Braithwaite; pioneering black physician May Edward Chinn; painter Aaron Douglas; scholar and sociologist W. E. B. Du Bois, a leading civil rights activist and founder of the NAACP; bandleader Jimmie Lunceford; lawyer Thurgood Marshall, who became the first African-American Supreme Court justice; civil rights leader and NAACP executive Walter White; and White's successor as head of the NAACP, Roy Wilkins.

471 **Chapel of the Intercession (Episcopal),** now the Church of the Intercession Complex, Broadway at West 155th Street (Bertram Goodhue of the firm Cram, Goodhue & Ferguson, 1910–14). The Church of the Intercession, a chapel of Trinity Church until 1976, is a remarkable complex of English Gothic inspiration, consisting of the main church, with its gabled front and tall tower, and a full cloister, vicarage, vestry, and parish house to the rear. Intercession has been called the quintessential Goodhue church, and was the architect's own favorite; he is, in fact, buried in the north transept.

472 **Macomb's Dam Bridge and 155th Street Viaduct,** spanning the Harlem River between West 155th Street and Saint Nicholas Place, Manhattan, and Jerome Avenue and East 162nd Street, the Bronx (Alfred Pancoast Boller, consulting engineer, 1890–95). Known until 1902 as Central Bridge, this is the oldest metal truss swing bridge and the third-oldest bridge in the city. The ensemble consists of a swing bridge over the Harlem River with an intricate latticework of steel crowned with four finials; stone end piers capped by shelter houses; a camelback span over the railroad tracks in the Bronx; the long 155th Street steel viaduct with tall stairways in Manhattan; and a shorter steel approach road in the Bronx.

■ *FREDERICK DOUGLASS BOULEVARD EAST TO LENOX AVENUE*

HISTORIC DISTRICT

36 **Saint Nicholas Historic District.** This district is an outstanding example of late 19th-century urban design in New York City. The four blockfronts, each a unified streetscape, were conceived by the developer David H. King, Jr., in 1891, "on such a large scale," he wrote, "and with such ample resources as to 'Create a Neighborhood' independent of surrounding influences." King was a builder who had previously worked on many important local projects and was familiar with the city's leading architects. He hired three distinguished architectural firms to design the 146 row houses and three apartment buildings. James Brown Lord designed the red brick and brownstone Georgian-inspired row on the south side of West 138th Street; Bruce Price was responsible for the yellow brick Colonial Revival houses with white limestone and terra-cotta trim on the north side of West 138th Street and the south side of West 139th Street; and McKim, Mead & White partner Stanford White designed the elegant Italian Renaissance–inspired row in dark mottled brick with brownstone and terra-cotta trim on the north side of West 139th Street. The houses were

equipped with up-to-date amenities and handsome woodwork and other details demanded by middle-class families. Service alleys, an extremely rare feature in New York City, run behind each row. Few houses were sold, and in 1895, during an economic depression, the mortgagor, the Equitable Life Assurance Company, foreclosed on almost all the properties. Equitable retained most of the buildings until 1919–20, when they were sold to African-Americans. Many became rooming houses, but others were home to prominent members of New York's black community, including, on West 138th Street, surgeon Louis T. Wright (No. 218), composer Will Marion Cook (No. 221), singer and songwriter Eubie Blake (No. 236), and Harry Pace (No. 257), the founder of the Black Swan Record Company, a pioneer in recording African-American singers and musicians; and, on West 139th Street, architect Vertner Tandy (No. 221), musician W. C. Handy (No. 232), bandleader Fletcher Henderson (No. 228), and boxer Harry Wills (No. 245). During the 1920s these houses became known as Striver's Row, a reference to the aspirations of many of the black residents who had recently moved into the area.

INDIVIDUAL LANDMARKS

473 **Wadleigh High School for Girls,** now Wadleigh School, 215 West 114th Street and 226–250 West 115th Street (C. B. J. Snyder, 1901–02). The construction of Wadleigh High School, a result of the increasing demand for advanced education for girls at the turn of the century, is named for Lydia F. Wadleigh, an early proponent of women's education. This was the first high school erected in New York City specifically for girls. The French Renaissance–style structure, with its picturesque dormers and tall tower, is one of the finest and most innovative designs of Superintendent of School Buildings C. B. J. Snyder. The seriously deteriorated building was restored in the early 1990s under the auspices of the New York City School Construction Authority.

474 **New York Public Library, 115th Street Branch,** 203 West 115th Street (McKim, Mead & White, Charles F. McKim, partner in charge, 1907–09). The 115th Street Branch Public Library was built as part of Andrew Carnegie's public library system (see No. 466). Many of the finest library buildings erected as a result of Carnegie's donation were designed by Charles F. McKim of the firm McKim, Mead & White. Among the finest of McKim's branch libraries is this building on West 115th Street. The emphatic rustication on the facade is reminiscent of that on the Palazzo Strozzi in Florence. A flamboyant shield bearing the seal of New York is balanced by a pair of putti above the central window on the ground floor.

475 **Regent Theater,** now First Corinthian Baptist Church, 1910 Adam Clayton Powell, Jr., Boulevard (Thomas W. Lamb, 1912–13). One of the first elaborately designed movie theaters in America, the Regent represents the transition of movie theaters from undistinguished nickelodeons to luxurious palaces. The facade, clad almost entirely in glazed, polychromatic terra cotta, is a fanciful version of a Venetian palazzo, meant to catch the attention of passersby. The Regent is an early work by theater specialist Thomas W. Lamb, who designed many of the finest theaters in America (see Nos. 224, 226, and 294). The theater was sold in 1964 to the First Corinthian Baptist Church, an African-American congregation established in Harlem in 1939.

476 **Graham Court Apartments,** 1923–1937 Adam Clayton Powell, Jr., Boulevard (Clinton & Russell, 1899–1901). Commissioned by William Waldorf Astor, whose family had owned this site in Harlem since the 1860s, Graham Court is one of the grandest courtyard apartment houses in New York and became the prototype for the Apthorp Apartments (see No. 335). The building, designed in the Italian Renaissance style, offers evidence of Harlem's early development as an affluent urban neighborhood.

477 **Washington Apartments,** 2034–2040 Adam Clayton Powell, Jr., Boulevard (Mortimer C. Merritt, 1883–84). The Queen Anne–style Washington Apartments, faced in red brick with terra-cotta trim and crowned by a pediment, is one of the oldest apartment houses in New York City and the earliest in Harlem planned specifically to house middle-class families. The construction of this building reflects the increasing popularity of Harlem as a residential community following the

opening of elevated rail lines through northern Manhattan in the late 1870s.

478 **Saint Paul's German Evangelical Lutheran Church,** now Greater Metropolitan Baptist Church, 147 West 123rd Street (Schneider & Herter, 1897–98). This neo-Gothic-style church, designed by German immigrant architects, was erected late in the 19th century as the German community in the Mount Morris area increased in size and wealth. The street facade of the building is Vermont marble. Saint Paul's remained in this building until 1939, long after most white church congregations had left Harlem. For forty-five years, beginning in 1940, this was home to the 12th Church of Christ, Scientist. In 1978 the Greater Metropolitan Baptist Church split from the Metropolitan Baptist Church (see No. 481), and in 1985 it purchased the West 123rd Street building.

479 **Hotel Theresa,** now Theresa Towers, 2090 Adam Clayton Powell, Jr., Boulevard (George & Edward Blum, 1912–13). The Hotel Theresa is one of the most prominent buildings in Harlem, a major work of the architectural firm George & Edward Blum and a key landmark in the cultural history of Harlem as an African-American community. Erected as Harlem's most prestigious hotel, the Theresa's white brick and terra-cotta facades are adorned with the distinctive geometric ornament favored by the Blums. The Theresa remained a segregated establishment until 1940 when the discriminatory policy was dropped and it rapidly became what *Ebony* called the "Waldorf of Harlem," hosting black celebrities and the social events of Harlem's African-American community. The hotel also contained the offices of A. Philip Randolph's March on Washington Movement and Malcolm X's Organization of Afro-American Unity. The Theresa is now an office building.

480 **Apollo Theater,** originally Hurtig & Seamon's New (Burlesque) Theater, 253 West 125th Street (George Keister, 1913–14). The Apollo became famous in the 1930s when the theater began to feature black entertainers. Today it is world renowned as a stage for African-American performing artists. In recognition of the Apollo's importance in the history of American entertainment and, more specifically, its central role in the pre-

165

sentation of major African-American performers, both the exterior and the neoclassical **interior** of the theater have been designated as landmarks.

481 **Metropolitan Baptist Church,** originally the New York Presbyterian Church, 151 West 128th Street (John R. Thomas, 1884–85; additions, Richard R. Davis, 1889–90). Although built in

two sections, this church reads as a single, unified structure. John R. Thomas was responsible for the chapel and lecture room on West 128th Street, while the main sanctuary on Adam Clayton Powell, Jr., Boulevard is attributed to the Harlem architect Richard R. Davis (who may have used Thomas's unexecuted design). The unusual building combines Romanesque-inspired massing and

Apollo Theater (No. 480). The historic and world-renowned venue for African-American performing talent. Photo by Carl Forster.

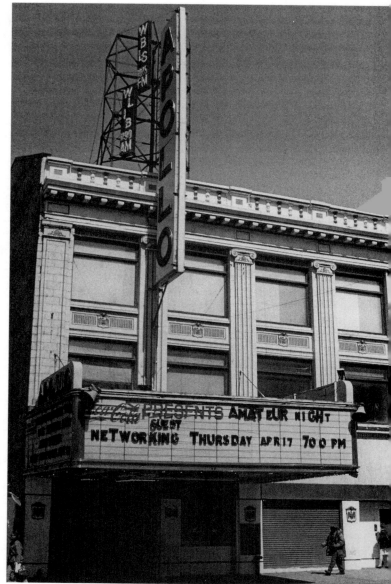

rough-textured stonework with such Gothic features as pointed arches and flying buttresses. In 1918 the building was sold to the Metropolitan Baptist Church, a reflection of the changing character of Harlem as it developed into America's most important African-American community. Metropolitan was one of the first black congregations established in Harlem and remains one of the most prestigious churches in the community.

482 **Saint Philip's Episcopal Church,** 214 West 134th Street (Tandy & Foster, 1910–11). This is the home of New York's oldest African-American Episcopal church congregation, established in 1818. Saint Philip's followed the city's black population north from Lower Manhattan to Mulberry Street, to West 25th Street, and finally to Harlem, where two of America's first African-American architects, Vertner Tandy and George W. Foster, Jr., designed a handsome neo-Gothic–style church building of Roman brick and terra cotta. Saint Philip's was an active supporter of the migration of New York's black community to Harlem, not only building an impressive new church but also purchasing apartment buildings that were rented to black households.

483 **New York Public Library, Schomburg Center for Research in Black Culture,** originally 135th Street Branch, 103 West 135th Street (McKim, Mead & White, Charles F. McKim, partner in charge, 1903–05). The 135th Street Branch was one of the first new libraries completed with money from the Carnegie grant (see No. 466). The building's design is loosely based on Michele Sanmicheli's Palazzo Canossa in Verona. Early in the 1920s, in response to changes in the surrounding Harlem neighborhood, the branch librarian Ernestine Rose began compiling a small collection of black literature and history books; in 1925 the branch was renamed the 135th Street Branch Division of Negro Literature. A year later the famed Schomburg Collection—a treasure trove of material on black culture and history, amassed by Arthur Schomburg—was purchased for the library. The facility was renamed for Schomburg in 1972, and eight years later a new building to house the research collection was completed on an adjacent site. The original building was restored in 1990 and is used by the Schomburg Center for exhibitions.

484 **Mother African Methodist Episcopal Zion Church,** 140 West 137th Street (George W. Foster, Jr., 1923–25). Mother A.M.E. Zion is the oldest African-American church congregation in New York and, as its name connotes, the "mother" church of the A.M.E. Zion denomination. The congregation relocated to Harlem in 1914 and eleven years later moved into this neo-Gothic stone church. George W. Foster, Jr., was one of the first black architects in America and one of the first two African-American architects registered in the state of New Jersey. Mother A.M.E. Zion has a long history of social activism in the black community and continues to be one of the most dynamic congregations in Harlem.

485 **Abyssinian Baptist Church and Community House,** 132 West 138th Street (Charles W. Bolton & Son, 1922–23). The second-oldest African-American church in New York City, Abyssinian is famous for its prominent ministers, notably Adam Clayton Powell, Sr., and his son Adam Clayton Powell, Jr., who became the first black congressman from New York City. Organized in 1808 by black worshipers who withdrew from the First Baptist Church, the congregation took a name associated with ancient Ethiopia. The neo-Gothic church complex was designed by a Philadelphia firm that specialized in church design.

486 **Dunbar Apartments,** West 149th Street to West 150th Street between Frederick Douglass and Adam Clayton Powell, Jr., Boulevards (Andrew J. Thomas, 1926–28). The Dunbar was the first major nonprofit cooperative apartment complex built specifically for African-Americans. Financed by John D. Rockefeller, Jr., the Dunbar consists of six five- and six-story walk-up buildings set around a landscaped central courtyard. Named for the poet Paul Laurence Dunbar, the cooperative (now rental buildings) attracted many of the most prominent members of the Harlem community, including W. E. B. Du Bois, A. Philip Randolph, Paul Robeson, and Bill ("Bojangles") Robinson.

487 **Harlem River Houses,** West 151st to West 153rd Streets, Macombs Place to Harlem River Drive (Archibald Manning Brown, chief architect, 1936–37). Harlem River Houses was one of the first two federally funded housing projects in New York City. Built in 1936 as "a recognition in brick and mortar of the special and urgent needs of Harlem," the project was an attempt to provide high-quality housing for African-American working people. The four- and five-story buildings of the nine-acre complex are set around large open areas that are landscaped with walkways as wide as streets, recreation sites, and lawns. The human scale, generous open space, and careful detailing of the project set a standard for public housing that has rarely been matched. Among the architects of Harlem River Houses was John Louis Wilson, Jr., one of the first African-American architects registered in New York State.

◼ *EAST OF LENOX AVENUE*

HISTORIC DISTRICT

⟨37⟩ Mount Morris Park Historic District. The streets of this district are lined with substantial masonry row houses interspersed with institutional buildings of exceptional quality, all reflecting Harlem's development as an affluent residential community following the extension of transit lines into the area around 1880. Initial construction in

the neighborhood was closely linked to Mount Morris Park (renamed Marcus Garvey Park in 1973 in honor of one of the first black nationalist leaders) and wide, tree-lined Lenox Avenue. Almost every street in the district contains fine examples of row houses in the neo-Grec, Romanesque Revival, and neo-Renaissance styles, designed primarily by architects who specialized in the creation of speculative row houses. In addition, the affluent Protestant and German-Jewish residents of the neighborhood in the late 19th and early 20th centuries commissioned major institutional buildings. These include the masterful Holy Trinity Episcopal Church (now Saint Martin's Episcopal Church; see No. 491); the picturesque Lenox Avenue Unitarian Church (now Bethel Gospel Tabernacle; Charles Atwood, 1889–91); the Gothic Revival Reformed Low Dutch Church (now Ephesus Seventh Day Adventist Church; John R. Thomas, 1885–87), with its soaring tower; the imposing Classical Revival Temple Israel (now Mount Olivet Baptist Church; Arnold W. Brunner, 1906–07); and the Queen Anne–style Harlem Club (now Bethelite Community Church; Lamb & Rich, 1888–89), all on Lenox Avenue, and the eccentric Harlem Presbyterian Church (now Mount Morris Ascension Presbyterian Church;

Harlem River Houses (No. 487). The human scale, generous open space, and careful detailing of one of the first two federally funded housing projects in New York City set a standard for public housing that has rarely been matched. Photo by Carl Forster.

Thomas H. Poole, 1905–06) on Mount Morris Park West. The evolving character of the area's population affected all these buildings. The Unitarian Church became an Orthodox synagogue in 1919 at a time when the area had a large immigrant Jewish population. In 1920, as Harlem was increasingly becoming the center of New York's black community, church congregations composed of African-Americans and Caribbean immigrants began to acquire these institutional buildings. Over the years many of the row houses were converted into rooming houses, while others remained single-family homes. Restoration work within the district has returned many buildings to their original character.

INDIVIDUAL LANDMARKS

488 New York Public Library, Aguilar Branch, 174 East 110th Street (Herts & Tallant, 1904–05). The Aguilar Free Library Society was founded in 1886 to serve the expanding population of Jewish immigrants and was named for Grace Aguilar, a popular early 19th-century English writer of Sephardic Jewish descent. The East Harlem branch was the society's fourth library. A building designed by Herts & Tallant was erected in 1898–99 and then totally redesigned and enlarged a few years later, after the Aguilar branches were incorporated into the New York Public Library system (see No. 466). The unusual Classical Revival facade consists of a grid of iron and glass framed by a pair of colossal limestone Ionic pilasters and a massive entablature. The building was renovated in 1993–96 (Gruzen Samton, architect).

489 Harlem Courthouse, 170 East 121st Street (Thom & Wilson, 1891–93). One of the most impressive buildings in East Harlem, the former Harlem Courthouse is an idiosyncratic Romanesque Revival brick structure with an octagonal tower and a four-faced clock. The building was erected to house the New York City Police Court and District Court, but since the reorganization of the court system in 1962, several other city agencies have used the building.

490 Watch Tower, Marcus Garvey Park (Julius Kroehl, 1855). Rising from a rocky outcropping

in what was originally known as Mount Morris Park, this three-tiered cast-iron structure, with its spiral staircase and octagonal lookout, is the only surviving fire tower in New York City. Use of the tower was discontinued in 1878, after the installation of fire alarm boxes.

491 Saint Martin's Episcopal Church Complex, originally Holy Trinity Episcopal Church, Rectory, and Parish House, 230 Lenox Avenue (William A. Potter, 1887–89). Known as Saint Martin's Episcopal Church since 1928, this prominent Harlem church is generally considered the finest Romanesque Revival religious complex in the city. The church and its related buildings have massive rough-hewn granite walls pierced by large rectangular and round-arched windows trimmed with brown sandstone. The complex was compactly planned; the parish house faces Lenox Avenue, and the sanctuary, with its tall square bell tower, and rectory are to the rear.

492 Mount Morris Bank Building, 81–85 East 125th Street (Lamb & Rich, 1883–84, enlarged 1889–90). This prominently sited Romanesque Revival–style building on the corner of Park Avenue and East 125th Street is one of the most impressive structures in Harlem. Built of brick and red sandstone, the building originally housed a bank and six apartments. Lamb & Rich created a boldly scaled structure with massive arched entries, picturesque oriels, and exceptional terracotta detail. The same architecture firm designed the 1889–90 expansion of the building along Park Avenue. The Mount Morris Bank became a branch of the Corn Exchange Bank in 1913 and then merged with Chemical Bank in 1954. The building has been vacant since the late 1970s.

493 Langston Hughes House, 20 East 127th Street (Alexander Wilson, 1869). Langston Hughes, one of the leading figures of the Harlem Renaissance, lived on the top floor of this Italianate brownstone from 1947 until his death in 1967. Hughes wrote many works while residing on East 127th Street, including his humorous pieces documenting the life of the common man in Harlem (as represented by Jess B. Semple) and a series of books exploring aspects of African-American culture.

494 Saint Andrew's Church (Episcopal), 2067 Fifth Avenue (Henry M. Congdon, 1872–73; enlargement, 1889–90). Saint Andrew's is one of the finest Victorian Gothic churches in New York City and one of the few 19th-century Protestant churches in Harlem that are still occupied by the original congregation. Henry Congdon designed Saint Andrew's for a site on East 127th Street between Park and Lexington Avenues, but by the late 1880s the congregation had outgrown the building. Congdon was rehired to dismantle the structure and supervise its reconstruction and enlargement on this more prestigious site at the corner of Fifth Avenue and East 127th Street.

495 17 East 128th Street House (c. 1864). In the mid-19th century, northern Manhattan was dotted with hundreds of wooden houses, few of which survive. This French Second Empire example is one of a handful of buildings still standing that relate to Harlem's early history as a rural village. The house is remarkably well preserved; it retains its original stoop, decorated porch, double doors, shutters, and multicolored slate roof.

496 12 West 129th Street House (c. 1863; alterations and additions: Edward Gustaveson, builder, 1882–83; Asbury Baker, 1896; c. 1920s). In the mid-19th century, modest suburban houses such as this residence were erected in increasing numbers in the village of Harlem. The house was originally a 2½-story structure erected around 1863. In 1882 piano merchant John Simpson, Jr., leased the property and commissioned additions, including the complex Moorish-inspired porch with its perforated detail cut by scroll saws. In 1896 an order of Franciscan Sisters moved in, added a full third story, and, in the 1920s, stuccoed the facade. The building has been undergoing restoration.

497 Astor Row, 8–62 West 130th Street (Charles Buek, 1880–83). The twenty-eight houses of Astor Row were erected in three campaigns on land owned by William Astor. The coherent blockfront of brick houses with wooden porches is unique in New York City. Nos. 8–22 were built in freestanding pairs, while the remaining twenty houses are linked at their rear sections. Most of the houses in the row have been rehabilitated and their porches restored as part of an ongoing project undertaken with private and public funding (Roberta Washington, architect).

498 369th Regiment Armory, 2360 Fifth Avenue (drill shed, Tachau & Vought, 1921–24; administration building, Van Wart & Wein, 1930–33). One of the last New York City armories to be constructed, the 369th Regiment was built in two campaigns. The massive administration building is unusual in its combination of the medieval motifs common to armory design and Art Deco features. The armory is the home of the renowned African-American regiment known as the Harlem Hell Fighters.

Astor Row (No. 497). The coherent blockfront of brick houses with wooden porches is unique in New York City. Photo by Carl Forster.

HISTORIC DISTRICT

38 **Jumel Terrace Historic District.** This small historic district consists largely of row houses erected adjacent to the Roger Morris House (see No. 500) after the former Morris estate was sold in 1882 by the heirs of Mme. Eliza Jumel. In that year the estate's carriage drive (now Sylvan Terrace) was built up with twenty two-story wooden houses (Albert Robinson, Jr., 1882–83) that were initially rented to working-class civil servants and laborers. Restored in 1979–81, these houses are among the few surviving examples of the frame dwellings once common in northern Manhattan. The remainder of the district contains Queen Anne, Romanesque Revival, and neo-Renaissance row houses erected between 1890 and 1902.

INDIVIDUAL LANDMARKS

499 **555 Edgecombe Avenue Apartments** (Schwartz & Gross, 1914–16). When this building, known as the Roger Morris, was completed in 1916, the apartments were leased to white tenants. In 1939–40, as the population of the surrounding area was changing, the tenants of 555 became exclusively African-American, soon including jazz great Count Basie, actor/producer Canada Lee, social psychologist Kenneth Clark, and actor/singer Paul Robeson and his wife, Eslanda, an anthropologist and author.

500 **Roger and Mary Philipse Morris House, Mount Morris,** also known as the Morris-Jumel Mansion, West 160th Street at Edgecombe Avenue

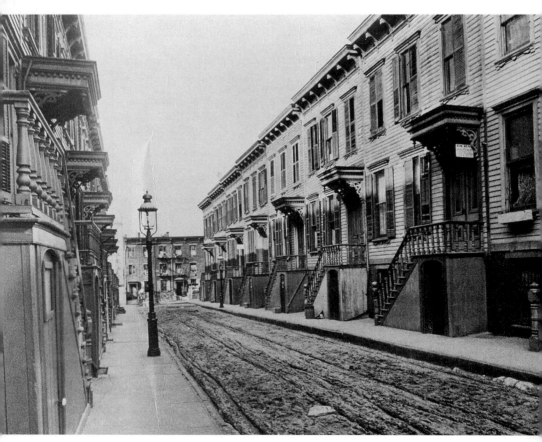

Jumel Terrace Historic District (H.D. 38). View of Sylvan Terrace about 1900. The houses were built in 1882. Photo: Landmarks Preservation Commission collection.

(1765; remodeling, c. 1810). Mount Morris was built as a summer villa by the British military officer Roger Morris and his American-born wife, Mary Philipse Morris. The house is an early example of the use of Palladian forms in North America; the double-height portico with a triangular pediment was an especially innovative feature in 1765. Historically, the house is famed for having served as General George Washington's headquarters for more than a month in 1776. Later used by the British, the house was confiscated at the end of the war. In 1810 Stephen Jumel, a wealthy French immigrant merchant, purchased the property and moved in with his wife (formerly his mistress), Eliza Bowen. The Jumels undertook some remodeling, including the addition of the handsome entrance in the Federal style. The house was purchased by New York City in 1903 and converted into a museum; operations were handed over to a women's group known as the Washington Headquarters Association. The mansion contains some of the finest Georgian **interiors** in America, including what is generally believed to be the country's first octagonal room.

Croton Aqueduct System. On July 4, 1842, amid great fanfare, the Croton Aqueduct was inaugurated, providing New Yorkers with pure water brought from the Croton Reservoir in northern Westchester County. Water was piped from the reservoir to the Harlem River, where it passed over the High Bridge (a temporary pipe served the system until the bridge was completed in 1848) and ran down Tenth Avenue to a receiving reservoir at West 79th Street (a site now in Central Park) and finally to the famous Egyptian Revival distributing reservoir on Fifth Avenue at West 42nd Street (the site of the New York Public Library). As the city grew, the water system expanded. In 1872 the High Bridge Water Tower was constructed as part of a northern Manhattan reservoir. By the 1870s it was clear that the original Croton system could not meet New York City's water needs, and the New Croton Aqueduct was proposed. Work on the new aqueduct, begun in 1883, included the construction of a major gatehouse at West 135th Street (see No. 462). After the turn of the century, New York City's water system expanded dramatically with the construction of the Catskill and Delaware water systems. The New York City buildings erected for the Croton system are no longer in active use.

Roger and Mary Philipse Morris House, Mount Morris (Morris-Jumel Mansion) (No. 500). This villa is an early example of the use of Palladian forms in North America. Photo by John Barrington Bayley.

501 **High Bridge Water Tower,** High Bridge Park (John B. Jervis, 1866–72). This 200-foot-high granite water tower was erected with a 47,000-gallon tank that provided gravity pressure for Manhattan's water supply, a necessity by the early 1870s as the use of flush toilets increased. Water was pumped into the tank from an adjacent reservoir, which was replaced by a swimming pool in 1934. Fifteen years later the tower was removed from service. In 1989–90 the stonework was cleaned and restored, and the cupola, which had burned, was reconstructed (William Hall Partnership, architect).

502 **High Bridge,** spanning the Harlem River between West 170th Street, the Bronx, and High Bridge Park, Manhattan (John B. Jervis, 1838–48; addition, 1860; replacement of central piers, 1923). Upon its completion, High Bridge was hailed as a feat of engineering. The stone arches of the bridge were modeled after such ancient Roman aqueducts as the Pont du Gard in southern France. The aqueduct on the bridge carried Croton water from the Bronx to Manhattan via two 36-inch mains. In 1860 a 90-inch main was installed atop the earlier two, and the walls of the bridge were raised. In 1923 the Navy removed the central piers and replaced them with a steel arch to improve navigation on the Harlem River.

503 **Washington Bridge**, spanning the Harlem River between West 181st Street, Manhattan, and University Avenue, the Bronx (Charles C. Schneider and Wilhelm Hildenbrand, 1886–89; modifications, Union Bridge Company, William J. McAlpine, Theodore Cooper, and DeLemos & Cordes, with Edward H. Kendall, consulting architect; reconstruction, 1989–93). The Washington Bridge is an important monument of 19th-century American engineering; its complex design and construction history includes the contributions of many engineers and architects. The bridge consists of arcaded masonry approaches leading to a pair of steel arches supported by masonry piers. The bridge was the first major link between Manhattan and the Bronx. A reconstruction of the roadway was undertaken in the late 1980s.

504 **Jeffrey's Hook Lighthouse**, also known as the Little Red Lighthouse, Fort Washington Park (1880; reconstruction, 1921). Erected in Sandy Hook, New Jersey, in 1880, this small conical iron lighthouse was moved to Jeffrey's Hook on Manhattan's Hudson River shore in 1921. The lighthouse, located beneath the George Washington Bridge, is best known as the subject of the children's book *The Little Red Lighthouse and the Great Gray Bridge,* written by Hildegarde Swift and published in 1942. Threatened with demolition after being taken out of service in 1951, the lighthouse was saved after an outcry from children led to its acquisition by New York City's Parks Department.

505 **Fort Tryon Park Scenic Landmark** (Olmsted Brothers, 1930–35). Fort Tryon Park is an outstanding example of the work of Olmsted Brothers, the successor firm to the one founded by Frederick Law Olmsted. The park occupies a portion of the site of the Revolutionary War Battle of Washington Heights; after the war the land was parceled into

several country estates. John D. Rockefeller, Jr., began buying the estates in 1917 with the intention of creating a park. In 1935 he presented Fort Tryon Park to the city. The park contains varied landscape features, among them a magnificent heather garden, and takes full advantage of its spectacular setting overlooking the Hudson River and the Palisades. In addition to the parkland, Rockefeller purchased a collection of medieval art, housed at the time in a nearby building, and donated it to the Metropolitan Museum of Art. The museum built the Cloisters, located within the park, for display of the collection (see No. 506).

506 **The Cloisters**, Fort Tryon Park (Charles Collens of Allen, Collens & Willis, 1934–39). The Cloisters, located in the midst of Fort Tryon Park (see No. 505), was designed by the Boston architect Charles Collens to house a portion of the Metropolitan Museum of Art's medieval art collection and to incorporate fragments from various cloisters and other medieval buildings that had been collected by the sculptor George Gray Barnard and purchased for the museum by John D. Rockefeller, Jr. The building, designed to resemble a French Romanesque abbey, has a tall tower that is an important focal point in the Fort Tryon Park landscape.

507 **Dyckman House**, Broadway at West 204th Street (c. 1785; restoration, Alexander M. Welch, 1915–16). The only farmhouse in the Dutch Colonial style surviving in Manhattan, the Dyckman House is constructed of fieldstone, brick, and wood and contains the gambrel roof, spring eaves, and porch typical of rural Dutch Colonial–style buildings. The house replaced an earlier building erected by the Dyckmans that was burned in the Revolutionary War. In 1915 when the house was threatened with demolition, two Dyckman sisters initiated a restoration project (under the architectural direction of the husband of one of the women) and presented the house to the city.

508 **University Heights Bridge.** See Bronx No. 22.

The Cloisters (No. 506). Besides housing a portion of the Metropolitan Museum of Art's medieval art collection, the Cloisters incorporates parts of cloisters and other medieval buildings from Europe. Photo by John Barrington Bayley.

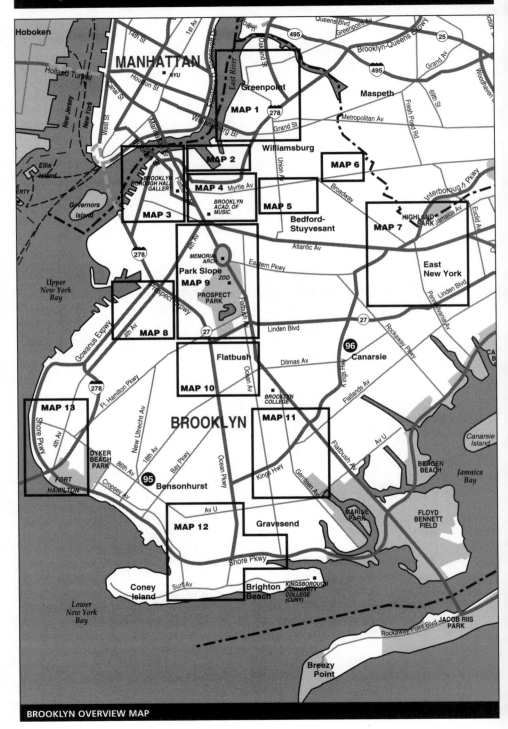

Hoboken

MANHATTAN

NYU

Holland Turnpke

New Jersey
New York

Ellis
Island

ERTY

Governors
Island

Upper
New York
Bay

14th St

1st Av

Houston St

Canal St

West St

Manhattan Br

BROOKLYN
BOROUGH HALL
GALLERY

MAP 3

278

Queens Blvd

Greenpoint

Grand St

MAP 1

278

Williamsburg Br

MAP 2

MAP 4   Myrtle Av

BROOKLYN
ACAD. OF
MUSIC

495

Oakland St

Greenpoint Av

Brooklyn-Queens Pkwy

Maspeth

Metropolitan Av

Williamsburg

Union Av

495

MAP 6

Grand Av

69th St

Fresh Pond Rd

25

Grand Av

Woodhaven

Interborough Pkwy

MAP 5

Broadway

Bedford-
Stuyvesant

Euclid Av

HIGHLAND
PARK Jamaica Av

MAP 7

278

4th Av

MEMORIAL
ARCH

Park Slope
MAP 9   ZOO

PROSPECT
PARK

Prospect Expwy

MAP 8

4th Av

27

Atlantic Av

Eastern Pkwy

Flatbush Av

Linden Blvd

East
New York

Linden Blvd

Pennsylvania Av

Gowanus Expwy

278

Ft. Hamilton Pkwy

New Utrecht Av

MAP 13

Shore Pkwy

4th Av

DYKER
BEACH
PARK

FORT
HAMILTON

86th Av

Cropsey Av

95

Bensonhurst

18th Av

Bay Pkwy

Flatbush
MAP 10

Ocean Av

MAP 11

Ocean Pkwy

Kings Hwy

Ditmas Av

BROOKLYN
COLLEGE

Av U

Kings Hwy

Gerritsen Av

27

Ditmas Av

Rockaway Pkwy

96   Canarsie

Flatlands Av

Flatbush Av

BERGEN
BEACH

MARINE
PARK

Canarsie
Island

CA
B

Jamaica
Bay

FLOYD
BENNETT
FIELD

MAP 12

Av U

Surf Av

Gravesend

Shore Pkwy

Coney
Island

Lower
New York
Bay

Brighton
Beach

KINGSBOROUGH
COMMUNITY
COLLEGE
(CUNY)

Rockaway Point Blvd   JACOB RIIS
PARK

Breezy
Point

176

HISTORIC DISTRICT

◆ **Greenpoint Historic District.** Unlike Brooklyn's other 19th-century residential historic districts, Greenpoint was not settled primarily by people who commuted to Manhattan. Rather, development in Greenpoint was closely linked to the prosperity of

the nearby industrial waterfront. The district contains a wide variety of buildings, reflecting the varied income levels of the local residents. Houses range from early examples of flats to modest frame dwellings to impressive masonry row houses. Construction boomed in the 1860s and early 1870s, and it was during these decades that some of the district's finest houses were erected. Among them are a large number of Italianate brick row houses with cast-iron window lintels and door hoods that were probably cast in local Greenpoint foundries. The houses at 128–132 Noble Street and 114–124 Kent Street (1867–68) are particulary notable. Also within the district are some of the most impressive ecclesiastical buildings in eastern Brooklyn, reflecting the importance of religious life to Greenpoint's residents. Among the major churches are the English Gothic–inspired Episcopal Church of the Ascension (Henry Dudley, 1865–66) and the High Victorian Gothic Reformed Church of Greenpoint (now Saint Elias Greek Rite Roman Catholic Church, William B. Ditmars, 1869–70; Sunday School, W. Wheeler Smith, 1879), both on Kent Street. Also of interest are the German Gothic–inspired Saint John's Evangelical Lutheran Church (Theobald Engelhardt, 1891–92) on Milton Street and the Early Romanesque Revival First Baptist Church of Greenpoint (now Union Baptist Church, 1863–65) on Noble Street. Most prominent is Saint Anthony of Padua Roman Catholic Church (1875) on Manhattan Avenue, the most distinguished of Brooklyn resident Patrick C. Keely's many local Gothic Revival churches.

INDIVIDUAL LANDMARKS

❶ **New England Congregational Church,** now Light of the World Church, 179 South 9th Street (Thomas Little, 1852–53). In the 19th century, numerous rural New Englanders settled in Brooklyn and built new Congregational churches. The former New England Congregational Church is one of these and is a rare example of an Italianate brownstone church building. The design and scale of the church, which occupies a midblock site, help to integrate the building into the surrounding urban fabric.

❷ **Williamsburgh Savings Bank,** now Republic National Bank, 175 Broadway (George B. Post, 1870–75; additions, Helmle, Huberty & Hudswell, 1905, and Helmle & Huberty, 1925). With its monumental arched entrance portico and towering dome, this early work by George B. Post is one of the first conscious expressions of the Italian Renaissance style erected in America. Post's design

anticipates the explosion of interest in Renaissance and classical architecture that culminated in the World's Columbian Exposition of 1893. The Williamsburgh Savings Bank was founded in 1851 to serve the rapidly growing independent city of Williamsburgh. This building was the bank's third home and served as its headquarters until its new tower (see No. 40) was completed in 1929. The vast **interior,** with its open plan, marble pilasters, and decorative iron grilles, contains one of the rare surviving examples of a post–Civil War ornamental scheme. This was designed by architect Peter B. Wight, with extraordinary neo-Grec and neo-Renaissance polychromatic stencil decoration in the cast-iron dome. Platt & Byard is the architect for the ongoing restoration of the building.

❸ **Kings County Savings Bank,** 135 Broadway (King & Wilcox, 1868). This former bank, built of light-colored sandstone, is one of New York's most magnificent French Second Empire buildings. The baroque quality of the design is accented by a projecting entrance portico, recessed loggias, a pair of projecting corner pavilions on the side facade, and beautifully executed carving on the ground floor.

❹ **Russian Orthodox Cathedral of the Transfiguration of Our Lord,** Driggs Avenue at North 12th Street (Louis Allmendinger, 1916–21). The Greek cross plan and the impressive scale of the onion domes of this small yellow brick church typify design in the Russian Orthodox tradition. The cathedral itself stands as a symbol of the importance of Eastern European immigrants in the history of northeastern Brooklyn.

❺ **19th Police Precinct Station House and Stable,** 43 Herbert Street and 512–518 Humboldt Street (George Ingram, 1891–92). In 1886 the Brooklyn Police Department began a campaign to expand the number of neighborhood precinct structures. George Ingram, the architect of this Romanesque Revival police station, with its bold arched entrance porch, prominent tower, and handsome ironwork, was the assistant engineer in the Brooklyn Department of City Works, where he developed the standard plan for Brooklyn's police station and stable complexes. Although no longer a precinct station, the building is still used by the Police Department.

Kings County Savings Bank (No. 3), one of the city's most magnificent French Second Empire buildings. Photo: Landmarks Preservation Commission collection.

❻ Winthrop Park Shelter Pavilion, now Monsignor McGolrick Park, bounded by Nassau and Driggs Avenues, Monitor and Russell Streets (Helmle & Huberty, 1910). For this small park in Greenpoint, Helmle & Huberty designed a curved pavilion that is reminiscent of such 17th- and 18th-century French garden structures as the Grand Trianon at Versailles. The use of Renaissance precedents can also be seen in other works by these architects, notably in the Brooklyn Central Office, Bureau of Fire Communications (see No. 67), and the Prospect Park Boathouse (see No. 72).

❼ Public School 34, also known as the Oliver H. Perry School, 131 Norman Avenue (Samuel B. Leonard, 1867; additions, Samuel B. Leonard, 1870, and James W. Naughton, 1887–88). Public education began in Brooklyn in 1816 and by the late 19th century had grown to the point that Brooklyn had one of the most extensive systems of public education in the country. As the population of Brooklyn increased and as more school buildings were needed, the office of superintendent of build-

ings was established. Samuel B. Leonard served as superintendent from 1859 to 1879 and was responsible for the design of many of Brooklyn's oldest surviving schools. He was succeeded by James W. Naughton, who retained the position until the Brooklyn school system was merged into that of the newly consolidated city in 1898 and New York's superintendent of school buildings, C. B. J. Snyder, took charge of school design and construction throughout the city. One of the oldest schools in continuous use in New York City, Greenpoint's P.S. 34 is an Early Romanesque Revival building that is similar in design to P.S. 9 (see No. 63).

❽ Sidewalk Clock, 753 Manhattan Avenue (early 20th century). This cast-iron sidewalk clock in Greenpoint is typical of the large clocks that were once commonly used to advertise jewelry stores and other businesses (see Manhattan No. 162).

❾ Astral Apartments, 184 Franklin Street (Lamb & Rich, 1885–86). The Astral is a significant example of "model tenement" design. Erected by

Charles Pratt and named for the "astral oil" manufactured by one of his companies in a nearby Greenpoint refinery, the building was planned as quality affordable housing for ninety-five families. Each apartment contained adequate windows, a toilet, hot and cold running water, and other amenities not usually provided to working-class families in the 19th century. The building was designed in the Queen Anne style by a Manhattan firm often engaged by the Pratt family.

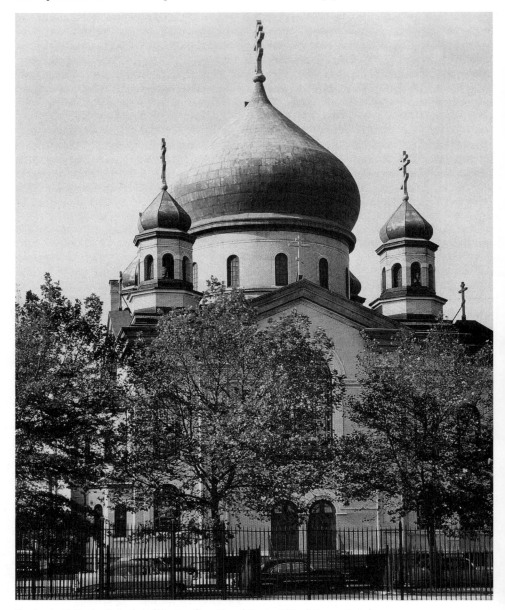

The Russian Orthodox Cathedral of the Transfiguration of Our Lord (No. 4) is a symbol of the importance of Eastern European immigration in the history of northeastern Brooklyn. Photo by John Barrington Bayley.

HISTORIC DISTRICT

2 **Vinegar Hill Historic District.** The three sections of this historic district—one of Brooklyn's oldest residential communities—are characterized by groups of brick and frame houses erected in the first half of the 19th century along the Brooklyn waterfront, just west of the Brooklyn Navy Yard. The area was named Vinegar Hill by John Jackson, one of its original developers, in commemoration of the Battle of Vinegar Hill of 1798, at which the English ended a rebellion by the Irish. Development began early in the 19th century, but the major period of residential construction was between the 1830s and early 1850s, when Greek Revival and Italianate houses were erected, including the impressive Greek Revival brick row at 237–249 Front Street and the frame houses with brick fronts at 51–59 Hudson Avenue, with Greek Revival and Italianate detail and ground-floor shop fronts. By the late 19th century, Vinegar Hill had so many residents of Irish background that it was often referred to as Irishtown. Industrial expansion along the waterfront replaced much of the surrounding residential community and is represented in the district by the factory building at 232–233 Front Street, designed by the prominent Brooklyn architect William Tubby in 1908 for Benjamin Moore & Co., paint manufacturers.

INDIVIDUAL LANDMARKS

Brooklyn Navy Yard. The Brooklyn Navy Yard was established in 1801 and rapidly grew into one of the busiest naval stations on the eastern seaboard. Some four hundred ships were fitted out at the navy yard during the Civil War, and during World War II the yard employed more than seventy thousand people. Although the navy yard is now an industrial center, most of its early buildings are extant.

10 **Commandant's House,** Evans Street at Little Street (1805–06). The design of this frame house has often been attributed to the Boston architect Charles Bulfinch, working in association with John McComb, Jr., but there is no evidence to support this attribution. The house is among the most elegant structures in the Federal style in New York. Of special note are the porches supported by slender colonnettes and the pair of especially fine fanlighted entranceways. The house was the residence of Matthew Perry when he served as commanding officer of the shipyard in the 1840s.

11 **Dry Dock #1,** Dock Street at the foot of 3rd Street (William J. McAlpine, chief engineer, 1840–51). The construction of Dry Dock #1

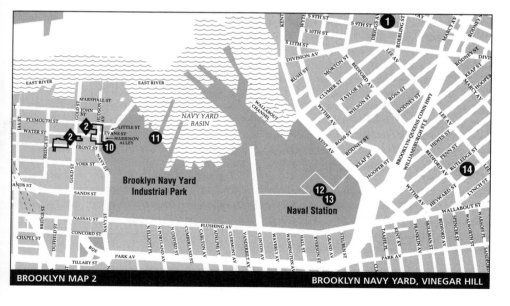

was one of the great feats of 19th-century American engineering. At a cost of more than $2 million, the dry dock was constructed of granite from Maine and Connecticut that was laid under the supervision of the master mason Thornton MacNess Niven.

⑫ Surgeon's House, Flushing Avenue opposite Ryerson Street (True W. Rollins and Charles Hastings, builders, 1863). This mansarded French Second Empire house, built for the chief surgeon of the nearby naval hospital (see No. 13), was erected during the Civil War, a period when the Brooklyn Navy Yard experienced extensive growth.

⑬ U.S. Naval Hospital, Hospital Road (Martin E. Thompson, 1830–38; wings, 1840 and c. 1862). Designed by one of the most prominent

architects of the pre–Civil War period, the former U.S. Naval Hospital is an austere yet impressive Greek Revival structure built of Westchester marble. It is distinguished by the eight square stone piers along its main facade. The building is vacant.

⑭ Public School 71K, now the Beth Jacob School, 119 Heyward Street (James W. Naughton, 1888–89). This French Second Empire structure in Williamsburg is one of the most beautiful schools designed by Naughton (see Nos. 52, 57, and 58; see also No. 7). The building is massed with projecting, pedimented end pavilions and a central frontispiece capped by a mansard roof, and it is articulated by large expanses of finely proportioned windows that permit a maximum amount of light to enter the classrooms. No longer owned by the city, the building now houses an Orthodox Jewish girls' school.

The elegant Commandant's House (No. 10), Brooklyn Navy Yard, was the residence of Matthew Perry when he commanded the shipyard in the 1840s. Photo by John Barrington Bayley.

HISTORIC DISTRICTS

3 **Fulton Ferry Historic District.** The development of Fulton Ferry, Brooklyn's only commercial area designated a historic district, is closely related to the advent of steam-powered ferry service between Brooklyn and Manhattan in 1814. The success of the ferry and resultant commuter traffic led business owners to erect new commercial structures. Among the district's notable early buildings are the Greek

Map 3: Fulton Ferry, Brooklyn Heights, and Downtown Brooklyn

Revival Long Island Insurance Company (1835) at 5–7 Front Street, thought to be New York City's earliest surviving office building; the row of Greek Revival stores at 7–23 Fulton Street, erected after the street was widened in 1835; the cast-iron Long Island Safe Deposit Company (William Mundell, 1868–69) at Fulton and Front Streets; and the Italianate Brooklyn City Railroad Building (see No. 16). The most impressive building on Fulton Street is the former Eagle Warehouse (now apartments), a massive Romanesque Revival brick structure designed in 1893 by Frank Freeman. Throughout much of the 19th century, the district's waterfront was lined with stores and warehouses used for the storage of produce and other goods that were shipped through the port. The monumental Empire Stores at 53–83 Water Street (1869; Thomas Stone, 1885), with their round-arched openings and iron shutters, are among the handful of port warehouses that survive. The opening of the Brooklyn Bridge (see No. 15) in 1883 doomed the ferry and the economic life of Fulton Street, but the area began to revive in the 1970s through the rehabilitation and adaptive use of many of the buildings in the district.

The imposing Romanesque Revival Eagle Warehouse, Fulton Ferry Historic District (H.D. 3). Photo by Carl Forster.

4 **Brooklyn Heights Historic District.** Brooklyn Heights, New York City's first historic district, is a rare example of a neighborhood where one can trace practically the entire history of urban residential design in New York City beginning in the 1820s. Following the establishment of the steam-powered Fulton Ferry in 1814, the Heights became the first area of Brooklyn to be urbanized. In the 1820s and early 1830s, elegant 2½-story houses in the Federal style were erected, primarily in the northern part of the Heights. Some of these were wooden buildings, notably the magnificent Eugene Boisselet House at 24 Middagh Street (c. 1829), with its detached carriage house, and 135 Joralemon Street (c. 1833), with its mid-19th-century iron veranda, while others were faced in brick laid in Flemish bond, notably the row of three at 155–159 Willow Street (c. 1826), each with an extraordinary doorway with elegant leaded sidelights and transom. By the 1830s and 1840s, large-scale speculative row-house construction was occurring in the Heights, and many three-story brick houses were erected in the Greek Revival style. These austere buildings generally have grand, often overscale brownstone entrance enframements, including those with massive pilasters, such as the long row at 35–75 Joralemon Street (c. 1844), others with eared enframements, such as the well-preserved row at 20–26 Willow Street (c. 1846), and a few with fluted columns, as at 173–175 Hicks Street (c. 1848). Brooklyn Heights also contains a rare surviving colonnaded row at 43–49 Willow Place (c. 1846), with monumental square piers, and the Adrien Van Sinderen House (c. 1839) at 70 Willow Street, a four-bay-wide Greek Revival mansion that is among the largest houses of the style in New York City. Besides these noteworthy individual houses and rows, there are several streets lined with three-story and basement brick houses that indicate the character of urban neighborhoods in the 1840s; this is evident on Clinton Street between Livingston and State Streets and Henry Street between Joralemon and State Streets. Gothic Revival row houses also appeared in Brooklyn Heights in the 1840s. Although this style was never overwhelmingly popular for row houses, one of the largest collections of these buildings can be found in this neighborhood. Many of these are early examples of the use of brownstone, and all are embellished with such Gothic-inspired features as pointed-arch openings and drip lintels. Notable Gothic Revival row hous-

es include the brick structures at 103–107 State Street (c. 1847), with their pointed-arch, cast-iron stoop and areaway railings and the quatrefoil-embellished iron balcony at No. 107; the unusual brick houses at 2–8 Willow Place (c. 1847), with their arched porticoes supported by clustered colonnettes; and the exceptionally well preserved brownstone rows at 118–122 Willow Street (c. 1845) and 131–135 Hicks Street (c. 1848). Also within the district is the George Hastings House at 36 Pierrepont Street, a large individual house with Gothic ironwork designed in 1846 by the prominent architect Richard Upjohn. By the time the brownstone-faced Italianate row house became popular in Brooklyn in the 1860s, much of Brooklyn Heights had already been developed, and there was little room for the long rows erected in neighborhoods such as Fort Greene and Clinton Hill (see Map 4). However, a few individual row houses were erected, and the neighborhood contains the two largest surviving Italianate mansions in New York, the Alexander M. White and Abiel Abbot Low houses (Frederick A. Petersen, c. 1857) at 2 and 3 Pierrepont Place. In the 1880s and 1890s, a few Queen Anne and Romanesque Revival row houses and mansions were erected. These include the exuberant Queen Anne row at 108–112 Willow Street (William Halsey Wood, 1880), the massive Romanesque Revival row at 262–272 Hicks Street (William Tubby, 1887), and one of the great masterpieces of Romanesque Revival design in New York City, the Herman Behr House (Frank Freeman, 1889) at 84 Pierrepont Street. The 1880s also mark the beginning of the development of middle-class apartment buildings in Brooklyn, with some of the finest early examples on Montague Street—the Queen Anne–style Montague, Grosvenor, and Berkeley (Parfitt Brothers, 1885), at Nos. 103, 115, and 117, and the Arlington (Montrose Morris, 1887) at No. 62. By the 20th century, large numbers of apartment houses were built, generally replacing earlier structures. Beaux-Arts apartment houses appeared in the northern end of the Heights early in the century. By the 1920s and 1930s, English Gothic-, Romanesque-, and Colonial-inspired apartment buildings were erected throughout the neighborhood, followed in the 1930s and 1940s by Art Deco structures. Brooklyn Heights also became a center for apartment hotels, with several of Brooklyn's most famous hotels erected early in the 20th century, in-

Brooklyn Heights
Historic District
(H.D. 4). Federal-style
houses at the
southeast corner of
Middagh and Willow
Streets in the city's
first historic district.
Photo by Caroline
Kane Levy.

cluding the Beaux-Arts Bossert (Helmle & Huberty, 1908–13) at 98 Montague Street with its famous rooftop restaurant, the Marine Grill, and the St. George on Clark Street between Hicks and Henry Streets, once New York's largest hotel (with what was reputed to be the world's largest saltwater swimming pool), composed of many buildings, including a high-rise tower (Emery Roth, 1929–30). Even in the post–World War II era a few important buildings appeared in Brooklyn Heights, notably the modern row houses at 40, 44, and 48 Willow Place (Joseph & Mary Merz, 1965–66). Brooklyn Heights also contains some of the most important institutional buildings in New York City which are individually discussed below.

A **Plymouth Church (Congregational)**, now Plymouth Church of the Pilgrims, Orange Street between Henry and Hicks Streets (Joseph C. Wells, 1849–50). After the organization of this congregation in 1847 as the third Congregational church in Brooklyn, Henry Ward Beecher was called to the ministry. Beecher was one of the most dynamic preachers of the 19th century, perhaps best known for his outspoken abolitionism. The church building is a simple barnlike structure with a seating plan consisting of pews arranged in arcs in front of the pulpit. Both the design and the plan became prototypes for churches erected by other evangelical Protestant congregations throughout the country. The entrance porch and stained-glass windows were added early in the 20th century, and the ad-

joining church house and arcade were built in 1913 (Woodruff Leeming, architect). The statue of Beecher in the church garden is by Gutzon Borglum (best known for his work at Mount Rushmore; he also did sculpture on the New York Evening Post Building—see Manhattan No. 46).

B **First Presbyterian Church**, 124 Henry Street (William B. Olmsted, 1846). This bold but somewhat naive Gothic Revival church is dominated by an exceedingly wide 90-foot-tall crenellated tower punctuated by a large pointed-arch window. The design reflects a greater freedom in the use of Gothic forms among Protestant denominations in contrast to the more strictly medieval inspiration of many contemporary Episcopal churches such as Grace (see entry H, below). First Presbyterian was established in 1822 just as Brooklyn was beginning its urban development and affluent Presbyterians were settling in the Heights.

C **First Unitarian Church of Brooklyn, Church of the Saviour**, Pierrepont Street at Monroe Place (Minard Lafever, 1842–44). The New Englanders who arrived in Brooklyn in the 1830s and 1840s not only established many Congregational churches (see Brooklyn Heights Historic District, entries A and F)

First Unitarian Church of Brooklyn, (Entry C).
A Gothic Revival masterpiece by architect
Minard Lafever. Photo by Caroline Kane Levy.

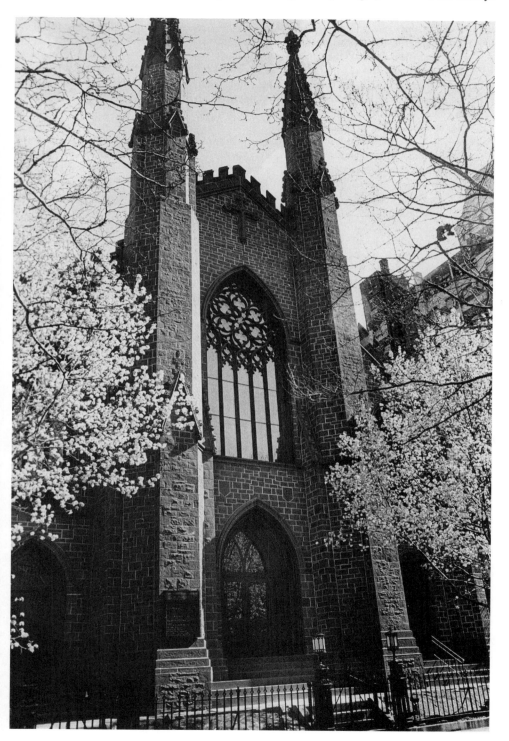

but also founded this Unitarian church in 1833. The brownstone church in the Gothic Revival style is among architect Minard Lafever's masterpieces. The form, with a gabled end flanked by turrets, is loosely based on King's College Chapel, Cambridge. The corner lot is marked by an exceptionally fine Gothic cast-iron railing. In 1995 a major restoration of the facade was undertaken (Robert Meadows, architect). As part of the congregation's efforts to improve conditions among Brooklyn's working poor, the church established a mission on the waterfront in 1865. Ten years later the **Willow Place Chapel**, now Alfred T. White Community Center (Russell Sturgis, 1875–76), was erected at 26 Willow Place, under the direction of Alfred Tredway White, who was also about to begin work on his pioneering Home and Tower model tenements in the Cobble Hill Historic District (see H.D. 5) and would later also erect the Riverside Homes on Columbia Place in Brooklyn Heights, completed in 1890 (partially extant; William Field & Son). Architect Russell Sturgis used a High Victorian Gothic style reflecting the ideas of English art theorist John Ruskin, as is evident in the chapel's brick facade with contrasting light-colored stonework, high clerestory, cusped arches, and dogtooth detail.

D **Long Island Historical Society,** now the Brooklyn Historical Society, 128 Pierrepont Street (George B. Post, 1878–81). Organized in 1863, the Long Island Historical Society soon grew into a leading library and museum of local history. Fourteen architects entered a design competition for the society's building in 1878. Post's Renaissance-inspired design won, and the new building, the first in New York to exploit ornamental terra cotta extensively, was dedicated in January 1881. It contains one of New York's great 19th-century **interiors.** The second-floor library retains its original furnishings and stained-glass windows; outstanding architectural features include columns, a gallery railing, and other woodwork carved of ash. The library houses an important collection of books, prints, photographs, and other material relating to Brooklyn. A major restoration and mechanical upgrading began in 1997 (Jan Hird Pokorny, architect).

E **Holy Trinity Church (Episcopal),** now Saint Ann and the Holy Trinity Episcopal Church, Clinton Street at Montague Street (Minard Lafever,

1844–47). Seven years after Holy Trinity parish was organized in 1837, construction began on this Gothic Revival church, chapel, and parish house funded by paper manufacturer John Bartow, who dreamed of erecting an Episcopal church in Brooklyn that would rival such New York City churches as Trinity (see Manhattan No. 15). At its completion, this was the largest church in Brooklyn. Lafever planned a spire, but it was not until 1866 that a spire designed by Patrick C. Keely (architect for many of Brooklyn's Roman Catholic churches; see Greenpoint Historic District, H.D. 1) was built; it was removed in 1905. The Havestraw red sandstone exterior deteriorated very badly and has been the subject of a major restoration project begun in 1979 with architect Mendel Mesick Cohen Waite. This has also entailed extensive restoration by the Greenland Studios of the stained-glass windows designed by William and John Bolton, which are among the earliest church windows produced in America.

F **Church of the Pilgrims (Congregational),** now Our Lady of Lebanon Maronite Rite Roman Catholic Church, Henry Street and Remsen Street (Richard Upjohn, 1844–46; rectory, Leopold Eidlitz, 1869). As Brooklyn was becoming urbanized in the pre–Civil War era, large numbers of New Englanders moved to the city, organizing many Congregational churches. This was the first Congregational church erected in Brooklyn and was a radical design. The church is the first round-arched, Early Romanesque Revival ecclesiastical building in America and became a model for many buildings erected by evangelical Protestant congregations in succeeding decades. The original corner steeple has been removed, as has the cap to the southern tower. In 1869 the church was expanded with a High Victorian addition that is one of the few surviving buildings by Leopold Eidlitz, a major figure in 19th-century American architecture. In 1944 the Church of the Pilgrims merged with Plymouth Church (see entry A, above), and this building was sold to a Lebanese Roman Catholic congregation. The medallions on the entrance doors, originally part of the main dining room doors on the French luxury liner *Normandie*, were purchased by Our Lady of Lebanon at an auction in 1945.

G **Heights Casino and Casino Mansions Apartments,** 75 Montague Street and 200 Hicks Street

(Boring & Tilton, 1905, and William A. Boring, 1910). Most affluent residential neighborhoods in the 19th and early 20th centuries were home to private clubs that catered to residents' social needs. The Casino is one of the few such clubs in Brooklyn still in use. The building is a Dutch Renaissance–inspired structure with brick laid in diaper patterns to enliven the blank walls where squash courts preclude the use of windows. Iron tie rods on the walls take the form of squash rackets. In 1910 William Boring designed the neighboring apartment building, the Casino Mansions, in conformity with the design of the club. With two apartments per floor, this was one of Brooklyn's most luxurious apartment houses.

H **Grace Church (Episcopal)**, Hicks Street at Grace Court (Richard Upjohn, 1847–49). Grace is one of the most mature Gothic designs in New York City by the prestigious architect Richard Upjohn, who was a resident of Brooklyn. Grace was organized in 1847 as an offshoot of Upjohn's own church, Christ Episcopal in the Cobble Hill Historic District (H.D. 5). The nave and chancel are clearly demarcated on the brownstone exterior, but a proposed corner tower was never built. A restoration by architect Page Ayres Cowley and Integrated Conservation Resources began in the early 1990s.

I **Packer Collegiate Institute For Girls,** now Packer Collegiate Institute, 170 Joralemon Street (Minard Lafever, 1853–56; additions, Napoleon Le Brun & Son, 1884 and 1886). The Brooklyn Female Academy, founded in 1844, burned in 1853, but Harriet L. Packer offered to reestablish the school in honor of her husband. Minard Lafever designed one of the finest Gothic Revival buildings of the 1850s, modeling his picturesque structure after college buildings at Oxford and Cambridge. The tall octagonal tower was originally capped and housed a telescope. Additions to the east and the west were designed by the Le Brun firm. Packer (now a coeducational school) has been a superb steward of its buildings and has carefully restored the brownstone facade and the Gothic cast-iron railings.

J **Saint Ann's Church (Episcopal)**, now part of Packer Collegiate Institute, Clinton Street at Livingston Street (Renwick & Sands, chapel, 1866–67; church, 1867–69). The former Saint Ann's is not

only a major work of James Renwick, Jr.'s, but one of the most important High Victorian Gothic churches in America. Saint Ann's was the first Episcopal congregation established in Brooklyn; this was its third home. The church is a complex Ruskinian building erected of contrasting Belleville sandstone from New Jersey with Cleveland stone trim from Ohio. It has a full tripartite horizontal massing with an arcade articulated by simple pointed-arch windows, a triforium with ornate tracery, and a clerestory with small windows set in horizontal frames. The roofline bristles with pinnacles and crockets. In the late 1960s Saint Ann's moved into the Holy Trinity Church (see entry E), and this building became the property of Packer Collegiate Institute (see entry I, above). The main sanctuary awaits a reuse.

5 **Cobble Hill Historic District.** The inauguration in 1836 of service on South Ferry, linking Atlantic Avenue and Whitehall Street across the East River, led to the development of what at the time was farmland into a middle-class residential neighborhood. The row houses of Cobble Hill are primarily Greek Revival, Italianate, and Anglo-Italianate in style; most are faced with brick or brownstone and feature high stoops with exceptionally fine ironwork. The district also includes two "model tenement" complexes that are among the most significant housing erected in the United States in the 19th century. The Home and Tower buildings, on Hicks Street at Baltic Street, designed by William Field & Son in 1876 and 1878, respectively, were erected by the Brooklyn businessman Alfred T. White as decent affordable housing for working people. The apartments were designed to provide plumbing and sufficient light and air, amenities that are often taken for granted today. Behind the Tower Apartments, stretching along Warren Place (a one-block street extending from Warren Street to Baltic Street between Henry Street and Hicks Street), White built two rows of 11-foot-wide houses facing onto a common garden. The district contains several religious structures designed by important New York architects—notably Christ Episcopal Church (1840–41) on the corner of Clinton and Kane Streets, an early Gothic Revival work by Richard Upjohn, and Minard Lafever's Gothic Revival Strong Place Baptist Church (now Saint Francis Cabrini R.C. Chapel; 1851–52) on the corner of Degraw Street and Strong Place.

❻ Boerum Hill Historic District. Located just south of busy Atlantic Avenue, Boerum Hill is a homogeneous district composed primarily of row houses with brick or brownstone facades. Designed in the Greek Revival and Italianate styles, most of the houses were erected between the 1840s and the early 1870s. The district contains unusually long rows for this period, accenting the cohesive nature of the blockfronts. The quality of the blocks is further enhanced by the survival of many cast-iron stoop and areaway railings, original wood double doors, and bluestone sidewalks.

❼ Carroll Gardens Historic District. This small district of row houses set behind deep front yards retains much of its 19th-century character. The impression of space is the result of the surveyor Richard Butts's plan, devised in 1846, which created building lots with especially deep front yards and a street pattern that protects President and Carroll Streets from through traffic. All the row houses in the district were erected between 1869 and 1884 by local builders, and most are brownstone-fronted buildings in the Italianate and neo-Grec styles.

INDIVIDUAL LANDMARKS

❶❺ Brooklyn Bridge, spanning the East River between Cadman Plaza, Brooklyn, and City Hall Park, Manhattan (John A., Washington, and Emily Roebling, 1867–83). The Brooklyn Bridge, one of the great engineering feats of the 19th century, was the first physical link between the independent cities of Brooklyn and New York (they merged in 1898). It not only became the world's longest suspension bridge but was also an aesthetic triumph, with its intricate web of cables and its bold Gothic-inspired piers serving as symbolic portals to the two cities. Conceived by a German immigrant engineer, John A. Roebling, who had previously designed suspension bridges in Cincinnati and Pittsburgh, the project was taken over by his son Washington after Roebling died from an injury sustained during construction. Even when Washington Roebling was later paralyzed by caisson disease, he continued, with the help of his wife, Emily, to oversee the project from the window of a house in Brooklyn Heights. In 1972–73 the bridge was repainted in historically accurate colors. The pedes-trian walkway was rebuilt in 1981–83, and the cables have been rehabilitated.

❶❻ Brooklyn City Railroad Company, 8 Cadman Plaza West (Old Fulton Street) (1860–61). Established in 1853, the Brooklyn City Railroad Company operated horse-car lines that brought people to and from the Fulton Ferry terminal. The company's headquarters building is an Italianate brick structure with granite trim and a cast-iron storefront. It has been converted into apartments.

❶❼ United States Post Office and Court House, Brooklyn Central Office, 271–301 Cadman Plaza East (Washington Street) (Mifflin E. Bell, 1885–91; extension, 1930–33). The office of the supervising architect of the U.S. Treasury was responsible for the design of many Romanesque Revival post offices in the United States. This Brooklyn building is one of the few such post offices still standing and still in use. The construction began during Mifflin E. Bell's brief tenure as supervising architect (1884–86); Bell's design was transformed into a boldly scaled Romanesque Revival work following his resignation. The complementary Depression-era addition was designed during James Wetmore's tenure as acting supervising architect. The upper floors, now vacant, were used for many years as offices. Plans call for the rehabilitation of the building.

❶❽ Brooklyn Trust Company Building, now Chase Bank, 177–179 Montague Street (York & Sawyer, 1913–16). The Brooklyn Trust Company, established in 1866, was responsible for the construction of the most beautiful building on Brooklyn's "bank row." York & Sawyer created an elegant structure modeled on Italian Renaissance designs, drawing especially from the Palazzo della Gran Guardia, often attributed to Veronese architect Michele Sanmicheli. The building set a precedent for the firm's largest Renaissance banks—the Central Savings Bank (see Manhattan No. 331) and the Federal Reserve Bank (see Manhattan No. 21). Both the exterior and the **interior** are magnificently crafted. The banking hall draws inspiration from ancient Roman and Italian Renaissance architecture. The monumentally scaled space has a vaulted, coffered ceiling with enormous chandeliers, grand arched windows, and a Cosmati-work floor of intricately patterned marble mosaic.

⑲ First Free Congregational Church, later the Bridge Street African Wesleyan Methodist Episcopal Church, now Polytechnic Institute, Wunsch Hall, 311 Bridge Street (1846–47). A rare surviving Greek Revival church structure in Brooklyn, this building first served as a Congregational church. Just seven years after its completion, it was sold to Brooklyn's oldest African-American congregation, the African Wesleyan Methodist Episcopal (A.W.M.E.) Church. This congregation, which soon became known as the Bridge Street A.W.M.E. Church, occupied the building for eighty-four years before moving to Bedford-Stuyvesant. The building eventually became a factory and was rehabilitated by Polytechnic Institute after it acquired the property in 1968. A more extensive restoration, overseen by architect James Wong, was completed in 1996 as part of a conversion into a student center.

⑳ Brooklyn Fire Headquarters, 365–367 Jay Street (Frank Freeman, 1892). The former headquarters of the Brooklyn Fire Department, designed by one of Brooklyn's most talented 19th-century architects, is a masterpiece of the Romanesque Revival. This powerful building is distinguished by its massive entrance arch and richly textured elevation, clad in rock-faced red sandstone and gold Roman brick and trimmed with terra cotta. The building is now an apartment house.

㉑ Brooklyn City Hall, now Brooklyn Borough Hall, 209 Joralemon Street (Gamaliel King,

Brooklyn City Hall (No. 21), built in 1845–48, when Brooklyn was an independent city. Photo by Caroline Kane Levy.

1845–48; alterations, Vincent Griffith and Stoughton & Stoughton, 1898). Brooklyn City Hall is an imposing Greek Revival structure. The exterior of the Tuckahoe marble building, with its Ionic portico and crisp window enframements, re-mained unaltered until its original cupola was destroyed by fire in 1895. The architects Vincent Griffith and Stoughton & Stoughton designed a new cast-iron cupola in 1898, the same year that Brooklyn was consolidated into Greater New York

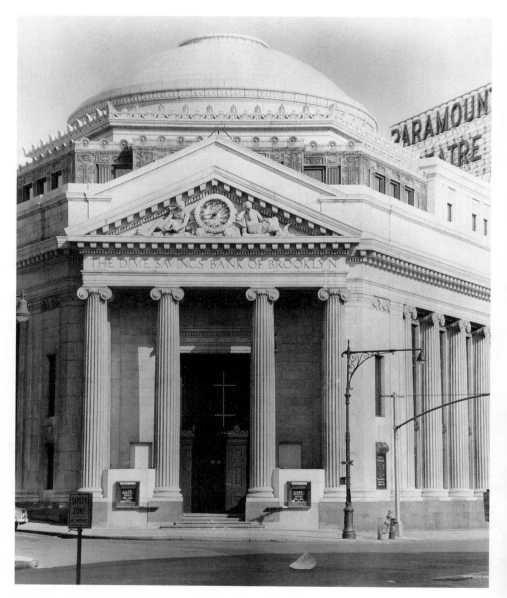

Dime Savings Bank (No. 24). The monumental design and grand interior were intended to attract small investors. Photo: Landmarks Preservation Commission collection.

and the building became Borough Hall. A restoration of the building was completed in 1989 under the direction of the architecture firm Conklin & Rossant; the copper shingles of the cupola were meticulously reconstituted by the French firm Les Metalliers Champenois (which also restored the Statue of Liberty), and a crowning figure of justice, planned in 1898, was finally installed.

㉒ Interborough Rapid Transit System Underground Station, Borough Hall. See Manhattan No. 7.

㉓ Gage & Tollner Restaurant, 372 Fulton Street (building, c. 1875; restaurant design, 1892). One of Brooklyn's most celebrated restaurants, Gage & Tollner opened at a nearby location in 1879. The restaurant moved to this brownstone building in 1892, at which time a new wooden shop front was added and the **interior** was redesigned. The dining room retains an authentic 19th-century character, with cherry wood trim, original furnishings and mirrors, Lincrusta (an imitation leather) wall covering, and graceful gaslight fixtures. In 1996 the interior was completely refurbished to enhance its historic character.

㉔ Dime Savings Bank, 9 DeKalb Avenue (Mowbray & Uffinger, 1906–08; enlarged, Halsey, McCormack & Helmer, 1931–32). This is one of New York City's most monumental banks, and it typifies early 20th-century savings bank architecture, which used impressive design to attract large numbers of small depositors. In 1906 the Dime purchased an oddly shaped lot on a triangular block and erected an imposing Classical Revival building faced with marble. The building was substantially enlarged in 1931–32, creating the present domed, temple-fronted building. The spectacular, richly detailed **interior,** focusing on a rotunda supported by twelve red German marble columns with gilded capitals displaying Mercury dimes, was created at this time.

㉕ Friends Meeting House, 110 Schermerhorn Street (attributed to Charles T. Bunting, 1857). Consistent with Quaker taste, the Brooklyn Friends Meeting House is a beautifully proportioned but severely simple brick structure. It is articulated by tall multipaned windows that allow light to flood the second-floor meeting room.

㉖ State Street Houses, 291–299 and 290–324 State Street (1847–74). These twenty-three row houses between Smith and Hoyt Streets reflect the development of this formerly rural section of Boerum Hill into a prosperous urban residential neighborhood in the mid-19th century. The brick- and brownstone-fronted houses are Greek Revival and Italianate in style.

㉗ South Congregational Church Complex, 358–366 Court Street and 253–269 President Street (chapel, 1851; church, 1857; ladies' parlor, F. Carles Merry, 1889; rectory, Woodruff Leeming, 1893). Located on a prominent corner in the old neighborhood of South Brooklyn—now generally known as Carroll Gardens—South Congregational is a brick church articulated by a series of arches expressive of the finest Early Romanesque Revival design. To the rear are the chapel, the Romanesque Revival ladies' parlor, and the neo-Gothic rectory. The church congregation now worships in the former parlor, and the church and the chapel have been converted into apartments.

㉘ John Rankin House, also known as the 440 Clinton Street House, now the F. G. Guido Funeral Home (c. 1840). This handsomely proportioned Greek Revival brick structure was erected for a wealthy merchant at a time when the area now known as Carroll Gardens was still largely rural. One of Brooklyn's largest residences of the 1840s, the house has an especially fine granite entrance surround and granite newel posts.

㉙ Carroll Street Bridge, spanning the Gowanus Canal (Robert Van Buren, chief engineer; George Ingram, engineer in charge, 1888–89). One of the oldest bridges in New York City and the oldest of the four known American examples of a "retractile" bridge, the Carroll Street Bridge rolls horizontally onto land whenever a barge needs to pass along the Gowanus Canal. The superstructure was manufactured by the New Jersey Steel and Iron Company, a subsidiary of Cooper, Hewitt & Company, one of the country's foremost iron and steel producers. The bridge was restored in 1989 by engineers in the city's Department of Transportation.

HISTORIC DISTRICTS

8 **Brooklyn Academy of Music Historic District.** This small district at the western edge of the Fort Greene neighborhood is composed of Italianate and Anglo-Italianate row houses erected primarily between 1855 and 1859 as residential development in Brooklyn was moving east across Flatbush Avenue. The streets are lined with row houses faced in either brick or brownstone and highlighted with fine wooden cornices, cast-iron railings, wood doors, and double-hung wood window sash. A small section of Fulton Street, Brooklyn's major 19th-century commercial thoroughfare, runs through the district and contains an unusual row of cast-iron buildings erected in 1882 that had stores on the ground floor and flats above. The three most prominent buildings in the district are the Williamsburgh Savings Bank's tower (see No. 40); the neo-Gothic Central Methodist Church (1929–31) on Hanson Place, designed by Halsey, McCormack, & Helmer, the same architecture firm responsible for the neighboring bank tower; and, most significant, the Brooklyn Academy of Music. The Brooklyn Academy of Music was established in 1859. Soon after its home on Montague Street burned in 1903, a decision was made to move to a site that was near the center of Brooklyn's population and was convenient to railroad, subway, and streetcar lines. The noted theater architecture firm Herts & Tallant designed the Italian Renaissance–inspired building, which opened in October 1908. The academy is faced in textured, sand-blasted cream-colored brick with extraordinary polychromatic terra-cotta detail, including entrances adorned with putti singing and playing musical instruments, inspired by the work of Renaissance master Luca Della Robbia. The Brooklyn Academy of Music continues to be one of New York's most vital cultural institutions.

9 **Fort Greene Historic District.** In the 1850s, as Brooklyn's population was expanding rapidly, middle-class residential development moved up the slope of Clinton Hill into the neighborhood now known as Fort Greene. A number of the streets in the area were named for the great Regency terraces of London (Portland, Oxford, Cumberland, Carlton, and Adelphi), and between 1855 and the early 1870s these and nearby streets were lined with fine row houses. Many of the early houses are simple brick buildings in the Italianate or transitional Greek Revival/Italianate styles; heavy concentrations of such row houses are found on Cumberland and Carlton Streets. By the 1860s grander Italianate and French Second Empire rows with brownstone facades and ornate carved detail were erected. The Italianate houses on South Portland Avenue are especially elaborate, as are the long rows of French Second Empire houses with mansard roofs that line Washington Park and Clermont Avenue between Willoughby and DeKalb Avenues. One of the most intact blockfronts of brownstone-fronted row houses in Brooklyn is that on the west side of Vanderbilt Avenue between Greene and Gates Avenues, built in 1872–79. A few important churches were erected to minister to the needs of the neighborhood's new residents. The most famous of these is the Lafayette Avenue Presbyterian Church (Grimshaw & Morrill, 1861–62), a

BROOKLYN MAP 4   CLINTON HILL, FORT GREENE, PRATT INSTITUTE

brownstone Early Romanesque Revival–style structure. The church was led by the Reverend Theodore L. Cuyler, one of New York's prominent mid-19th-century ministers. The focus of the new neighborhood was (and still is) Fort Greene Park, designed by Frederick Law Olmsted and Calvert Vaux in 1867 on the site of a Revolutionary War fort. In the center of the park is McKim, Mead & White's Prison Ship Martyrs' Monument of 1906–09, an enormous Doric column commemorating the American patriots who died on British prison ships in nearby Wallabout Bay during the Revolutionary War. A few single-family houses and apartment buildings were erected in the district later in the 19th century and in the early 20th century, and two prestigious institutions were built on Lafayette Avenue between Clermont and Vanderbilt Avenues—the Brooklyn Masonic Temple (Lord & Hewlett, 1906), a grand Classical Revival structure built of brick with exceptional polychromatic terra-cotta detail, and Queen of All Saints

Roman Catholic Church and School (Reiley & Steinback, 1910), an imposing French Gothic structure built of cast stone. Even with these additions to the area, the character of the district remains one of cohesive mid-19th-century row houses.

10 Clinton Hill Historic District. Clinton Hill is unusual among Brooklyn residential neighborhoods in that it has undergone many periods of development and redevelopment, creating a varied character along the streets. Clinton Avenue, at the crest of Clinton Hill, was laid out in 1832 as a wide boulevard for large suburban residences; several of these survive, notably the wooden Gothic Revival house erected at No. 284 (Field & Correja, c. 1854, with later additions) and the brick and stone Italianate villa at No. 447 (c. 1850). In the 1860s long rows of Italianate brick or brownstone houses were erected. Grand Avenue, Cambridge Place, and Saint James Place contain some of New York's most intact mid-19th-century row houses. In the

The Clinton Hill Historic District (H.D. 10) contains the magnificent mansions of the Pratt family, once Brooklyn's wealthiest citizens. Photo by Carl Forster.

1870s Clinton Avenue and Washington Avenue began to attract many of Brooklyn's wealthiest citizens. Charles Pratt erected a large but restrained neo-Grec mansion at 232 Clinton Avenue in 1874 (Ebenezer L. Roberts, architect), and he was followed in the next half century by other wealthy industrialists who established Clinton Avenue as Brooklyn's "Gold Coast." Some of these mansions were designed by prominent Manhattan architects, including Herts & Tallant (the Liebman House at 384 Clinton Avenue; 1907), Babb, Cook & Willard (the Frederick B. and George DuPont Pratt houses at 229 and 245 Clinton Avenue; 1895 and 1901), and Dwight James Baum (the Van Glahn House, 367 Washington Avenue; 1921–22), but other mansions and groups of late 19th-century row houses were the work of such talented Brooklyn architects as William B. Tubby (notably the Charles Millard Pratt House of 1890 at 229 Clinton Avenue) and Montrose Morris (the row houses at 285–289 and 282–290 DeKalb Avenue of 1889–90). In the late 19th century, small apartment houses were built in the neighborhood, and in the 1920s many larger six-story buildings were erected, often replacing mansions. Apartment-house construction culminated with the erection of the Clinton Hill Houses on Clinton Avenue (Harrison, Fouilhoux & Abramovitz), a group of towers planned during World War II for workers in the nearby Brooklyn Navy Yard (see Nos. 10–13). The mix of row houses, mansions, apartment buildings, and a few institutional structures (see Emmanuel Baptist Church, No. 34), designed in a variety of styles, contributes to the unique character of Clinton Hill's streets.

INDIVIDUAL LANDMARKS

③⓪ Saint Mary's Episcopal Church, 230 Classon Avenue (Richard T. Auchmuty, 1858–59). One of New York's most original but least well known Gothic Revival churches, Saint Mary's was designed by a partner in the firm Renwick & Auchmuty. Executed in brownstone, the church was erected to minister to the population that settled near the bustling Brooklyn Navy Yard.

③① Pratt Institute: Main Building Complex, 215 Ryerson Street (Main Building, Lamb & Rich, 1885–87; South Hall, William B. Tubby, 1891; porch, William B. Tubby, 1894; Memorial Hall, John Mead Howells, 1926–27). Pratt Institute was founded in 1884 by the wealthy Brooklyn manufacturer Charles Pratt as a school to train men and women in the manual arts. Pratt recognized the growing need for skilled industrial workers, and he believed that the best way to help people was to teach them to help themselves. The institute buildings were erected only a few blocks from Pratt's home on Clinton Avenue and originally faced onto city streets; the current campus environment was not created until the 1950s. The Main Building is an imposing Romanesque Revival brick and stone structure that originally housed all institute functions. The bold arched entrance porch, perhaps the building's most striking feature, is an addition designed by Tubby in 1894. Tubby's South Hall is a modest Romanesque Revival work that was originally used as the Pratt Institute High School. The neo-Romanesque Memorial Hall, commemorating Charles Pratt's second wife, Mary Richardson Pratt, was planned as an assembly hall; the brick and stone building is adorned with sculpted figures by Rene Chambellan. Memorial Hall was restored by H & H Building Consulting in 1996–97.

③② Pratt Institute Library, 224–228 Ryerson Street (William B. Tubby, 1896; north porch, John Mead Howells, 1936). Charles Pratt organized Brooklyn's first free library, open to all citizens over the age of fourteen, as part of the institute. Originally located in the Main Building (see No. 31), the library received its own home in 1896. This transitional Romanesque Revival/Renaissance Revival structure is one of many designed by Tubby for the Pratt family. When this library was removed from the Brooklyn Public Library system in 1940, it became the home of the Pratt Institute library.

③③ Pratt Row Houses, 220–234 Willoughby Avenue, 171–185 Steuben Street, and 172–186 Emerson Place (Hobart A. Walker, 1907). The Pratt family built a large number of row houses in the Clinton Hill neighborhood. These three rows, encompassing twenty-seven houses, survive from an original complex of thirty-eight houses that were planned for "people of taste and refinement, but of moderate means." Of Northern Renaissance–inspired design, the complex was built with rear service alleys and a central heating plant. The houses soon became popular with people affiliated with Pratt Institute; they are currently used as faculty housing.

㉞ Emmanuel Baptist Church, 279 Lafayette Avenue (Francis H. Kimball, 1886–87; chapel, Ebenezer L. Roberts, 1882–83; school, 1925–27). The construction of the imposing Emmanuel Baptist Church was financed largely by Charles Pratt, a Standard Oil vice president and Brooklyn's wealthiest citizen, who resided nearby. Built of a light-colored Ohio sandstone, the church recalls the medieval Gothic cathedrals of France. The complex consists of a towered chapel on Saint James Place; the sanctuary, which is Kimball's largest ecclesiastical design; and the neo-Gothic school building to the west of the church.

㉟ Joseph Steele House, 200 Lafayette Avenue (c. 1850). Erected early in the 1850s, this frame house is a magnificent example of a residence in a transitional style, combining Greek Revival and Italianate elements. Of special interest are the handsome Greek Revival entrance and the Italianate cupola. The small wing at the east side of the house may date from as early as 1812.

㊱ Royal Castle Apartments, 20–30 Gates Avenue (Wortmann & Braun, 1911–12). One of the earliest elevator apartment houses in Clinton Hill, the Royal Castle, faced in brick and limestone, is embellished by a series of fanciful corbels in the form of building masons. The building has a striking roofline with projecting arched gables reminiscent of early 20th-century Viennese architecture.

㊲ Saint Luke's Episcopal Church, now the Church of Saint Luke and Saint Matthew, 520 Clinton Avenue (John Welch, 1888–91). Saint Luke's, built at the time when Clinton Avenue was Brooklyn's "Gold Coast," is one of the grandest 19th-century ecclesiastical buildings in Brooklyn. The design of the church and its adjoining chapel is loosely based on the Romanesque churches of Northern Italy. The building is faced with six materials carefully modulated in color and texture to create a dramatic street facade.

㊳ Lincoln Club, now Mechanics Temple, Independent Order of Mechanics of the Western Hemisphere, 65 Putnam Avenue (Rudolph L. Daus, 1889). The former home of the Lincoln Club is a flamboyant Queen Anne brick, stone, and terra-cotta structure designed by one of Brooklyn's most original late 19th-century architects. The club was organized in 1878 by a group of affluent local gentlemen who sought to band to-

Joseph Steele House (No. 35), an excellent example of a building containing Greek Revival and Italianate elements. Photo: Landmarks Preservation Commission collection.

Williamsburgh Savings Bank Building (No. 40). Brooklyn's tallest building contains marvelous exterior and interior detailing and a monumental four-faced clock. Photo by Caroline Kane Levy.

gether for social purposes and to further the interests of the Republican Party (political activities were soon dropped). The Lincoln Club disbanded in 1931. In the 1940s the clubhouse was acquired by the Mechanics. This is a rare example of a 19th-century clubhouse that still serves its original social function.

39 Hanson Place Baptist Church, now the Hanson Place Seventh Day Adventist Church, 88 Hanson Place (George Penchard, 1857–60). This unusual church building combines the austere round-arched brick forms of the Early Romanesque Revival, a style popular with Protestant denominations in the 1850s, with a grand Corinthian temple front. A restoration of both the exterior and the interior was undertaken in the late 1970s.

40 Williamsburgh Savings Bank Building, 1 Hanson Place (Halsey, McCormack & Helmer, 1927–29). In 1929 the Williamsburgh Savings Bank moved its headquarters from Broadway in Williamsburg (see No. 2) into Brooklyn's tallest building. The bank's new home consisted of a domed tower soaring 512 feet above Hanson Place. The skyscraper is famous for its monumental four-faced clock, the largest in the world at the time of the building's completion. At its base, the building is embellished with relief carving—much of it evoking themes related to saving and thrift, including figures of bees, pelicans, and squirrels—and metal grilles depicting four continents. The **interior** lobby and banking hall are among the finest 20th-century interiors in Brooklyn, finished in quality materials and ornamented with symbolic decoration. The lobby is divided into a series of groin vaults covered with blue mosaics highlighted with gold stars. The doors leading into the banking hall are ornamented with figures in metal by Rene Chambellan representing the working men who might deposit their savings at the bank. The basilica-like form of the banking hall gives this space the feel of a cathedral of thrift. Twenty-two marbles were employed on the interior, for the walls, floors, columns, and decorative trim. Ornament includes symbols of commerce, thrift, industry, education, and finance; a mosaic ceiling with signs of the zodiac by Angelo Magnenti; and a mosaic mural showing an aerial view of Brooklyn executed by Ravenna Mosaics of Berlin.

HISTORIC DISTRICT

 Stuyvesant Heights Historic District. This residential district is a part of the larger Bedford-Stuyvesant community. Early development in the district took place in the 1860s, when freestanding suburban houses were erected at 87 MacDonough Street (1863) and 97 MacDonough Street (1861). A few row houses were built in the early 1870s, but most of the district's row houses and mansions were built between about 1880 and the first years of the 20th century. Within the district are fine examples of French Second Empire, neo-Grec, Romanesque Revival, and neo-Renaissance houses, all designed by Brooklyn architects. There are also a number of early apartment houses for middle-class residents, most located on corner sites. As is true of most of Brooklyn's 19th-century residential neighborhoods, this district also contains several architecturally distinguished churches: the Victorian Gothic–style Our Lady of Victory Roman Catholic Church (Thomas F. Houghton, 1891–95) and the neo-Gothic-style Saint Philip's Episcopal Church (Arni Delhi, 1899), both on MacDonough Street, and the handsome Embury Methodist Church (now Mount Lebanon Baptist Church), in the Romanesque Revival style, designed in 1894 by the prominent Brooklyn firm Parfitt Brothers and located on Decatur Street.

INDIVIDUAL LANDMARKS

41 Antioch Baptist Church, originally the Greene Avenue Baptist Church and Church House, 828 and 826 Greene Avenue (church, Lansing C. Holden and Paul F. Higgs, 1887–92; church house, Langston & Dahlander, 1891–93). The Greene Avenue Baptist Church built this Romanesque Revival/Queen Anne building at a time when this section of Bedford-Stuyvesant was being rapidly developed as a row-house neighborhood. The manner in which the midblock church is massed to resemble a group of row houses reflects the architect's effort to design a building that would fit within its urban context. Holden prepared a design, but only the extant basement can definitively be attributed to him. The upper church is either a new design by Higgs or an adaptation by Higgs of Holden's original scheme. The church was sold in 1950 to the Antioch Baptist Church, an African-American congregation established in downtown Brooklyn in 1918. The church has hosted many leaders of the civil rights movement, including Martin Luther King, Jr., as well as many important politicians and notable African-Americans. The Romanesque Revival church house is one of a row of seven houses designed in 1891.

42 Magnolia Grandiflora and Magnolia Tree Earth Center, 677, 678, and 679 Lafayette Avenue (tree, c. 1885; houses, 1880–83). This magnificent tree, which grows at the northern edge of its species' range, was planted around 1885 from a slip brought from North Carolina. The preservation of the tree and the reuse of the three adjacent late 19th-century houses, now converted into a center for environmental education, were the inspiration of Hattie Carthen, who began a grassroots campaign to revitalize Bedford-Stuyvesant in 1969.

43 Saint George's Episcopal Church, 800 Marcy Avenue (R. M. Upjohn, 1887–88, and Sunday school, 1889). This late High Victorian Gothic design is a striking example of the vivid polychromy characteristic of the style. The building also reflects the idiosyncratic nature of R. M. Upjohn's work, notably at the entrance porch, with its stout dwarf columns, and the octagonal chimney tower. Upjohn, an architect of national prominence, lived in Cobble Hill, Brooklyn.

44 Boys' High School, now the Street Academy, Brooklyn Literacy Center, and Outreach Program, 832 Marcy Avenue (James W. Naughton, 1891–92; additions, C. B. J. Snyder, c. 1905–10). In the late 19th century, Boys' High School was considered one of the most important public schools in Brooklyn; its new home was therefore conceived as a major architectural monument visi-

ble throughout much of central Brooklyn. The focus of this Romanesque Revival building is its dynamic roofline, with gables, dormers, round tower, and lofty corner campanile, all modeled on the public buildings of Henry Hobson Richardson. The school initially housed 782 students in 22 classrooms; as enrollment increased, several additions were constructed early in the 20th century. Boys' High and the nearby Girls' High (see No. 45) were organized in 1878 as separate departments of the Central Grammar School. The building has been restored by Beyer Blinder Belle, architect.

45 Girls' High School, now the Board of Education Brooklyn Adult Training Center, 475 Nostrand Avenue (James W. Naughton, 1885–86, and rear addition, 1891; Macon Street addition, C. B. J. Snyder, 1912). The roots of Girls' High School extend back to the organization of the Central Grammar School, Brooklyn's first public high school, in 1878. As the student population increased, a new school was erected on Nostrand Avenue between Halsey and Macon Streets. Only the Girls' Department of Central Grammar School moved to this facility; the Boys' Department later moved to Boys' High School (see No. 44). The Nostrand Avenue building, popularly known as Girls' High School (the name was made official in 1891), is the oldest surviving structure in New York City erected as a high school. The design of the Victorian Gothic building focuses on the central entrance pavilion with its tall cupola. The building was restored by the School Construction Authority.

46 Renaissance Apartments, 488 Nostrand Avenue and 140–144 Hancock Street (Montrose Morris, 1892). The Renaissance was commissioned by the developer Louis F. Seitz, who was responsible for some of Brooklyn's finest late 19th-century apartment houses. The design of this pale yellow brick and terra-cotta structure is closely related to that of Morris's contemporaneous Imperial Apartments (see No. 50). The vacant and deteriorated

Boys' High School (No. 44). The grand design reflects the building's status as an important public school in Brooklyn in the late 19th century. Photo by Caroline Kane Levy.

Imperial Apartments (No. 50). One of a trio of fine apartment houses for affluent middle-class Brooklynites designed by Montrose Morris for developer Louis F. Seitz. Photo by Carl Forster.

building was rehabilitated for housing in 1995–96 by Anderson Associates, architect and developer.

47 Alhambra Apartments, 500–518 Nostrand Avenue and 29–33 Macon Street (Montrose Morris, 1889–90). The earliest of the three major apartment houses designed by Morris for the developer Louis F. Seitz (see Nos. 46 and 50) and an early example of a Brooklyn apartment house for affluent middle-class tenants, the Alhambra displays rich textural contrasts and is notable for its six towers, steep roof slopes, gables, loggias, arcades, and lively terra-cotta detail. A restoration of the vacant building was scheduled to begin in 1997.

48 23rd Regiment Armory, 1322 Bedford Avenue (Fowler & Hough and Isaac Perry, 1891–95). Designed to resemble a medieval fortress, the 23rd Regiment Armory is a vast and impressive example of late 19th-century military architecture. With its corner tower rising 136 feet, its great arched entrance, and its enormous drill shed, this building is the most imposing of Brooklyn's 19th-century armories. Fowler & Hough were local architects responsible for several important late 19th-century Brooklyn buildings; Isaac Perry was the architect for New York State (the state financed the construction of most armories) and a specialist in armory design.

49 **Saint Bartholomew's Church (Episcopal)**, 1227 Pacific Street (George P. Chappell, 1886–90). Chappell, one of Brooklyn's most creative late 19th-century architects, was responsible for this quirky English-inspired Queen Anne design. The asymmetrically massed church, with its richly textured stone and brick walls, tile cladding, and picturesque tower, is set behind a garden that creates the illusion of a rural church in this urban neighborhood.

50 **Imperial Apartments**, 1198 Pacific Street and 1327–1339 Bedford Avenue (Montrose Morris, 1892). The success of the Alhambra Apartments (see No. 47) led the developer Louis F. Seitz to commission this apartment house and the Renaissance (see No. 46) in 1892. The light-colored brick building, with its terra-cotta trim, metal bay windows, tall arcades, and round corner tower, is an important presence on Grant Square. This relatively early example of a prestigious apartment house in Brooklyn was built at a time when hundreds of handsome row houses were being erected on the surrounding streets of the Crown Heights neighborhood.

51 **Weeksville Houses**, also known as the Hunterfly Road Houses, 1698–1708 Bergen Street (1840–83). These four small frame houses are all that remains of the 19th-century African-American community of Weeksville. Initially settled in the 1830s by free blacks, Weeksville grew by the 1870s into a community of several hundred, with its own public school, church, and other institutions. The surviving houses are located in the middle of a block, facing onto Hunterfly Road, a country road that predates Brooklyn's street grid. The old houses have been restored by Li-Saltzman Architects and serve as a living museum of African-American history and culture.

The Weeksville Houses (No. 51) are the remnant of a 19th-century African-American community. The four houses are now a museum of African-American history and culture. Photo by Caroline Kane Levy.

INDIVIDUAL LANDMARKS

52 **Public School 86,** also known as the Irvington School, 220 Irving Avenue (James W. Naughton, 1892–93). Naughton's creative use of Romanesque Revival forms is evident on this relatively small school in Bushwick, with its rough stone base, trios of arched windows, and large central gable articulated by a massive semicircular arch and flanked by pedimented dormers. (See also No. 7.)

53 **20th Precinct Police Station House and Stable,** later the 83rd Precinct Station House, now Brooklyn North Task Force, 179 Wilson Avenue (William B. Tubby, 1894–95). Tubby, one of Brooklyn's most inventive late 19th-century architects, designed this fanciful police station as a mock-medieval fortress, complete with crenellations and a round corner tower; the building is entered through an eccentric Doric entrance porch embellished by a beautifully carved frieze. An exceptional restoration by Ehrenkrantz & Eckstut returned the deteriorated building to active use in 1996.

54 **Reformed Church of South Bushwick,** 855–867 Bushwick Avenue (Messrs. Morgan, 1853; chapel and Sunday school, J. J. Buck, 1881;

church enlargement, 1883). This imposing church is unusual in its combination of austere Greek Revival forms, still popular in the 1850s in outlying areas such as Bushwick, with the type of Georgian-inspired tower and steeple that had gone out of fashion in most areas more than twenty-five years earlier. The church's records note that the design was "drawn up by Messrs. Morgan"; just who these men were is not known.

BROOKLYN MAP 6   BUSHWICK

The 20th Precinct Police Station House and Stable (No. 53) is a mock-medieval fortress. Photo by Carl Forster.

INDIVIDUAL LANDMARKS

55 **Engine Company No. 252**, originally Fire Engine Company 52, later Engine Company 152, 617 Central Avenue (Parfitt Brothers, 1896–97). One of Brooklyn's most talented architecture firms created this whimsical brick, red sandstone, and terra-cotta firehouse for the Brooklyn Fire Department (the initials BFD are carved on the facade) at a time of major expansion. The Flemish Revival style, evident in the scrolled and stepped gables, links the building to Bushwick's history as a 17th-century Dutch settlement.

56 **Public School 73**, 241 MacDougal Street (James W. Naughton, 1888, and addition, 1895). The construction and rapid expansion of this school reflect the fact that the area where Bedford-Stuyvesant meets East New York underwent significant development following the opening of the elevated rail lines on Fulton Street and Broadway in the 1880s. The tall central tower of P.S. 73 is a focal point in the neighborhood; the school is ornamented with handsome terra-cotta detail. (See also No. 7.)

57 **Public School 108**, 200 Linwood Street (James W. Naughton, 1895). The imposing yellow brick Romanesque Revival mass of P.S. 108 in Cypress Hills rises from a rough stone base to a steeply sloping roof that is punctuated by gables and dormers. (See also No. 7.)

58 **Public School 65K,** 158 Richmond Street (Samuel Leonard, 1870; facade, James W. Naughton, 1889). The earliest part of P.S. 65K in Cypress Hills was built in 1870, but the unpretentious Romanesque Revival–style Richmond Street

facade, with its striking Gothic-inspired detail was not constructed until 1889. (See also No. 7.)

59 **New Lots Reformed Dutch Church,** now New Lots Community Church, 630 New Lots Avenue (1823–24). This simple wood building, with Gothic-inspired pointed windows and a modest cupola, was erected to serve a small farming community. It has been transformed into an important historic presence in a struggling inner-city neighborhood.

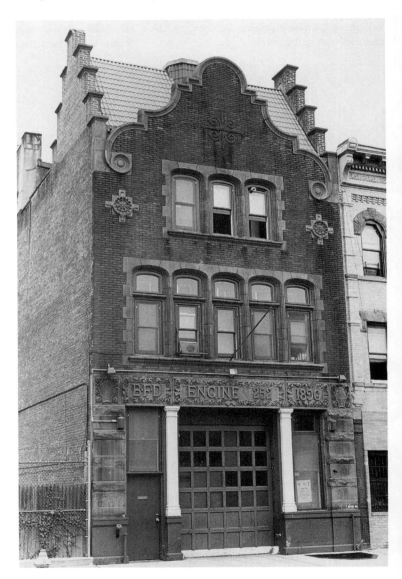

Engine Company No. 252 (No. 55). The Flemish Revival design reflects Bushwick's history as a 17th-century Dutch settlement. Photo by Andrew S. Dolkart.

INDIVIDUAL LANDMARKS

60 **Weir Greenhouse,** now McGovern-Weir Greenhouse, Fifth Avenue at 25th Street (G. Curtis Gillespie, 1895). Located across from the main entrance gates to Green-Wood Cemetery (see No. 61), this structure is a rare surviving example of a 19th-century commercial greenhouse. Erected by James Weir, Jr., a member of a Brooklyn family long involved in horticulture, the greenhouse is a wood and glass structure with projecting corner pavilions and an octagonal dome. Since its completion, the greenhouse has catered to those seeking to purchase plants and flowers to embellish grave sites.

61 **Green-Wood Cemetery Gate,** Fifth Avenue at 25th Street (Richard Upjohn & Son, 1861–65). The design of this spectacular Gothic Revival gate is generally attributed to R. M. Upjohn, as opposed to his more famous father, Richard Upjohn. The two entrance arches with their soaring pinnacled gables and the adjoining pavilions are intri-

cately carved from New Jersey brownstone. Above the arches are four panels of Nova Scotia sandstone carved with scenes evoking themes relating to death and resurrection; these are the work of John Moffit. A restoration of the gates was completed in 1996 (Platt, Byard & Dovell, architect).

62 **18th Police Precinct Station House and Stable,** later 68th Police Precinct House and Stable, now the Sunset Park School of Music, 4302 Fourth Avenue (George Ingram, 1890–92). This former police station is one of several station houses in Brooklyn designed by police department architect George Ingram (possibly with the assistance of Emile Gruwé) late in the 19th century to resemble a medieval fortress. The impregnable quality is emphasized by the presence of a massive arched entry and a corner tower. The fortresslike design is offset by the use of such details as complex pointed-arch windows, exuberant iron tie rods, and fanciful carved heads. The stable and main building have been converted into a school of music.

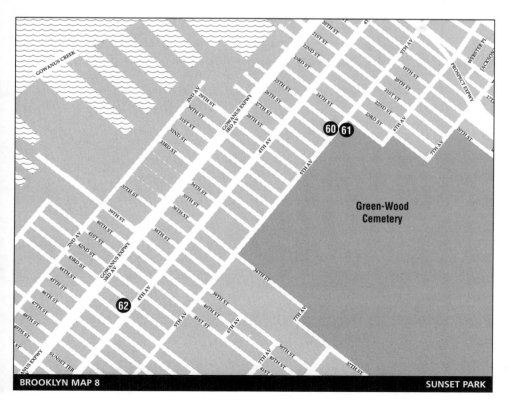

The spectacular Green-Wood
Cemetery Gate (No. 61) is carved
with scenes relating to death and
resurrection. Photo by Carl Forster.

HISTORIC DISTRICTS

12 **Park Slope Historic District.** Park Slope is situated along the western edge of Prospect Park (see No. 69). Located several miles from Brooklyn's 19th-century ferry terminals, Park Slope owes its development as a prestigious neighborhood to the opening of the Brooklyn Bridge (see No. 15) in 1883; the convenience of commuting over the bridge permitted people to live in locations that were farther from Manhattan than previously developed areas. The Slope contains a mix of mansions, row houses, apartment houses, and institutional buildings, almost all of which were erected in

the final decades of the 19th century and the first years of the 20th century. These include many rows of brownstone houses as well as some of the most outstanding Romanesque Revival and Queen Anne residences in the United States. The brick and stone houses on Carroll Street and Montgomery Place designed by C. P. H. Gilbert in the late 1880s are especially distinguished, as is Montrose Morris's Henry Hulbert House, now the Poly Prep–Woodward School (1892) at 49 Prospect Park West. The district's fine institutional structures include a cluster of three Gothic-style churches at Saint John's Place and Seventh Avenue—Saint John's Episcopal (Edward T. Potter, 1889; nave, John Rochester

Thomas, 1885), Grace Methodist (Parfitt Brothers, 1882–83), and Memorial Presbyterian (Pugin & Walter, 1882–83); the imposing Classical Revival Beth Elohim Synagogue (Eisendrath & Horowitz, 1908–10; Temple House, Mortimer Freehof and David Levy, 1928) on Eighth Avenue and Garfield Place; and the architect Francis H. Kimball's spectacular Venetian Gothic Montauk Club (1889–91) on Eighth Avenue and Lincoln Place, with its superb terra-cotta detail.

⑬ Prospect–Lefferts Gardens Historic District. At the time when suburban development was sweeping through Flatbush, the northern edge of the area was built up primarily with blocks of modest row houses. This movement was initiated in the 1890s by James Lefferts, who subdivided eight blocks of his family's ancestral farm (see No. 71) into Lefferts Manor, a development with restrictive covenants that required the construction of single-family houses. Between 1897 and the mid–1920s,

row houses and a few freestanding houses were erected in Lefferts Manor and on some of the adjoining streets. Among the outstanding houses are the neo-Renaissance limestone rows on Maple and Midwood Streets designed by Axel Hedman in the first years of this century and the Colonial Revival and neo-medieval brick houses from the 1920s that Slee & Bryson designed for sites on Fenimore and Midwood Streets and Rutland Road.

INDIVIDUAL LANDMARKS

㊺ Public School 9, later Public School 111, now Public School 340, 249 Sterling Place (Samuel B. Leonard, 1867–68; additions, James W. Naughton, 1887). This Early Romanesque Revival school was constructed in conjunction with the development of the surrounding Prospect Heights community in the 1860s. The focus of the building is a central gabled pavilion with fine brick arches. (See also No. 7.)

Park Slope Historic District (H.D. 12), Montgomery Place. The district contains some of the country's finest examples of Romanesque Revival and Queen Anne residences. Photo by Carl Forster.

64 Public School 9 Annex, 251 Sterling Place (James W. Naughton, 1895). As the population of Prospect Heights increased in the late 19th century, P.S. 9 (see above) became overcrowded, and this handsome Romanesque Revival brick and stone annex with brownstone Renaissance-inspired detail was erected. The building has been converted into apartments.

65 Eastern Parkway Scenic Landmark, between Grand Army Plaza and Ralph Avenue (Frederick Law Olmsted and Calvert Vaux, 1870–74). Eastern Parkway was part of a regional system envisioned by Olmsted and Vaux in 1866 as a means of introducing open space, fresh air, and greenery into the city's residential neighborhoods. The idea of a tree-lined boulevard with a central roadway flanked by access roads was new to the United States; Olmsted coined the term *parkway* in 1868 to describe this new type of urban thoroughfare. The parkway begins at Prospect Park and originally extended eastward to Ralph Avenue. It was intended that the parkway would continue north to the East River and then, on the other side of the river, extend to Central Park and the Hudson River; to the south the system runs from Prospect Park, via Ocean Parkway (see No. 91), to the Atlantic shore.

66 Brooklyn Museum, now Brooklyn Museum of Art, 200 Eastern Parkway at Washington Avenue (McKim, Mead & White, 1893–1915; removal of front stairs, 1934–35). In 1893 McKim, Mead & White won a competition for the new home of the Brooklyn Institute of Arts and Sciences. The firm's winning entry proposed a monumental Classical Revival structure, only a small portion of which was eventually erected. The building is enhanced by extensive sculptural embellishment undertaken by a group of artists supervised by Daniel Chester French. The museum was originally entered via a grand flight of stairs leading to the Ionic portico; these stairs were removed in 1934–35. The museum, housing one of the country's finest art collections, is especially famous for its American, Egyptian, and African holdings.

67 Brooklyn Central Office, Bureau of Fire Communications, 35 Empire Boulevard (Frank J. Helmle, 1913). Designed in a Florentine Early Renaissance style, this elegant building serves as a communications center for the New York City Fire Department. Helmle was responsible for many of Brooklyn's finest early 20th-century Renaissance-inspired landmarks, including buildings in Prospect Park (see No. 72) and Winthrop Park (see No. 6) and several Roman Catholic churches.

68 Soldiers' and Sailors' Memorial Arch, Grand Army Plaza (John H. Duncan, 1889–92; alterations, McKim, Mead & White, 1894–1901). Designed in the tradition of Roman imperial arches, this Civil War memorial is the centerpiece of one of the finest formal civic design projects in the United States. The construction of Duncan's arch, the winning entry in a competition, was completed in 1892. Two years later Stanford White planned alterations to allow the addition of sculpture: heroic bronze groups representing the army and the navy, as well as the arch's crowning Victory quadriga, all by Frederick MacMonnies; a pair of bronze relief panels depicting Lincoln and Grant on horseback (the horses were modeled by Thomas Eakins, the figures by William O'Donovan); and carved spandrel figures by Philip Martiny.

69 Prospect Park Scenic Landmark, bounded by Flatbush Avenue, Parkside Avenue, Prospect Park West, and Prospect Park Southwest (Frederick Law Olmsted and Calvert Vaux, designed 1865; constructed 1866–73). Prospect Park is generally considered the masterpiece of designers Frederick Law Olmsted and Calvert Vaux. Planned as Brooklyn's counterpart to Central Park (see Manhattan No. 315), Prospect Park is a milestone in the movement to create naturalistic parks in America's cities as a response to the increasing industrialization and congestion of the urban environment. A Brooklyn park was initially authorized in 1859, but the Civil War delayed work. In 1864 James S. T. Stranahan, later known as the Father of Prospect Park, approached Vaux, who in turn persuaded Olmsted to assist with the design. Their plan, submitted in 1866, divided the park into three zones: meadows (notably the Long Meadow, which at ninety acres is the largest lawn in New York), forests, and water bodies. Vaux was responsible for a series of splendid structures, including several bridges, the Oriental Pavilion (restored, following a fire, by the New York City Department of General Services), and the terraces of the Concert Grove (designed in conjunction with Jacob Wrey Mould). The park's classical entrances, designed between 1889 and 1907 by McKim, Mead & White in conjunction with prominent sculptors (notably Brooklyn-born Frederick MacMonnies), reflect a late 19th-century shift in ideas about landscape design away from the picturesque in favor of increased formality. In addition to the gates, classical pavilions were erected within the park based on designs by McKim, Mead & White and the local architecture firm Helmle & Huberty.

70 **Edwin Clarke and Grace Hill Litchfield House, Grace Hill,** also known as Litchfield Villa, now the Brooklyn Headquarters of the New York City Department of Parks and Recre-

ation, Prospect Park West at 5th Street (A. J. Davis, 1854–57). The lawyer and railroad financier Edwin Clarke Litchfield purchased a good deal of land in Brooklyn in the 1850s. At the crest of Prospect Hill, Litchfield erected one of the finest Italianate villas in the United States. Originally clad in stucco tinted to simulate stone, the building has a picturesque silhouette; its towers and projecting bays were planned to take advantage of views of the surrounding landscape and of New York Harbor. On the south side is a porch supported by columns with corncob capitals. Part of the grounds were incorporated into Prospect Park when the park site was acquired and the house was converted in 1913 for use by the Parks Department.

71 **Peter Lefferts House,** also known as the Lefferts Homestead, Flatbush Avenue near Empire Boulevard (1777–83). Peter Lefferts built this farmhouse in the traditional Dutch Colonial style to replace an earlier dwelling that was burned by American troops during the Battle of Brooklyn in 1776. Originally located on Flatbush Avenue between Maple and Midwood Streets, the house was moved to Prospect Park in 1918 to save it from destruction; it is now a museum specializing in children's educational programs.

72 **Boathouse,** Lullwater (Helmle & Huberty, 1904). As is appropriate for a building located at water's edge, this white terra-cotta-clad pavilion

was modeled on the Renaissance palaces that line the Grand Canal in Venice.

73 **Croquet Shelter,** Parkside Avenue (McKim, Mead & White, 1904). The Croquet Shelter, also known as the Grecian Shelter, is a beautifully proportioned Corinthian temple reminiscent of 18th-century French neoclassical garden pavilions.

74 **Public School 39,** also known as the Henry Bristow School, 417 Sixth Avenue (Samuel B. Leonard, 1876–77). Located in Park Slope, this building in the French Second Empire style displays typically French features—the projecting central frontispiece and end pavilions and the crowning mansard roof with iron cresting that were adapted by Leonard to the demands of public school design. (See also No. 7.)

75 **William B. Cronyn House,** also known as the 271 Ninth Street House (1856–57). This French Second Empire suburban villa was erected by a wealthy Wall Street merchant. The stucco-covered house is especially notable for its central cupola lit by a clerestory and its slate mansard roof with end pavilions and iron cresting. When the house was built, the surrounding area was largely open farmland, but by the end of the 19th century, the neighborhood had become industrialized and the house served as the headquarters for Charles M. Higgins's india ink company. Today the house is again in residential use.

76 **Public Bath No. 7,** 227–231 Fourth Avenue (Raymond F. Almirall, 1906–10). Early in the 20th century, New York City erected an extensive system of public bathhouses in neighborhoods where most of the residences lacked indoor plumbing. The bathhouse on Fourth Avenue served the Gowanus community. The building is faced in brick and terra cotta with glazed white surfaces that connote cleanliness. Its ornamental forms evoke bathing and the sea. These include fish, tridents, shells, and streams of water, many of them in polychromatic terra cotta.

Prospect Park Scenic Landmark (No. 69). The masterpiece of renowned landscape architects and park designers Frederick Law Olmsted and Calvert Vaux. Photo: Landmarks Preservation Commission, from the collection of the Long Island Historical Society.

HISTORIC DISTRICTS

14 **Albemarle–Kenmore Terraces Historic District.** This small historic district, nestled behind the grounds of the Flatbush Reformed Dutch Church (see No. 77), consists of two culs-de-sac lined with houses designed by the local firm Slee & Bryson. Albemarle Terrace (1916–17) has charming Colonial Revival brick row houses, while the Garden City–inspired Kenmore Terrace (1917–18, with two houses from 1919–20) is an early example of the influence of the automobile on American architecture; each house on the south side of Kenmore Terrace incorporates a garage into the ground story.

15 **Prospect Park South Historic District.** Prospect Park South, Brooklyn's most imposing suburban neighborhood, was a development scheme initiated by Dean Alvord, who sought "to create a rural park within the limitations of the conventional city block and city street." After purchasing approximately sixty acres of farmland in 1899, Alvord laid out all the utilities, erected brick gateposts, planned lawns and malls, and hired the

Scottish landscape gardener John Aitkin to supervise the plantings. Alvord also hired an architectural staff, which was headed by the talented John J. Petit, to design large, comfortable houses in a wide variety of styles. Petit was responsible for some of the finest houses in the district (as an alternative, owners could hire their own architects), including examples of the Colonial Revival (for example, 1510 Albemarle Road), neo-Tudor (183 Argyle Road), and Queen Anne (1423 and 1501 Albemarle Road) styles, as well as several more uncommon examples, most notably a Swiss chalet (100 Rugby Road) and a house modeled on a Japanese pagoda (131 Buckingham Road). Within a few years Alvord had created a community that, in his words, was "acceptable to people of culture with means equal to some of the luxuries as well as the necessities of life."

16 **Ditmas Park Historic District.** Following the success of Prospect Park South (see H.D. 15), much of Flatbush was developed with freestanding suburban homes. Ditmas Park was a real-estate venture planned by the developer Lewis H. Pounds in 1902. Pounds graded the land, divided the area into lots, and planted the magnificent trees that still grace the streets. He then erected houses or sold lots to other builders. Most of the houses in the district are wood-frame structures in the Colonial Revival style, although there are also a few examples of neo-Tudor and neo-Renaissance design. Most of them were designed by local Brooklyn architects such as A. White Pierce, Arlington Isham, Benjamin Driesler, and Slee & Bryson who were responsible for residential work throughout Brooklyn in the early 20th century. The most unusual houses in the district are Arlington Isham's Arts and Crafts bungalows on East 16th Street, all built in 1909, and the romantic English cottage, designed in 1931 by Frank J. Forster and R. A. Gallimore for legendary baker Arthur Ebinger, located at 415 East 19th Street. The most prominent building in the district is the imposing neo-Georgian Flatbush Congregational Church, designed in 1910 by the Boston architecture firm Allen & Collens working in collaboration with the local architect Louis Jallade. The adjacent parish house, designed by Whitefield & King and built in 1899, is an unusual polygonal Shingle Style structure.

INDIVIDUAL LANDMARKS

77 **Flatbush Reformed Dutch Church Complex,** 890 Flatbush Avenue (church, Thomas Fardon, 1793–98; cemetery, first burial, 17th century; parsonage, at 2101–2103 Kenmore Terrace, 1853; church house, Meyer & Mathieu, 1923–24). This church, the third to be erected at this location, occupies the site in longest continuous use for religious purposes in New York City. The stone and brick building in the Federal style has an elegant clock tower and steeple. To the south and west is a cemetery that contains the graves of members of local families; familiar names include Vanderbilt, Lott, Lefferts, Cortelyou, and Bergen. The parsonage is an exceptional example of a vernacular house in a transitional style, with both Greek Revival and Italianate features. A Colonial Revival brick church house completes the complex.

78 **Erasmus Hall Academy,** now Erasmus Hall Museum, in the courtyard of Erasmus Hall High School, 911 Flatbush Avenue (1786). Erasmus Hall, the first secondary school chartered by the New York State Board of Regents, was originally a private school for boys. Founded with the assistance of Alexander Hamilton, Aaron Burr, John Jay, and others, the school was housed in this Federal-period wooden building until Erasmus Hall High School, the surrounding Collegiate Gothic complex, was erected early in the 20th century.

79 **Flatbush Town Hall,** 35 Snyder Avenue (John Y. Culyer, 1874–75). Designed in a High Victorian Gothic style by Culyer, an engineer, this brick and stone structure, with its prominent tower and gables, is a reminder of the period when Flatbush was an independent community. The building, which was restored in the late 1980s after years of standing vacant, is currently used by the New York City Board of Education.

Prospect Park South Historic District (H.D. 15). Brooklyn's most imposing suburban neighborhood contains a varied mixture of architectural styles, including this idiosyncratic Japanese-style house at 131 Buckingham Road. Photo by Caroline Kane Levy.

215

INDIVIDUAL LANDMARKS

80 **Johannes Van Nuyse House,** also known as the Van Nuyse–Magaw House, 1041 East 22nd Street (1800–03). With its wide gambrel roof, this house is an especially fine example of a traditional Dutch Colonial farmhouse. Moved to this site in 1916 from its original location several blocks to the south, the house was erected by Johannes Van Nuyse, the son of Joost Van Nuyse (see No. 81), and his bride, Nellie Lott. Between 1844 and 1909, the house and its surrounding farmland were owned by Robert Magaw and his descendants.

81 **Joost and Elizabeth Van Nuyse House,** also known as Coe House, 1128 East 34th Street (before 1792). Joost Van Nuyse is recorded as having died in this building in 1792. With its characteristic Dutch Colonial design, the house is the sole remnant of Joost's 85-acre Flatlands farm.

82 **Flatlands Dutch Reformed Church,** Kings

Highway at East 40th Street (1848). With its simple clapboard siding, multipaned windows, and tall steeple, the Flatlands church is a notable example of rural Greek Revival design. The church, which is the third building to occupy this site, was restored after a fire in 1977.

83 John and Altje Baxter House, also known as Stoothoff-Baxter-Kouwenhoven House, 1640 East 48th Street (wing, c. 1747; main house, 1811). The small wing of this house was probably erected by Wilhelmus Stoothoff. His granddaughter Altje married John Baxter, and in 1811 they moved the small building, connecting it to a new, larger house. The entire house was reoriented on the lot around 1900. The steeply pitched roof, projecting eaves, and end chimneys are typical features of Dutch Colonial design.

84 Hendrick I. Lott House, 1940 East 36th Street (east wing, 1720; main section and west wing, 1800). The Lott family first settled in what is now Brooklyn in 1652. In 1720 Johannes Lott erected a small house in the village of Flatlands. Eighty years later his grandson Hendrick built a new house that incorporated the earlier building as its east wing. The house, designed in traditional

Dutch Colonial style, remains on its original site and is virtually unaltered on the exterior, retaining its gambrel roof, spring eaves, and shingled siding. The large site gives a sense of the house's original setting. The house has been vacant for many years.

85 Henry and Abraham Wyckoff House, also known as the Wyckoff-Bennett Homestead, 1669 East 22nd Street (c. 1766). Built by Henry and Abraham Wyckoff, this house is generally considered to be the most beautiful of the surviving Dutch Colonial farmhouses in Brooklyn. During the Revolutionary War, Hessian soldiers were quartered on the premises. In 1835 the house was sold to the Bennett family, and it remained in their possession until the 1980s. The house has a long porch sheltered by a curved roof that rests on columns, and it retains its original double Dutch door. It was reoriented on the site in the 1890s.

86 Elias Hubbard Ryder House, 1926 East 28th Street (1834). An extremely late example of a house designed in the Dutch Colonial style, the Ryder House displays such characteristic features as a sloping roof and deep projecting eaves. The house was slightly altered when it was moved to its present site in 1929.

The Henry and Abraham Wyckoff House (No. 85) is generally considered the most beautiful Dutch Colonial farmhouse in Brooklyn. Photo by Caroline Kane Levy.

INDIVIDUAL LANDMARKS

87 **Gravesend Cemetery,** Gravesend Neck Road at McDonald Avenue (c. 1650s). Gravesend was the first English settlement in the New Netherlands and the first European community in the New World established by a woman—Lady Deborah Moody. This small cemetery of 1.6 acres may date back to the 1650s, but all the gravestones predating the 18th century have been lost.

88 **Parachute Jump,** Riegelmann Boardwalk at West 16th Street (James H. Strong, inventor; Elwyn

E. Seelye & Co., engineers, 1939). Originally constructed at the New York World's Fair of 1939–40, the Parachute Jump was rebuilt in 1940 at Coney Island's Steeplechase Park, where it continued to thrill riders for twenty-eight years. Although the jump has long been closed, the tapered steel structure with its radiating crown remains one of the borough's most visible landmarks. The Parks Department stabilized the structure in the early 1990s.

89 **Wonder Wheel,** 3059 West 12th Street (Charles Herman, inventor; Eccentric Ferris Wheel Amusement Co., manufacturer, 1918–20). The Wonder

The wood-track Cyclone (No. 90) is one of America's most famous roller coasters.
Photo by Janet Adams.

Wheel is a variant of the typical Ferris wheel. The 150-foot-tall, 200-ton steel wheel has 24 passenger cars and can hold up to 160 passengers. While 8 of the cars are stationary, the remaining 16 are swinging cars that slide along serpentine tracks. The Wonder Wheel has excited Coney Island visitors since the park opened on Memorial Day in 1920.

90 **The Cyclone,** 834 Surf Avenue (Harry C. Baker, inventor; Vernon Keenan, engineer, 1927). The Cyclone at Coney Island, one of America's most famous roller coasters (it has been called the world's best), is one of a vanishing breed of wood-track coasters. The Cyclone is a gravity ride. A chain pulls the three-car train to the top of the first plunge; the train then runs on its own momentum, reaching a speed of up to 68 miles per hour as it proceeds through nine drops and six curves.

91 **Ocean Parkway Scenic Landmark,** south of Prospect Park extending from Church Avenue to Seabreeze Avenue (Frederick Law Olmsted and Calvert Vaux, 1874–76). Ocean Parkway was planned as part of an extensive system of parkways that would extend the rural beauty of Prospect Park

into Brooklyn's residential neighborhoods and that were eventually to connect with Manhattan's Central Park. The road—with its central drive, landscaped malls, bridle path (now paved), pedestrian promenade, and narrow access roads—originally ran from the park to Coney Island and was a companion to Eastern Parkway (see No. 65). The northernmost section was destroyed in the 1950s for the construction of the Prospect Expressway.

92 **F.W.I.L. Lundy Brothers Restaurant,** 1901–1929 Emmons Avenue (Bloch & Hesse, 1934). Lundy's, one of New York's best-loved seafood palaces, is a major cultural and architectural presence in the waterfront community of Sheepshead Bay. The Spanish Colonial Revival–style restaurant, thought to be the largest restaurant in the country at its completion, was erected by Frederick Lundy at the time when the federal government was investing in the reconstruction of the area's waterfront. The restaurant boomed during the 1950s, serving fifteen thousand people on holidays such as Mother's Day. The restaurant closed in 1979 but reopened in 1996 after major restoration (Van J. Brody, architect).

93 Howard E. and Jessie Jones House, also known as the 8200 Narrows Avenue House (J. Sarsfield Kennedy, 1916–17). Arts and Crafts design is rare in New York City, but this house built of boulders is a striking example of the type. Erected for a successful shipping merchant, the house is set on a large landscaped plot and contains a series of homey details, including an asphalt roof designed to simulate thatch.

94 Fort Hamilton Casemate Fort, now the Officers' Club, Whiting Quadrangle (1825–31). Fort Hamilton and its companion, Fort Wadsworth on Staten Island (see Staten Island No. 26), were erected to protect the Narrows at the entrance to New York Harbor. The granite casemate fort, erected as part of the Totten system of seacoast fortifications, is an impressive example of 19th-century military architecture. The fort was altered in 1937–38 when it was converted for use as an officers' club.

95 New Utrecht Reformed Church, 18th Avenue at 83rd Street (1828). Reusing rubble stone from an earlier octagonal church of 1699 in its construction, the New Utrecht church is attractively sited on a landscaped plot. The building has Gothic pointed arches, a square tower, and a pedimented front elevation articulated by a beautifully proportioned roundel window in the Federal style.

96 Pieter Claesen Wyckoff House, 5900 Clarendon Road at Ralph Avenue (c. 1652; additions, 1740 and 1820). The Pieter Claesen Wyckoff House includes the oldest surviving built structure in New York State; fittingly, the house was the first New York City landmark to be designated after the establishment of the Landmarks Preservation Commission in 1965. The west wing of the Wyckoff House appears to have been built around 1652, with the main section added around 1740. The house was owned by Wyckoff descendants until 1901, repurchased by the Wyckoff Family Foundation in 1961, and donated to the city in 1970. It has been largely reconstructed (Oppenheimer, Brady & Vogelstein, architect) and is now a museum.

BROOKLYN MAP 13

The Pieter Claesen Wyckoff House (No. 96) contains the oldest surviving built structure in
New York State. It is now a museum. Photo: Landmarks Preservation Commission collection.

QUEENS OVERVIEW MAP

tone ⑤ ②

14th Av

Blvd

Francis Lewis Blvd

Crocheron Av

m Blvd

②⑤A

46th Av

KISSENA PARK

Expwy

St

73rd Av

Utopia Pkwy

Hollis Ct Blvd

②⑨⑤

④⑨⑤

CUNNINGHAM PARK

ST. JOHN'S UNIV. ■

Union Tpk

Grand Central Pkwy

②⑤

Hillside Av

Jamaica Av

③①-③⑨
Jamaica

Liberty Av

QUEENS

Merrick Blvd

Guy Brewer Blvd

Linden Blvd

Baisley Blvd

Farmers Blvd

Southern Pkwy

JOHN F. KENNEDY
INTERNATIONAL

Cross Island Pkwy

Cleanview Expwy

Bell Blvd

Springfield Blvd

②⑦

Little
Neck
Bay

②⑥

ALLEY PARK

②⑧ ②⑨

Great Neck
Plaza

Neck Rd

Bayview Av

Northern Blvd

Long Island Expwy

Northern State Pkwy

Little Neck Pkwy

③⓪

Hillside Av

②⑤

Francis Lewis

Hempstead Av

Murdock A

Rockaway Blvd

Northern Blvd

Comm Dr

①⑨⑤
④⑨⑤

LAKE SUCCESS PARK

New Hyde Pk Rd

Marcus Av

Union Tpk

②⑤B

Jericho Tpk

Tulip Av

New Hyde Pk Rd

BELMONT RACE ■

PARK RACE ■

Plainfield Av

FLORAL PARK

JOHN F. KENNEDY
INTERNATIONAL
AIRPORT
④⓪

Inwood

Burnside Av

Sheridan Blvd

Empire Av

Broadway

ROCKAWAY COMMUNITY PARK

Far
Rockaway
④①

LAWRENCE VILLAGE PARK

Seagirt Blvd

❶ Adrian and Ann Wyckoff Onderdonk House, 1820–1836 Flushing Avenue, Ridgewood (c. third quarter 18th century). This is a rare example of a surviving farmhouse built of stone in the Dutch Colonial, or "Dutch American," tradition. The gambrel-roofed structure faces Flushing Avenue, a colonial-era road connecting the Dutch town of Bushwick and the English settlement of Newtown. The house was built for members of the Van Ende family and was sold to the Onderdonks in 1821. The building was reconstructed by architect Giorgio Cavaglieri in 1980–82 following a disastrous fire.

❹ Hunter's Point Historic District. This district, extending along facing blockfronts, is an unusual example of 19th-century middle-class rowhouse construction in Queens. The urbanization of Hunter's Point followed the 1861 inauguration of ferry service between 34th Street in Manhattan and the nearby Long Island Railroad terminus. Development began in the historic district in the early

1870s and continued until 1890. Among the earliest houses are ten faced with Tuckahoe (or Westchester) marble, at 21-12–21-20 and 21-21–21-29 45th Avenue (1871–72). This material, common on mid-19th-century commercial buildings, was rarely used for entire row-house facades.

❷ New York State Supreme Court, Queens County, Long Island City Branch, 25-10 Court Square, Long Island City (George Hathorne, 1872–76; reconstruction, Peter M. Coco, 1904–08). In 1870 the seat of Queens County was moved from Jamaica to Long Island City; shortly thereafter a new courthouse was erected. Following a disastrous fire in 1904, the building was rebuilt and enlarged in a Beaux-Arts manner by the local architect Peter M. Coco. A parking garage was built at the rear of the courthouse in 1988–90 (Skidmore, Owings & Merrill, architect), replacing two jail structures.

❸ New York Architectural Terra Cotta Company Building, 42-10–42-16 Vernon Boulevard, Long Island City (Francis H. Kimball, 1892). The New York Architectural Terra Cotta Company was one of the leading manufacturers of ornamental terra cotta between 1886, when the firm was founded, and 1928, when it went bankrupt. The company manufactured the terra cotta for such landmarks as the Ansonia Hotel (see Manhattan No. 329) and Carnegie Hall (see Manhattan No. 300). This small office building displays the range and potential of the products manufactured by the company. Its architect was a pioneer in the use of ornamental terra cotta, as can be seen, for example, at his Montauk Club (1889–91) in Park Slope (see Brooklyn H.D. 12), with its Venetian-inspired terra cotta also fabricated by this New York firm. The building has been vacant for many years.

❹ Queensboro Bridge, spanning the East River between 11th Street and Bridge Plaza North and Bridge Plaza South, Queens, and East 59th Street, Manhattan (Gustav Lindenthal, engineer; Henry Hornbostel, architect, 1901–08). Inspired by the Pont Mirabeau in Paris, the Queensboro Bridge is a "through-type" cantilevered structure; that is, the roadway runs between the structure's piers and trusses. As the third bridge to span the East River and the first to connect Queens and Manhattan, it

was a potent influence on the development of the borough of Queens. The heavy steel towers and frame rest on stone piers. Beneath the bridge are tall vaulted spaces faced with Guastavino tiles.

❺ Famous Players–Lasky Studio, later Paramount Studios Building No. 1, now Kaufman's Astoria Motion Picture and Television Center, 35-11 35th Avenue, Astoria (Fleischman Construction Company, 1919–21). Built at a time when New York City was a major center for motion picture production, the former Famous Players–Lasky Studio is once again one of America's most active film and television production centers. Between 1921 and 1927, more than 110 silent features were filmed here, including movies starring Gloria Swanson, Rudolph Valentino, W. C. Fields, and Dorothy Gish. Following the introduction of sound, films such as the Marx Brothers' *Animal Crackers* and Paul Robeson's acclaimed version of Eugene O'Neill's *The Emperor Jones* were shot at the studio.

❻ Sidewalk Clock: 30-78 Steinway Street (1922). Many of New York's commercial streets were once graced by cast-iron sidewalk clocks, generally erected as advertisements by local banks and stores (see Manhattan No. 162). Two of these clocks survive in Queens (see No. 35). This clock was erected by Wagner's Jewelers in 1922. The clock was purchased secondhand by Edward Wagner and moved from Manhattan to its present site.

7 **Lawrence Family Graveyard,** southeast corner of 20th Road and 35th Street, Steinway (1703–1975). This small private cemetery is the resting place of eighty-nine members of the distinguished Lawrence family, including twelve high-ranking American military officers. Oliver Lawrence, who died in 1975, was the last family member buried at the site.

8 **Benjamin T. Pike House,** later the William Steinway House, 18-33 41st Street, Steinway (c. 1858). Pike, a manufacturer of scientific instruments, erected this magnificent Italianate stone villa, with its tall square tower and cast-iron porches, on what at the time was a beautiful riverfront site. The house was purchased in 1870 by William Steinway, whose piano factory is still located nearby.

9 **Abraham Lent House,** also known as the Lent Homestead, 78-03 19th Road, Steinway (c. 1729). One of the few surviving dwellings in Queens built in the Dutch Colonial tradition, the Abraham Lent House has walls of rough stone and contrasting wooden shingles and a steeply sloping roof with deep front and rear overhangs.

10 **Marine Air Terminal, La Guardia Airport** (Delano & Aldrich, 1939–40). The Art Deco Marine Air Terminal evokes the glamour of early air travel. It was a principal feature of Mayor Fiorello La Guardia's plan to build a major airport in New York City. North Beach Airport (as La Guardia was originally called) was the largest single undertaking financed by the Works Progress Administration (WPA). The Marine Air Terminal was built for Pan American's luxurious transatlantic seaplanes, known as clipper ships. The terminal is massed

Benjamin T. Pike House (No. 8), a magnificent Italianate stone villa.
Photo by Stephen Senigo.

around a central circular core, with a rectangular entrance pavilion and two symmetrically disposed wings. Its exterior ornament includes a polychromatic terra-cotta frieze of flying fish. The **interior** consists of a small foyer and vestibule with stainless steel detail and a spectacular central rotunda encircled with James Brooks's *Flight,* a 12-foot-high, 237-foot-long mural commissioned by the WPA. The mural, which was painted over in the 1950s, was restored by Alan Farancz in 1980. In 1996 Beyer Blinder Belle, architect, undertook a restoration of other interior features as well as the exterior.

❷ **Jackson Heights Historic District.** The Jackson Heights Historic District celebrates the innovative garden apartment and garden home development undertaken by the Queensboro Corporation on the former farm fields of north central Queens, primarily in the 1910s and 1920s. The opening of the Queensboro Bridge (see No. 4) in 1909 and the inauguration of service on the elevated Interborough Rapid Transit line (now the No. 7 train) in 1917 made this outlying region of Queens County a prime location for the construction of homes for middle-class New Yorkers. The Queensboro Corporation began purchasing land in 1910 and erected a few traditional row houses and apartment buildings, such as the row at 37-46–37-60 83rd Street (Charles Peck, 1911) and the Laurel Court apartments (George H. Wells, 1913–14) at 33-01–33-21 82nd Street. Beginning in 1917, with the construction of architect George H. Wells's

Jackson Heights Historic District (H.D. 2), an innovative development in the early 20th century, contains garden apartment buildings like the Greystone Apartments, pictured here. Photo: Courtesy Jackson Heights Beautification Group collection.

Greystone Apartments on both sides of 80th Street between 35th and 37th Avenues, the Queensboro Corporation pioneered in the design of garden apartment complexes with five- and six-story buildings erected in groups. They had large land-scaped gardens at the rear that increased light and air and created a suburban atmosphere within the neighborhood's gridded urban street pattern. The most interesting of the apartment complexes were those erected on a single block with shared, undivided rear gardens. This plan was initiated by architect Andrew J. Thomas at Linden Court (1919–21) on 84th and 85th Streets between 37th and Roosevelt Avenues and reached its peak at Jackson Heights's most spectacular apartment complexes, including Wells's Cambridge Court (1922–23) on 85th and 86th Streets and Thomas's Chateau (1922) and Towers (1923–25), both of which line 80th and 81st Streets. The apartment complexes were designed, primarily by Wells and Thomas, in eclectic and conservative styles, including English Gothic/Tudor (Greystone), French

Gothic (Chateau), neo-Georgian (Cambridge Court), and Italian Romanesque/Renaissance (Towers). To attract middle-class households that might otherwise have moved out of New York City to single-family suburban homes, the Queensboro Corporation organized its apartments as cooperatives, so that residents would also be owners. These are among the first cooperatives in New York City planned for the middle class. In addition to apartment buildings, the Queensboro Corporation built attached and semidetached single-family houses (some were planned so they could easily be converted into two-family units) in picturesque ensembles with brick facades and traditional American Colonial and English Tudor detail. These rows had combined rear yards or rear alleys leading to garages designed in the same style as the houses. Mostly erected in the mid-1920s, these houses can be seen between 84th and 88th Streets. The depressed economic conditions of the 1930s led the Queensboro Corporation to build more traditional six-story apartment houses on its vacant sites,

229

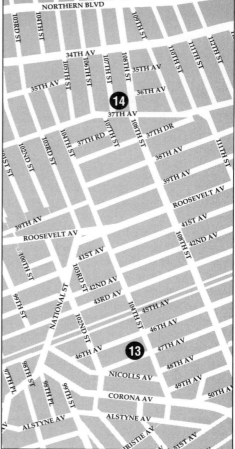

including neo-Georgian, Mediterranean, and neo-Tudor buildings designed by apartment-house specialists, many with offices in Brooklyn, such as Cohn Brothers and Seelig & Finkelstein. An exception was Dunolly Gardens, Thomas's last garden apartment complex (1939), on the block between 78th and 79th Streets and 34th and 35th Avenues, which was given a modernistic architectural treatment. Small-scale apartment-house construction continued into the 1950s, by which time almost all the vacant land in the neighborhood was filled with an extraordinary array of high-quality middle-class housing. The southern intersection of 37th Avenue, the commercial spine of the district, and 82nd Street is distinguished by a group of picturesque neo-Tudor commercial buildings dating from between the World Wars. These complement the residential buildings in their design.

⑪ Reformed Dutch Church of Newtown and Fellowship Hall, 85-15 Broadway, Newtown (church, 1831; hall, 1860). This wooden church building displays a late use of the Georgian style; its cupola is a prominent feature of the Newtown community. Fellowship Hall, originally a chapel designed in the Greek Revival style, was moved to the site in 1906.

⑫ Remsen Cemetery, adjacent to 69-43 Trotting Course Lane, Newtown (c. 1790–). The Remsens, among the earliest settlers of Queens, may have established this private cemetery in the mid-18th century, although the earliest extant gravestone dates from 1790. The main focus of the small plot is a World War I memorial with a flagpole and two statues of doughboys.

Louis Armstrong House (No. 14). Home of famed jazz trumpeter Louis Armstrong, the house is now a museum devoted to Armstrong's career and the history of jazz. Photo by Janet O'Hare.

🔟 **Edward E. Sanford House,** also known as the 102-45 47th Avenue House, Newtown (c. 1871). This small two-story house is one of the last intact 19th-century frame houses in Queens. Designed in a vernacular Italianate style, the house is especially notable for its decorative porch, gable, and fence, all of which display fanciful wooden detail.

🔟 **Louis Armstrong House,** 34-55 107th Street, Corona (Robert W. Johnson, 1910). One of the world's most renowned jazz musicians and enter-

tainers purchased this modest house in 1943 and occupied it until his death in 1971. Armstrong—or Satchmo, as he was commonly known—gained world fame as a jazz trumpeter and bandleader onstage (notably at the Savoy Ballroom and other Harlem nightspots), in recordings, and in Hollywood films. In 1983 Armstrong's widow, Lucille, willed the house and its contents to New York City for the creation of a museum and study center devoted to Armstrong's career and the history of jazz.

Flushing Meadows Corona Park

15

thought to have been the first American free kindergarten for the children of working mothers was housed in this French Second Empire structure. The building was designed by a Brooklyn architecture firm that specialized in institutional work. The institute, which still occupies the premises, continues to provide services to the community. In 1996 Page Ayres Cowley Architects began a restoration of the building.

17 **Lewis H. Latimer House,** 34-41 137th Street, Flushing (c. 1887–89). The renowned African-American inventor Lewis H. Latimer lived in this house from 1902 until his death in 1928. Latimer was a specialist in electric lighting and invented the long-lasting carbon filament, which made possible the production of affordable electric lightbulbs. During his long career, Latimer worked with Alexander Graham Bell and Thomas Alva Edison and was active in civil rights and black history organizations. Threatened with demolition, the house was moved to its present site from Holly Avenue, west of Kissena Boulevard, in 1988 and is scheduled for restoration and reuse as a museum.

15 **Unisphere and Surrounding Reflecting Pool,** Flushing Meadows–Corona Park (Gilmore D. Clarke, landscape architect; United States Steel Company, engineering and fabrication, 1963–64). The Unisphere, symbolizing peace through understanding, was the centerpiece of the 1964–65 New York World's Fair. The monumental steel globe surrounded by satellite rings stands in the center of a reflecting pool with fountains spraying water twenty feet into the air. It was fabricated and donated to the fair by the U.S. Steel Corporation. The city restored the ensemble in 1993–94.

18 **RKO Keith's Flushing Theater (interior),** 135-29–135-45 Northern Boulevard, Flushing (Thomas Lamb, 1927–28). The ticket lobby, grand foyer, promenade, and lounges of the former RKO Keith's Flushing Theater, designed in a fanciful Mexican Baroque style, are a reminder of the grandeur of movie palaces in the 1920s. The space is currently vacant and closed to the public.

16 **Poppenhusen Institute,** 114-04 14th Road, College Point (Mundell & Teckritz, 1868). The Poppenhusen Institute was established by the German-born Conrad Poppenhusen, founder in 1853 of the U.S. hard-rubber industry, as a vocational school for the workers in his nearby plant. What is

19 **Flushing Town Hall,** later Flushing Municipal Courthouse, now Flushing Council on Culture and the Arts, 137-35 Northern Boulevard, Flushing (1862). Before the consolidation of Greater New York in 1898, each town in the region had its own governmental center. This Early Romanesque

Flushing Town Hall (No. 19), one of the few local town halls left in Queens, is now a cultural center. Photo by John Barrington Bayley.

Revival masonry building is one of the few such town halls still standing. The German-inspired design is striking in its use of round-arched forms for windows and doors, its entrance portico, and its corbeled cornice. The Flushing Council on Culture and the Arts acquired the building in 1991. Platt & Byard, architects, have undertaken a major restoration.

20 **Flushing High School,** 35-01 Union Street (C. B. J. Snyder, 1912–15). Flushing High School, incorporated in 1875, is the oldest public secondary school in New York City. Its present home is an impressive Collegiate Gothic structure designed by the city's superintendent of school build-

ings. Like Snyder's earlier Curtis High School (see Staten Island No. 9) on Staten Island, Flushing High School was given a campus setting. The choice of style and setting evokes the great Gothic colleges of Oxford and Cambridge.

21 **Friends Meeting House,** 137-16 Northern Boulevard, Flushing (1694; additions, 1716–19). The eastern third of the Friends Meeting House in Flushing is New York City's oldest structure in continuous use for religious purposes. In its proportions and framing system, this austerely simple wooden building offers evidence of the survival of medieval building techniques in the American colonies.

John Bowne House (No. 22). The house is significant as an example of 17th-century colonial construction and as a monument to religious freedom. Photo by Janet O'Hare.

㉒ **John Bowne House,** 37-01 Bowne Street, Flushing (1661; additions, 1680, 1696, and c. 1830). The kitchen wing of the Bowne House is the oldest surviving structure in Queens and one of the oldest in New York City. The house is significant both as an example of 17th-century colonial construction and as a monument to religious freedom. John Bowne was arrested in 1662 for permitting the Quakers to hold meetings in the house. After appealing to the Dutch government in Holland, Bowne was acquitted, thus establishing the right to freedom of worship. Exterior stabilization and conservation began in 1994 by Page Ayres Cowley Architects.

㉓ **Kingsland Homestead,** 143-35 37th Avenue, Flushing (1785). This vernacular frame house, the second oldest in Flushing, was erected by Charles Doughty shortly after the Revolutionary War. The house is named for Doughty's son-in-law, Joseph King, who purchased the property in 1801. Moved from 40-25 155th Street to its current site in 1968, the Kingsland Homestead is now the headquarters of the Queens Historical Society. The building was restored in 1996 by the Department of Parks.

㉔ **Weeping Beech Tree,** Weeping Beech Park, 37th Avenue between Parsons Boulevard and Bowne Street, Flushing (1847). This weeping beech was planted in 1847 by Samuel Parsons, owner of a large nursery in Flushing and supplier of original plant stock to both Central and Prospect Parks. Intrigued by word of the existence of an exotic new variety of beech tree in Belgium, Parsons acquired a tiny shoot; the shoot has matured into this magnificent specimen. Parsons was one of several individuals who established Flushing as a mid-19th-century horticultural center.

㉕ **Arthur and Dorothy Dalton Hammerstein House, Wildflower,** 168-11 Powells Cove Boulevard, Beechhurst (Dwight James Baum, 1924 and pre-1930). Although not as well known as his father, Oscar Hammerstein I, or his nephew, Oscar Hammerstein II, Arthur Hammerstein was a successful theatrical producer who sponsored twenty-six Broadway shows, including works by Victor Herbert, George Gershwin, and Jerome Kern (see Hammerstein's Theater, Manhattan No. 297). Following the success of the musical *Wildflower* in 1923, and his marriage to the actress and film star Dorothy Dalton, Hammerstein purchased a waterfront plot in Queens and erected this sprawling neo-Tudor house, which was enlarged prior to 1930. The house is one of many mansions erected along the north shore of eastern Queens and adjacent sections of Long Island in the early decades of the 20th century. The building is currently vacant and in poor condition, but permits have been issued to restore it.

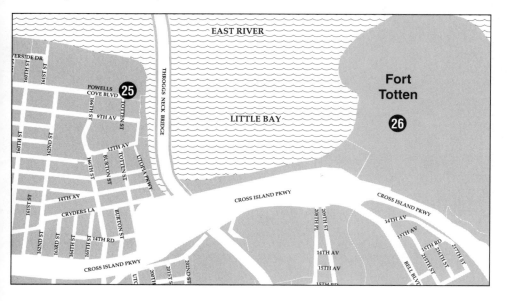

26 Fort Totten, U.S. Government Reservation, Bayside. Between 1857 and 1863, the federal government purchased land in Queens for a fort that, along with Fort Schuyler (see Bronx No. 48) in the Bronx, would protect the mouth of the East River. In 1898 the fort was named for Joseph Gilbert Totten (1788–1864), the military engineer responsible for planning the nation's 19th-century seacoast defense.

Battery (William Petit Trowbridge, engineer, 1862–64). This massive battery consists of two tiers of gun emplacements set into the hillside on the East River shoreline at Willets Point. The seaward wall is constructed of beautifully cut rough granite blocks with small square openings.

Officers' Club (c. 1870; enlargement, 1887). Originally a one-story building, this picturesque Gothic Revival frame structure was enlarged in

1887. Its mock-medieval features include a crenellated roofline, a pointed-arch portico, and drip lintels.

27 Lawrence Graveyard, 216th Street at 42nd Avenue, Bayside (1832–1925). The land on which this cemetery is located was given to the Lawrence family in 1645. Used for many years as a picnic ground, the plot became a graveyard in 1832. Forty-eight members of the Lawrence family, including one mayor of New York, were interred at the site between 1832 and 1925.

28 Cornelius Van Wyck House, 37-04 Douglaston Parkway (126 West Drive), Douglaston (c. 1735; addition, mid-18th century). Set at the edge of Little Neck Bay, this house, built by the farmer Cornelius Van Wyck in the traditional Dutch Colonial mode with hand-hewn scalloped shingles, is one of the finest residences of its type on Long Island. A Georgian-style extension was added to the west and south at some point before 1770. Additions were also made early in the 20th century when the structure served as a clubhouse, but these were removed during a restoration, early in the 1920s, by the architect Frank J. Forster.

㉙ Benjamin P. Allen House, also known as the Allen-Beville House, 29 Center Drive, Douglaston

(c. 1848–50). Allen acquired property in Douglaston in 1847 and is thought to have erected this house shortly thereafter. The house, one of the few surviving 19th-century buildings in Queens constructed as a farm dwelling, was designed in a transitional style; the basic form is Greek Revival, but the cornices on the main house and its porches display Italianate brackets.

㉚ Jacob Adriance Farmhouse, also known as the Creedmoor Farmhouse, now the Queens County Farm Museum, 73-50 Little Neck Parkway, Floral Park (1772; additions, c. 1835 and later). The Adriance House is a rare example of a New York City farmhouse that is still set in a rural landscape. The original house, with its Dutch and English Colonial features, was greatly enlarged in the 19th century, giving the structure the Greek Revival character now evident.

㉛ First Reformed Church of Jamaica, 153-10 Jamaica Avenue, Jamaica (Sidney J. Young, 1858–59; addition, Tuthill & Higgins, 1902). The bold massing and complex use of arched motifs mark this red brick building as one of the finest Early Romanesque Revival churches in New York. It was designed by master carpenter Sidney J. Young, a member of the congregation, who had visited other local churches for inspiration, possibly including the Church of the Pilgrims (see Brooklyn H.D. 4, entry F) and South Congregational (see

First Reformed Church of Jamaica (No. 31), one of the finest Early Romanesque Revival churches in New York. Photo by Carl Forster.

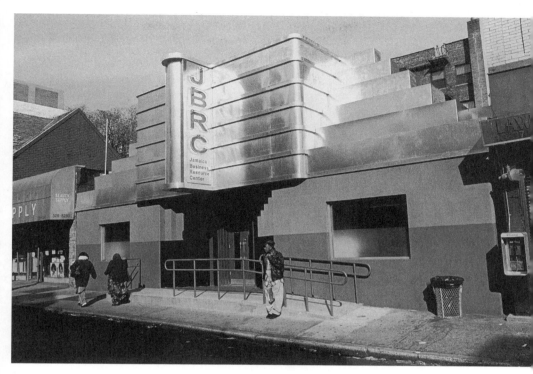

La Casina (No. 34), a jazzy, streamlined nightclub from the 1930s. Photo by Carl Forster.

Brooklyn No. 27) in Brooklyn. This was the third church on this site of a congregation established in 1702.

32 **Rufus King House,** also known as the King Manor Museum, Jamaica Avenue and 150th Street, King Park, Jamaica (1733–55; additions, 1806, 1810, and c. 1830s). Rufus King—Massachusetts delegate to the Continental Congress, antislavery advocate, and three-term senator from New York —purchased a modest gambrel-roofed farmhouse and adjacent acreage in Jamaica in 1805. King immediately added a kitchen wing to the house; in 1810 he undertook major alterations, including the addition of a new dining room with chambers above and the construction of a new front elevation. Rufus King's heir, John Alsop King, was probably responsible for the Greek Revival additions, notably the front porch supported by four Doric columns. After 1896, when the last member of the King family died, the house became the property of New York City. In 1989–90 the city undertook a

major restoration of the exterior and the **interior,** which features fine plasterwork, woodwork, and marble mantels.

33 **Grace Episcopal Church and Graveyard,** 155-03 Jamaica Avenue, Jamaica (Dudley Fields, 1861–62; chancel, Cady, Berg & See, 1901–02; graveyard, c. 1734–). Grace Church was founded in 1702 as the official church of the British colonial government. The congregation has worshiped at this site on the main street of Jamaica since 1734. The present church, a rough-cut brownstone Early English Gothic–inspired structure with a tall spire, is the third at this location. The early 20th-century chancel complements the design of the original building. Among those buried in the graveyard are Rufus King, whose house (see No. 32) still stands 200 yards to the west.

34 **La Casina,** (also known as La Casino), now Jamaica Business Resource Center, 90-33 160th Street, Jamaica (c. 1933). A rare surviving example of Streamlined Moderne design, this metal and stucco facade was designed for a nightclub and restaurant and reflects the jazzy, streamlined motifs fashionable for Depression-era nightspots. Erected in the heart of Jamaica's commercial center, the building was restored by Li-Saltzman Architects in 1994–95.

㉟ Sidewalk Clock, 161-11 Jamaica Avenue (1900). This handsome clock, one of two surviving in Queens (see No. 6), was probably erected by a jewelry store. The clock is crowned by a Greek-inspired acroterion. (See also Manhattan No. 162.)

㊱ J. Kurtz & Sons Store, 162-24 Jamaica Avenue, Jamaica (Allmendinger & Schlendorf, 1931). The former J. Kurtz & Sons furniture store is one of the finest examples of Art Deco architecture in Queens and a building of great prominence on the commercial thoroughfare of Jamaica Avenue. As one of the architects recalled, the brick building, with its black-and-white glazed tile pylons, polychromatic terra-cotta panels, and prominent vertical sign, was designed to be as "modern and colorful" as the contemporary furniture displayed inside.

㊲ The Register, now the Jamaica Arts Center, 161-04 Jamaica Avenue, Jamaica (A. S. Macgregor, 1898). An excellent example of a public building in the neo–Italian Renaissance style, the former deeds registry, designed by a Queens architect, was erected in the year that Queens became a part of New York City.

㊳ Saint Monica's Church (R.C.), 94-20 160th Street, Jamaica (Anders Peterson, builder, 1856–57). This brick church has a distinctive central campanile that is reminiscent of the Romanesque architecture of northern Italy. Erected by the master mason Anders Peterson under the supervision of the Reverend Anthony Farley, Saint Monica's is one of the oldest surviving examples of Early Romanesque Revival architecture in New York, and one of the few Roman Catholic churches in the city executed in this style. Owned by New York State and now located on the campus of York Community College, the building has been vacant since 1973 and is severely deteriorated.

㊴ Prospect Cemetery, 159th Street at Beaver Road, Jamaica (c. 1668–). This four-acre plot is the oldest cemetery in Queens. Established before 1668, the cemetery is the final resting place of many Revolutionary War veterans as well as members of such prominent Queens families as the Sutphins, Van Wycks, and Merricks. A small Romanesque Revival chapel was erected in 1857 by Nicholas Ludlum in memory of his three daughters.

㊵ Trans World Airlines Flight Center at New York International Airport, now TWA Terminal A, John F. Kennedy International Airport (Eero Saarinen & Associates, 1956–62). The TWA Terminal is one of the great masterpieces of expressionistic modern design and is a major work by Eero Saarinen (with codesigner Kevin Roche), one of the leading modern architects in the United States. Built of carefully engineered concrete and glass, the distinctive winged form of the building reflects Saarinen's desire "to interpret the sensation of flying." The terminal was among the first planned with the satellite gates, jetways, and baggage carousels now common in airports. The dynamism of the design continues on the **interior,** where the terminal is massed with a powerful series of curved concrete forms on the walls, stairs, balconies, and ceiling vaults of the main hall, jetways, and satellite gates.

Trans World Airlines Flight Center at New York International Airport (No. 40), one of the great masterpieces of expressionistic modern design. Photos by Carl Forster.

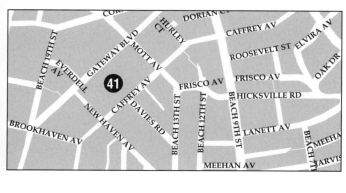

41 **Richard Cornell Graveyard**, adjacent to 1463 Gateway Boulevard, Far Rockaway (18th to 19th centuries). Named for the first European settler in the Rockaways, this small graveyard was established early in the 18th century and was used by the Cornell family into the 19th century.

BRONX OVERVIEW MAP

HISTORIC DISTRICTS

❶ **Bertine Block Historic District.** This small historic district centers on a row at 414–432 East 136th Street, called the Bertine Block. These ten Queen Anne–style houses form one of the most exceptional late 19th-century residential groups in New York City. The houses, erected in 1891 by developer Edward D. Bertine (who moved into No. 416), were designed by Manhattan architect George Keister, who was responsible for several important landmark buildings (see Manhattan Nos. 218, 219, and 480). The narrow houses are faced with tawny brick with brownstone trim and massed with a diverse array of window openings, gables, mansards, corbeled cornices, and tall chimneys. Development in this district began in 1877 with a trio of neo-Grec row houses at Nos.

408–412 designed by Rogers & Browne, but further construction awaited the opening of a rail line in 1886, connecting the Mott Haven area to business districts in Manhattan. Following the completion of the centerpiece Bertine Block, Edward Bertine erected two other rows—the Romanesque Revival single-family houses at Nos. 415–425 designed in 1892 by John Hauser and the two-family neo-Renaissance houses at Nos. 434–440 designed by Adolph Balschun, Jr. Finally, eight tenements were erected in the district, between 1897 and 1899, all designed by local Bronx architect Harry T. Howell.

❷ **Mott Haven Historic District.** This district, named for Jordan Mott, who established the Mott Iron Works at East 134th Street and the Harlem River in 1828, contains the finest 19th-century row houses in the Bronx. Of particular note are two rows of brick houses on Alexander Avenue between East 139th and 140th Streets: a ten-house unit on the east side, built in 1863–65, that is among the earliest row houses in the Bronx; and a twelve-house row across the street, designed in 1881 by Charles Romeyn. The district also includes two imposing turn-of-the-century churches—Saint Jerome's Roman Catholic (Delhi & Howard, 1898) and the Third Baptist (Frank Ward, 1901)—a Carnegie public library branch (Babb, Cook & Willard,

1905; see Manhattan No. 466), and a police station (Thomas O'Brien, 1924).

◆ **3** **Mott Haven East Historic District.** This small district, facing onto East 139th and East 140th Streets, exemplifies urban residential development in the southern part of the Bronx in the final years of the 19th century and the first years of the 20th century as new mass transit lines made this area accessible to working- and middle-class New Yorkers. The earliest buildings in the district are single-family

The Mott Haven East Historic District (H.D. 3), East 140th Street between Willis and Brook Avenues, contains the finest 19th-century row houses in the Bronx. Photo by Katherine Khan Reed.

neo-Grec-style row houses erected by architect/builder William O'Gorman in 1887–92 at 403–445 East 139th Street and 406–450 East 140th Street. An additional row, built by O'Gorman in 1897–1900 at 409–427 East 140th Street, has picturesque facades with Romanesque and Renaissance detail designed by Walter Hornum. By the late 1890s, speculative builders were erecting tenements, rather than row houses, in Mott Haven. O'Gorman and Hornum were responsible for a tenement at 407 East 140th Street. The remaining nine tenements in the district were designs of two of the most prolific apartment-house architects in New York City—George Pelham (Nos. 441–461 East 140th Street, 1902–03) and Neville & Bagge (Nos. 465–481 East 140th Street, 1901–02). Many of the early residents of the district were of German birth or descent. They commissioned the Second Saint Peter's German Evangelical Lutheran Church, a neo-Gothic-style complex designed by Louis Allmendinger and built in 1911 at 435 East 140th Street.

INDIVIDUAL LANDMARKS

❶ Bronx Grit Chamber, 158 Bruckner Boulevard (McKim, Mead & White, 1936–37). The Bronx Grit Chamber is a primary component of the Ward's Island Sewage Treatment Works, New York City's first major project to alleviate water pollution. The exterior of the building, a late work of McKim, Mead & White, is within the tradition of the monumental public buildings designed by the firm and is evidence of the fact that even the most utilitarian buildings were deemed worthy of impressive architectural expression.

❷ Saint Ann's Church (Episcopal) and Graveyard, 295 Saint Ann's Avenue (1840–41). The oldest surviving church in the Bronx, Saint Ann's was erected on the country estate of Gouverneur Morris, Jr., as a memorial to his mother. The Morrises, for whom the neighborhood of Morrisania is named, were a prominent colonial family. (Gouverneur Morris, Sr., was one of the framers of the Constitution.) The simple vernacular fieldstone church is articulated by Gothic windows and is capped by a Greek Revival steeple. The cemetery contains the graves of many members of the Morris family.

❸ Public School 27 (Saint Mary's Park School), originally Public School 154, 519 Saint Ann's Avenue (C. B. J. Snyder, 1895–97). One of the earliest designs of C. B. J. Snyder, then superintendent of school buildings, this limestone, brick, and terra-cotta school was designed with a combination of elements derived from Dutch and English colonial sources, including scrolled gables and an octagonal bell tower. The school is representative of the impressive neighborhood buildings erected by the city at the turn of the century as symbols of the importance of education to New York's citizens.

❹ 614 Courtlandt Avenue Building (1871–72). Erected by the saloon keeper Julius Ruppert as a saloon and meeting hall serving the German community of Melrose South, this building is a simple French Second Empire structure with cast-iron window lintels and a handsome two-story mansard roof.

❺ Public School 31, 425 Grand Concourse (C. B. J. Snyder, 1897–99). Public School 31 is one of a large number of schools erected in the Bronx around the turn of the century to accommodate the waves of people moving to the borough from other parts of New York City and abroad. A relatively early work of the school architect C. B. J. Snyder, Public School 31 was one of the first Collegiate Gothic public schools in New York, and it set the stage for Snyder's better-known examples of the style, including Morris High School (see No. 9 and H.D. 5).

❻ Bronx Post Office, 560 Grand Concourse, at East 149th Street (Thomas Harlan Ellett, 1935–37). The Bronx Post Office, the largest of New York's twenty-nine Depression-era post offices, was designed by Thomas Harlan Ellett as part of a Department of the Treasury program to employ out-of-work architects. Almost as soon as it was completed, the gray brick edifice was proclaimed a "significant example of an evolving American style, a new classicism free of dependence on the works of antiquity." Important works of art were commissioned for many of the post offices of this period. On the exterior of the Bronx Post Office are a pair of limestone panels, *The Letter* by Henry Kreis and *Noah* by Charles Rudy; the lobby contains a significant series of murals by Ben Shahn on the theme of America at work.

HISTORIC DISTRICTS

 Longwood Historic District. The Longwood Historic District, located in the Morrisania section of the South Bronx, was almost entirely developed by George B. Johnson, who purchased the land in 1898. The cohesive character of the area can be traced to the fact that the majority of the houses were designed by the same architect, Warren C. Dickerson, one of the most active architects in the

Longwood Historic District (H.D. 4), Beck Street between Longwood Avenue and East 156th Street. The cohesive character of the district is the result of the work of Bronx architect Warren C. Dickerson. Photo by Paul Sachner.

Bronx at the turn of the century. Most of the houses in the historic district are semidetached two- and three-family neo-Renaissance structures. Especially fine examples line Dawson, Kelly, Beck, and East 156th Streets. Among the distinctive features are the use of Roman brick and the roofs with false mansards capped by polygonal or cone-shaped peaks. Also in the district are a series of simple single-family houses on Hewitt Place, designed by the Bronx architect Charles S. Clark; several apartment houses; a church; and a former synagogue.

❺ Morris High School Historic District. The Morris High School Historic District focuses on the architect C. B. J. Snyder's masterful Collegiate Gothic school building (1900–04; see No. 9) but also contains rows of neo-Renaissance houses on Jackson and Forest Avenues that were erected in this section of Morrisania around the same time as Morris High. The houses were designed by four local Bronx architects. The majority are the work of the prolific Warren C. Dickerson, with additional designs by John H. Lavelle, Harry T. Howell, and Hugo Alden. Construction in the district responded to the rapid population growth in the southwest Bronx in the early 20th century as subway and elevated train lines began to link this area to Manhattan. The district contains one survivor from Morrisania's rural past—the High Victorian Gothic red brick Trinity Episcopal Church of 1874.

INDIVIDUAL LANDMARKS

❼ Peter S. Hoe House, Sunnyslope, later Temple Beth Elohim, now the Bright Temple A.M.E. Church, 812 Faile Street (c. 1860). This picturesque Gothic Revival villa is an extraordinary survivor from the mid-19th century. Built for Peter S. Hoe, a member of the firm R. M. Hoe & Co., manufacturers of printing equipment, Sunnyslope was part of a 14.6-acre estate in rural West Farms. Although the architect is not known, this compact, asymmetrical stone house is in the style of Calvert Vaux and may have been inspired by one of the designs Vaux published in his 1857 book *Villas and Cottages.* Most of the other country houses in West Farms were destroyed as the area was urbanized after 1900, but Sunnyslope was

saved when it was converted into a synagogue in 1919.

❽ 62nd Police Precinct Station House, later 41st Police Precinct Station House, 1086 Simpson Street (Hazzard, Erskine & Blagden, 1912–14). As the West Farms neighborhood rapidly developed in the early 20th century, new civic structures were required, and the police department erected this imposing limestone-fronted Italian Renaissance–inspired precinct house. The design reflects the City Beautiful notion of erecting sophisticated buildings to ennoble the civic sector and to provide beauty for all citizens. The building, which underwent major interior rehabilitation beginning in 1992 (Cabrera/Barricklo Architects), is still in use by the police department.

❾ Morris High School Auditorium (interior), East 166th Street at Boston Road (C. B. J. Snyder, 1900–04; 1926). The Collegiate Gothic–style Morris High School, located within the Morris High School Historic District (see H.D. 5), was the first major public secondary school in the Bronx and is one of the masterpieces of the New York City school architect C. B. J. Snyder. The auditorium (now Duncan Hall), a high churchlike space with a balcony, is perhaps the finest interior in any city school. The room contains elaborate Gothic plasterwork, steel-ribbed vaults set within Tudor arches, stained-glass windows, and a series of organ pipes. It is decorated with several murals, most prominently the French artist Auguste Gorguet's monumental 1926 World War I memorial entitled *After Conflict Comes Peace.* The New York City School Construction Authority restored the auditorium in 1991.

❿ Second Battery Armory, 1122 Franklin Avenue (Charles C. Haight, 1906–11; addition, Benjamin W. Levitan, 1926–28). This boldly massed brick structure is the earliest permanent armory erected in the Bronx. The building, with its crenellated roofline and restrained Gothic detailing, was designed by Charles C. Haight, one of New York's leading architects and a specialist in the use of Gothic design. The narrow wing on Franklin Avenue contains offices and company rooms (a story was successfully added in 1926–28) with a vast drill shed behind.

⓫ Herman Ridder Junior High School, 1619 Boston Road (Walter C. Martin, 1929–31). Herman Ridder was the first "modernistic" Art Deco public school in New York City and one of the first schools erected specifically for use as a junior high. The building, faced with limestone and yellow brick enlivened by subtle polychromatic trim, has dramatically massed vertical buttresses and an entrance tower capped by setbacks modeled on the form of contemporary skyscrapers. The ornamentation incorporates abstract Art Deco elements and such iconographic features as stylized figures of male and female students, open books, and lamps of knowledge.

Sunnyslope (No. 7), a picturesque mid-19th-century Gothic Revival villa. Photo by Carl Forster.

HISTORIC DISTRICT

6 Clay Avenue Historic District. The two blockfronts of Clay Avenue between East 165th and East 166th Streets make up one of the most unified and harmonious streetscapes in the Bronx. The district contains thirty-two residential buildings—twenty-eight semidetached two-family houses designed by Bronx architect Warren C. Dickerson in 1901, a single-family house erected for hardware merchant Francis Keil in 1906 (Charles S. Clark, architect), and three corner apartment buildings designed by Neville & Bagge in 1909–10. Dickerson's houses are a picturesque group of transitional Romanesque Revival/neo-Renaissance-style dwellings with brick facades, limestone trim, and a variety of peaked and scrolled gables and angled and rounded towers. The district is located on the site of Fleetwood Park, a trotting-horse park that ceased operations in 1898 just as this section of Morrisania was being intensively developed as a residential neighborhood.

INDIVIDUAL LANDMARKS

⓬ **Bronx Borough Courthouse,** East 161st Street at Third Avenue (Oscar Bluemner and Michael J. Garvin, 1905–15). The former Bronx Borough Courthouse was erected to serve the judicial needs of the rapidly growing borough. Garvin, a close political associate of the borough president, received the commission for the building, but he retained Bluemner to undertake the actual design work. Bluemner, who was trained as an architect in Europe and designed only a few buildings in New York, is best known as a pioneer of modern American painting. The Beaux-Arts courthouse is a massive granite structure embellished with overscaled French-inspired detail. The building has been vacant for many years.

⓭ **Bronx County Building,** also known as the Bronx County Courthouse, 851 Grand Concourse (Max Hausle and Joseph H. Freedlander, 1931–35). This monumental limestone-faced structure is an impressive example of the austere classicism popular for public edifices in the 1930s. Its sculptural program is especially striking. The carved detail includes Charles Keck's frieze of heroic figures symbolically engaged in various modes of productive employment (e.g., agriculture, industry, the arts). Eight freestanding groups of figures carved in pink Georgia marble (two flanking each of the four entrances) represent such themes as achievement, progress, and the majesty of law. The sculptor Adolph Weinman carved two of these compositions and also supervised the work of three other artists: Edward F. Sanford, George H. Snowden, and Joseph Kiselewski. The

building was restored by the New York City Department of General Services (now the Office of Construction and Design).

⓮ **Macomb's Dam Bridge and 155th Street Viaduct,** see Manhattan No. 472.

⓯ **Park Plaza Apartments,** 1005 Jerome Avenue (Horace Ginsberg and Marvin Fine, 1929–31). As one of the first and most prominent Art Deco apartment houses in the Bronx, the Park Plaza ushered in the style that was to change the face of much of the borough. The facade was designed by Marvin Fine, who noted the direct stylistic influence of the new Chrysler and American Radiator Buildings (see Manhattan Nos. 279 and 234). The orange brick structure contains fine polychromatic terra-cotta ornament, including panels that depict an architect presenting a model of his building to the Parthenon.

⓰ **Andrew Freedman Home,** 1125 Grand Concourse (Joseph H. Freedlander and Harry Allan Jacobs, 1922–24; wings, David Levy, 1928–31). At his death in 1915, Andrew Freedman left most of his money for the establishment of a home for the elderly, with the unusual proviso that it care for poor people who had once been affluent. Freedman was a wealthy capitalist and Tammany Hall leader who was involved in financing the construction of the IRT subway and was, from 1894 to 1902, the controversial owner of the New York Giants baseball team. The design of the limestone-clad building is a free interpretation of Italian Renaissance architecture, combining the balanced rectilinearity of urban palazzi with the setting and terraces of a rural villa. The building continues to serve the elderly but now draws its residents from a broader spectrum of the community.

⓱ **Public School 91,** now Public School 11, 1257 Ogden Avenue (George W. Debevoise, 1889; additions, C. B. J. Snyder, 1905, and Walter C. Martin, 1930). As the population of the West Bronx rapidly increased late in the 19th century, the New York City Board of Education planned several new schools. Former Public School 91, one of the few surviving early school buildings in the borough, is a Romanesque Revival structure with a massive stone base, brick upper stories, and a mansard roof. The Ogden Avenue wing was added in 1905; the gymnasium/auditorium wing was built along Merriam Avenue in 1930.

18 **High Bridge,** see Manhattan No. 502.

19 **Washington Bridge,** see Manhattan No. 503.

Park Plaza Apartments (No. 15), one of the first and most prominent Art Deco apartment houses in the Bronx. Photo: Landmarks Preservation Commission collection.

HISTORIC DISTRICT

7 **Morris Avenue Historic District.** This one-block-long historic district is a notable example of a uniformly planned streetscape, developed by a single speculative builder working with one architect. In 1906–07 August Jacob purchased both sides of

Morris Avenue between East Tremont Avenue and East 179th Street. John Hauser designed the two- and three-story neo-Renaissance two-family brick row houses with their projecting, full-height, angled or rounded bays; all the houses were built before 1910. Hauser was also responsible for the pair of tenements at the Tremont Avenue end of the street.

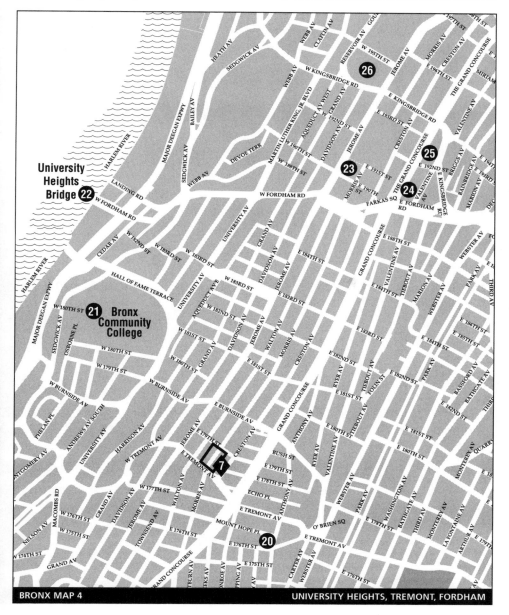

INDIVIDUAL LANDMARKS

⑳ Edwin and Elizabeth Shuttleworth House, also known as the 1857 Anthony Avenue House (Neville & Bagge, 1896). One of the few surviving suburban residences in the southern Bronx, this house was built for a prosperous stone dealer and his wife. While the firm Neville & Bagge was responsible for the basic design, it is probable that Shuttleworth specified the use of one of the varieties of stone that he sold (stone houses were uncommon in the Bronx) and commissioned the sculpted detail from one or more of his most talented carvers. The idiosyncratic ornament, including male and female figures, marine elements, and portrait busts, survives as a monument to the anonymous stone carvers who created some of New York's finest architectural detail.

㉑ New York University, now the Bronx Community College of the City University of New York, Hall of Fame Terrace at Sedgwick Avenue (McKim, Mead & White, Stanford White, partner in charge; plan, 1892–94; construction, 1894–1912). Dramatically sited on a terrace placed at the crest of a steep ridge overlooking the Harlem River, with the Hudson River and the New Jersey Palisades beyond, the former Bronx campus of New York University is a triumph of turn-of-the-century American architecture and a masterpiece of Stanford White's. In 1892 NYU decided to move its undergraduate school from its urbanized Washington Square site to a more rural location "suggestive of academic seclusion." White laid out the new campus and designed its classical and Renaissance-inspired buildings, all constructed of yellow Roman brick with terra-cotta and limestone trim. In 1973 New York University left the campus, and it was acquired by the City University of New York.

Gould Memorial Library (1894–99). One of White's greatest buildings, this library is both the physical and the symbolic center of the campus. The library, with its temple front and

New York University (No. 21), the Gould Memorial Library. This late masterpiece by noted New York architect Stanford White is the physical and symbolic center of the campus. Photo: Landmarks Preservation Commission collection.

dome, was clearly modeled on the Roman Pantheon. Set at the edge of the terrace, the building was designed to blend with, rather than overpower, its spectacular site. The importance of this design in White's work was recognized in 1919 when his peers chose to create a pair of bronze doors for the library as a White memorial. The Gould Memorial Library contains monumental **interior** spaces. Richly detailed in marble, stone, mosaic, wood, and bronze, with Tiffany glass highlights, the interior was planned as a single unified whole. A long Renaissance-inspired staircase rises from the entrance to the rotunda of the library's main reading room. The rotunda has sixteen columns of green Irish Connemara marble; sculpted, classically garbed figures; and a coffered dome. The building is no longer used as a library.

Hall of Fame (1900–01). White initially designed an ambulatory at the rear of the library that would take advantage of the superb views to the west; in 1900 the university chancellor, Henry MacCracken, suggested instead the creation of a Hall of Fame commemorating great Americans. White's magnificent colonnade was dedicated in 1901, although construction was not completed until 1912. The open terrace with Guastavino vaults and a tile roof contains the busts of noted scientists, writers, educators, and others who have made their mark on American culture.

Hall of Languages (1892–95) **and Cornelius Baker Hall of Philosophy** (1892–1912). Although completed seventeen years apart, these twin classroom buildings, standing to either side of the library, complete the west range of White's 1892 campus plan. They are simpler than the library and serve as foils for that structure, accentuating its grandeur.

㉒ **University Heights Bridge,** spanning the Harlem River between West Fordham Road, the Bronx, and West 207th Street, Manhattan (William H. Burr, consulting engineer, with Alfred P. Boller and George W. Birdsall, 1893–95; relocation and extension, Othniel F. Nichols, chief engineer, 1905–08; widening and reconstruction, 1987–92). The University Heights Bridge is a steel-truss structure consisting of a central revolving swing span, three masonry piers, and steel approach spans. The central span and two flanking approach spans were originally located at Broadway (at the northern tip of Manhattan Island) and made up the Harlem Ship Canal Bridge. In 1905–08 the bridge was floated south to its present location, and a second west approach span was constructed. The bridge is especially notable for the aesthetics of its design, a particular concern of the engineer Alfred P. Boller. It has a graceful curved profile, two stone pavilions, four sidewalk shelters with cast-iron piers, and ornate iron railings. As part of a reconstruction project in 1987–92, the entire structure was widened.

㉓ **Saint James Episcopal Church and Parish House,** 2500 Jerome Avenue (church, Henry M. Dudley, 1864–65; parish house, Henry F. Kilburn, 1891–92). Designed for a rural parish in what at the time was part of Westchester County, Saint James is a major work by Dudley, one of the leading Gothic Revival church architects of the mid-19th century. It is noteworthy for its straightforward use of materials (fieldstone, red sandstone, wood, and slate) and for the expression of interior spaces (nave, side aisles, transepts, chancel, and porch) on the exterior massing. The Gothic-inspired parish house complements the church building.

㉔ **Dollar Savings Bank,** now Emigrant Savings Bank, 2516–2530 Grand Concourse (Halsey, McCormack & Helmer, Adolph L. Muller, architect in charge, 1932–33; additions, 1937–38 and 1949–52). The Dollar Savings Bank's building grew in three stages from a small granite structure in a Modern Classical style into one of the most impressive buildings on the Grand Concourse. Organized in 1890, the Dollar was the first savings bank chartered in the Bronx. When the bank decided to open a branch near the busy corner of the Grand Concourse and Fordham Road, it hired a firm that specialized in savings bank design. The Dollar prospered and expanded its branch in 1937–38 and then erected a 10-story tower with a four-faced clock for its headquarters. On the **interior,** the rectangular banking hall is boldly detailed in marble, limestone, terra cotta, bronze, and gold-and silver-leafed plaster, and contains five murals by Angelo Magnanti depicting scenes from early Bronx history.

25 **Poe Cottage,** Poe Park, 2640 Grand Concourse (c. 1812). In 1846 Edgar Allan Poe moved from New York City to this small cottage located in the village of Fordham. He lived in the house until his death in 1849, (in Baltimore); it was while he resided here that he wrote such masterpieces as "Annabel Lee" and "The Bells." As development swept through Fordham later in the century, the house was slated for demolition, but a public outcry led to its preservation in 1902. In 1913 this shrine to one of America's great writers was moved by the city from its original location across the street to its present site at the north end of Poe Park. The cottage is operated as a historic house museum by the Bronx County Historical Society.

26 **Eighth Coastal Artillery Armory,** later the Eighth Regiment Armory, now the Kingsbridge Armory, 29 West Kingsbridge Road (Pilcher & Tachau, 1912–17). Pilcher & Tachau's design, centering on two tall round towers, was inspired by French architect Eugène-Emmanuel Viollet-le-Duc's mid-19th-century reconstruction of the great French medieval castle at Pierrefonds. At the time of its completion, the armory boasted the world's largest drill hall; measuring 300 by 600 feet, the hall is set beneath a vaulted roof supported by a double-truss steel frame.

The Dollar Savings Bank (No. 24), one of the most impressive buildings on the Grand Concourse, contains fine details, including this bronze door. Photo by Carl Forster.

INDIVIDUAL LANDMARKS

㉗ New York, Westchester & Boston Railroad, Administration Building, now the East 180th Street (No. 2 and No. 5) Subway Station, 481 Morris Park Avenue (Fellheimer & Long and Allen H. Stem, 1910–12). The short-lived New York, Westchester & Boston Railroad ran from Manhattan, through the Bronx, to White Plains and Port Chester, from 1912 until 1937. The stations, designed by a nationally known firm of railroad architects, were modeled after Florentine villas. The 180th Street building, which served as both station and offices, has an arcade, arched windows, and two square towers. In 1941 the section of "the Westchester" located within city limits was incorporated into the IRT system; it is now a part of the No. 2 and No. 5 lines.

㉘ Old West Farms Soldiers' Cemetery, 2103 Bryant Avenue (1815–). Situated in a modest landscaped enclosure, this cemetery is the oldest public veterans' burial ground in the Bronx. It serves as the last resting place of veterans of four wars—the War of 1812, the Civil War, the Spanish-American War, and World War I.

㉙ New York Zoological Park, now the Wildlife Conservation Society, Bronx Park, south of East Fordham Road. The New York Zoological Park, better known as the Bronx Zoo, was founded in 1895. The New York Zoological Society immediately acquired a 250-acre site in Bronx Park and began the construction of the world's first zoological research center.

Paul J. Rainey Memorial Gates, park entrance at East Fordham Road (Paul Manship, sculptor, and Charles A. Platt, architect, 1929–34). This pair of monumental bronze gates is one of the finest examples of Manship's elegant public sculpture. The work consists of two gates with stylized plant and animal motifs. The gates were set within Platt's architectural framework. They were a gift of Grace Rainey Rogers in memory of her brother, Paul Rainey, a big-game hunter and supporter of the zoo.

New York Zoological Park (No. 29), Paul J. Rainey Memorial Gates. One of the finest examples of Paul Manship's sculpture, at the world's first zoological research center. Photo by Joseph Brooks.

Rockefeller Fountain, inside entrance at East Fordham Road (Heins & La Farge, 1910). A gift of William Rockefeller, this 18th-century Italian fountain is set onto an exuberant basin designed by Heins & La Farge.

㉚ New York Botanical Garden, Bronx Park, north of East Fordham Road. The organization of the New York Botanical Garden in 1891 was inspired by the success of the Royal Botanic Garden at Kew, England. The garden and nearby New York Zoological Park (see No. 29) were founded shortly after New York City acquired Bronx Park. The parkland had been part of the Lorillard estate, and the Botanical Garden incorporates the former Lorillard Snuff Mill. The 250-acre Botanical Garden was planned in 1895–96, but landscape and construction work did not actually begin until 1899.

Conservatory, now the Enid A. Haupt Conservatory, Kazimiroff Boulevard (Lord & Burnham, William R. Cobb, architect in charge, 1896–1902). The magnificent conservatory consists of a central domed rotunda (known as the Palm House) and ten connecting greenhouses. Cobb is credited with the design and the structural system, which was originally steel, cast iron, wood, and glass and was inspired by mid-19th-century exposition halls and horticultural structures, notably the Palm House at Kew. The conservatory was rehabilitated in 1976–78 under the direction of the architect Edward Larrabee Barnes and was renamed for the philanthropist who provided much of the funding. In 1997 a more extensive rehabilitation project was completed by Beyer Blinder Belle, architect, which entailed the disassembly of the building and the replacement of the wooden framing with aluminum, as well as a complete upgrading of the technical systems.

Lorillard Snuff Mill, now the Snuff Mill River Terrace Cafe, Bronx River (c. 1840). One of the rare surviving examples of early industrial architecture in the city, this fieldstone and brick mill used the water power of the Bronx River to grind tobacco into snuff. The mill was in operation until 1870, when the Lorillard company moved to New Jersey. The building was rehabilitated in the 1950s and is now a public cafeteria.

㉛ Fordham University, East Fordham Road at East 191st Street. Fordham University, originally known as Saint John's College, received its first students in 1841. The campus is located on the former Rose Hill estate of the Brooklyn merchant Horatio S. Moat, which was purchased by Bishop John Hughes (later New York's first Catholic archbishop) in 1839.

Horatio Shepheard Moat House, Rose Hill, now the Fordham University Administration Building (1836–38; additions, 1907). The central part of this fieldstone building was originally a freestanding country house erected on the Rose Hill estate by Horatio S. Moat. It is a superb example of the Greek Revival style, distinguished by a fine Ionic entrance portico and an octagonal cupola. The building became the nucleus of Saint John's College, later Fordham University; the wings were added by the university in 1907.

Outbuilding, also known as Alumni House, now the Fordham University Housing Office (c. 1840). Although a stone plaque clearly dates this small fieldstone building to 1840, the exact date that construction began and what the building's original use was are not known. The austere rectilinear structure is a vernacular example of Greek Revival design, notable for the simplicity of its massing and fenestration.

Saint John's Church, now the Fordham University Chapel (William Rodrigue, 1841–45; enlargement, Emile Perrot, 1928–29). Rodrigue, a teacher at Saint John's College, as well as the brother-in-law of Bishop John Hughes, designed this Gothic Revival stone church with its tall pinnacled tower as the focal point of the campus of this new Catholic university. The chapel and nearby residence hall form the northern arm of the U-shaped complex known as Queen's Court (formerly the "Old Quad"). The chapel was enlarged in 1928–29 with the addition of the large transept.

Saint John's Residence Hall (William Rodrigue, 1841–45). This fieldstone building was the first dormitory on the Fordham campus. It was designed in a Gothic Revival style that is reminiscent of English collegiate architecture.

32 **52nd Police Precinct Station House,** 3016 Webster Avenue (Stoughton & Stoughton, 1904–06). This romantic red brick police station was modeled on the Italian Renaissance villas of Tuscany, as is especially evident in the gabled roof slopes and the square four-faced clock tower. The modestly scaled civic structure gains stature from the architects' exploitation of inexpensive materials—brickwork laid in a diaper pattern, terra-cotta plaques, and blue tile window spandrels.

33 **United Workers Cooperative Colony (The "Coops"),** 2700–2774 Bronx Park East (Springsteen & Goldhammer, 1925–27) and 2846–2870 Bronx Park East (Herman Jessor, 1927–29). The United Workers Cooperative Association was founded by left-wing secular Jewish garment workers who purchased land across from Bronx Park to erect high-quality housing with large apartments and plenty of fresh air and light. The earliest buildings form a neo-Tudor complex set around a large garden. The multiple entrances are ornamented with smoking factories, a hammer and sickle, and other details consistent with the group's beliefs. Architecturally, the second complex is more radical, adapting the expressive brickwork employed on contemporary workers' housing in Vienna and elsewhere in Europe. While the cooperative failed during the Depression, the buildings survive as a testament to a commitment to quality housing for all people.

United Workers Cooperative Colony (No. 33). The brickwork reflects contemporary European design for workers' housing. Photo by Carl Forster.

INDIVIDUAL LANDMARKS

34 **High Pumping Station,** 3205 Jerome Avenue (George W. Birdsall, 1901–06). The High Pumping Station, constructed as part of the Jerome Reservoir complex, pumped water to consumers throughout the Bronx, providing the necessary pressure to permit water to reach the upper floors of the borough's many new apartment houses. Birdsall, an engineer for the Department of Water Supply, Gas, and Electricity, was responsible for the station's construction; it is not known whether he actually undertook the design of the late Romanesque Revival structure.

The building has a utilitarian form enlivened by expressive brick detail.

35 **Isaac Valentine House,** now the Valentine-Varian House, 3266 Bainbridge Avenue (1758). This pre–Revolutionary War vernacular Georgian house, constructed of fieldstone, was built for the blacksmith and farmer Isaac Valentine and was sold in 1791 to Isaac Varian. Saved from demolition when it was moved in 1965 onto city-owned property, the house has been restored and is owned and operated by the Bronx County Historical Society as the Museum of Bronx History.

Issac Valentine House (No. 35). Constructed before the Revolutionary War, the building is now home to the Bronx County Historical Society. Photo: Bronx County Historical Society.

BRONX MAP 6

BEDFORD PARK, NORWOOD

HISTORIC DISTRICT

◆8 **Riverdale Historic District.** Encompassing approximately fifteen acres of sloping land overlooking the Hudson River, the Riverdale district includes thirty-four buildings on landscaped sites.

It is the nucleus of the parcel purchased in 1852 by five wealthy and influential businessmen who intended to create a suburban summer community named Riverdale that could be reached conveniently from Manhattan by the Hudson River Railroad. Riverdale was the first railroad suburb in

Riverdale Presbyterian Chapel (No. 37), a picturesque amalgamation of architectural styles. Photo by Carl Forster.

New York City. The district includes seven original estates linked by a carriage alley (now Sycamore Avenue) and one parcel subdivided from the adjacent Wave Hill estate (see No. 44). All the estates, including that of William and Ann Cromwell (see No. 45), were developed in the 1850s. Several early estate houses in the Italianate and French Second Empire styles remain, as do stables and carriage houses (now converted for residential use), stone walls, iron fences, and important landscape elements. Notable among the carriage houses are that of the Cromwell estate (c. 1856–58) at 5286 Sycamore Avenue, designed in an Italianate style that matches that of the mansion, and, from a later period, the Queen Anne–style example at 5286 Sycamore Avenue, designed by Frederick Clarke Withers (1886) for William S. Duke. Later residences in the district illustrate the changing nature of suburbanization from the mid-19th century to the present. From the 20th century are a series of Colonial Revival houses, including examples by such prominent suburban home designers as Dwight James Baum (5200 Sycamore Avenue, 1922–24) and Julius Gregory (5249 Sycamore Avenue, 1937; and 5294 Sycamore Avenue, 1938).

INDIVIDUAL LANDMARKS

36 40th Police Precinct Station House, later the 50th Police Precinct Station House, 3101 Kingsbridge Terrace (Horgan & Slattery, 1900–02). This

former police station is a small-scale Beaux-Arts structure with a dramatic curved corner and bold sculptural detail. It reflects the explicit intention of New York's leaders at the turn of the century to erect civic buildings throughout the five boroughs that would symbolize the importance of municipal government. The building is now a Parks Department community center.

37 Riverdale Presbyterian Chapel, now Edgehill Church of Spuyten Duyvil (United Church of Christ), 2550 Independence Avenue (Francis H. Kimball, 1888–89). The Edgehill Church, originally built as a chapel of the nearby Riverdale Presbyterian Church (see No. 41), is a survivor from the period when Spuyten Duyvil was a sparsely populated area at the northern edge of New York City. Kimball's masterful design for this small, asymmetrical church nestled into a hillside combines elements from the Romanesque Revival, neo-Tudor, and Shingle styles in an extremely picturesque manner.

38 Christ Church (Episcopal), 5040 Riverdale Avenue (R. Upjohn & Son, 1865–66). As might seem appropriate for a church built in the suburban community of Riverdale, this High Victorian Gothic stone structure was designed to resemble a medieval English rural parish church. With its clearly delineated nave, transepts, chancel, and porch, its steep polychromatic slate roof (restored in 1991), its bell cote, diminutive crossing tower, and pointed-arch openings, Christ Church is among the most beautiful early designs of R. M. Upjohn, the son of Richard Upjohn, architect of Trinity Church, Manhattan (see Manhattan No. 15).

39 Frederick and Frances Jay Van Cortlandt House, also known as the Van Cortlandt Mansion, Van Cortlandt Park, Broadway at West 242nd Street (1748–49). Solidly built of locally quarried fieldstone with contrasting brick trim, Frederick Van Cortlandt's mansion is one of the handsomest Georgian manor houses of the era. The formidable size of the house and the quality of its interiors are evidence of the great wealth amassed by a few prominent 18th-century New York families. The **interior** combines the formal elegance of the Georgian style with features typical of the older, more conservative Dutch Colonial tradition. The mansion was saved thanks to the creation of Van Cortlandt Park, and it has been maintained since 1896 by the Society of Colonial Dames.

40 William E. and Melissa Phelps Dodge House, Greyston, 690 West 247th Street (James Renwick, Jr., 1863–64). In the 1860s Riverdale-on-Hudson became a popular country retreat for wealthy New Yorkers. William E. Dodge, Jr., who together with his father-in-law founded the mining firm Phelps, Dodge & Co., was among the first to build here, commissioning this stone villa from the prominent architect James Renwick, Jr. The angular detail, quirky silhouette, and polychromatic slate roof mark this house as one of Renwick's earliest High Victorian Gothic designs and reflect Renwick's understanding of contemporary English design ideas. In 1961 the Dodge family gave the property to Columbia University Teachers College, which used it as a conference center until the late 1970s, at which time it was sold to a Zen Buddhist community. Having undergone extensive rehabilitation by architect Joseph Pell Lombardi, the house is now once again a private home.

41 Riverdale Presbyterian Church and Manse, 4765 Henry Hudson Parkway (James Renwick, Jr., 1863–64). Renwick's English-inspired Gothic Revival stone church was built in 1863 with funding provided by local estate owners, including William E. Dodge, Jr., whose Renwick-designed house, Greyston (see No. 40), was under construction nearby. In the adjoining stone manse, now known as Duff House, Renwick combined Gothic Revival forms with a French-inspired mansard roof.

42 Anthony Campagna Estate, now Yeshiva of Telshe Alumni School, 640 West 249th Street (Dwight James Baum, 1929–30; landscape, Vitale & Geiffert). Anthony Campagna, a prominent Italian-born builder of apartment houses in the early decades of the 20th century, erected this vast Tuscan-inspired villa for his own family. It is a major design of Dwight James Baum, an architect whose career centered on the design of historically inspired homes, many in the Riverdale area. Baum's limestone and stucco house with sloping tile roof is perched on a site overlooking the Hudson River and is set amid a formal Italian Renaissance–inspired landscape.

43 Spaulding Estate Coachman's House, 4970 Independence Avenue (Charles W. Clinton, 1880). This small Stick Style cottage was built as the coachman's residence for Parkside, the estate of the businessman Henry Foster Spaulding. Lively and varied textures are created by board-and-batten siding on the first floor, crossed sticks above, dormer windows with jigsaw ornament, and a slate roof with overhanging eaves.

44 Wave Hill, William Lewis Morris House, 675 West 252nd Street (1843–44; later additions). This imposing stone mansion, the focus of a magnificent estate overlooking the Hudson, is operated as part of the Wave Hill Center for Environmental Studies, an educational-cultural center with an arboretum, greenhouses, art galleries, and a sculpture garden on the grounds. The original (central) section of the house was built for the jurist William Lewis Morris in 1843–44 using locally quarried Fordham gneiss. In 1866, following Morris's death, the house was sold to the publisher William Henry Appleton. George W. Perkins, one of America's leading financiers, purchased the property in 1893. Between the time of his acquisition of Wave Hill and his family's donation of the estate to New York City in 1960, the side wings and main entrance enframement were constructed and the grounds relandscaped. In 1932 Perkins's tenant, Bashford Dean, built the armor hall at the north end of the house (Dwight James Baum, architect); Dean's armor collection is now at the Metropolitan Museum of Art.

45 William D. and Ann Cromwell House, Stonehurst, later the Robert Colgate House, 5225 Sycamore Avenue (1856–58). The importer William Cromwell was one of the original investors who helped to establish Riverdale as a suburban enclave in 1852 (see H.D. 8). He sold his interest a year later, then purchased another plot of land in 1856 for the construction of this villa. After Cromwell's death in 1859, his widow sold the property to the paint manufacturer Robert Colgate. Stonehurst is one of the most elegant mid-19th-century country houses along the Hudson and is unusual within the Italian villa tradition for its classical symmetry. The house derives its name from the beautifully dressed gray stone used in its construction.

INDIVIDUAL LANDMARKS

46 **Fonthill, the Edwin Forrest House,** now the Admissions Office of the College of Mount Saint Vincent, West 261st Street at Palisade Avenue (1848–52). Located on a bluff overlooking the Hudson, Fonthill is a country house designed to resemble a medieval castle. The building consists of six interlocking octagonal units of varying height, which culminate in a tall, slender tower. Fonthill was erected for the famed Shakespearean tragedian Edwin Forrest (see Manhattan No. 210) by a local builder, Thomas C. Smith, and was named for the English house Fonthill Abbey, built in 1796–1812. In 1856 Forrest sold the property to the Sisters of Charity of Saint Vincent-de-Paul, who have used the house at various times as administrative offices, a chaplain's residence, and a library. Fonthill's stone **carriage house/ stable,** now Boyle Hall, and its **cottage** (c. 1848–52) combine Gothic and Italianate features in a manner representative of the finest in 19th-century rural design.

47 **Mount Saint Vincent Academy,** now the College of Mount Saint Vincent Administration Building, West 261st Street at Palisade Avenue (Henry Engelbert, 1857–59; additions, 1865, 1883, and 1906–08). The main building on the campus of the College of Mount Saint Vincent is dramatically situated on a hill commanding a sweeping view of the Hudson River and the Palisades. With its complex round arches, tall tower, beautifully articulated brickwork, and two-story verandas, the building is a masterpiece of the Early Romanesque Revival. The expansive structure houses a wide variety of college activities.

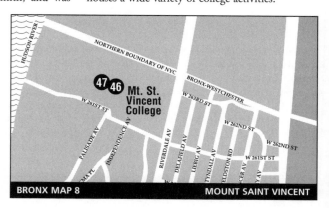

BRONX MAP 8   MOUNT SAINT VINCENT

Fonthill (No. 46), consisting of six interlocking octagonal units, designed to resemble a medieval castle, was built for the famed Shakespearean actor Edwin Forrest. Photo by Carl Forster.

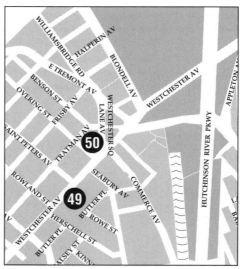

48 Fort Schuyler, now the State University of New York Maritime College, east of the Throgs Neck Bridge (Captain I. L. Smith, 1833–56). Fort Schuyler and its companion across Long Island Sound, Fort Totten (see Queens No. 26) in Queens, were erected to protect the eastern entrance to New York Harbor from Long Island Sound. The massive fort, built of Connecticut granite, has walls up to 11 feet thick and once mounted more than 300 guns. The fort was abandoned in 1870. In 1934 the Works Progress Administration (WPA) rehabilitated the structure for use as a school. The architect William A. Hall converted the gun galleries into a library in 1966–67.

49 Saint Peter's Church (Episcopal), Westchester, Complex and Cemetery, 2500 Westchester Avenue (church, Leopold Eidlitz, 1853–55; alterations, Cyrus L. W. Eidlitz, 1879; Sunday school and chapel building, Leopold Eidlitz, 1867–68; cemetery, 1702–). Saint Peter's congregation was established in the village of Westchester in 1693. Leopold Eidlitz's impressive Gothic Revival stone edifice was the third church building on the site. In its straightforward use of materials and its emphasis on structural clarity, the building is characteristic of the work of Eidlitz, who was one of the most

talented and influential American architects of the 19th century. After part of Saint Peter's was destroyed by fire in 1877, the church was rebuilt and somewhat altered by Leopold's son Cyrus in 1879. Leopold's nearby Sunday school and chapel building (now called Foster Hall) is a superb example of High Victorian Gothic design. The cemetery contains many 18th-century gravestones.

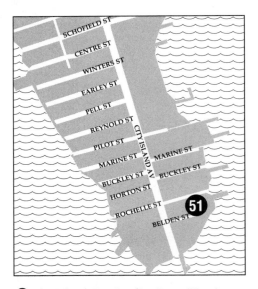

road magnate Collis P. Huntington purchased, enlarged, endowed, and renamed the structure. The institution continues to serve as a noncirculating library open to the public.

⑤ 175 Belden Street House, City Island (c. 1880). This small clapboard house, with its superb jigsaw-cut struts and brackets and a slate roof, is one of the finest picturesque cottages in New York City. Although the exact date of construction is not documented, the house was erected during City Island's heyday as a maritime community supported by fishing, shellfishing, sail-making, and shipbuilding.

⑤ Robert and Marie Lorillard Bartow House, now the Bartow-Pell Mansion Museum, Shore Road, Pelham Bay Park (1836–42). Located near Long Island Sound, on land that was once part of the Manor of Pelham, this magnificent neoclassical country seat was built by Robert Bartow, who was descended from the Pell family. The house was purchased by the city in 1888, and after several decades of neglect, restoration was undertaken in 1914 by the International Garden Club under the direction of the architecture firm Delano & Aldrich. The elegant stone house faces a terraced garden dating from 1914–16. The exceptionally fine Greek Revival **interiors** were designed in the manner of Minard Lafever. The site includes an original stone stable/carriage house, later walled gardens, and a small family memorial plot.

⑤ Van Schaick Free Reading Room/Huntington Free Library and Reading Room, 9 Westchester Square (Frederick Clarke Withers, 1882–83; addition, William Anderson, 1890–92). In 1882 local philanthropist Peter C. Van Schaick built a free noncirculating library for the village of Westchester, twelve years before it became part of the City of New York. He commissioned a picturesque little brick building from Frederick Clarke Withers, one of the most prominent American architects of the time. The citizens of Westchester rejected the gift, and the building remained vacant until rail-

Bartow House (No. 52), now the Bartow-Pell Mansion Museum, a neoclassical country manor house. Photo by John Barrington Bayley.

53 **Public School 15**, 4010 Dyre Avenue (Simon Williams, 1877). At the time of its construction, Public School 15—a rare example in New York City of the rural red brick schoolhouse—was largely surrounded by an undeveloped section of Westchester County. The Victorian Gothic building, with its paired gables supported by large brackets and its central bell tower, was designed by Simon Williams, who became the school's principal.

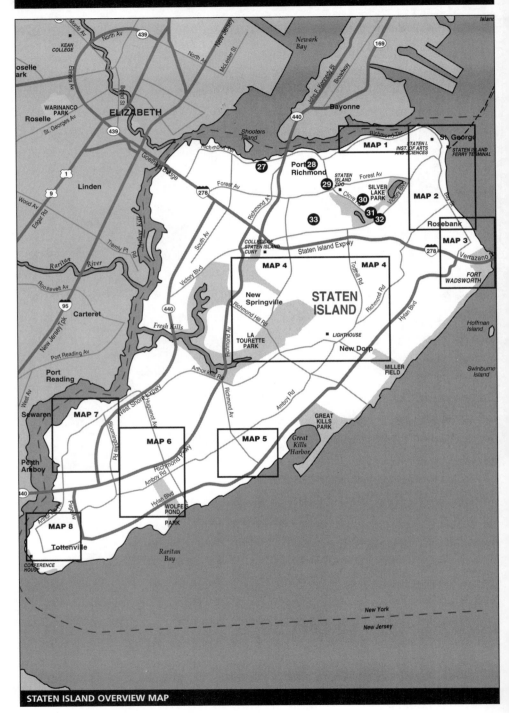

STATEN ISLAND OVERVIEW MAP

INDIVIDUAL LANDMARKS

❶ Cornelius Cruser House, also known as the Kreuzer-Pelton House, 1262 Richmond Terrace (1722; additions, 1770 and 1836). Three construction phases are clearly visible on the exterior of this house. Cornelius Van Santvoord, minister of the Dutch Reformed Church in Port Richmond, erected the original one-room section in the Dutch Colonial tradition. The steep-roofed central wing was added by Cornelius Cruser, and the two-story brick end section in the Federal style was built by Daniel Pelton.

❷ 69 Delafield Place House, also known as the Samuel MacKenzie Elliott House (possibly Calvin Pollard, c. 1850). This beautifully proportioned stone house was built as a real-estate investment by Samuel MacKenzie Elliott, a prominent oculist and eye surgeon and a vocal abolitionist. Elliott, who began purchasing property in northern Staten Island in 1839, built so many suburban houses in the vicinity that the area became known as Elliottville. The Scottish-born doctor/developer is known to have commissioned several designs from the prestigious New York City architect Calvin Pollard, and this Gothic Revival house may be one of them.

❸ Sailors' Snug Harbor, now the Snug Harbor Cultural Center, 914–1000 Richmond Terrace. Sailors' Snug Harbor was established with an 1801 bequest from the merchant Robert Randall, who left a large plot of land north of Washington Square in Manhattan for the establishment of an institu-

tion for the care of "aged, decrepit and worn-out sailors." Randall's bequest was challenged in court, and it was not until 1830 that the case was settled, by which time the Washington Square area was being developed as a prestigious residential neighborhood. Realizing that their Manhattan property was extremely valuable, the trustees of Sailors' Snug Harbor leased the land and in 1831 purchased a large farm on the north shore of Staten Island, where they proceeded to erect a complex of buildings. Sailors' Snug Harbor housed retired seamen at this location until 1976, when it moved to North Carolina. Following a series of court challenges that upheld the validity of landmarks regulation and devised tests to determine its effects on property devoted to charitable purposes, the Sailors' Snug Harbor facility was sold to New York City. The complex is now a cultural center.

Main Buildings, Buildings A through E (Administration Building, Minard Lafever, 1831–33; interior renovation, 1884; dormitories, Minard Lafever, 1831–41, and Richard P. Smyth, 1879–81). The centerpiece of the Sailors' Snug Harbor complex is the former Administration Building (Building C), Minard Lafever's earliest surviving work. This magnificent Greek Revival structure, with its monumental Ionic portico, was constructed of Westchester marble. It originally housed all of the institution's functions except for cooking. The plan of the **interior** is Lafever's, but the rectangular hall, second-floor gallery, and elliptical dome were redecorated in 1884 with stained glass, murals, and other painted details in the neo-Grec style. The murals were painted by the

Sailors' Snug Harbor (No. 3). Established as a home for "aged, decrepit and worn-out sailors," Sailors' Snug Harbor contains a group of exquisite 19th-century Greek Revival buildings. Photo by Carl Forster.

New York firm Artman & Fechteler and restored in 1993 by the EverGreene Painting Studios. As the number of residents at Sailors' Snug Harbor increased, new dormitory buildings were erected. The pavilions (Buildings B and D) that flank the main building were designed by Lafever in 1831 in a simplified Greek Revival style but were not built until 1839–41. The end pavilions (Buildings A and E), designed by Richard Smyth, echo the form of the central building. Together the buildings form a masterpiece of the Greek Revival.

Chapel, now Veterans Memorial Hall (James Solomon, 1854–56; interior renovation, 1873; addition, 1883). The Manhattan builder James Solomon erected this Italianate chapel in 1855–56; the bell tower that he had recommended was not built until 1883. The chapel was an important aspect of life at Sailors' Snug Harbor, since daily attendance was mandatory for all residents. The **interior** of this deconsecrated chapel has a simple rectangular layout with three aisles, a raised platform and shallow apse, and a balcony supported by cast-iron columns. In 1873 the decorator Charles Berry refurbished the chapel, adding trompe l'oeil architectural elements that include the recently restored pilasters and entablature.

Fence (Frederick Diaper, 1841–45). This monumental iron fence, erected to keep residents from unauthorized excursions, extends for more than a third of a mile along Richmond Terrace. The fence was designed by the British-born Diaper, who derived inspiration from the Cumberland Gates in Hyde Park, London; the fence was fabricated by William Alexander of Manhattan.

North Gatehouse (Richard P. Smyth, 1873). The Italianate gatehouse, with its arched central tunnel and diminutive cupola, gave access to the main building complex from Richmond Terrace. It was one of four gatehouses erected in an effort to prevent liquor from being brought onto the property illicitly.

❹ **Tysen-Neville House,** also known as the Neville House and the Old Stone Jug, 806 Richmond Terrace (c. 1800). The builders of this exceptional farmhouse of rough sandstone (now whitewashed) were probably Jacob and Mary Tysen. Rehabilitation work on the facade in 1991 revealed that the unusual two-story veranda, which was added at an unknown date, perhaps in the late 19th century, assumed its present configuration around 1910, and that the hexagonal cupola was added at that time. For part of the 19th century, the house was used as a tavern, known as the Old Stone Jug, which was frequented by residents of Sailors' Snug Harbor (see No. 3). The building is often referred to as the Neville House, after Captain John Neville, a retired naval officer who purchased the property in the 1870s.

❺ New Brighton Village Hall, 66 Lafayette Avenue (James Whitford, 1868–71). This small but impressive French Second Empire brick building was erected at a time when the northern Staten Island village of New Brighton was the suburban home of many prominent New Yorkers. Whitford was a local architect who arrived in Staten Island from England in 1852. The building has been vacant since 1968.

❻ 105 Franklin Avenue House, also known as Hamilton Park Cottage (Carl Pfeiffer, c. 1864). Hamilton Park (originally known as Brighton Park) was one of the earliest suburban residential parks on Staten Island and one of the first self-contained, limited-access suburban subdivisions in the United States. Laid out around 1851–52 by Charles Hamil-

ton, Hamilton Park had dwelling sites set on curving drives amid a naturalistic landscape. Development proceeded slowly; only three or four houses were erected in the 1850s, but in the 1860s the German-born architect Carl Pfeiffer designed twelve additional residences. The Hamilton Park cottages were among Pfeiffer's first American commissions. Somewhat simpler and less picturesque than the earlier Harvard Avenue House (see No. 7), this Italianate brick building has a magnificent arcaded loggia.

❼ 66 Harvard Avenue House, also known as the Pritchard House (c. 1853). This Italianate stuccoed house, with its stone trim and its notable wooden porch, balcony, and projecting window hood, is the only intact survivor of Hamilton Park's original suburban residences, which predate the houses designed by Carl Pfeiffer in the 1860s (see No. 6).

❽ 22 Pendleton Place House, also known as the W. S. Pendleton House (attributed to Charles Duggin, c. 1855). This Gothic Revival house—with its tower, oriel, varied windows, and steeply pitched gables—commands a high elevation above the Kill van Kull. The house was one of a number of suburban dwellings in New Brighton built as rental units by William S. Pendleton. Several of these houses are known to have been designed by the English-born and -trained architect Charles Duggin, and although there is no specific documentation for this house, it is probably one of his buildings.

The 105 Franklin Avenue House (No. 6) is located in one of the first limited-access suburban developments in America. Photo by Peter Choy.

HISTORIC DISTRICT

1 Saint George/New Brighton Historic District. The genesis of this district extends back to the 1835 creation of New Brighton, one of the earliest planned suburban communities in the

STATEN ISLAND MAP 2   NORTH SHORE—EAST

New York area. New Brighton was established by Thomas E. Davis, an English immigrant who named his projected summer retreat for the famous English seaside resort. Davis erected several houses, including the district's earliest building, the Greek Revival house at 404 Richmond Terrace (c. 1835), before selling the property to a group of investors who laid out the curving streets that survive to this day. A few houses were erected in the late 1830s, but a financial panic in 1837 eventually led to a foreclosure action. Over the next several decades, scattered development occurred in New Brighton, notably a group of semidetached French Second Empire–style houses, such as those at 36–38 and 60–62 Westervelt Avenue, probably dating from the late 1860s. The establishment of a unified ferry terminal at Saint George and the opening of the Staten Island Rapid Transit's rail lines in the mid-1880s led to major development in the northern portion of Staten Island as an increasing number of middle-class families moved there. A real-estate boom in the late 1880s and 1890s, including the construction of a group of Queen Anne, Shingle Style, and Colonial Revival houses, established the dominant character of the district. Most notable are those designed by Edward A. Sargent, Staten Island's leading architect of the late 19th century, who was responsible for such superb Shingle Style dwellings as the Rodewald House (c. 1890) at 103 Saint Marks Place and the Camman House (1895) at No. 125. In the early 20th century, suburban residential development continued with several fine Colonial Revival houses, such as 65 Westervelt Avenue (Thomas C. Perkins, 1908). The district also contains one important institutional complex, Saint Peter's Roman Catholic Church and Rectory. Saint Peter's is the oldest Catholic parish on Staten Island. The neo-Romanesque church, with its soaring tower visible from a distance, was designed by Harding & Gooch in 1900 to replace an earlier building that had burned.

INDIVIDUAL LANDMARKS

9 Curtis High School, 105 Hamilton Avenue at Saint Marks Place (C. B. J. Snyder, 1902–04; additions, 1922, 1925, and 1937). Staten Island's first secondary school building, Curtis High School was

Saint George/New Brighton Historic District (H.D. 1). The district contains several groups of Shingle Style houses on Westervelt Avenue. Photo by Caroline Kane Levy.

built following the consolidation of Greater New York. It was part of a plan to erect a major high school in each of the outlying boroughs—Erasmus Hall, Morris (see Bronx No. 9), and Flushing (see Queens No. 20) High Schools were the other three. The school is named for the nationally prominent writer and orator George W. Curtis, who lived nearby. The Collegiate Gothic school is situated in an appropriate campuslike setting.

🔟 Richmond County Courthouse, 12–24 Richmond Terrace (Carrère & Hastings, 1913–19). Shortly after Staten Island became a part of New York City, a new civic center was planned. This impressive temple-fronted L-shaped limestone courthouse and the Staten Island Borough Hall (see No. 11) are the only two major features of the plan that were erected. Carrère & Hastings, one of the preeminent early 20th-century American architecture

firms, received the commission for both civic center buildings, probably because John M. Carrère was a resident of Staten Island.

🔟 Staten Island Borough Hall, 2–10 Richmond Terrace (Carrère & Hastings, 1904–06). Borough Hall is the most prominent feature of Staten Island's governmental center and one of the great early 20th-century civic monuments of New York City. Carrère & Hastings designed Borough Hall in a style reminiscent of the brick-and-stone châteaux erected in France during the early 17th century. This is especially evident on the east elevation, facing New York Harbor, where the facade consists of a central pavilion flanked by projecting wings, all crowned by a mansard roof. The massing creates a courtyard reached by a long flight of stairs. A tall clock tower, visible from the harbor, rises from the center of the west elevation.

⑫ U.S. Light-House Service, Third District, Staten Island Depot Office Building, later the U.S. Coast Guard Station Administration Building, 1 Bay Street (Alfred B. Mullett, c. 1865–71; wings, 1901). The relatively small but boldly detailed granite and red brick office building (now painted) is one of the few surviving examples of the French Second Empire buildings designed by A. B. Mullett during his tenure as supervising architect of the Treasury. The Staten Island lighthouse depot complex was established for the storage of materials destined for East Coast lighthouses and as an experimental station for the testing of new materials and methods of lighthouse operation. The office building was constructed, beginning in 1868, as a fireproof facility for the storage of the depot's records. It has stood vacant for many years.

⑬ Public School 15 (Daniel D. Tompkins School), now Staten Island Area Office, Office of Building Services, Division of School Facilities, 98 Grant Street (Edward A. Sargent, 1897–98). This district school commissioned by Middletown Township was completed just as Staten Island became a part of New York City and was renamed P.S. 15. The picturesque building, with its chamfered pavilions, Queen Anne detail, and tall clock tower, was designed by Staten Island's most talented late 19th-century architect, many of whose residential works are in the Saint George/New Brighton Historic District (see No. 1).

⑭ Saint Paul's Memorial Church (Episcopal) and Rectory, 217–225 Saint Pauls Avenue (Edward T. Potter, 1866–70). Saint Paul's Memorial Church and Rectory form one of the finest High Victorian Gothic religious complexes in New York City. The noted architect Edward T. Potter created a dynamic work using a dark gray stone with lighter-colored Connecticut brownstone banding and polished granite dwarf columns on the entrance porch. The church was damaged by fire in 1940 and again in 1985; restoration took place following both fires. The 2½-story rectory, resembling a rural English parish house, complements the church.

⑮ Caleb T. Ward House, 141 Nixon Avenue (Seth Geer, c. 1835). Located at the crest of Ward's Hill, with a magnificent view of New York Harbor, this monumental mansion is the finest Greek Revival country house surviving in New York City. The house has brick walls stuccoed to simulate stone and an impressive two-story portico. Geer, the builder of Colonnade Row (see Manhattan No. 129) in Manhattan, was involved in a number of Staten Island building projects.

⑯ 364 Van Duzer Street House (c. 1835). This house is a fine example of Staten Island vernacular construction that combines the traditional curved overhanging eaves of the Dutch Colonial style with a two-story Greek Revival portico. It is one of three dwellings erected by Robert M. Hazard, an early Stapleton developer, shortly after he purchased the site in 1834.

⑰ 390 Van Duzer Street House. This house of indeterminate history no longer occupies its original site. The house is thought to be an 18th-century structure onto which a Greek Revival porch, possibly salvaged from another house, was added.

⑱ Edgewater Village Hall, 111 Canal Street in Tappan Park (Paul Kühne, 1889). This Romanesque Revival brick building with a square central tower was erected to house the civic functions of the village of Edgewater. It is one of only two village halls built on Staten Island (see No. 5). Restoration has been undertaken by John Ellis Associates, and the building is to be converted into a community center.

⑲ Dr. James R. Boardman House, also known as the 710 Bay Street House (1848). Boardman, the resident physician at the nearby Seaman's Retreat hospital (see No. 20), built this wood-frame Italianate house atop a steep bluff overlooking the Narrows. In 1894 the house was purchased by Captain Elvin Mitchell with money received from the Cunard Lines in recognition of his heroism in saving the lives of all 176 people aboard the SS *Oregon,* which sank off Fire Island.

⑳ Seamen's Retreat, now Bayley-Seton Hospital, 732–738 Bay Street. The Seamen's Retreat was founded by the New York State Legislature in 1831 to care for sick and disabled merchant seamen. The institution served seamen for 150 years. Run by the state until 1883, the facility became a

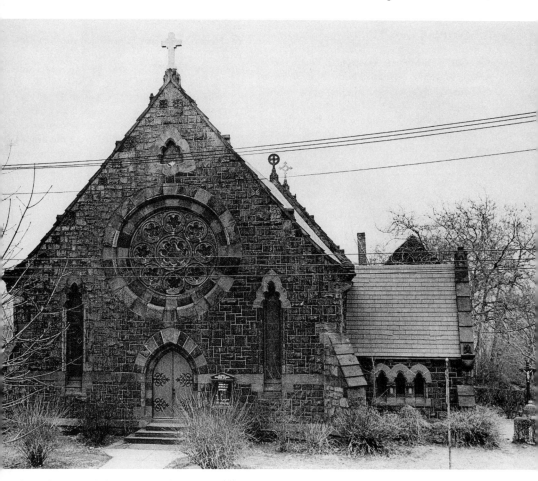

Saint Paul's Memorial Church (Episcopal) and Rectory (No. 14). One of the finest High Victorian Gothic religious complexes in New York City. Photo: Landmarks Preservation Commission collection.

U.S. Marine Hospital and then a U.S. Public Health Service Hospital; government use ceased in 1981. As befits a hospital for sailors, the Seamen's Retreat enjoys a waterfront location with fine harbor views. The retreat's physicians were in the forefront of medical research and reform, campaigning for improved conditions for sailors on ship and in port and undertaking bacteriological research that laid the groundwork for the public health endeavors later carried out by the National Institutes of Health.

Main Building (Abraham Maybie, builder, 1834–37; additions, 1848, 1853, and 1911–12).

This imposing Greek Revival hospital, constructed of granite ashlar, originally consisted of a central pavilion (with Doric entrance portico) projecting forward from flanking wings with two-story porches. As the hospital expanded, matching end pavilions were constructed in 1848 and 1853, and an additional story was added to the flanking wings in 1911–12.

Physician-in-Chief's Residence (Staten Island Granite Company, builder, 1842). Designed to harmonize with the nearby hospital building, this house is a severe granite structure in the Greek Revival style.

INDIVIDUAL LANDMARKS

㉑ Garibaldi-Meucci Museum, 420 Tompkins Avenue (c. 1845). This small house is preserved by the Sons of Italy as a memorial to two great Italians. Giuseppe Garibaldi, the liberator of Italy, lived in the house in 1851–53 while in exile in the United States. Garibaldi was a guest of Antonio Meucci, one of the early developers of the telephone.

㉒ Henry McFarlane House, later the New York Yacht Club, also known as the McFarlane-Bredt House, 30 Hylan Boulevard (c. 1841–45; additions, c. 1860, c. 1870s, and c. 1890s). The site of this villa adjoining the Alice Austen House (see No. 23) property enjoys commanding views across the harbor. The house has had many owners and has been substantially enlarged since the original cottage was constructed, apparently by the mer-

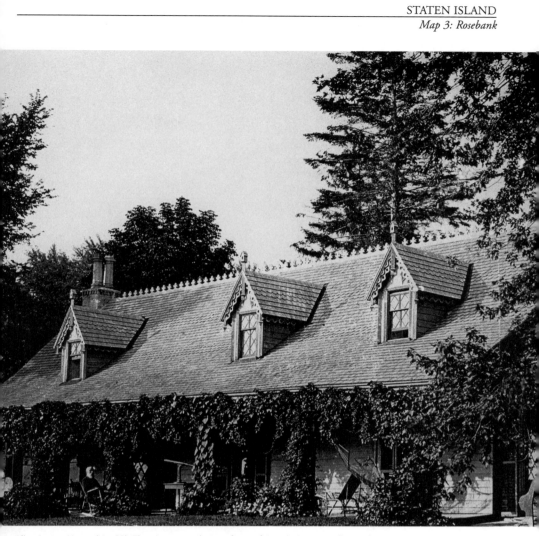

Alice Austen House (No. 23). The picturesque home of one of America's outstanding early photographers is now a museum. Photo courtesy of the Staten Island Historical Society.

chant Henry McFarlane. The earliest addition was built around 1860 when the dry goods merchant Henry Dibblee doubled the size of the dwelling, copying the original detail so that the house appeared to be a single structure. Between 1868 and 1871, the house served as the headquarters of the New York Yacht Club (see Manhattan No. 243); it was during its tenancy that the club first successfully defended the America's Cup. The house is owned by the New York City Parks Department and is being occupied by residential tenants until it can be restored.

㉓ Alice Austen House, 2 Hylan Boulevard (c. 1700–50; remodeling, 1846, c. 1852, and 1860–78). This picturesque house overlooking the Narrows was the home of Alice Austen (1866–1952), one of America's outstanding early photographers. The original one-room Dutch Colonial house was erected in the early 18th century and gradually enlarged. In 1844 Alice Austen's grandfather purchased the property, renamed it Clear Comfort, and remodeled it in the Gothic Revival style. The house was restored by New York City and is now a museum commemorating Alice Austen's artistry.

㉔ Woodland Cottage, also known as the 33–37 Belair Road House (c. 1845; addition, c. 1900). In the 1830s Staten Island's farms began to undergo suburban development. Woodland Cottage, which was built as a rental unit, is one of the few surviving examples of the picturesque Gothic Revival houses that were quite common in Clifton in the early years of the area's suburbanization. The original cross-gabled section has steep roof slopes outlined by bargeboards; the house features diamond-paned casement windows with drip moldings. Between 1858 and 1869, the cottage served as the rectory of Saint John's Church (see No. 25).

㉕ Saint John's Church (Episcopal), 1331 Bay Street (Arthur D. Gilman, 1869–71). Arthur D. Gilman's Gothic Revival granite structure, whose tall spire serves as a prominent landmark to ships arriving in New York Harbor, was planned to resemble a medieval English parish church. The design reflects 19th-century theories of Episcopal church architecture, especially in its clear delineation of such building parts as nave, side aisles, transepts, chancel, and tower. Gilman was a well-known architect in Boston before moving to Staten Island and receiving the commission for this church, which replaced an 1844 wooden church building.

㉖ Fort Richmond, now Battery Weed (Joseph G. Totten, 1845–61) and **Fort Tompkins,** Hudson Road (1858–76), Fort Wadsworth. Built at a crucial site on the edge of the Narrows at the entrance to New York Harbor, Fort Richmond was designed in 1845 by the army's chief engineer, but construction did not begin until two years later. Due to inadequate funding, work dragged on until 1861. The trapezoidal granite building, named for General Stephen Weed after his death at Gettysburg in 1863, is a magnificent example of military architecture. Fort Tompkins, a pentagonal granite structure, is set on a hill above Fort Richmond. The fort contained gun emplacements that were burrowed into the hill.

Fort Tompkins at Fort Wadsworth (No. 26). A magnificent example of military architecture. Photo: Landmarks Preservation Commission collection.

27 **Stephen D. Barnes House,** 2876 Richmond Terrace (c. 1853). One of the few survivors on "Captain's Row," which runs along the shore road opposite the Kill van Kull, this large Italianate brick house was erected by Stephen D. Barnes, a prosperous oysterman.

28 **Northfield Township District School 6,** later Public School 20 Annex, now Parkside Senior Housing, 160 Heberton Avenue (1891; addition, James Warriner Moulton, 1897–98). This structure is among the most impressive of the public school buildings erected on Staten Island before its consolidation with New York City. The Romanesque Revival school, which has a wealth of sculptural ornament, was built in two sections, each with a tower that is visible throughout the neighborhood. In 1993–94 the architecture firm Diffendale & Kubec converted the vacant building to low-income housing for the elderly.

29 **752 Delafield Avenue House,** also known as the Scott-Edwards House, 752 Delafield Avenue (early 18th century; remodeling, 1840). The original one-story brownstone house on this site was probably erected in the first part of the 18th century, possibly by Captain

Northfield Township District School 6 (No. 28) is an impressive early example of public school architecture on Staten Island. Photo by Carl Forster.

Nicholas Manning. At a later date the second story was added; the Greek Revival portico was most likely placed on the building in the 1840s, perhaps by Ogden Edwards, the first New York State supreme court justice from Staten Island, shortly after he purchased the house.

30 Julia Gardiner Tyler House, originally the Elizabeth Racey House, also known as the Gardiner-Tyler House, 27 Tyler Street (c. 1835). This Greek Revival mansion with a portico supported by four Corinthian columns was purchased by Juliana and David Gardiner and given to their daughter Julia, the wife of President John Tyler. Julia did not occupy the house until 1868, after her husband's death, when she moved to Staten Island with her seven stepchildren.

31 John King Vanderbilt House, 1197 Clove Road (c. 1836). A representative example of Greek Revival design on Staten Island, this house reflects the transition of the northern part of the island from a rural area into a region of suburbs and villages. The building was restored in 1955 by Dorothy Valentine Smith, who lived next door (see No. 32) and who was a descendant of the house's original owner.

32 John Frederick Smith House, later the Dorothy Valentine Smith House, 1213 Clove Road (1893–95). The prominent local banker and insur-

ance dealer John F. Smith erected this house in a restrained version of the Queen Anne style. The house was the lifelong home of Smith's daughter Dorothy, the author of several books and articles on Staten Island's history and a founder of Richmondtown Restoration (see No. 41).

33 Peter Housman House, 308 Saint John Avenue (c. 1730; addition, c. 1760). The small one-room stone wing of this 18th-century vernacular house was erected around 1730 on the Dongan estate. (Shortly after his appointment as royal governor of New York in 1683, Thomas Dongan acquired approximately 5,100 acres on Staten Island.) Thirty years later Peter Housman, a prosperous millwright, erected a large clapboard extension. With its steep roof and unusually deep overhang, the addition matches the architectural form of the original building.

Map 4: Seaview, Richmondtown, Todt Hill

HISTORIC DISTRICT

2 **New York City Farm Colony–Seaview Hospital Historic District.** This historic district, consisting of the buildings and grounds of two municipal institutions, illustrates the commitment made

by New York City at the turn of the century to improve social and health-care services for the needy. Construction began at the Farm Colony in 1904 on a series of striking Colonial Revival dormitories and other structures built of local rubble stone. These buildings, designed by Renwick, Aspinwall

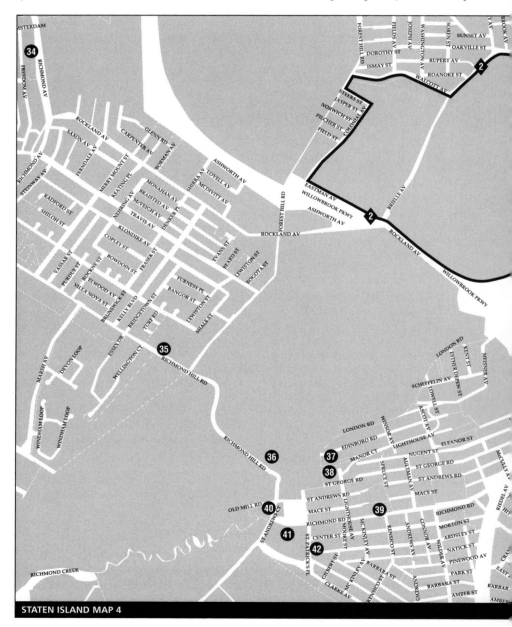

STATEN ISLAND MAP 4

284

& Owen, set the style for buildings by other architects erected during the following ten years. The New York City Farm Colony was established in 1902 by the New York City Department of Public Charities. Able bodied paupers were sent to the facility to learn discipline and self-sufficiency, raising vegetables for themselves and for other public institutions. Between 1930 and 1934, the capacity of the farm colony was doubled with the construction of a series of Colonial Revival brick structures designed by Charles B. Meyers. The entire complex is bordered by fields that were farmed by the colony's

SEAVIEW, RICHMONDTOWN, TODT HILL

residents. Separated from the farm colony by Brielle Avenue, Seaview Hospital was founded in 1905 for the treatment of tuberculosis. The architect Raymond F. Almirall conceived the plan for the hospital and designed the original facility. Later additions include Renwick, Aspinwall & Tucker's two groups of small open-air pavilions designed in 1917 for ambulatory patients. The hospital buildings were all set within a therapeutic environment that provided abundant fresh air and landscaped vistas. Most of the buildings are no longer in use.

INDIVIDUAL LANDMARKS

❸❹ Asbury Methodist Church, now Son-Rise Interfaith Charismatic Church, 1970 Richmond Avenue (1849; remodeling, 1878). This church was named for Francis Asbury, a preacher sent to America by John Wesley, the founder of Methodism. Asbury, who was consecrated in 1784 as the first bishop of the American Methodist Episcopal Church, preached on Staten Island for forty-five years. This simple vernacular brick church building, constructed by a mason named Riker and the carpenter J. L. Richards, follows in the traditions of Federal architecture. The front was rebuilt and the tower added in 1878.

❸❺ Decker Farmhouse, 435 Richmond Hill Road (c. 1810; expansion, c. 1840). This simple clapboard building is typical of the small farmhouses that once dotted Staten Island. The modest early 19th-century house was expanded in 1840 when the front porch and other additions were constructed. The building is now a farm museum operated by the Richmondtown Restoration (see No. 41).

❸❻ David Latourette House, now the Latourette Park Golf Course Club House, Latourette Park, Richmond Hill Road (c. 1836; alterations, 1936). The Latourette House, an especially imposing example of a Greek Revival residence, is one of the few early 19th-century brick country houses on this scale to survive in New York City. In 1928 the Latourette farm was sold to the city for use as a park and golf course. The Parks Department subsequently undertook a series of alterations that included the removal of dormer windows; the reconstruction of the four tall chimneys; the replacement or reconstruction of the floor, cornice, and railings at the original front porch; and the extension of the porch along the south elevation.

❸❼ Staten Island Lighthouse, Edinboro Road (1912). This octagonal brick tower rising from a rusticated limestone base houses a 350,000-candlepower beacon that guides ships into New York Harbor.

❸❽ William and Catherine Cass House, The Crimson Beech, 48 Manor Court (Frank Lloyd Wright, 1958–59). The only residence in New York City designed by Frank Lloyd Wright, this house is an example of the prefabricated houses Wright initially designed in 1956 for the builder Marshall Erdman of Madison, Wisconsin. These prefabs were the last of Wright's many attempts at designing moderate-cost housing. The components were shipped from Madison and assembled on Lighthouse Hill under the supervision of Wright's associate Morton H. Delson.

❸❾ Reverend David Moore House, also known as the Moore-McMillen House, 3531 Richmond Road (1818). This frame farmhouse with a gambrel roof and an elegant entranceway is one of the few buildings in the Federal style on Staten Island. The house was built by Saint Andrew's Church (see No. 40) for its minister, David Moore. Moore served the church for forty-eight years and was eventually given the house; his descendants occupied the premises until 1943. In the following year the prominent Staten Island historian Loring McMillen purchased the property and lived here until his death in 1990.

❹❶ Saint Andrew's Church (Episcopal), 50 Old Mill Road at Arthur Kill Road (attributed to George Mersereau, 1872). This stone edifice housing Staten Island's oldest Episcopal congregation is located just outside the Richmondtown Restoration (see No. 41). Construction of the original church began in 1709. This structure burned in 1867 and again in 1872; surviving sections of the original walls are encased in the present stonework. With its rounded windows and carefully delineated nave, tower, and entrance porch, the church resembles the Norman parish churches erected in 12th-century England.

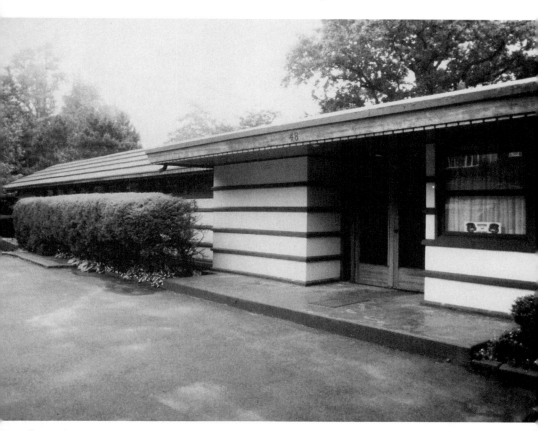

William and Catherine Cass House, the Crimson Beech (No. 38). The only residence in the city designed by noted architect Frank Lloyd Wright, the house is an example of Wright's attempts to design moderate-priced housing. Photo by Carl Forster.

④ Richmondtown Restoration, Richmond Road, Richmondtown. Due to its central location, the town of Richmond became the seat of county government on Staten Island in 1729. Richmondtown's importance declined after Staten Island joined New York City in 1898, although its courthouse remained in use until the Richmond County Courthouse (see No. 10) opened. In 1939 the Staten Island Historical Society inaugurated the preservation of Richmondtown, including the restoration of historic village buildings and the relocation of endangered buildings from other Staten Island sites. The museum village, which is owned by New York City and operated by the historical society, recalls three centuries of life on Staten Island. The names and dates given below are those currently used by the Richmondtown Restoration historic village and museum complex.

Basketmaker's House (c. 1810–20). Originally located in New Springville, this modest clapboard Dutch Colonial cottage was erected for the basketmaker John Morgan.

Bennett House (c. 1839; addition, c. 1854). This clapboard house with Greek Revival elements is located on its original site. Built as a residence with a cellar bakery, the house belonged to the shipping merchant John Bennett and his family from the late 1840s through the early 20th century.

Boehm House (c. 1750; addition, c. 1840). This extremely simple pre–Revolutionary War

Map 4: Seaview, Richmondtown, Todt Hill

Richmondtown Restoration (No. 41), a museum village, also contains historic buildings that were relocated from other parts of the island. Pictured is the Voorlezer's House, the oldest surviving elementary school building in the country. Photo by Carl Forster.

clapboard house, the home of the teacher Henry M. Boehm from 1855 to 1862, was moved to this site from Greenridge.

Britton Cottage (c. 1670; additions, c. 1755, c. 1765, and c. 1800). Built in four stages, this wood and stone farmhouse was moved from New Dorp Beach in 1967. The central stone section, which was probably built around 1670, may have served as Staten Island's first government building. The Britton family owned the house from 1695 to 1714 and again from 1895 to 1915.

Christopher House (c. 1720; addition, 1730). Originally a one-room-and-attic structure on the Dongan estate (see Peter Housman House, No. 33), this vernacular stone house was the home of the patriot Joseph Christopher during the Revolutionary War and is said to have been the meeting place of the American Committee of Safety. It was moved to Richmondtown in 1969.

Eltingville Store (c. 1860). This modest board-and-batten commercial building was originally a one-room grocery store in the village of Eltingville.

Guyon-Lake-Tysen House (c. 1740; additions, c. 1820 and c. 1840). A superb Dutch Colonial–style house erected in the New Dorp–Oakwood area by the Huguenot settler Joseph Guyon, this building was moved to Richmondtown in 1962.

The gambrel roof, spring eaves, and front porch are especially notable. The kitchen wing was added around 1820 and the dormer windows twenty years later.

Historical Museum, originally the Richmond County Clerk's and Surrogate's Office (1848; additions to c. 1918). This simple brick building, constructed in the tradition of the Federal style, served the county government until around 1920, when civic functions moved to Saint George. The building was converted into a museum in the 1930s.

Kruser-Finley House (c. 1790; additions, c. 1820 and c. 1850–60). Endangered by the construction of the Willowbrook Parkway, this modest clapboard building was moved from Egbertville in 1965. Originally a one-room house, the structure was extended around 1820 and again around 1850–60, when a shop, thought to have been used by a cooper, was added.

Parsonage (c. 1855). Located on its original site, this vernacular Gothic Revival clapboard building with gingerbread detail was originally the parsonage of the Reformed Dutch Church of Richmondtown.

Rezeau–Van Pelt Cemetery (1780s to 1860s). A rare surviving 18th-century private graveyard, this cemetery was used by two families who occupied the Voorlezer's House (see below) in the

18th and 19th centuries, after the house ceased to be used as a school.

Stephens-Black House (c. 1838–40). Stephen D. Stephens erected this simplified Greek Revival house, and his family lived here until 1870, operating the one-story general store (reconstructed in 1964) that was added to the rear at some point after the main house was completed.

Third County Courthouse, now the Visitors Center (1837). With its Doric portico and square cupola, this Greek Revival courthouse was the centerpiece of Richmondtown during its period as a governmental center. The courthouse remained in use until 1919.

Treasure House (c. 1700; additions, c. 1740, c. 1790, and c. 1860). Still on its original site, this modest clapboard building was the house and workshop of Samuel Grasset, a tanner and leatherworker. The Treasure House derives its name from the local legend that a $7,000 cache of British coins was found hidden in its walls around 1860.

Voorlezer's House (c. 1695). Built by the Reformed Dutch Church as a school, church, and home for the "voorlezer," or lay reader and teacher, this two-story clapboard structure is the oldest surviving elementary school in the country and the oldest surviving building from the settlement of Richmondtown. Its restoration in 1939–42 was Richmondtown Restoration's first project.

㊷ Saint Patrick's Church (R.C.), 45 Saint Patrick's Place (1860–62). Located across the street from the Richmondtown Restoration (see No. 41), Saint Patrick's is an integral part of the old community of Richmondtown. The church is a dignified example of the Early Romanesque Revival style.

㊸ Lane Theater (interior), 168 New Dorp Lane (John Eberson, 1937–38). Designed by one of the preeminent theater architects of the 20th century, the Art Moderne foyer, lounge corridor, and auditorium of the Lane Theater make up one of the last surviving historic theater interiors on Staten Island. The theater has been vacant for several years.

㊹ Gustave A. Mayer House, originally the David R. Ryers House, 2475 Richmond Road (1855–56). With its boxy massing, arcaded porch, deep bracketed eaves, round-arched openings, and square cupola, this house, built for David R. Ryers, epitomizes the Italian villa form that became popular in the United States in the 1850s. In 1889 the property was purchased by Gustave A. Mayer, the confectioner who invented the Nabisco sugar wafer. Mayer used the basement of the villa as a workshop to experiment with novelties for his business. The house was occupied by members of the Mayer family for one hundred years.

㊺ New Dorp Light, 25 Boyle Street, New Dorp Heights (c. 1854). Now converted into a residence, this vernacular clapboard cottage with a tall square tower served for almost ninety years as a beacon to ships entering New York Harbor.

㊻ Ernest Flagg Estate, Stone Court, now the Scalabrini Fathers of Saint Charles and the Copperflagg Residential Development, 209 Flagg Place (Ernest Flagg, 1898 to c. 1917). Stone Court was built as the country estate of the prominent American architect Ernest Flagg. Flagg was introduced to Staten Island in 1897, and a year later he began to purchase land in a section of Todt Hill with splendid ocean views. Here he erected a large house that was indebted to the form of Staten Island's early Dutch Colonial–style dwellings, with their steep, sloping gambrel roofs and deep eaves (the roof slope was somewhat altered when the house was enlarged in 1907–09). Flagg extensively landscaped his grounds and also erected a series of other structures, including the extant gatehouse, stable, water towers, retaining wall, gardener's cottage, palm house, garage, and storage house, all of which were originally faced with whitewashed fieldstone. Much of the estate is now occupied by a complex of large suburban houses designed by Robert A. M. Stern and built in the 1980s.

㊼ Ernest Flagg Estate Cottage: Bowcot, 95 West Entry Road (Ernest Flagg, 1916–18). Flagg not only built his own large estate on Todt Hill, but he also used the area to experiment with the construction of innovative low-cost dwellings of modular design that embodied his pioneering vision of affordable middle-class housing. Although Flagg

Ernest Flagg Estate, Stone Court (No. 46). The country estate of the prominent American architect Ernest Flagg contains an impressive estate house as well as a myriad of experimental and model buildings. Photo by Andrew S. Dolkart.

erected only a few cottages, his ideas were widely disseminated through popular magazines and his book *Small Houses.* Three of the houses are landmarks. Bowcot was the earliest of Flagg's experimental stone cottages. Built into a curved section of the stone wall of his estate (thus the name Bowcot, a diminutive for "bowed cottage"), the small house is carefully integrated with its setting. Among Flagg's innovations was the use of "mosaic rubble," a technique of setting rubble stone into a concrete wall.

48 **Ernest Flagg Estate Cottage: Wallcot,** also known as House-on-the-Wall, 285 Flagg Place (Ernest Flagg, 1918–21). Wallcot is a simple dwelling erected in conjunction with flanking walls. Both the cottage and the walls were built of Flagg's mosaic rubble. The house has the picturesque sloping roofs and dormers that Flagg favored for their evocation of "home."

49 **Ernest Flagg Estate Cottage: McCall's Demonstration House,** 1929 Richmond Road (Ernest Flagg, 1924–25). In 1924–25 Flagg built a model house for the benefit of the readers of *McCall's* magazine. A series of articles detailing the construction of this cottage served to popularize Flagg's ideas on residential design. When the house was completed, Flagg leased it to his secretary.

50 **Pierre Billiou House,** also known as the Billiou-Stillwell-Perine House, 1476 Richmond Road (c. 1660s; additions, c. 1680 to c. 1830). The original stone section of this house was erected by Pierre Billiou in the 1660s, shortly after the first permanent settlement was founded in the region known as Olde Dorp. Constructed according to medieval building traditions, the house is the oldest surviving building on Staten Island. Billiou's daughter married Thomas Stillwell, and they built the first of several additions to the house. For 150 years, beginning in 1764, the house was owned by members of the Perine family. In 1919 this became the first site on Staten Island to be acquired by a historical society for use as a house museum.

INDIVIDUAL LANDMARKS

51 **Saint Alban's Episcopal Church,** originally the Church of the Holy Comforter (Episcopal), 76 Saint Alban's Place (R. M. Upjohn, 1865; enlargement, R. M. Upjohn, 1872). Saint Alban's in Eltingville, a rare example of board-and-batten construction in New York City, is one of the city's finest rural Gothic Revival wood-frame buildings. The church was built in 1865; in 1872 it was moved to its present site and enlarged by the insertion of transepts between the nave and chancel. In 1951 the Holy Comforter parish merged with Saint Anne's, Great Kills, to form Saint Alban's. In 1990 the church completed a restoration (Li-Saltzman Architects) that included repainting in historically accurate colors.

52 **Frederick Law Olmsted House,** also known as the Poillon House, 4515 Hylan Boulevard (early 18th century; additions, 1830s). The high stone base of the present house was probably erected in the early part of the 18th century and used as a barn. The building appears to have been converted into a residence by the addition of the frame upper stories in the 1830s. In 1839 the house and surrounding land were purchased by Samuel Akerly, a renowned agricultural reformer. Nine years later the young Frederick Law Olmsted bought the property; over the next few years he relandscaped the site and undertook a variety of agricultural ex-

periments. In 1853 Olmsted moved to Manhattan, where he would eventually embark on a career as America's first landscape architect.

STATEN ISLAND MAP 5   ELTINGVILLE

Saint Alban's Episcopal Church (No. 51), one of New York City's finest rural Gothic Revival wood-frame buildings. Photo: Andrew S. Dolkart.

291

OMBAY ST
RVIL ST
MASON BLVD
McBAINE AV
ROSSVILLE AV
ALVERSON AV
GILROY ST
MARCY AV
WEST CASTOR PL
VENUS PL
WOODROW RD
MARCY AV
DESFRE AV
POWELL ST
WALKER PL
ELLSWORTH AV
HUGUENOT AV
CROWN AV
VINELAND AV
STAFFORD AV
SINCLAIR AV
SHELDON AV
RENSSELAER AV
NIPPON AV
RATHBUN AV
RAMONA AV
DELMAR AV
LAMONT AV
IONA AV
EDGEGROVE AV
DARLINGTON AV
HEENAN AV
RICHMOND PKWY
IDA CT
ELFIELD AV
SINCL
SHELDO

53

WOODROW RD
WIELAND AV
RAMAPO AV
ANTHONY ST
STAFFORD AV
SINCLAIR AV
SHELDON AV
RENSSELAER AV
RATHBUN AV
RAMONA AV
LAMONT AV
LENEVAR AV
IONA AV
EDGEGROVE AV
DARLINGTON AV
CARLTON AV
DRUMGOOLE RD WEST
DRUMGOOLE RD E
MAGUIRE AV
MINTURN AV
FOSTER RD
VERNON AV
ELLSWORTH AV
RICHMOND PKWY
WEST TERRACE
HUGUENOT AV
AMBOY RD
BENNETT AV
COLLYER AV
DAN ST
ARBUTUS AV
SALA CT

54

BRADFORD AV
ASHLAND AV
ALBOURNE AV
VICTOR ST
GOFF AV
MAGUIRE AV
TERRACE AV
CLEARMONT AV
UNCAS AV
VOGEL AV
PARKWOOD AV
SCUDDER AV
FOSTER RD
VALDEMAR AV
MADERA ST
AMBOY RD
VERNON AV
WOODHULL AV
ADDISON AV
KELLER AV
HAWLEY AV
CHISHOLM ST
LUTEN AV
ANDROVETTE AV
PRALL AV
ALGOKIN ST
BILLOU ST
COMELY ST
DEISIUS ST
TUCKAHOE AV
HUGUENOT AV
KINGDOM AV
STECHER ST
COLON AV
EYLANDT ST
CAPELLIAN ST
JANSEN ST
TUCKAHOE AV
KINGDO
HUGUENOT AV
CHISHOLM ST

55

AMBOY RD
AMBOY RD
BAYVIEW AVE
WATERBURY AV
FLORENCE PL
MACCREGOR ST
KNOX ST
SINGLETON ST
HATHAWAY AVE
WOLF'S POND PARK
SHADYSIDE AV
EXCELSIOR AV
S GOFF AV
CORDELIA AV
SHARROTT AV
FINLAY AV
BURTON AV
EVERETT AV
VAIL AV
WOODVALE AV
KENNETH PL
SHERWOOD AV
DIRENZO CT
HANOVER AV
ATKINS ST
HYLAN BLVD
SEGUINE AV
HOLTEN ST
WOLF'S POND PARK
HYLAN BLVD
MAXWELL AV
CORNELIA AV
IRVINGTON ST

CASE AV
MEMO ST
MELVILLE ST
HANK PL
WILBUR ST
TRENTON CT
MARSCHER PL
VAN WYCK AV
PURDY PL
JOHNSTON

56

57

BAYVIEW AV
WOODVALE AV
HYLAN BLVD
NSTON TERR

INDIVIDUAL LANDMARKS

53 **Woodrow Methodist Church,** 1101 Woodrow Road (1842). This simple Greek Revival country church was built in 1842 on the site of Staten Island's first Methodist church. The tower was added in 1876.

54 **Memorial Church of the Huguenots,** now the Reformed Church of Huguenot Park, 5475 Amboy Road (Ernest Flagg, 1923–24; assembly hall, James Whitford, Jr., 1954–55; library, 1903–05). Dedicated in 1924 as the National Monument of the Huguenot–Walloon–New Netherlands 300th Anniversary of Religious Freedom, this stone church is both a testament to a significant aspect of Staten Island's early history and an important late work by Ernest Flagg (see No. 46). The design, reminiscent of the vernacular Norman architecture of England and northwestern France, offers evidence of Flagg's interest in medieval design and his experimentation with economical means of construction. Like the Ernest Flagg Estate Cottages (see Nos. 47–49), the building is a concrete structure set with rubble stone (quarried on Flagg's nearby estate) and built on the modular system first used at the estate cottages. The site also includes an assembly hall that was added to the west side of the church in 1954–55 and a small wooden public library built in 1903–05 and moved to this site shortly thereafter. The former library was once the smallest branch of the New York Public Library system.

55 **Abraham J. Wood House,** also known as the 5910 Amboy Road House (c. 1840). This house was erected by the farmer and oysterman Abraham Wood shortly after he purchased the property in 1840. The main section of Wood's new Greek Revival house may have been an addition to an earlier building (now part of the west wing). The house, which has many features typical of vernacular Greek Revival design on Staten Island, is notable for its entranceway.

56 **Joseph H. Seguine House,** 440 Seguine Avenue (1837). This sophisticated Greek Revival country house is located at the highest point on the Seguine family's ancestral farm. The farmer, shipping merchant, and industrialist Joseph Seguine, born in the nearby Abraham Manee House (see

Memorial Church of the Huguenots (No. 54). The design of this church is reminiscent of Norman architecture of England and northwestern France. Photo by Kevin McHugh.

No. 57), belonged to the fifth generation of his family to live on Staten Island.

57 **Abraham Manee House,** also known as the Manee-Seguine Homestead, 509 Seguine Avenue (late 17th to early 19th centuries). Located on Prince's Bay near the southern tip of Staten Island, this house has a complex building history that may extend back to the construction of a one-room dwelling by Paulus Regrenier in the late 17th century. A major rubble-stone addition was constructed early in the 18th century by Abraham Manee. Further additions were made early in the next century by the Seguine family, who acquired the property in the 1780s.

INDIVIDUAL LANDMARKS

58 Sleight Family Graveyard, also known as the Rossville or Blazing Star Burial Ground, Arthur Kill Road at Rossville Road (1750–1850). This small graveyard, which served the village of Rossville, is one of the earliest community cemeteries on Staten Island.

59 Rossville A.M.E. Zion Church Cemetery, Crabtree Avenue (1852–). This cemetery is a major surviving element of Sandy Ground, a 19th-century settlement of free black oystermen and their families who moved to Staten Island from Maryland. The cemetery contains the burial sites of members of at least thirty-four African-American families, some of whose descendants still reside in the area.

60 Westfield Township School No. 7, later Public School No. 4, 4210–4212 Arthur Kill Road, Charleston (1896; enlarged, C. B. J. Snyder, 1906–07). Kreischerville, or Charleston, the seventh school district of Westfield Township, erected

STATEN ISLAND MAP 7   ROSSVILLE, KREISCHERVILLE

this school during the years of peak employment at the Kreischer Brick Works and accompanying village development. The association with the company is evident on the front facade, which employs two colors of ironspot brick and uses brick to spell out the name and date of the building. It remains in use as Public School 25, Annex D, under the jurisdiction of the Board of Education's Division of Special Education.

61 **Saint Peter's German Evangelical Reformed Church of Kreischerville**, now Free Magyar Reformed Church, Parish Hall, and Rectory, 19–25 Winant Place, Charleston (church, Hugo Kafka, 1883; parish hall, 1898; rectory, Royal Daggett, 1926). This small wooden church complex reflects the immigrant history of the Kreischerville area. The church was a gift of Balthasar Kreischer, owner of the Kreischer Brick Works, to the many German workers in his factory. By the early 20th century, the work force was increasingly Hungarian, and in 1919 the Carpenter Gothic church and parish hall were sold to the Magyar Reformed Church.

62 **Kreischerville Workers' Houses**, 71–73, 75–77, 81–83, and 85–87 Kreischer Street,

Charleston (c. 1890). These four identical pairs of houses are rare surviving examples of their type. Built by prominent local landowner Peter Androvette as housing for workers in the adjacent Kreischer Brick Works, they, along with the nearby Kreischer House (see No. 63), reflect the evolution of a Richmond County hamlet into a company town. Although the houses are clad in wood shingles, the sidewalks are paved in Kreischer brick.

63 **Charles Kreischer House**, 4500 Arthur Kill Road (attributed to Palliser & Palliser, c. 1888). In 1854 Balthasar Kreischer established the Kreischer Brick Company in southwestern Staten Island. He built a villa at the top of a hill overlooking his factory, and around 1888 a pair of houses was erected at a lower elevation for his two sons. One of the houses was this exuberant Stick Style structure built for Charles Kreischer; it is the only one of the Kreischer family houses that survives. The Kreischer Brick Company was an important late 19th-century Staten Island industry, producing a variety of architectural materials, including terra-cotta ornament and many types of bricks. Ronald Victorio was the architect for the conversion of this house into a restaurant.

The Kreischerville Workers' Houses (No. 62) are remnants of this once bustling company town. Photo by Carl Forster.

INDIVIDUAL LANDMARKS

64 **New York Public Library, Tottenville Branch,** 7430 Amboy Road (Carrère & Hastings, 1903–04). With Andrew Carnegie's $5 million gift, the New York Public Library erected branches in Manhattan (see Nos. 466, 474, and 483), the Bronx, and Staten Island. This handsome Classical Revival building is the oldest public library on Staten Island and was the work of Carrère & Hastings (John Carrère was a resident of the island), architect of the main Fifth Avenue Library (see Manhattan No. 237). The building was restored in 1991–93 by architect John Ellis.

65 **Westfield Township District School No. 5,** now Public School 1 Annex, Yetman Avenue and Academy Avenue (1878; enlarged, Pierce & Brun, 1896–97). Prior to becoming a borough of New York City, Staten Island had its own school system organized by township. Westfield, the southernmost town on the island, had seven districts; Tottenville was No. 5. This modest neo-Grec school of brick with stone trim was originally capped by an open belfry. It is the oldest school building on Staten Island remaining in use. An addition was erected in 1896–97 for a two-year high school.

66 **Henry Hogg Biddle House,** 70 Satterlee Street (late 1840s). The Biddle House, overlooking the Arthur Kill, exemplifies an unusual aspect of vernacular design on Staten Island—the combining of Dutch Colonial–style spring eaves with Greek Revival columned porticoes. This structure is the only extant local house with two-story porticoes and spring eaves on both the front and rear elevations. These elements add a sense of grandeur to the relatively small waterfront dwelling.

STATEN ISLAND MAP 8
TOTTENVILLE

67 Conference House, also known as Bentley Manor, the Christopher Billopp House, 7455 Hylan Boulevard (c. 1675). This house is historically significant as the site of a conference on September 11, 1776, between three delegates of the Continental Congress—Benjamin Franklin, John Adams, and Edward Rutledge—and the British Admiral Lord Howe that proved an unsuccessful effort to avert the Revolutionary War. The house was built by naval captain Christopher Billopp, who was granted a patent on sixteen hundred acres of southern Staten Island in 1676. Because of its historical importance, efforts were made to preserve the site as early as 1888, but it was not until 1926 that it was acquired by the city and restoration began.

Henry Hogg Biddle House (No. 66), a vernacular design that has an unusual combination of Dutch Colonial and Greek Revival elements. Photo by Carl Forster

Governors Island Historic District. Governors Island, located one-half mile from Manhattan in New York Harbor, was used by the United States military for almost two hundred years. In 1637 the island, called Pagganck by the Canarsee Indians and Nutten by the Dutch, became the private property of Wouter Van Twiller, the director general of the New Netherlands. It remained in the hands of succeeding Dutch and English governors, thus accounting for its name. The island was initially fortified by American and later British troops during the Revolutionary War. The first permanent fortifications were erected by the United States government in 1794–96 and named Fort Jay in 1798. In 1800 the island was ceded by New York City to the federal government, along with Ellis and Bedloe's (now Liberty) Islands (see below). Between 1807 and 1811, as tensions between the United States and Britain increased, a series of for-

tifications were built in New York Harbor, including Fort Columbus, to replace Fort Jay (the name Fort Jay was later restored; see below), and Castle William (see below). As the importance of the island in the defense of New York Harbor waned in the mid-19th century, the island was adapted for other army uses, notably as an arsenal. Twelve buildings were erected for the arsenal, including seven that survive. Barracks, a hospital, officers' housing, and other buildings in the Greek Revival style were also built for troops stationed at Fort Columbus. Under the command of General Winfield Scott Hancock, the island became an army administrative center, and a series of officers' quarters, including a group of picturesque clapboard houses set around Nolan Park (1878–1902), and large brick houses, known as Regimental Row (1893–1917), were erected. Also dating from this period is the Chapel of Saint Cornelius the Centu-

GOVERNOR'S ISLAND

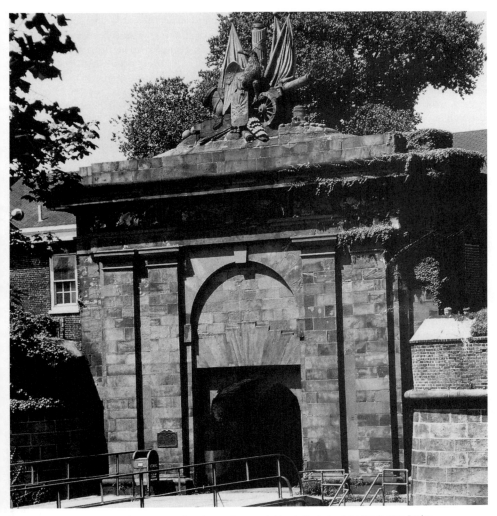

The impressive French-inspired entrance to Fort Jay on Governor's Island. Photo by John Barrington Bayley.

rion, a neo-Gothic church designed by Charles C. Haight in 1905. In the early 20th century, the island was enlarged through landfill, and Charles F. McKim of the firm of McKim, Mead & White was hired to plan for additional troop facilities. It was not until 1928 that work began on the first buildings designed by the McKim, Mead & White firm. These include a neo-Georgian-style model barracks (Building 400) that was the longest military building in the world at the time of its completion and a similarly styled officers' quarters (Building 12) built with a U-shaped plan in seven sections. The

construction of neo-Georgian-style buildings in the 1930s, some according to McKim's plan, included quarters for officers and their families and nurses' quarters designed by Rogers & Poor; the First United States Army headquarters building, designed by Lorimer Rich; and Public School 26, designed by Eric Kibbon. In 1966, after over 150 years on Governors Island, the army left the island and the United States Coast Guard established it as the Atlantic Area headquarters. The Coast Guard has ceased operations on the island, and its future is undetermined.

Prior to the designation of the Governors Island Historic District, which incorporates the portion of the island northeast of Division Road, five buildings were designated as individual landmarks; in recent years much new information has come to light on these buildings, based on an extensive study in archival documents by the Historic American Buildings Survey:

❶ **Commanding Officer's Quarters,** Nolan Park, west of Barry Road (Martin E. Thompson, 1843; south wing, 1886; porch, c. 1893–1918). This building served as the home of the island's commanding officer from the time of its completion until the summer of 1996. The building was originally a rectangular Greek Revival–style structure with a porch. A wing was added to the south in 1886, and sometime between 1893 and 1918 the original front porch was altered to incorporate the present slender Tuscan columns with a balustrade above. With funding from the Works Progress Administration in 1936–37, Charles O. Cornelius redesigned the rear of the house and embellished the building with ironwork, giving it an "early American" character. The house was the site of a historic 1988 luncheon meeting between President Ronald Reagan and President Mikhail Gorbachev of the Soviet Union.

❷ **Governor's House** (originally a guardhouse), Nolan Park, corner of Barry Road and Andes Road (c. 1805–13). Previously thought to have been erected in around 1708, this Georgian-style house was actually built in the early 19th century and was originally Governors Island's main guardhouse. In 1824 the building became the quarters of the island's commanding officer. By 1839 the roof slope had been altered to the present combination of hipped and gabled slopes. The building later served again as a guardhouse and then as the post headquarters, and in the 1920s it became the residence of the army's post commander. A one-story addition was added at the rear in the 1930s. The entrance portico with Ionic columns and pilasters may also date from this period.

❸ **Post Hospital,** also known as the Block House, Nolan Park, northwest of Barry Road (1839). This two-story Greek Revival building with a fieldstone base and granite entrance en-

framement served as a hospital until 1878 and was later used as an army headquarters building and as apartments. The austerity of the design has led to its being popularly named the Block House. The building originally had a flat roof, but this had been replaced by 1863 (or earlier) with the present shallow hipped roof to prevent damage caused by leaks.

❹ **Fort Columbus,** now Fort Jay, Andes Road (Lieutenant Colonel Jonathan Williams, 1806–09). In 1794–96 an earthen fortification, known as Fort Jay, was erected on this site as part of the earliest attempt to fortify New York Harbor. In 1806 this was replaced by Fort Columbus, an impressive star-shaped structure inspired by French fortifications; only a few sections of the earlier fort were saved and incorporated into the new structure. Lieutenant Colonel Jonathan Williams, who designed this and other contemporary forts, had lived in France in 1776–85 under the auspices of his great-uncle Benjamin Franklin; there he gained familiarity with French military design. The sandstone structure has four bastions enclosed by a dry moat. The impressive French-inspired entrance is crowned by a large sandstone trophy sculpture with an eagle and military symbols. The interior of the fort contains Greek Revival barracks with impressive colonnaded porticoes that were constructed in 1834–36. The fort was renamed for John Jay in 1904.

❺ **Castle Williams,** Hay Road (Lieutenant Colonel Jonathan Williams, 1807–11). Castle Williams is a massive bastion forming three-fifths of a circle, with a two-story entrance pavilion filling in the remainder of the form. Erected to support more than one hundred cannons, it is one of a series of forts, including Castle Clinton (see Manhattan No. 3), just across New York Harbor, built to fortify New York as tensions rose between America and the British in the early 19th century. At the time of its construction, it served as a prototype for seacoast fortifications in America and is today one of the best examples of its type in existence. The imposing three-tiered fort was constructed of red Newark sandstone with walls that are eight feet thick at the base and seven feet thick at the top. During the Civil War,

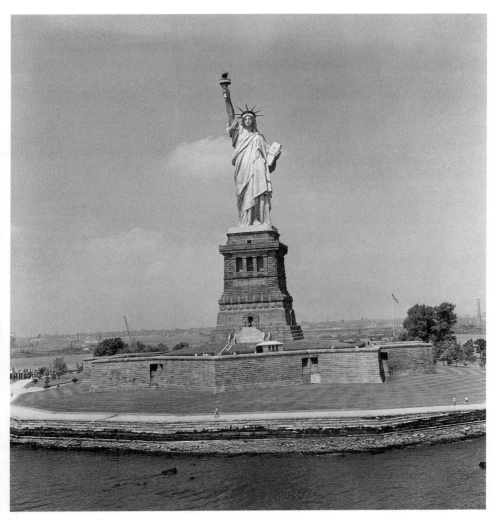

The Statue of Liberty. Photo courtesy of the National Park Service.

the fort served as a prison for Confederate soldiers; it was later used as quarters for new recruits, as a military prison, and for storage.

Liberty Island. Known as Bedloe's Island until 1956, this island was the site of Fort Wood, a structure in the shape of an eleven-pointed star, erected in 1806–11 to fortify the entrance to New York Harbor. The fort was incorporated into the plans for the base of the Statue of Liberty. Although located within New Jersey's territorial waters, the island itself has

been considered a part of New York City since the late 17th century. An agreement of 1834 provides that the island is in New York above the mean low-water mark and in New Jersey below it.

Statue of Liberty (Frédéric Auguste Bartholdi, sculptor, and Gustave Eiffel, engineer, 1871–86; base, Richard Morris Hunt, 1881–86). This portrait of Liberty, famed the world over as a symbol of the United States of America, was a gift from the people of France. The idea for the statue originated with a group of French intellectuals who advocated republican rule in France during the Second Empire. They hoped that inspiration provided by the ideals associated with the construction of the statue would lead to the expansion of democracy in France. It was not until 1903, when Emma Lazarus's famed poem "The New Colossus" was inscribed on a tablet at the base of the pedestal, that the Statue of Liberty became the symbol of American immigration. The Alsatian sculptor Frédéric Auguste Bartholdi started work on the statue in 1871 and by 1875 was ready to begin construction. Money was raised in France for the casting of the colossal piece. The beaten copper exterior was placed on a wrought-iron armature designed by Gustave Eiffel to support the statue's weight and to provide bracing against the winds that would batter the statue at the mouth of New York Harbor. Construction of the base was the responsibility of the United States. Appropriately, the design was undertaken by the French-trained architect Richard Morris Hunt, with money raised through contributions encouraged by Joseph Pulitzer in his newspaper, the *New York World*. In 1885 the statue arrived from France in hundreds of crates and was assembled under the supervision of General Charles P. Stone, an army engineer. A major restoration of the statue was completed in time for its centennial in 1986. This work was directed by Swanke Hayden Connell, architect, with the engineering firm Ammann & Whitney; the French metalworkers Les Metalliers Champenois also contributed their expertise.

ELLIS ISLAND

Ellis Island Historic District. The Ellis Island Historic District commemorates the significance of immigration to the history of the United States. Beginning in 1892, when Ellis Island first became an immigrant station, more than twelve million poor immigrants from all over the world came through Ellis Island before settling in New York City or continuing their journeys to every corner of the nation. Ellis Island had been a fort (Fort Gibson) before it was converted into an immigrant arrival station, replacing Castle Clinton (see Manhattan No. 3) as the site for the federal registration of immigrants. After the original wooden facility burned in 1897, the present Beaux-Arts-style complex was erected to the designs of the New York City architecture firm Boring & Tilton (1897–1900). The immigration station focuses on the main building, a monumental brick and limestone structure with prominent corner towers where the immigrants were received, registered, and examined, where their baggage was stored, and were some were detained in dormitories. Most of those who came to Ellis Island were soon sent on their way, but a small percentage of prospective immigrants were held on the island or sent back to their place of embarkation. The most prominent space on the **interior** of the main building is the double-height Registry Room on the second floor. The vast open space, lit by natural light entering from large windows, was originally divided by iron railings into alleys where immigrants lined up for inspection. The railings were replaced by benches in 1911. In 1916 an explosion in New Jersey, caused by German saboteurs, damaged the building, and in 1918 the damaged plaster ceiling and asphalt floor were replaced by a spectacular Guastavino tile arched ceiling and a floor of red Ludowici tile. Adjoining the main building are Boring & Tilton's kitchen and laundry building (1898–1901) and powerhouse (1900–01) and a baggage and dormitory building designed by Supervising Architect of the Treasury James Knox Taylor (1907–09). Boring & Tilton was also responsible for the original hospital (1901–09) located across the ferry slip from the main building. To accommodate the increasing number of immigrants arriving at Ellis Island, the island was enlarged through landfill, and many new buildings were erected. The hospital was enlarged, and a contagious disease complex was built early in the 20th century, all to designs by James Knox Taylor. The passage of re-

Ellis Island, gateway to America. Photo by Carl Forster.

strictive immigration legislation in 1924 and the institution of immigration checks at United States consulates changed the use of Ellis Island. It became largely a center for the deportation of aliens, usually illegal immigrants. In 1934–36 the Public Works Administration allocated funds for the construction of additional buildings, including another immigration building, ferry house, and recreation building, all designed in a Modern Colonial idiom by architect Chester H. Aldrich of the firm Delano & Aldrich. In 1954 the island was closed, but eleven years later President Lyndon B. Johnson made it a part of the Statue of Liberty National Monument. A restoration undertaken by Beyer Blinder Belle began in the 1980s, and in 1990 the main building at Ellis Island reopened as a museum of immigration history that is now one of the most popular sites in New York City. The remainder of the island, including the majority of the buildings, awaits restoration and reuse.

Roosevelt Island. The six landmark structures on Roosevelt Island, dating from the late 18th century to the early 1890s, illustrate the transformation of this 107-acre island from a farm to the home of

several large institutions. In 1676 the Blackwell family took possession of the island, and it remained in their hands until it was purchased by the city in 1828 for the construction of hospitals, asylums, and a prison. Long known as Blackwell's Island, the name was changed to Welfare Island in 1921 and to Roosevelt Island in 1973. The island now houses several institutions as well as a planned residential community that opened in 1975. In conjunction with the residential development, several of the older buildings were restored or stabilized by Giorgio Cavaglieri.

❶ **Lighthouse** (James Renwick, Jr., supervising architect, 1872). The 50-foot-tall lighthouse was erected on what was once a separate tiny island. The octagonal shaft, faced with rough stone blocks of gray gneiss quarried on the island by convict labor, is enlivened by Gothic detail, notably a gabled entrance and a band of foliate ornament.

❷ **New York City Lunatic Asylum,** now Octagon Tower (A. J. Davis, 1835–39; alterations, Joseph M. Dunn). The Octagon Tower—the

303

LIGHTHOUSE
PARK
❶

BIRD S
COLER
MEMORIAL
HOSPITAL

❷

RIVER RD

FDR DRIVE

MOTORGATE
PLAZA

ROOSEVELT
BRIDGE

❹

MAIN ST

❸

VERN

QUEENSBORO BRIDGE

GOLDWATER
MEMORIAL
HOSPITAL

WEST RD

EAST RD

❺

❻

ROOSEVELT ISLAND

sole surviving portion of the city's insane asylum—was originally the central section of a larger structure planned by Davis in 1835–36. As completed in 1839, the complex consisted of the octagon and two patient wings. In 1879 the wings were enlarged and a dome was added. The building is now badly deteriorated.

❸ **James Blackwell House** (between 1796 and 1804). This simple Georgian-vernacular clapboard farmhouse, the oldest building on the island, was erected by descendants of the island's original European settlers.

❹ **Chapel of the Good Shepherd,** now Good Shepherd Community Ecumenical Center (Frederick Clarke Withers, 1888–89). Withers's design for this late Victorian Gothic chapel combines the traditions of English parish churches with the demands of an unusual commission. The chapel was a gift of the banker George M. Bliss to the Episcopal City Mission Society and was intended for use by inmates of the nearby city institutions. The stone building has a clearly delineated nave, chancel, and tower, as well as a pair of entrance porches—for male and female inmates, respectively.

❺ **Strecker Laboratory** (Withers & Dickson, 1892; third floor, William Flanagan, 1905). This small Romanesque Revival graystone and orange-brick building was originally a pathology laboratory for the nearby Charity Hospital. The seriously deteriorated building is to be reconstructed by the New York City Transit Authority (Page Ayres Cowley Architects) and converted into an electrical substation.

❻ **Smallpox Hospital** (James Renwick, Jr., 1854–56; south wing, York & Sawyer, 1903–04; north wing, Renwick, Aspinwall & Owen, 1904–05). Now a picturesque ruin that was stabilized in the 1970s, this Gothic Revival stone structure was built for the treatment of smallpox patients. In 1903–05, by which time the hospital served as a nurse's residence, the facility was enlarged to form a U-shaped structure. Additional stabilization of the ruin is planned.

A GUIDE TO ROW-HOUSE ARCHITECTURAL STYLES

New York City is world famous for its skyline of glass and steel, yet architecturally it is in large part a 19th-century city. A great deal of its architectural character derives from the numerous blocks of row houses, the standard, narrow three- to five-story houses built throughout the 19th century for the city's expanding middle class. Such row houses are the predominant building type within a majority of New York's historic districts and the most common type of single-family residence in the city as a whole.

During the 19th century, New York City and neighboring Brooklyn (independent until 1898) grew extraordinarily in both wealth and influence and surged ahead of the great colonial centers of Philadelphia, Boston, and Charleston, South Carolina, to become the commercial center of America. At this time, New York City also experienced an unprecedented increase in population, as both Europeans and rural Americans arrived. New York became a city of the poor, with tenements and shanties; a city of the rich, with enormous mansions located on the finest avenues; and a city of the vast middle class, who lived in comfortable, if not luxurious, row houses.

The row house is a three- to five-story narrow residence with windows on only the front and rear elevations (corner buildings often have windows on a side elevation). Each house in a group is similar to and shares sidewalls with its neighbor. Even when built singly, row houses did not feature side lot-line windows, as developers assumed that the neighboring property would also be developed with row houses. Although widely used in New York, the row house was not invented here. It was imported from Europe, where it was common in the great urban centers, especially London and Paris. Because land is expensive in dense urban areas, row houses are cheaper to build, since no land is left open between buildings. Further economies, relative to

comparable freestanding residences, result from the row house sharing common, or party, walls with its neighbors.

Most of New York's row houses were erected by developers who purchased large plots of open land and built houses on speculation, usually in groups of two to thirty-five. These row houses were intended for sale or rent to families moving into newly developing areas. Frequently, the developers were also builders. If they were not, they hired builders to erect the rows. Architects were not involved with the design of the average row house until the late 19th century. The builders were primarily responsible for the floor plans and window pattern of the facade; specific decorative details were probably left to the anonymous craftsmen.

Because the row house was such an enduring type of middle-class residence in New York City, with construction spanning more than a century, from 1800 to 1930, it was built in a variety of styles as architectural tastes shifted. Examples of almost every major 19th- and early 20th-century style—Federal, Greek Revival, Italianate, and Romanesque Revival, to name but a few—can be encountered in the historic districts scattered throughout the city. The following styles are the most significant and the most common. The accompanying illustrations, elevation drawings of particular New York City row houses, show the most common identifying features of each style. It must be remembered, however, that architecture is a creative endeavor; not all houses of a particular style will exactly fit the description given. Architectural styles evolve slowly. Many row houses are transitional buildings, with forms and details characteristic of two or more styles. In addition, many of New York City's row houses have been altered since they were built. Often the change was the addition of one or more elements to make an older row house more stylish.

THE FEDERAL STYLE (1800–1835)

The Federal style became popular in New York around 1800, coinciding with the beginning of New York's rise to economic power and wealth and the growth of the city's population. When New York recovered from the Revolutionary War, most building was undertaken in the Federal style, although few buildings were constructed on the grander scale of Federal-style residences in Boston, Philadelphia, or Charleston. The style came late to New York and lingered longer than in other cities. A large number of Federal-style residences were erected as far north as 14th Street, with scattered examples even farther uptown. A few of these buildings survive, some still set on gracious residential streets, others hemmed in by factories, lofts, and various commercial structures. The largest concentration of Federal row houses is in Greenwich Village, and the most extraordinary examples are on Charlton and Vandam Streets between Varick Street and Sixth Avenue. They can also be found in and around SoHo and the Lower East Side.

Most of the Federal-style row houses in SoHo and Greenwich Village are modest 2½-story buildings. New York's grandest Federal-style row houses were 3½-story residences, usually built in long terraces. Many existed in the elegant Bond Street neighborhood, now part of the East Village. Most, however, were replaced by industrial buildings and tenements in the late 19th century, after the affluent residents had moved uptown.

The popularity of the Federal style coincided with the beginning of major urban development in Brooklyn. The catalyst for Brooklyn's residential development was the establishment of a reliable ferry service between Brooklyn and Manhattan in 1814. By the 1840s, fast, safe, and reliable steamboats were traveling regularly between New York and Brooklyn, making it possible to live in Brooklyn and work in Manhattan. This service brought with it an unprecedented population boom; in only a few decades Brooklyn grew from a small rural village to the third-largest city in America. Brooklyn's urban development began in Brooklyn Heights, which was near the original ferry docks at Fulton Street. In the 1820s modest Federal-style houses were erected in Brooklyn Heights, and a few notable examples survive today, particularly on Middagh, Hicks, and Willow Streets.

8 GROVE STREET, MANHATTAN

The Federal style is characterized by modest scale and simple architectural ornament inspired by ancient Greek and Roman architecture; two to three stories high, with basement and an attic half-story with dormer windows; metal or slate peaked roof; brownstone base with red brick upper facade (laid in Flemish bond pattern); low stoop with wrought-iron handrails, fence, and newels; six- or eight-paneled wood entrance door, sometimes with a leaded transom, sidelights, and colonnettes; six-over-six double-hung wood windows (often flanked by paneled shutters); stone window sills and paneled stone window lintels; classical wood cornice with dentils, modillions, and moldings.

THE GREEK REVIVAL STYLE (1830–1850)

In the 1830s the popularity of the Federal style waned, and the Greek Revival style, another classically based architectural mode with its antecedents in British architecture, emerged. Like the Federal style, the Greek Revival style came late to New York. While more austere in ornament, New York's Greek Revival–style residences tend to be larger and grander than its Federal-style buildings. The newer houses reflected the great wealth that was pouring into the city. Most Greek Revival–style buildings were erected in long rows, and many of them survive relatively intact.

The Greek Revival style was popular in New York during the 1830s and 1840s, when Greenwich Village and Chelsea in Manhattan and Brooklyn Heights and Cobble Hill in Brooklyn were being built up. Although thousands of row houses of the period have been demolished, the city has retained several grand Greek Revival–style groupings, three of which are of special note. In the 1830s New York's grandest row of houses was La Grange Terrace, also known as Colonnade Row, a rare example of nine houses set behind a monumental Corinthian colonnade. Four of these great houses survive, at 428–434 Lafayette Street. Other good examples of Greek Revival–style rows are found on Washington Square North, residences with magnificent cast- and wrought-iron railings, and on West 20th Street in Chelsea, the group known as Cushman Row at Nos. 408–418. The Chelsea row, which was erected between 1839 and 1840, exemplifies the typical Greek Revival–style residence in New York: a rectilinear building with a flat roofline, simple cornice, projecting stoop, grand stone entrance enframement, recessed doorway, and elegant ironwork. Of particular note in Brooklyn are the colonnade row at 43–49 Willow Place (c. 1846) and the austere row of four houses at 20–26 Willow Street (c. 1846), which is intact in almost every detail.

414 WEST 20TH STREET, MANHATTAN

The Greek Revival style is characterized by simple and bold architectural elements, imitating Greek motifs; three to three and one-half stories high with basement, sometimes an attic story below the cornice; brownstone base with brick upper facade (laid in English bond pattern); stoop of medium height with wrought- or cast-iron handrails, fence, and newels; vertical paneled wood door; grand entrance pilasters, sidelights, and stone enframements; six-over-six double-hung wood windows, often six-over-nine on the parlor floor, and sometimes small attic windows; modest molded stone window lintels and sills; wood dentiled cornice.

THE GOTHIC REVIVAL STYLE (1840–1860)

In the 1840s and 1850s the Gothic Revival style was used for row houses, but it never attained the popularity or widespread use of other 19th-century architectural styles. The Gothic Revival style is characterized by architectural elements inspired by organic and natural forms, medievalism (Tudor arches), and the picturesque. The Gothic Revival

The Gothic Revival style is characterized by architectural elements inspired by organic and natural forms, medievalism, and the picturesque; bold, projecting ornament; three stories plus basement; flat roof; brick with brownstone trim or full brownstone facade; stoop of medium height with cast-iron handrails, fence, and newels with elaborate Gothic motifs; recessed doorway with paneled wood door with pointed arches and occasional trefoils or quatrefoils; door surmounted by horizontal hood molding or low Tudor arch or combination of the two with foliated spandrel carving; picturesque hooded stone window lintels; multipaned double-hung wood windows or multipaned wood casement windows; plain Greek Revival–style or bold projecting Italianate-style cornice.

131 HICKS STREET, BROOKLYN

style was contemporary with the Greek Revival style, and it is found in some of the same neighborhoods. The major concentration of surviving Gothic Revival–style row houses, with their brick or brownstone facades, pointed arches, drip lintels, and fanciful Gothic railings, is in Brooklyn Heights, on Hicks, Willow, and State Streets. A few examples can also be found in Greenwich Village.

THE ITALIANATE STYLE (1840–1870)

In the 1850s the Italianate style and related modes became popular, coinciding with the tremendous growth in New York's wealth and a desire among many of the city's more affluent residents to build grand residential structures that reflected their newfound social position. The Italianate style is characterized by elaborate, bold projecting ornament with an emphasis on repetitive forms. Beginning in 1854 with the Herman Thorne Residence, on West 16th Street off Fifth Avenue (now demolished), thought to be the first Italianate-style residence in the city, this became the style of choice for most New Yorkers. The Italianate style and related Anglo-Italianate, French Second Empire, and neo-Grec styles remained popular until well into the 1880s.

Most Italianate-style residences were faced with brownstone. This material became so widespread that in New York the term *brownstone* has become synonymous with *row house*. Brownstone held great appeal in the mid-19th century because the dark, subtly textured stone gave a romantic appearance to buildings. A more important reason for its popularity, however, was that it was plentiful in Connecticut and New Jersey and thus could easily be transported to the city. Brownstone row houses are actually brick houses with a brownstone veneer front a few inches thick.

The Italianate style is characterized by elaborate, bold projecting ornament with an emphasis on repetitive forms; two to four stories high with brownstone basement; usually a full brownstone facade; high and wide stoop with elaborate cast-iron handrails, balusters, fence and newels; deeply recessed doorway with heavy protruding door hood and console brackets; round-headed double-leaf doors with heavily molded arched panels; large double-hung two-over-two or one-over-one wood windows, or multipaned double-hung windows with a wide central muntin to imitate casement windows; heavy, projecting stone window lintels and sills (sometimes resting on brackets) or full window enframements; and heavy, imposing, projecting cornice, embellished with moldings and supported by rectangular or scroll-shaped brackets.

Thousands of row houses were built in the Italianate style as both New York City and Brooklyn grew. In Manhattan most of these buildings were erected in midtown, but because of the extensive 20th-century redevelopment of this area, few survive. Manhattan's finest surviving Italianate-style rows are in Greenwich Village. Of special interest is the north side of Saint Luke's Place, where a row

325 PRESIDENT STREET, BROOKLYN

of brick houses with brownstone entrance en-framements, heavy cast-iron railings, and wooden cornices lines almost the entire blockfront. Anoth-er notable row, among the earliest in the Yorkville area, is at 208–218 East 78th Street.

In Brooklyn, entire Italianate-style streetscapes remain virtually as they were in the mid-19th cen-tury. These streets, mostly in the Clinton Hill and Fort Greene areas, give some idea of what mid-Manhattan must have looked like at the time of the Civil War. The most unusual Italianate-style row houses in the city, for both their facade materials and their location, are the marble residences on 45th Avenue in Hunter's Point, a rare late 19th-cen-tury urban enclave in Long Island City, Queens.

THE ANGLO-ITALIANATE STYLE (1840–1860)

Anglo-Italianate-style row houses, with ground-floor entrances and terraced groupings, were far less com-mon than their Italianate-style cousins with high stoops leading to parlor-floor entrances. Two superb groups of Anglo-Italianate-style row houses survive in Greenwich Village: at 20–38 West 10th Street, a series of 1856–58 brownstone-fronted houses with rusticated ground floors and iron balconies, and "The Triangle" (1860–61) on Stuyvesant and East 10th Streets near Second Avenue, an unusual group of narrow five-story brick houses with rusticated brownstone bases. There is a large concentration of Anglo-Italianate-style residences in Chelsea, and others were erected in the Gramercy Park area. In Brooklyn, fine Anglo-Italianate-style houses can be seen in Cobble Hill and Fort Greene.

THE SECOND EMPIRE STYLE (1860–1875)

The French Second Empire style gained popularity after the Civil War, when mansard roofs were added to basically Italianate-style row houses to give them more grandeur. These are now quite rare in Manhattan. Most were in Midtown, and few have survived. The finest surviving rows of Second Empire–style row houses are in Park Slope, Brook-lyn. In the 1860s French roofs were added to many Federal- and Greek Revival–style row houses to modernize them and provide another floor. This type of alteration is easy to detect because usually only the roof was changed; the door surrounds, window lintels, and cornice below retain their Fed-eral or Greek Revival style. Many examples of these

55 SOUTH ELLIOT STREET, BROOKLYN

The Anglo-Italianate style is generally three to five stories high; narrow width; rusticated brownstone basement and first story with smooth brownstone or brick upper facade; low stoop; round-headed, double-leaf wood door with arched panels; round-arched door surround; square-headed, round-arch, or segmental-headed window openings; two-over-two, one-over-one, or multipaned wood windows; simple brownstone window lintels and sills; and bracketed cornice with recessed panels and an arched fascia.

French Second Empire mansard-roofed Federal- and Greek Revival–style buildings can be found in Greenwich Village and in Brooklyn Heights.

THE NEO-GREC STYLE (1865–1885)

Similar in basic form to the Italianate-style row houses, but different in detail, are the neo-Grec-style structures popular in the 1870s and 1880s. These houses, most of which have brownstone fronts, are identifiable by the quality of their ornament, which tends to be angular and stylized and exhibit a widespread use of incised detailing. Rows of neo-Grec-style row houses were erected after the recovery from the financial panic of 1873. They were once common on the Upper East Side; Madison Avenue and side streets in the East 70s retain many of these rows.

The Second Empire style is similar to the Italianate style and is generally three to five stories high; brownstone facade; wide stoop with classically inspired iron handrails, fence, and newels; mansard roof (usually slate with iron cresting); and doorway with stone pilasters, consoles, and segmental arched pediment.

179 WASHINGTON PARK, BROOKLYN

Other examples can be found in Harlem and on the Upper West Side. There are also fine examples of neo-Grec-style streetscapes in Park Slope and Bedford-Stuyvesant, Brooklyn. In the Bronx, comparable examples of the neo-Grec style can be found in Mott Haven East on East 139th and 140th Streets, and at the Bertine Block on East 136th Street.

THE QUEEN ANNE (1870–1890) AND ROMANESQUE REVIVAL (1880–1890) STYLES

The brownstone row-house era ended in the 1880s when the rhythmically massed and carefully balanced Italianate-style, Second Empire–style, and neo-Grec-style rows were supplanted by freer and far livelier Romanesque Revival– and Queen Anne–style buildings. The brownstone front had been the primary row house type for over three decades, and miles of New York's streets were lined with these row houses. The change that occurred in the 1880s was dramatic and is attributable partly to the growth of architecture as a profession and the enactment of building laws that required the use of an architect and minimum construction standards, and partly to the greater availability of substitute materials.

The Romanesque Revival and Queen Anne styles were popular during the same years and share many design attributes, including a wide variation in materials, massing, and texture. The Romanesque Revival style is characterized by heavy forms, asymmetry, and polychromatic materials. The Queen Anne style features eccentric details, often with Classical or Renaissance precedents and often mixed with Romanesque Revival–style forms. These styles became possible, in part, because of a greatly expanding and developing economy. As railroads were extended, it became possible for New York's architects and builders to use materials imported from far-off places. Stone quarried in the Midwest was shipped to New York, and bricks made from distant clay deposits became popular. Thus the color and texture of New York's buildings became much more varied, including rock-faced brownstone; granite; limestone; elongated red, yellow, and brown brick; and terra cotta. In addition, American industry began mass-producing ornamental materials such as wrought iron and stained glass, which were used in abundance on Romanesque Revival– and Queen Anne–style residences.

330B PRESIDENT STREET, BROOKLYN

The Neo-Grec style is characterized by extremely stylized, classical details, angular forms, and incised detailing formed by mechanical stone cutting; three to five stories high with basement; brownstone and/or brick facade with simplified ornament, including single-line incised cuttings in the stone; high stoop with massive, heavy, angular cast-iron handrails, fence, and newels; massive door hood and enframement with angular decorative elements resting on stylized brackets; double-leaf wood entrance doors with angular ornament; stylized, angular incised window surrounds; two-over-two or one-over-one double-hung windows; projecting angular bays; projecting wood or metal cornice resting on angular brackets.

245 WAVERLY PLACE, MANHATTAN

The Romanesque Revival style is characterized
by heavy forms, asymmetry, polychromatic
materials, and a straightforward use of materials
and expression of structure; tonal and textural
juxtaposition of materials: rock-faced brownstone,
granite, limestone, elongated red, yellow, and
brown brick, and terra cotta; use of stone to
evoke a sense of solidity; Byzantine-style carved
ornament; spiny, interlaced vegetal forms,
abstract patterns, and grotesque human and
animal heads; massive arches; deeply recessed
round-arched door and window openings;
multipaneled wood double doors; elaborate,
stained-glass transom lights; Spanish tile roofs.

214 LINCOLN PLACE, BROOKLYN

The Queen Anne style is characterized by asymmetric
massing of forms and details; contrasts of varied materials,
colors, and textures; eccentric details, often with Classical or
Renaissance precedents and often mixed with Romanesque
Revival–style forms; use of terra cotta; three-sided projecting
bay windows; whimsical juxtaposition of window pane size,
usually double-hung windows with small pane upper sash;
wrought iron used at doorways and railings; L-shaped stoops
or straight stoops; multipaneled wood doors; gable roofs
covered with tiles or slate and featuring dormers and chimneys.

In Manhattan, buildings in these styles are prevalent on the Upper West Side and in Harlem, two neighborhoods that attracted thousands of middle-class families during the late 19th century. A small enclave in the Mott Haven section of the Bronx, along Alexander Avenue, was also built up with this style of row house. One of America's greatest collections of Romanesque Revival– and Queen Anne–style dwellings is in Brooklyn. Carroll Street in Park Slope, DeKalb Avenue in Clinton Hill, Hancock Street in Bedford-Stuyvesant, and Dean Street in Crown Heights exemplify the inventiveness of the architects working in the Romanesque Revival and Queen Anne styles. Interestingly, most of these buildings were designed by Brooklyn architects and not by their better-known Manhattan contemporaries. In the Bronx, many fine examples of the Romanesque Revival/neo-Renaissance style are found on Clay Avenue and the Bertine Block on East 136th Street, and examples of the Queen Anne style are found on the Bertine Block on East 136th Street.

EUROPEAN REVIVAL STYLES (1880–1925)

The popularity of the Romanesque Revival and Queen Anne styles waned in the 1890s when these idiosyncratic design modes were replaced by classical and Renaissance-inspired work that gave each streetscape a more regular appearance. The styles that became popular in the last decade of the 19th century and the first three decades of the 20th century were directly inspired by European buildings. American architects and patrons had visited Europe or had seen pictures of European buildings and were familiar with the masterpieces of classical, Renaissance, Baroque, and neoclassical architecture. These buildings became the new inspiration for American architects. McKim, Mead & White's Villard Houses complex, for example, one of the pioneering examples of the neo–Italian Renaissance style in America, was modeled after the Palazzo della Cancelleria in Rome. The complex, built in 1882–85 on Madison Avenue between East 50th and East 51st Streets, adapted the forms of the Roman work to the needs of late 19th-century American life. The use of European architectural motifs was viewed by the wealthy as a symbol of their success—their houses befitted an American royalty.

The Renaissance Revival style is characterized by simple, restrained Renaissance design forms and an interest in classicism. The neo-Renaissance style

597 2ND STREET, BROOKLYN

The Renaissance Revival style is characterized by simple, restrained Renaissance design forms and an interest in classicism; two to three stories high; brownstone, limestone or light colored brick facade; subdued Classical ornament concentrated around door and window openings; applied detail includes motifs of wreaths, baskets of fruit, and garlands of flowers; L-shaped stoop, often with two landings; entrance surround features full stone enframement; wood double-leaf doors with glazed openings, sometimes with iron grilles; and simple cornice with Renaissance-inspired ornament.

(1890–1920) was a later outgrowth of the Renaissance Revival style. Neo-Renaissance-style row houses are similar to Renaissance Revival row houses but are more academic in their use and expression of classical ornament.

The Upper East Side of Manhattan has New York's largest concentration of buildings from the late 19th and early 20th centuries. Most were built for the rich and were designed by prominent architects. The greatest Beaux-Arts-style mansions, the grandest French and English neoclassical-style town houses, and the most monumental neo–Italian Renaissance–style palazzi are located in this district, and all these styles are characterized by an academic classicism and an ordered, uniform appearance.

However, these new styles also filtered down to the middle class, and thousands of middle-class row houses were designed with French, English, and Italian forms. The World's Columbian Exposition in Chicago in 1893 brought Renaissance design to the attention of most Americans, and Renaissance-inspired buildings began to appear all across the country. On the Upper West Side and in West Harlem, rows of these houses were erected for the middle class. Perhaps the greatest example is the King Model Houses, designed by McKim, Mead & White in 1891 on West 139th Street between Seventh and Eight Avenues in Harlem. A large number of neo-Renaissance-style houses were also constructed in Brooklyn's Park Slope, Crown Heights, and Prospect–Lefferts Gardens. Most of these houses, faced with white Indiana limestone, are middle-class versions of the great Upper East Side mansions and town houses. Clay Avenue in the Bronx also has a high concentration of neo-Renaissance-style row houses.

The Beaux-Arts style is characterized by an academic classicism, symmetry of design, and an ordered, uniform appearance; five stories high; steep mansard roof with ornate dormers, or flat or low-pitched roof; white marble, limestone, or a light color brick facade; bold, three-dimensional stone carving; use of cartouches as ornament; lacks high stoop, entrance door is one or two steps above the sidewalk; main floor is often one floor above the entrance and usually has large windows with balconies; double-hung and casement wood windows; curved or three-sided projecting bay windows; sheet metal cornice with console brackets embellished with friezes.

TOWNHOUSE, UPPER EAST SIDE, MANHATTAN

315

The English Neoclassical style is characterized by the pure design and accurate replication of 18th-century English town house architecture; subdued classical ornament; four to five stories high; full brick facade laid in Flemish bond style or limestone facade; projecting entrance portico at ground level with full entablature; double-leaf glass and iron entrance doors; modestly projecting window and door surrounds with hoods, and eared surrounds; florid wrought iron; roof may be flat, steeply pitched with dormers, or steeply pitched with a triangular pediment set before it; cornice set on modillions and surmounted by a balustrade.

124 EAST 80TH STREET, MANHATTAN

COLONIAL REVIVAL STYLES (1880–1930)

At the same time that these European-inspired works were being built, American architects were examining our colonial past. The Colonial Revival style was popularized by the Centennial Exhibition of 1876 in Philadelphia, which focused national attention on the nation's 18th-century past. Architects began to admire the restrained and thoroughly American dwellings of the colonial past. Row houses and freestanding dwellings in the Colonial Revival, neo-Georgian, and neo-Federal styles were the result. The grandest row houses in these styles are on the Upper East Side; most notable is Park Avenue between East 68th and East 69th Streets. More modest examples are found on the Upper West Side and in Brooklyn's Crown Heights and Prospect–Lefferts Gardens.

THE END OF AN ERA

In the late 19th century, the apartment house began to replace the row house as the most common type of urban residence. As it became more expensive to build and to maintain row houses, many of those in Manhattan were demolished and tall apartment buildings erected in their stead. These apartment houses were designed in many of the same styles that had been popular for row houses. Although many row houses remained single-family residences, others were converted to multiple dwellings or businesses, often with the loss of important design features, such as the stoop. By the end of the 1930s, the era of the row house was over.

2119 ALBEMARLE TERRACE, BROOKLYN

The **Colonial Revival style** is characterized by the use of colonial design motifs, a combination of elements from the Federal and Greek Revival styles; symmetrical red brick facade laid in Flemish bond style; high stoop or simple steps; stone trim around doorway and windows; six- or eight-paneled wood door with leaded fanlight or rectangular sidelights and transom; simple iron handrails and fences; multipaned double-hung wood windows; Classical details often include urns, festoons, and broken pediments; delicate, slender moldings; a simple cornice.

WHAT IS THE NEW YORK CITY LANDMARKS PRESERVATION COMMISSION?

What does the Landmarks Preservation Commission do?

The Landmarks Preservation Commission is the New York City agency that is responsible for identifying and designating local landmarks and historic districts. The Commission also regulates changes to designated buildings.

Who are the Landmarks Commissioners?

According to the Landmarks Law, the eleven Commissioners that make up the Commission must include at least three architects, one historian, one city planner or landscape architect, and one realtor. There must be at least one resident of each borough on the Commission. Ten Commissioners serve part-time and receive no salary; the Chairman is a full-time, paid Commissioner. The Commissioners are appointed by the Mayor for three-year terms. The Chairman and the Vice-Chairman are designated by the Mayor.

What are the Commissioners' duties?

The Commissioners meet several times a month for public hearings and public meetings. On these occasions, they address Commission policies; review, discuss, and vote on landmark designations and applications to make changes to designated properties; and establish guidelines for future alterations to designated buildings. Sub-committees of Commissioners are sometimes created to review particular items and to make recommendations to the full Commission. There is, for instance, a Designation Committee, as well as committees to review particular Parks Department applications or specific applications from the public.

Who are the Commissions's staff members?

The agency's staff, headed by the Executive Director, includes architects, architectural historians, restoration specialists, planners, and archaeologists, as well as administrative, legal, and clerical personnel. Although it is one of the smallest New York City agencies, the Commission is the largest municipal preservation agency in the United States.

What does the Commission's staff do?

The Research Department carries out research and makes presentations to the Commissioners on the history and significance of proposed landmarks and historic districts. Members of the public can request the Commission to consider designating a particular building or area as a landmark or historic district.

The Preservation Department is the regulatory arm of the agency. It works with applicants who propose alterations or additions to designated properties or new construction in historic districts, and issues permits for changes that the Commission has found to be appropriate.

The Commission administers several other programs such as the Historic Preservation Grant Program, which awards restoration grants to low and moderate-income homeowners and not-for-profit organizations. The Commission's Architectural Salvage Warehouse Program retrieves architectural elements from buildings that are about to demolished and then sells them to city residents for restoration purposes.

When was the Commission established?

The Landmarks Preservation Commission was established in 1965 when Mayor Robert Wagner signed the local law creating the Commission and giving it its power.

Why was the Landmarks Law enacted?

The Landmarks Law was enacted in response to New Yorkers' growing concern that important buildings and other physical elements of the city's history were being lost despite the fact that these structures could be reused or adapted for other uses.

Events like the demolition of the architecturally distinguished Pennsylvania Station in 1963 increased public awareness of the need to protect the city's architectural, historical, and cultural heritage.

Why is it important to designate and protect landmarks and historic districts?

As the Landmarks Law explains, protection of these resources serves the following important purposes:

* safeguarding the city's historic, aesthetic and cultural heritage;

* helping to stabilize and improve property values in historic districts;

* encouraging civic pride in the beauty and accomplishments of the past;

* protecting and enhancing the city's attractions for tourists, thereby benefiting business and industry;

* strengthening the city's economy; and

* promoting the use of landmarks for the education, pleasure, and welfare of the people of the city.

What is a landmark?

A landmark is a building, property, or object that has been designated by the Landmarks Preservation Commission because it has a special character or special historical or aesthetic interest or value as part of the development, heritage, or cultural characteristics of the city, state or nation.

Landmarks are not always buildings. A landmark may be a bridge, a park, a water tower, a pier, a cemetery, a building lobby, a sidewalk clock, a fence, or even a tree. A property or object is eligible for landmark status when at least part of it is thirty years old or older.

What types of designations can the Commission make?

There are three types of landmarks: individual (exterior) landmarks, interior landmarks, and scenic landmarks. The Landmarks Preservation Commission may also designate areas of the city as historic districts.

1. *An individual landmark* is a property, object, or building that has been designated by the Landmarks Commission. These properties or objects are also referred to as "exterior" landmarks because only their exterior features have been designated.

The Roosevelt Island Lighthouse, the Edgewater Village Hall on Staten Island, Grand Central Terminal, and Old West Farms Soldiers' Cemetery in the Bronx are examples of individual landmarks.

2. *An interior landmark* is an interior space that has been designated by the Landmarks Commission. Interior landmarks must be customarily accessible to the public.

The lobby of the Woolworth Building, the dining room of the Gage & Tollner restaurant in Brooklyn, and the waiting room of the Marine Air Terminal at LaGuardia Airport are examples of interior landmarks.

3. *A scenic landmark* is a landscape feature or group of features that has been designated by the Landmarks Commission. Scenic landmarks must be situated on city-owned property.

Prospect Park and Ocean Parkway in Brooklyn, Verdi Square at Broadway and 73rd, and Central Park are examples of scenic landmarks.

4. *A historic district* is an area of the city designated by the Landmarks Commission that represents at least one period or style of architecture typical of one or more eras in the city's history; as a result, the district has a distinct "sense of place."

Greenwich Village and SoHo, Mott Haven in the Bronx, Jackson Heights in Queens, Saint George in Staten Island and Fort Greene in Brooklyn, are examples of sections of the city that contain historic districts.

How many buildings has the Commission designated?

Between 1965 and February 1997, the Commission has designated almost 1,000 individual landmarks, 68 historic districts (containing over 20,000 properties), 9 scenic landmarks, and 99 interior landmarks. These buildings are a small percentage of New York City's 850,000 building lots, but they are most important to the city's historic, aesthetic, and cultural heritage.

How can I learn more about the Landmarks Preservation Commission?

If you would like more information, call or write the Landmarks Commission at 100 Old Slip, New York, NY 10005; telephone: 212-487-6800; fax: 212-487-6776.

NEWLY DESIGNATED LANDMARKS

The reader should be aware that the Commission continues to designate new landmarks and historic districts. Between February 1997, when this book went into production, and December 1997, the Commission designated 21 individual landmarks and 1 historic district, as well as 66 historic lampposts and fixtures. The new landmarks and historic district are listed below. The reader should contact the Commission for more information about any of these new designations.

(Former) Stuyvesant High School, 345 East 15th Street, Manhattan

Pike Street Synagogue (Congregation Sons of Israel Kalwarie), 13–15 Pike Street, Manhattan

New School for Social Research (Interior), 66 West 12th Street, Manhattan

Jonathan W. Allen Stable, 148 East 40th Street, Manhattan

George S. Bowdoin Stable, 149 East 38th Street, Manhattan

Fire Hook and Ladder Company No. 14 (now Fire Engine Company No. 36), 120 East 125th Street, Manhattan

Fire Engine Company No. 47, 500 West 113th Street, Manhattan

Fire Engine Company No. 84 and Hook and Ladder Company No. 34, 513–515 West 161st Street, Manhattan

American Surety Company Building, 100 Broadway, Manhattan

American Bank Note Company Office Building; 70 Broad Street, Manhattan

(Former) Scheffel Hall, 190 Third Avenue, Manhattan

New York Training School for Teachers/New York Model School (now A. Phillip Randolph Campus High School); 443–464 West 135th Street, Manhattan

CBS Building, 51 West 52nd Street, Manhattan

Manufacturers Trust Company Building (now Chase Manhattan Building), 510 Fifth Avenue, Manhattan

Ford Foundation Building and Interior Atrium, 321 East 42nd Street/320 East 43rd Street, Manhattan

Loew's Paradise Theater, 2401–2419 Grand Concourse, Bronx

Messiah Home For Children, 1771–1777 Andrews Avenue South, Bronx

Brooklyn Public Library, Central Building, 2 Eastern Parkway/415 Flatbush Avenue (Grand Army Plaza), Brooklyn

John and Elizabeth Truslow House, 96 Brooklyn Avenue, Brooklyn

Moore-Jackson Cemetery, 51st to 54th Streets between 31st Avenue and 32nd Avenue, Queens

Douglaston Historic District, Queens

GENERAL INDEX

Page numbers in *italic* type indicate a full entry on the landmarked property or interior, historic district, or scenic landmark. Page numbers in **bold** type indicate a photograph of the building,

INDEX OF STREET ADDRESSES

Page numbers in *italic* type indicate a full entry on the landmarked property or interior.
Page numbers in **bold** type indicate a photograph or drawing of the building,

East 44th St.
No. 304, *97*
Nos. 307 and 310, *97*
West 44th St., **74**
No. 20, *86–87*
No. 27, *86*
No. 37, *86*
No. 42, *86*
Nos. 59–61, *86*
Nos. 111–121, *78*
No. 123, *79*
No. 128, *78*
Nos. 139–141, *79*
No. 238, *74*
Nos. 221–233, *74*
Nos. 235–243, *74–75*
Nos. 245–247, *75*
Nos. 246–256, *74*
No. 432, *75*
West 45th St.
Nos. 149–157, *79–80,* **79**
Nos. 222–232, *76*
Nos. 239–247, *76*
Nos. 234–240, *76*
Nos. 242–250, *76*
No. 249, *76*
Nos. 252–256, *76*
Nos. 302–314, *75–76,* **75**
West 46th St.
No. 120, *80*
Nos. 133–145, *80*
Nos. 203–217, *77*
Nos. 226–236, *76*
West 47th St.
Nos. 243–251, *77*
Nos. 256–262, *77*
Nos. 261–265, *77*
East 48th St.
No. 211, *97–98,* **98**
West 48th St.
Nos. 138–146, *80*
Nos. 220–228, *77*
East 49th St.
Nos. 211–215, *98*
West 49th St.
Nos. 215–223, *77–78*
Nos. 230–238, *77*
East 51st St.
No. 24, *90*
West 51st St.
Nos. 217–239, *102–03*
East 52nd St.
Nos. 2–4, *90*
No. 99, *100*
West 52nd St.
No. 51, 320
Nos. 244–254, *103*
Nos. 243–259, *103*
East 53rd St.
312 East 53rd St. House, 100
East 54th St.
No. 4, *91*
West 54th St., *91*
No. 1. *91*
5 West 54th St. House, *91*
7 West 54th St. House, *91–92*
9–11 West 54th St. House, *92*
13 and 15 West 54th St. Houses, *92*
No. 17, *92*
No. 314, *103*
East 55th St.
No. 2, 92
West 55th St.
No. 24, 92
No. 131, *103*
West 56th St.
Nos. 12–14, *93*

East 57th St.
No. 41, *93*
West 57th St.
No. 200, *104–05*
No. 205, *105*
No. 215, *105–07,* **105**
East 58th St.
311 and 313 East 58th St. Houses, *139*
West 58th St.
No. 182, **106,** *107*
No. 213, *107*
No. 215, *107*
West 59th St.
No. 400, *108*
East 60th St.
Nos. 1–11, *130–31*
East 61st St.
No. 250, 139
No. 421, *139*
West 61st St.
Nos. 33–43, *111*
East 62nd St.
No. 2, *131*
No. 11, 127, **127**
No. 36, 129
East 63rd St.
No. 2, 127
No. 153, *134*
East 64th St.
No. 3, 127
No. 112, 129
Nos. 401–423, *139*
West 64th St.
No. 2, *111*
East 65th St.
45 East 65th St. Apts., *131–32,* **131**
Nos. 47–49, *131*
Nos. 141–151, *134–35*
Nos. 402–416, *139*
East 66th St.
No. 5, 127
Nos. 131–135, *135–36*
West 66th St.
No. 56, *111*
East 67th St.
130–134 East 67th St. Apts., *136*
Nos. 149–151, *138*
No. 163, *138*
East 68th St.
No. 49, *132*
East 70th St.
No. 1, *133–34*
11th East 70th St. House, *133*
15 East 70th St. House, *133*
No. 17, *133*
No. 19, *133*
No. 21, *133*
No. 124, 129
No. 107, *127–29*
East 71st St.
No. 10, *133–34*
West 71st St.
No. 171, *115*
East 72nd St.
No. 7, *134*
No. 9, *134*
West 72nd St.
No. 1, *113*
309 West 72nd St. House, *115*
311 West 72nd St. House, *115*
Nos. 340 and 344, *115*
East 73rd St.
No. 11, 127
161–179 and 166–182 East 73rd St. Bldgs., *138*
No. 321, *139*

East 74th St.
No. 32, 129
East 75th St.
No. 1, *134*
East 77th St.
Nos. 507–523, *152*
West 77th St.
No. 44, 111
East 78th St.
No. 1, *143*
No. 4, 141
Nos. 22 and 26, 142
157, 159, 161, 163, and 165 East 78th St. Houses, *151*
208, 210, 212, 214, 216, and 218 East 78th St. Houses, *151*
Nos. 501–555, *152*
Nos. 508–522, *152*
East 79th St.
No. 53, *148*
59 East 79th St. House, *148*
63 East 79th St. House, *148*
67–69 East 79th St. House, *148*
No. 222, *152–53*
Nos. 502–540, *152*
East 80th St.
116 East 80th St. House, *148*
120 East 80th St. House, *148*
124 East 80th St. House, *148,* 316, **316**
No. 130,, *148–49*
West 80th St.
Nos. 307–317
West 81st St.
Nos. 308–314, 114
West 83rd St.
332 West 83rd St. House, *117*
East 84th St.
No. 3, 142
No. 55, *149*
East 85th St.
No. 100, *149*
West 85th St.
316, 318, 320, 322, 324, and 326 West 85th St. Houses, *122*
329, 331, 333, 335, and 337 West 85th St. Houses, *122*
No. 350, *122*
East 86th St.
No. 9, 142
West 86th St.
Nos. 201–225, *122*
East 87th St.
No. 6, 142
No. 12, 142
East 88th St.
No. 15, 142
Nos. 316–332, *153*
West 88th St.
Nos. 267–271, 121
East 89th St.
Nos. 12–16, 142
146, 148, 150, 152, 154, and 156 East 89th St. Houses, *154*
West 89th St.
No. 175, *119*
No. 346, *122–23*
East 90th St.
No. 9, 146
11 East 90th St. House, *144–46*
15 East 90th St. House, *146*
17 East 90th St. House, *143*
East 91st St.
No. 1, *146,* **147**
No. 2, *146*
No. 7, *146*
No. 9, *146–47*

No. 11, *147*
No. 20, 143
West 91st St.
Nos. 121–147, *119,* **119**
East 92nd St.
Nos. 6–14, 142
Nos. 20–24, 143
120 and 122 East 92nd St. Houses, *149*
160 East 92nd St. House, *154*
East 93rd St.
No. 56, *150,* **150**
No. 60, *149–50*
Nos. 67, 69, and 75, *149*
East 94th St.
Nos. 5–25, 142
East 95th St.
No. 3, *156*
No. 7, *156*
West 95th St.
No. 143, *119*
East 96th St.
No. 7, *156*
No. 15, *156*
West 96th St.
No. 1, *120*
East 97th St.
No. 15, *156–57,* **156**
West 100th St.
No. 206, *124*
West 102nd St.
254 West 102nd St. House, *124*
East 106th St.
Nos. 112–120, *157*
West 108th St.
No. 301, *124*
East 110th St.
No. 174, *169*
West 113th St.
No. 500, 320
West 114th St.
No. 215, *164*
West 115th St.
No. 203, *164–65*
Nos. 226–250, *164*
East 121st St.
No. 170, *169*
West 123rd St.
No. 147, *165*
East 125th St.
Nos. 81–85, *169*
No. 120, 320
West 125th St.
No. 253, *165–66,* **166**
East 127th St.
No. 20, *169*
East 128th St.
17 East 128th St. House, *170*
West 128th St.
No. 151, *166–67*
West 129th St.
12 West 129th St. House, *170*
West 130th St.
Nos. 8–62, *170,* **170**
West 134th St.
No. 214, *167*
West 135th St.
No. 103, *167*
Nos. 443–464, 320
West 137th St.
No. 140, *167*
West 138th St.
No. 132, *167*
No. 218, 164
No. 221, 164
No. 236, 164
No. 257, 164
West 139th St.
No. 221, 164

INDEX OF CHURCHES AND SYNAGOGUES

Page numbers in *italic* type indicate a full entry on the landmarked church or synagogue.
Page numbers in **bold** type indicate a photograph of the building.